Optimizing Windows for Games, Graphics, and Multimedia

Optimizing Windows for Games, Graphics, and Multimedia

David L. Farquhar

O'REILLY®

Beijing · Cambridge · Farnham · Köln · Paris · Sebastopol · Taipei · Tokyo

Optimizing Windows for Games, Graphics, and Multimedia
by David L. Farquhar

Copyright © 2000 O'Reilly & Associates, Inc. All rights reserved.
Printed in the United States of America.

Published by O'Reilly & Associates, Inc., 101 Morris Street, Sebastopol, CA 95472.

Editor: Robert Denn

Production Editor: Madeleine Newell

Cover Designer: Ellie Volkenhausen

Printing History:

January 2000: First Edition.

ISBN: 1-56592-677-3
[M]

Table of Contents

Preface .... *ix*

1. *System Optimization Theory* *1*
   What Makes a Computer Fast? 3
   The Ideal Operating System 4
   Working Within Windows' Limitations 5
   Is My Computer Getting Slower? 7
   What You Can Expect to Get from This Book 8
   Requirements for This Book 9
   Measuring the Improvement 11

2. *First Steps* *13*
   Check Your Free Disk Space 14
   Lose autoexec.bat and config.sys 17
   Make Sure Your System Is Using 32-bit Drivers 17
   Clean Out Your Startup Group 17
   Optimize Your Swap File 18
   Optimize Your Disk Cache (and Get a UPS!) 20
   Tune the Hidden Windows Disk Cache Settings 21
   Tune Your CD-ROM Caching 22
   Turn Off CD-ROM Autoplay 23
   Optimize Your Multimedia Settings 23
   Turn Off Power Management 24
   Take Down Your Wallpaper 25
   Use Hotkeys Instead of Desktop Icons 25
   Lose the Screen Savers 26

Lose the System Sounds and Desktop Schemes *26*

Turn Off the Windows 98 Animations *27*

Turn Off Windows 98 Tooltips *27*

Find the Fastest Settings for Your Video Card *28*

Enable Your Hard Drive's DMA Setting *29*

Shrink Your Start Menu *29*

A Primer on Regedit and the Registry *30*

Turn Off Windows 95's Window Animation *35*

Turn Off Pause in Menus *35*

Turn Off Click Here to Begin *36*

Tune Windows 9x to Your Modern CD-ROM Drive *36*

Recover That Wasted CD-ROM Cache Memory *38*

Improve the Windows 9x Server Template Even More *38*

Reduce Filesystem Fragmentation *39*

3. *Disk Optimization* ***41***

Directory Optimization *42*

Taking Care of Fragmentation *50*

Working Within the Physical Limitations of the Disk *56*

Living with FAT *57*

Other Disk Performance Tools *69*

How Much Difference Will This Make? *73*

Getting Rid of Disk Compression *74*

4. *Speeding Up the Boot Process* ***76***

The Boot Process Explained *76*

Speeding Up the Boot Process *78*

msdos.sys Options *79*

Wringing That Last Ounce of Speed from msdos.sys *86*

Speeding Up autoexec.bat *87*

Getting By with Less in Your Startup Group *87*

Speeding Up POST *89*

Compacting the Registry *91*

5. *Utilities* ***93***

What Tools You Need and How to Use Them *93*

Should I Upgrade to Windows 98? *94*

The Big Three Utilities Suites *95*

Uninstallation Programs *105*

Anti-Virus Software *107*

Freeware and Shareware Utilities *109*

6. *Replacement Windows Shells* *119*
Program Manager *120*

EVWM *123*

StarOffice *125*

LiteStep *126*

7. *Optimizing DOS* *134*
Try It *135*

"Insufficient Memory?" I Have 64 Megs! *135*

When DOS Programs Are Sluggish *140*

Running DOS Programs in DOS Mode *141*

A Pseudo-Dual Boot *143*

Dual-Booting Windows 9x and True DOS *145*

Tweaks You'll Want Even If You Never Run DOS Software *148*

What to Do When DOS Games Run Too Fast *148*

Putting It into Practice *150*

Running DOS Games from a RAM Disk *155*

8. *Modems and the Internet* *157*
Idealistic General Principles *158*

Finding Your Modem and Optimizing Your Port Speed *158*

Optimizing Your Port *159*

So What's This UART Business? *159*

A Bit of Low-Tech: Your Phone Connection *160*

Download the Newest Drivers for Your Modem *161*

Tune Your Connection via Software *161*

Speed Up DNS Lookups *163*

Lose the Ads Altogether *165*

Preloading and Caching Utilities *168*

Taking Full Control of Your Internet Connection ... *169*

The Value of Free Software *171*

Which Web Browser Should I Use? *171*

Tune Your Web Browser *172*

9. *Home Networking* *174*
Requirements *174*

Using Networks to Save Disk Space *184*

Some Networking Tips *185*

10. Clean Windows Installation *188*

First Steps with Windows 95 .... *188*

Hacking Out MSN and the Exchange Client *190*

OSR2.x's Excess Baggage *191*

Installing Windows 98 .... *192*

Installing Windows 98 Without Internet Explorer *195*

Removing Internet Explorer from an Existing
Windows 98 Installation *197*

Installing Device Drivers *197*

Performing the Installation *198*

Post-Installation Magic *201*

Stupid Installation Tricks *202*

Multi-Booting Windows 95 and 98 .... *204*

11. RAM Disks *206*

Advantages of RAM Disks *206*

Special Considerations for Windows 98 and RAM Disks *214*

12. Hardware Upgrades *217*

Prudence in Hardware Upgrades *218*

Realistic Memory Requirements *218*

Video Cards *226*

Modems *231*

Printers *233*

The PCI Bus *233*

Straight Talk on CPU Upgrades *234*

Motherboards *239*

CD-ROM and DVD Drives *245*

External Removable-Media Drives *248*

Scanners *248*

Monitors *248*

Input Devices *249*

Buying New Systems *250*

Scavenging *251*

What Do I Do with This Old 486? *252*

Appendix: Useful Web Resources *255*

Index *261*

Preface

Windows 95 and 98 have earned a reputation for being bloated, antiquated, and slow. To a degree, this image is deserved, as the minimum system requirements for the venerable Windows 9x operating system have grown significantly since its release in the late summer of 1995.

Windows 9x rolls on, however, for a variety of reasons. Its installed base is much larger than that of Windows NT, and while hard-core gamers praise NT as a better platform for running certain games, 9x is overall a much better platform for home use, games included. Consumer hardware and software that work only with great effort (or not at all) under NT works under 9x.

In its default configuration, Windows 9x probably deserves every snide comment it gets. However, it is certainly possible to transform this behemoth into a much sleeker package that makes you feel almost as if you got a new computer. In this book, I'll show you how to do just that.

Who's This Book For?

This is not a beginning book on Windows. While most of the book is within the grasp of the intermediate user, I don't spend any time explaining what right-clicking is, or much of anything about the user interface itself. This is also not a book for the timid. If you want your system to run in a state that's completely supported by both Microsoft and your hardware manufacturer, you won't get the most out of this book.

If, on the other hand, you buy all those magazines with articles on how to tune Windows for performance, and you have all those articles in a stack somewhere in your computer room for reference, this book is for you. I've collected hundreds of such tips over the years from both magazines and web sites, well known and obscure, and added some of my own discoveries.

This book targets the home user. Although the tricks in this book will also make Microsoft Office run faster on the aging workstations in your office, I don't spend much time talking about the work environment. Your support contract may require you to run your PCs in standard configurations. While I've found the recommendations in this book to be safe and reliable (I keep all of my PCs, plus most of my friends' PCs, configured the way I describe here), your IT department and/or your third-party support vendor will probably not want you to run your PC in a configuration that they haven't tested themselves.

What's Not in This Book

There are more Windows 95 and 98 books on the market than I can count, and many of them try to cover every possible aspect of Windows. It's an admirable goal, but Windows has become such a complex beast that any effort to cover it comprehensively is going to fall short in most areas, even if the book is 2,000 pages in length. Instead, I have chosen to cover a single topic and do the best job I can in that specialized area.

I also don't spend any time talking about Windows NT. Although some of these tips and many of the concepts in this book will work under Windows NT (the concepts behind getting computers to run fast are surprisingly universal), NT has almost as much in common with OS/2 as it does with Windows 9x, especially once you start digging under the hood.

How This Book Is Organized

This book is broken into 12 chapters and one appendix. In general, the chapters start with the simplest concepts, and get increasingly complicated as the book goes on. Here's a brief summary of each chapter's contents:

- Chapter 1, *System Optimization Theory,* introduces the concepts of system optimization in terms that apply not only to Windows 9x, but also to other operating systems.

- Chapter 2, *First Steps,* is a huge collection of settings, registry hacks, and tips to speed up any Windows 9x-based PC, including many tips I've never seen published anywhere else.

- Chapter 3, *Disk Optimization,* discusses advanced disk optimization, starting with defragmentation utilities, then moving into file placement and directory optimization to increase performance further. This chapter also discusses strategic partitioning of hard drives to reduce fragmentation.

- Chapter 4, *Speeding Up the Boot Process,* discusses the boot-up process, all of the known settings in the mysterious *msdos.sys* file, and how to reduce your system boot time from minutes to seconds.

- Chapter 5, *Utilities,* discusses and compares the big three utilities suites, including which suite to buy and what components to install, as well as other useful third-party commercial, shareware, and freeware utilities.

- Chapter 6, *Replacement Windows Shells,* discusses the use of replacements for Microsoft's Explorer shell to decrease your PC's memory usage, increase your system's customizability, or both.

- Chapter 7, *Optimizing DOS,* covers the difficult topic of configuring the MS-DOS 7 operating system that lies beneath Windows 9x, as well as getting those stubborn classic DOS games to run.

- Chapter 8, *Modems and the Internet,* discusses optimization of your modem for maximum speed, including free and inexpensive utilities that give you all the functionality (or more) of commercial modem accelerators.

- Chapter 9, *Home Networking,* describes how to set up a home network for maximum efficiency, which allows you to share peripherals among multiple PCs without slowing all of them to a crawl.

- Chapter 10, *Clean Windows Installation,* explains how to install or reinstall Windows 9x for the most efficient system possible. This chapter includes information on removing MSN, the Exchange client, and Internet Explorer from Windows 95 or 98.

- Chapter 11, *RAM Disks,* covers the use of RAM as a high-speed disk drive for the fastest possible speed, including how to boot and run Windows from a huge RAM disk.

- Chapter 12, *Hardware Upgrades,* discusses what to do when changing your software configuration just isn't enough and how to get the most for your upgrade dollar.

- The appendix, *Useful Web Resources,* lists a large number of web sites I've found helpful over the course of the past few years. Many of them provide downloadable software, useful software settings, hardware advice, or all three.

Conventions in This Book

The following typographical conventions are used in this book:

Constant width
> is used to indicate command-line computer output and code examples.

Constant width italic
> is used to indicate variables in examples.

Italic

> is used to introduce new terms and to indicate URLs, variables, user-defined files and directories, file extensions, filenames, directory or folder names, and UNC pathnames.

We'd Like Your Feedback!

The information in this book has been tested and verified to the best of our ability, but mistakes and oversights do occur. Please let us know about errors you may find, as well as your suggestions for future editions, by writing to:

O'Reilly & Associates, Inc.
101 Morris Street
Sebastopol, CA 95472
800-998-9938 (in the U.S. or Canada)
707-829-0515 (international or local)
707-829-0104 (fax)

You can also send us email messages. To be put on our mailing list or to request a catalog, send mail to:

info@oreilly.com

To ask technical questions or to comment on the book, send email to:

bookquestions@oreilly.com

To find out about errata and any plans for future editions, you can access the book's web site at:

www.oreilly.com/catalog/win9x

To find links to the author's web site and email address, you can visit:

www.daynotes.com

For more information about this book and others, see the O'Reilly web site:

www.oreilly.com

Acknowledgments

A large number of people contributed in one way or another to this book—if I truly were to thank everyone who deserves thanks, the acknowledgments would easily be the biggest section of this book. The book started with a discussion with Robert Denn, my editor at O'Reilly. Despite the press reports at the time, I didn't believe Windows 9x was going away any time soon, and the events of the past six months have only reinforced that belief. I'm glad he agreed with me, and I appreciate his patience as I adjusted to writing a book.

At O'Reilly, an entire production crew labored to turn my original drafts into a finished product. I especially want to thank Steven Abrams, who made sure I had everything I needed to finish this book and spent many hours helping me get the manuscript into a usable form.

I also want to thank my excellent technical reviewers: Sam Kalat, a game developer at Red Storm Entertainment; Steve DeLassus; John Meyer, a systems analyst at the University of Missouri-Columbia School of Journalism and Tom Gatermann all pored over the manuscript in search of errors, omissions, and misguided ideas. Their suggestions immensely improved this book.

Without the support and encouragement of my mentors, this project would have been much more difficult. It was Jerry Pournelle's essay titled "How to Get My Job" that got me thinking about writing about computers again. A virtual community sprung up around his web site, known collectively by some as "The Daynotes Gang"; they also deserve thanks. Authors Robert Bruce Thompson and Tom Syroid provided invaluable advice on how to approach a project like this, as did Dan Bowman, a frequent contributor to their sites. I also want to thank several of my past teachers, who taught me about writing, computers, life, or all three: Debbie Schulte, Duane Giesselmann, The Rev. Merlen Wegener, Elizabeth Spencer, Bob Sullivan, Brian Brooks, and Byron Scott.

My mother and sister were extremely supportive and understanding during this project, which frequently kept me from visiting them as often as we would have liked. I am thankful and grateful for their love and encouragement. Lastly and most importantly, I want to thank the Lord for his guidance and many blessings during this and every other endeavor.

1

System Optimization Theory

One web site changed my whole way of looking at computers.

I was looking for sites about Windows 98. I got a site about cars. If there was ever any doubt in my mind that there's a web site about everything, this site erased it. Before I knew it, I was reading about tweaking out Dodge Spirits and racing them. One fan of the site wrote in, criticizing some aspects of the Spirit's design. Another buff said that without cutting down the springs, modifying the gizmo that holds the air filter to get more air flowing into the engine, and other less-than-trivial modifications, the car was "totally inadequate" for stop-and-go city driving.

I related the story to a couple of friends who don't exactly share my love of computers and asked if that was what I sounded like when I started talking about computers. Both agreed adamantly.

Would I know a totally inadequate car if I drove one? My Spirit always seemed fine to me. But what do I know? I'm sure if I let real car buffs have a week with my car to do anything possible to improve it, they would make a zillion little changes, then try to explain them to me and I wouldn't understand. But I'd notice the difference when I got behind the wheel.

Then I'd turn the tables and sit down at the car buff's computer. Chances are, it would seem slow to me, I'd call it "totally inadequate," and then I'd go to town making change after change.

That's what this book is about—fine-tuning your computer to be an awesome machine. Maybe you're like me: you know a good computer when you see one, but if it's sluggish, it bugs you. You want to get in there and dig and tweak until it feels just right. Or maybe you use your computer the way I drive my car. You appreciate it when it works; you know it could be a little bit better, but you don't want to dedicate your life to reengineering your computer. Similarly, I appreciate not having to walk eight miles to work every morning, but I don't want to be an automotive engineer. You don't have to be an aspiring computer scientist to enjoy video games, and you shouldn't have to be a computer scientist in order to have your games play well.

You'll learn a few things about computers from reading this book, just as I learned a few things about cars from reading that web site. Take what you want from the experience. If you just want a faster computer, I can help you get there. If you want a faster computer but also want to know why you should do certain things, that's fine too. I explain why this stuff works. Do with it what you will. Maybe get a job maintaining computers. Take bottom-line PCs and make them perform like machines that cost four times as much, if you want. Pull neglected four-year-old PCs off the scrap heap and put them to use. Or just get back to your serious work or play.

At least once a year, most of the major U.S. computer magazines publish a list of tricks that purport to make Windows run faster. I imagine those issues sell briskly. I don't think I've ever met anyone who complained about a computer being too fast, and most of the people who brag about their computers just bought theirs. I imagine that, in reality, they're secretly dissatisfied with the speed of their computers (or will be in a couple more months), but who wants to talk about a $3,000 computer being too slow when you still have ten months' worth of payments to go on it?

The tricks presented in those magazine articles generally work pretty well, but a ten-page feature article with lots of slick four-color art can only cover a very limited amount of ground. The art of making a computer run faster (and it is as much an art as a science) just can't be confined to such a small space.

Books on the topic are much harder to come by. I've seen a couple of books with the words "Windows optimization" in their titles, but I've always been disappointed by them. Typically, they spend only one chapter talking about optimization, and the rest of the book talks about work habits and user interface tutorials. They're useful books, but calling them optimization guides is a misnomer. They have more in common with David Karp's *Windows Annoyances* (O'Reilly & Associates) than with this book.

This isn't a book about how to use Windows more effectively. It's a book about performance tuning.

What Makes a Computer Fast?

There's a lot of misinformation out there on this topic. A good friend recently told me about a conversation he had in the camera store where he works. It seems most people who like cameras also like computers these days, and this customer was no exception. He'd been a Macintosh fanatic for some time, and had just bought his first PC: a 400 MHz Pentium II. He just wouldn't stop talking about how fast it is. My friend, who's somewhat of a performance tweaker himself, kept trying to get more details.

> "What kind of hard drive does it have?" he asked.
> "Eight-point-four gigabytes," the customer answered. "That's fast!"
> My friend tried not to roll his eyes. "How much memory?"
> "One hundred twenty-eight megabytes," the customer answered.
> Before he could add, "That's fast!" the store owner appeared, having caught enough of the conversation to know the customer had just bought a new computer.
> "What kind of computer is it?" she asked.
> "Pentium II 400," he said.
> "Oh, that's all that matters," she said.

Intel's marketing hype would have you believe that CPU speed is all that matters, and as long as you have a 550 MHz Pentium III, you don't have to worry about anything else. As long as people think of computers only in terms of microprocessors, they're going to have overpriced, underachieving computers.

But a system doesn't have to cost a fortune to be fast. As I was finishing this book, I bought two new Celeron 400 systems for $650 each. They're more than adequate for almost everything I do—and I'm a computer professional. It would be nice if they had better video and sound cards, and I may replace those soon. For $200, I can add good stuff; for $300, I can add the best stuff. If and when I do, I'll have an $850 or $950 system that plays like a $1,500 system.

The Computer Is a Team

Although the computer looks like just a box sitting there on the desk or on the floor, it actually consists of many discrete components that work together like a team. The CPU is the big-money player on the team, the flamboyant player who gets all the headlines and is expected to carry the team.

But without adequate memory, video and sound cards that do a lot of the work on their own, a fast hard drive, and a motherboard that provides fast and reliable data paths between the components, that big-money player won't make a huge difference in the computer's performance. How often does a faltering sports team, or, to a certain degree, a failing television show, go looking for a big name to come on board and turn everything around? If the real problem is something relatively minor, a new face can inject some new perspective and make a difference. But all too often, a big name comes in, finds the problems are bigger than one person can solve, and becomes a symbol of futility. What had been a bad team becomes just a bad team with a big star.

A lot of computers are a bad team with one big star. They have one big-ticket item in a fast CPU, but they have an inadequate amount of memory and a slow hard drive. A 450 MHz Pentium II with 32 MB of RAM and a Quantum Bigfoot hard drive will usually be outclassed by a $399 AMD- or Cyrix-based eMachines PC upgraded with 128 MB of RAM.

Dumping buckets of money for a big-ticket CPU is even more foolhardy than buying a big-ticket athlete, because the big-ticket CPU will be the mid-range CPU in six months and entry-level six months after that.

Every computer has limited resources. Linux runs faster than Windows, especially on low-end hardware, precisely because it makes better use of limited resources than Windows 9x does. But it's possible to make Windows scrappier and more efficient if you shift your mindset from a CPU-centric approach to more of a whole-system approach. Think of the computer as a big pool of megahertz, available RAM, and disk throughput. The more water in the pool, the faster your computer runs, but everything you do takes a little bit of water from the pool. When you upgrade your computer, you make that pool last longer because you make it bigger. You need to consider two things: you can make the pool bigger by adding memory or disk throughput, and it's usually less expensive than adding more CPU speed (megahertz). But consider that you can make the pool last longer by making everything that drinks from it drink less.

The Ideal Operating System

I recently ran across a quote from Leo Tolstoy's "An Afterword to the Kreutzer Sonata." Tolstoy was talking about his own religious ideals, but his words seem applicable to ideals in general.

"The test of observance," Tolstoy wrote, "is our consciousness of failure to achieve an ideal perfection. The degree to which we draw near to this perfection cannot be seen; all we can see is the extent of our deviation."

Tolstoy was trying to measure up to an ideal that he couldn't really see. He knew he wasn't perfect, and even at his best, he couldn't see how close to perfect he was. He could only measure imperfection, and he was more likely to notice his shortcomings on a bad day than on a good day.

The ideal operating system is something we can't really see. In this case, it's an abstract thing that exists only in computer programmers' minds. I'm not about to jump into the Windows-versus-Macintosh-versus-Linux-versus-whatever debate, because all of those operating systems have shortcomings that sometimes drive me up the wall. The ideal operating system becomes a useful concept when we take the system in question—in this case, Windows 9x—and hold it up to the ideal, then measure the deviation and do what we can to close the gap.

I think everyone who's used computers heavily for more than a few months has a picture of the ideal operating system. I can think of six characteristics my ideal operating system would have. My ideal operating system:

- Is stable.

- Makes the most efficient use of memory possible. It makes good use of as much memory as it can, but wastes very little on superfluous features.

- Compensates for the slow speed of hard drives and CD-ROM drives by using disk caching, but isn't obsessed with this task.

- Uses as few CPU cycles as possible, leaving them available for the applications' use.

- Fragments the disk as little as possible, so as to keep I/O operations fast and efficient.

- Uses disk space efficiently so as to not slow down dramatically as the disk fills up.

Every operating system on the market today falls short of these ideals. The key to making the best of any operating system, Windows or otherwise, is to work within its limitations in order to make it come as close to the ideal as possible.

Working Within Windows' Limitations

I've used a number of different operating systems. My first computer with a hard drive was an Amiga 2000. I used Macintoshes in high school, and I used a variety of computers in college: PCs running Windows 3.1, PCs running OS/2, NeXTs running NeXTstep, and SGIs running Irix. Unlike many authors of Windows books, I was a latecomer to the Windows 9x game. I used Windows 95 a few times in the fall of 1995, but at the time my PC ran OS/2. I was working part-time in an OS/2 shop, and OS/2 did an excellent job of running the programs I needed to run, so I saw little reason to switch.

I finally switched in late 1996, when 32-bit Windows programs started becoming commonplace and I realized I needed them. I found Windows 95 to be somewhere between Windows 3.1 and OS/2 in terms of both speed and stability.

Comparing its speed to NeXTstep, Irix, and AmigaOS was difficult, since those systems ran on different hardware, but they were definitely more stable.

I had accumulated a collection of OS/2 speedup tricks over the course of the two years I ran that operating system, and I found many of those tricks applied to Windows 9x as well. This made sense, as Windows and OS/2 are cousins and run on the same hardware.

Then I took a long look at the other operating systems that had visible advantages over Windows. AmigaOS was designed to run off floppy disks, so to get around that huge speed deficiency, it stored things like temporary files and preferences (the closest Amiga equivalent to the Windows registry) in a RAM disk. It also stored large portions of the operating system in ROM.

When I looked at Unix-derived operating systems like NeXTStep, Irix, and Linux, I noticed a tendency to put everything in its own isolated partition. You didn't have to work that way, but everyone did. Unix has a definite isolationist mentality, roping off every task and function to prevent tasks from interfering with one another. This process increases reliability and it can't help but improve speed as well. If the operating system, applications, data, swap space, and temporary space are all on separate partitions, the likelihood of one corrupting another is reduced, and so is the possibility of fragmentation. Fragmentation-prone filesystems don't fragment as much, and fragmentation-resistant filesystems don't have to work as hard.

As I examined other operating systems, one common thread popped up over and over. These other operating systems have a much greater tendency to take the underlying hardware into consideration. I wondered what would happen if I tried to add similar behavior to Windows.

My conclusions shouldn't be too surprising. Making Windows take the underlying hardware into greater consideration results in a system that performs much better. How much better depends on what you do, but in extreme cases, such as low-end Pentiums without any high-speed cache memory, you can make Windows perform 40% faster.

Working within the limits of your PC and its operating system can force you to think a bit differently and perhaps will make the computer a little bit less user-friendly at first. The difference in performance is so staggering, however, that I doubt you'll mind.

Radical Changes . . . or a Return to the Past?

Some of the techniques I present here will come across as a bit radical and may go directly against common practice. For instance, most computer writers and editors recommend formatting hard drives as one big drive because it's less confusing. In Chapter 3, *Disk Optimization*, I recommend exactly the opposite, suggesting that a single hard drive ought to be split into at least four chunks of varying sizes. This configuration is less confusing for the computer, and I would argue that it can be less confusing for human beings as well. How many of us have a file cabinet with just one drawer in it?

I tend to dedicate partitions of a hard drive to single tasks: one for the operating system, one for programs, one for data, one for temporary files, and possibly one for virtual memory. DOS and Windows have never operated this way by default; I'm suggesting that should change. Some of the fastest and most reliable computers in the world run on Unix systems, which are often split up into this type of partition configuration. My proposal to suddenly change something over to the Unix way of doing things may sound radical—after all, PCs have been operating their own way since 1981. However, I would argue that I'm being conservative, not radical, because Unix has been doing things its way since 1970.

Is My Computer Getting Slower?

If your computer just doesn't seem as zippy today as it did the day you unpacked it, it probably isn't all in your head. I'm sure some of it is simply the result of seeing faster computers. In 1993, I honestly believed a 66 MHz 486 would be all the computer most people would ever need. Then I saw a Pentium being used for something other than playing Windows Solitaire and changed my mind. Today, that Pentium seems slow enough that I wouldn't even want it on my desk as my day-to-day PC. But the gradual decline in your computer's speed over time definitely isn't 100% psychological.

Windows experts have talked about this phenomenon, commonly called "OS rot," for years. I've been reading suggestions ever since 1996 that the "95" in Windows 95 stands for the number of days you should go before reformatting and reinstalling your drive. This approach would work—even a 33 MHz 486 isn't too bad with a clean installation of Windows containing a minimal number of optional components—but it's extreme. This cure could be worse than the disease for many people.

To a certain degree, all Microsoft operating systems exhibit this kind of behavior under the right circumstances. Windows 9x just happens to be more vulnerable than Windows NT and much more widespread than NT or earlier versions of Windows. I've never seen any verifiable evidence that Windows regularly and consistently corrupts itself to the point that a complete reinstall is the only possible remedy. Rather, OS rot seems to be due to a combination of factors, most of them unavoidable if you use your computer for even the most basic tasks.

For instance, sometimes programs will dump junk files into your system's Windows directory, which slows the system down. Junk files also accumulate every time you install software. Be aware that you can be installing software without realizing it. If you download the newest version of RealPlayer so you can listen to RealAudio over the Web, you're installing software. If a piece of software makes a change to any Windows configuration file, chances are that it will dump a backup copy of that file in your Windows directory. Some programs install large pieces of themselves in the Windows directory; Microsoft's own software especially tends to exhibit this trait. Installing Office 97 results in more changes to the Windows system directories than installing some versions of Internet Explorer, which Microsoft bills as an upgrade to the operating system.

A computer is worthless without software, so I'm not saying that installing software is a bad idea. But when you upgrade a piece of software, uninstall the old version before you install the new one. And if possible, monitor every software installation with a third-party uninstallation program.

Regular maintenance can pretty much eradicate the threat of OS rot from your system. This concept is covered throughout the book. In Chapters 10 and 11, I suggest reinstalling whatever version of Windows you use, and I present strategies for doing so. If after performing this installation you follow the rest of the advice in this book, you won't have much problem with OS rot.

What You Can Expect to Get from This Book

I admit that setting computers up in the fashion described in this book is a lot of work. It will take at least twice as long as just accepting the defaults and going on. It's also not a flashy method. This book takes a very utilitarian approach to computing. Many of the whiz-bang features in Windows slow the program down. If I can gain some speed by sacrificing some glitz, I always do it, and recommend that you do it, too. If you're used to having your computer play audio clips and spin icons and use the mouse cursor to wink back at you every time you launch a program, you might even say computers that are set up my way are boring.

But there are tremendous benefits as well. I don't even look at the hardware requirements when I buy a new piece of software. Honestly. I just install the new software and run it, and then sometimes find out later, when I bother to take a look at the box, that my system doesn't meet the supposed minimum requirements. Right after I got Railroad Tycoon II and Alpha Centauri, I installed them on a 75 MHz Pentium. Railroad Tycoon II seemed a little bit slow, so I took a look at the system requirements: both stated a minimum of a Pentium 133. I laughed. From the way they played on my machine, I would have guessed a minimum for Alpha Centauri should be a Pentium 60, or maybe even a 486DX4-120, and the minimum for Railroad Tycoon a Pentium 75. But after I thought about it some more, I realized that if the computers are set up in typical fashion, I can certainly see how a Pentium 120 would be inadequate for these games.

Most people consider a 120 MHz Pentium obsolete now. But properly configured, a Pentium 120 still does a good job with the majority of everyday tasks. I consider a Pentium 100 a little too slow for me to want to use one every day, but it's adequate for most things. Even a 486 can surprise you.

Requirements for This Book

I spend a great deal of time discussing software that doesn't ship with Windows. When possible, I stay with software that's available free of charge. An example of this is Chapter 8, *Modems and the Internet*, where I tell you how to get the functionality of the commercial Internet speedup programs for free. But in some cases, there are no truly adequate free alternatives. For peak performance, your system absolutely needs one of the big three utilities suites (Symantec's Norton Utilities, *www.symantec.com*; Network Associates' Nuts & Bolts, *www.mcafee.com*; or Mijenix's Fix-It, *www.mijenix.com*) and one of the two major uninstallation programs (CleanSweep, formerly marketed by Quarterdeck but now available from Symantec, *www.symantec.com*; or UnInstaller, formerly from MicroHelp but now available from Network Associates, *www.mcafee.com*). Additionally, you'll need an anti-virus program. These tools are discussed in more detail in Chapter 5, *Utilities*.

It might seem ridiculous to buy a $399 computer, then turn around and spend another $150 on software that doesn't even do any day-to-day work. But think of it another way: that $150 worth of software will make your $399 PC run as well as an unenhanced $799 PC. And if you just plunked down $3,499 for the best PC available today, that $150 will give you the performance you paid for. In either case, the investment will delay obsolescence for your shiny new PC.

The most important requirement for this book, however, is multiple backup copies of your Windows directory. Info-ZIP's free command-line Zip and UnZip utilities are excellent choices. Download them from *www.cdrom.com/pub/infozip*. You'll want the 32-bit Windows versions of Zip and UnZip, as well as the 16-bit DOS version of UnZip (which will allow you to restore Windows from a boot floppy if things go wrong). The 32-bit *Unzip.exe* is a self-extracting file. Open a command line, change to the directory where you saved the file, then execute the file (the current version is called *unz540x3.exe*) by typing the filename. You can then use *Unzip.exe* to extract the files from the other archive. Type:

```
Unzip filename
```

Since the current version filename for Zip is *Zip22x3.exe*, you would type:

```
Unzip zip22x3.exe
```

Now copy the 32-bit versions of *Zip.exe* and *Unzip.exe* to *C:\Windows\Command* by typing:

```
copy zip.exe c:\windows\command
```

and pressing Enter. Then type:

```
copy unzip.exe c:\windows\command
```

and press Enter.

Now insert a blank floppy disk and issue the following commands:

```
Sys a:
Unzip zip22x.zip
Copy zip.exe a:\
```

Keep this disk in a safe place. Creating a backup copy of your Windows configuration is easy. Type the following commands:

```
C:
CD\
Zip -R -S windows.zip c:\windows\*.*
```

You will now have a file called *Windows.zip* in the root directory. If you mess up your Windows installation, boot off the floppy disk you just made, then type the following line:

```
Unzip c:\windows.zip -d c:\windows
```

As long as you're careful and follow the instructions in this book exactly, your chances of messing up your system are minimal. If you have a current backup copy, you don't have to worry about it. Experienced computer technicians and administrators keep a series of backup copies as they configure a system, so they can always revert back a step or two when something goes wrong. If you want to keep multiple backup copies, just append a number to the end of the first occurrence of the word "windows" in the preceding lines. For example:

```
C:
CD\
Zip -R -S windows2.zip c:\windows\*.*
```

and:

```
Unzip c:\windows2.zip -d c:\windows
```

This procedure will permit you to keep multiple backups. You can substitute whatever number you wish. You are limited only by the amount of free disk space you have. Once you make a change and verify that the system is indeed working better, I suggest you discard the prior series of backups.

Alternatively, you can use a program like Symantec's Norton Ghost (*www.symantec.com*) or PowerQuest's Drive Image (*www.powerquest.com*) to make backup copies of your entire hard drive to an image file. This is a little bit easier than using Info-ZIP, but it requires you to have more disk space available, and these utilities cost money, whereas Info-ZIP is free.

Whichever method you choose, I cannot possibly overemphasize the importance of making backup copies. I've taken every step possible to minimize or eliminate the problems you might have implementing the suggestions in this book. That said, you probably will still run into problems, and I don't want you to run into a problem you can't reverse.

Measuring the Improvement

I don't talk much about benchmarking programs in this book, because most benchmarking programs seem to be designed for comparing hardware. They're useful for giving you an idea of how much better Quake II will run if you replace your video card with this month's model, but they don't do a very good job of telling you how much faster your system runs right after you defragment your drive. There's no denying that your system runs faster, but the difference doesn't register in the benchmark.

In the June 14, 1999 issue of *InfoWorld*, columnist Brian Livingston proposed an ingenious benchmarking method: set your PC to load all of your largest documents at startup, then restart, and use a stopwatch to measure the time from startup to the instant the Windows hourglass disappears and the hard drive stops churning. Optimize, then repeat the process and compare the two numbers.

The best thing about this method is that it doesn't require you to download or install any software. The method isn't perfect—it's not a thorough test of how quickly the programs perform tasks like accepting input, and it's worthless for gamers who may not keep very many word processing files—but it's a good exercise for most of the components in your system. Best of all, it's specific to how your system is operating *now*—not its ideal condition, its typical condition.

Here's the method, modified slightly in order to be useful for gamers as well. Right-click your Start menu, then click Explore. Double-click Startup. Resize this window so it doesn't fill your entire screen. Now, press Start → Programs → Windows Explorer. Navigate to the directory where you store your data files (probably *C:\My Documents*, but this can vary depending on what programs you run). Select View → Details. Now click Size twice. Take the largest document of each type (your largest word processing document, your largest spreadsheet, your largest newsletter, your longest-playing MP3 file, etc.) and drag it to the window that's displaying your Start menu's Startup group. (Don't worry, you're just creating shortcuts to these files; you're not moving them.) Close that window. Now, right-click your Start menu again, select Explore, and drag your web browser's icon over into the Startup window. If you're a gamer, take the game that takes the longest period of time to load and drag it into the Startup window.

Grab your stopwatch, then restart your computer and time it. You'll probably feel that a calendar would be a more appropriate measuring tool than a stopwatch—these load times can get very long and tedious—but be patient. When the load finishes, write down the time. Now, to return your system to normal, close all of the programs that just loaded. Right-click your desktop, select New → Folder, and name the folder *Startup*. Right-click your Start menu, select Explore, and double-click *Startup*. Drag all those things you just added into the new folder on your desktop. Now you can quickly switch your computer from test mode to general usage mode and back just by dragging those icons between the two folders.

After you've done some performance tuning and you want to measure the results, drag the contents of the *Startup* folder on your desktop to the *Startup* folder in your Start menu, then restart.

2

First Steps

When Windows sets itself up, it makes a number of assumptions about what you want to do with your computer. I have installed Windows 95 on literally hundreds of computers since its introduction, and I have yet to see one installation where those assumptions were correct. Windows' incorrect assumptions come at a price—they consume memory, CPU cycles, or both.

Computer manufacturers make a set of assumptions as well. Frequently, their decisions about setup seem to be aimed at making their computers look flashiest in the store—of course *that* computer has to be the best, just look at all the spinning icons and listen to all the cool sounds! The result is a system that's hopelessly overburdened.

What this means is that no matter who you are and no matter what you do with your computer, there are probably a few adjustments you can make to your system's configuration that will make the system run better.

As I said in Chapter 1, *System Optimization Theory,* computer speed is a complex formula, with CPU speed, amount of memory, memory speed, motherboard speed, video card speed, and hard disk speed being the major variables. Before spending money on hardware upgrades, it makes sense to take what's already there and maximize it.

Every major computer magazine publishes a yearly list of Windows tips, including a handful of speedup tips. These tips work, though their effectiveness tends to vary a bit. The biggest problem is that there just isn't enough room in a magazine to go into much depth about why these tricks work, so the magazine articles end up being a bit superficial.

Chances are, if you're reading this book, you're dissatisfied with your computer's performance. Having seen Pentium systems that run slower than the typical 486, I understand that. I've seen it often. That said, I've also seen overachieving 90 MHz Pentiums that certainly felt much faster, usually because someone beat me to optimizing them. This chapter begins to explain what I do when I sit down in front of a computer and the user or owner complains about it being too slow—or I get sick of waiting on it. Like me, you may find that an overachieving 90 MHz Pentium isn't half bad.

Most of these tricks are easy to implement, so let's start off with the classic, easy-to-implement tips that make a difference right away. Many of these changes will require you to restart the system in order for them to take effect. Unless I tell you specifically to reboot immediately, answer no when given the choice. Make all the changes you want, then restart, and the changes will all take effect at once. While this goes against standard troubleshooting advice, most of these tips won't cause problems, and none cause any problems that later chapters don't tell you how to solve.

Check Your Free Disk Space

I'll talk about how to minimize the importance of checking your free disk space in Chapter 3, *Disk Optimization*, but I'll shoot for the quick fix for now, because if you're having this problem, the implementation of every other trick is going to be downright painful. If the free space on a hard disk falls to below 10% of the size of the drive or 100 MB (whichever is smaller), performance slows to an absolute crawl. The easiest way to quickly check your available disk space is to double-click My Computer, hit F5, and click once on C:. The drive's capacity and free disk space will appear in the lower pane of the window.

If the space is too low, you need to do some quick-and-dirty housecleaning. Leaving the My Computer window open, Start → Find → Files or folders → *.tmp will probably turn up some temp files. Ctrl-A-Shift-Del-Enter will banish them without sending them to the Recycle Bin. To see how much disk space you have freed, click back on the C: icon in the My Computer window and hit F5.

CHK files also tend to clutter up hard drives—these are the lost clusters ScanDisk finds and saves unless told otherwise. Start → Find → Files or folders → *.chk may turn up some more candidates for deletion. Ctrl-A-Shift-Del-Enter disposes of them properly.

If you're still short on space, try Start → Run → c:\Windows and, while holding down the Control key, click once on the folder labeled *Temporary Internet Files* and once on the folder labeled *Cookies*. If you have settings that are saved in cookies, such as logon IDs for password-protected web sites, don't select *Cookies*. Shift-Del will throw away your Internet Explorer cache (IE uses an inordinately high 10% of your available disk space for cache by default) and your Internet

Explorer cookies. Internet Explorer will rebuild this folder the next time it's launched.

If you use Netscape Navigator or Communicator instead of Internet Explorer, try to find your Netscape cache. I suggest Start → Find → Files or Folders → Named → cache → Find in → c:\Program Files\Netscape → Find Now. When you find it, click on it once, then hit Shift-Del.

Should all of this prove inadequate, proceed to the next two tips, which also deal with free disk space.

Uninstall Unneeded Applications

To see what's installed on the system, run Windows 9x's native uninstallation program by pressing Start → Settings → Control Panel → Add/Remove Programs. If you have seldom-used programs there, uninstall them. You can always reinstall a seldom-used program from the original CD or floppy disks if it turns out you need it later.

Installed applications will slow down your hard drive even if you aren't running them. This phenomenon is described in detail in Chapter 3, but as a general rule, the fewer applications you have installed on your system, the faster it will run. Leaving software installed just because you think you might need it someday is usually a bad idea. When programs used to come on stacks of ten or more floppy disks, this made more sense. But now that programs come on CD-ROM and install in a minute, it just doesn't make much sense to leave those programs you only run once a year installed all the time.

We also buy some packages that we use only once—tax preparation software comes to mind. Once your tax return is filed, uninstall your tax preparation software. The uninstall program will leave your data files alone, so if you reinstall the software, your return is still there. This is good, because it means next year's edition will be able to find your return to import data, and in the case of an IRS audit (gulp), you can reinstall and the program will find your data.

Other examples of good candidates for uninstallation would include games you rarely play anymore and previous versions of software packages you've upgraded. Chapter 5, *Utilities*, will deal with the problems of disk bloat in more detail.

If you have a small number of applications that you rarely use but never know when you'll need them, you might want to consider installing a second copy of Windows and installing them under that copy, keeping a cleaner copy for general use. This advanced technique is covered in Chapter 10, *Clean Windows Installation.*

Get Rid of Excess Fonts

Windows 9x is better at font management than Windows 3.1 was, but this platform still has difficulty managing large numbers of fonts. Fonts consume disk space and chew up CPU cycles whether you're using them or not. If you have hundreds of fonts, either get a package like Adobe Type Manager Deluxe that lets you group and categorize them for special projects, or group and categorize them into folders yourself, dragging their contents into your fonts folder as you need them. As long as fonts aren't in the *C:\Windows\Fonts* directory, they're just occupying disk space, and they're not consuming any CPU cycles.

For general home use, the default set of fonts installed with Windows is adequate: Arial, Courier New, Marlett, Symbol, Times New Roman, Verdana, Wingdings, and Webdings. (Windows 95 doesn't come with Marlett, Verdana, and Webdings by default.) Having an additional serifed font (a font with feet and ears like Times New Roman) and an additional sans-serif font (a clean font like Arial) won't drag your system down a noticeable amount, and using fonts other than Arial and Times will give your documents a distinctive look. Chances are you will want a handful of novelty fonts—those fun fonts you use on greeting cards—as well. But by all means, if there's a font on your system that you don't like and can't imagine using, get rid of it. Windows 9x can handle a few dozen fonts without much difficulty, but hundreds of fonts will take its toll.

If you have a low-resource system like an old 486, or if you are short on disk space, strip out any unused fonts, including rarely used bold and italic variations of fonts you do use. Windows can generate draft-quality bolds and italics from the base font when needed. And the only people likely to need the Symbol font are mathematicians, college students living in Greek houses, and students studying the Greek language. If you don't fall into any of those three categories, you can ditch Symbol as well.

Defragment Your Hard Drive

After you maximize your free space, you want to defragment your drive using Start → Programs → Accessories → Disk Defragmenter. Defragment whether Windows says you need to or not. There are strategies for defragmenting, third-party utilities that do a better job, and strategies for reducing the frequency with which you will need to defragment your drive. These are covered in Chapters 3 and 5. For now, blind optimization is far better than no optimization.

Defragment your drive after you remove any large quantity of data from your hard drive, as well as any time you install software. You should also make a habit of defragmenting your drive once a month.

The need to defragment a drive is one point that the popular computer press has done a good job of driving home. The reasons why fragmentation happens and the reasons it can slow your computer down are discussed in detail in Chapter 3.

Lose autoexec.bat and config.sys

Chapters 3 and 7 discuss the creation of optimal configuration files, but because the configuration files most PCs come with from the manufacturer are worse than no configuration files at all, rename *autoexec.bat* to *autoexec.xyz* and rename *config.bat* to *config.xyz* and restart. If you don't run DOS programs, this trick is a double blessing: you speed up your system, and you don't have to change the way you work at all. Renaming the files like this allows you to keep the files for reference, but keeps the system from finding them and using the configuration data in them. You could use your initials as the extension; I suggest using the letters "xyz."

Be sure to restart immediately after you do this procedure, because it can have a dramatic effect on your system speed. It can also prevent the problem described in the next section.

Make Sure Your System Is Using 32-bit Drivers

If the system is much slower than it should be, there's a good chance that Windows isn't using its native 32-bit drivers for disk access. Another common symptom of this problem is a nonfunctioning CD-ROM drive. To check for more symptoms, press Start, then proceed to Settings → Control Panel → System → Performance. If you see a message that says certain drives are using MS-DOS compatibility mode, you have a problem. Switch over to Device Manager → Hard Disk Controllers. If you see yellow exclamation points, you may have one very common (but perplexing) Windows 9x problem. To fix it, press Start, then proceed to Run → Regedit, then Ctrl-F-NoIDE-Enter. We'll talk about Regedit in a little bit more depth later in this chapter. For now, if Regedit comes back with a key labeled NoIDE highlighted in blue, right-click on it and select Delete. Now restart immediately. You should see an immediate, dramatic improvement in disk performance.

Clean Out Your Startup Group

There may be programs Windows is loading at startup that you don't need. Right-click Start → Explore → Programs → Startup. Take a look around at the items in your *Startup* folder. Perhaps two of the most common are Microsoft Find Fast and

Office Startup. Both are components of Office 95 and Office 97. Find Fast indexes the files on your hard drive at certain intervals. This process speeds up the Start menu's Find operation somewhat and allows you to search the text of your files, but at the expense of making Pentiums feel half as fast as their rated speed. If these features are less important to you than system speed, remove Find Fast. Office Startup makes Office load slightly faster, but Office can run without it, and Office Startup consumes memory. Unless you use your computer almost exclusively for Office-based applications, remove Office Startup. If there are other programs running at startup that you don't need to load automatically, get rid of them.

There are two other places from which programs can run at startup. Press Start → Run → sysedit → win.ini → Search → Find → run= → Next. Step through and delete (or comment out by preceding with a semicolon) any line that runs a program you don't want starting automatically. Startup programs can also hide in the registry. Press Start → Run → regedit. Navigate to HKEY_LOCAL_MACHINE\SOFTWARE\ Microsoft\Windows\CurrentVersion\Run and examine any RunOnce, RunServices, and RunServicesOnce keys.

Digging around in *win.ini* and in the registry can be cumbersome, and putting deleted programs back if necessary is even more cumbersome. To make life easier, download a freeware program called Startup Manager from *www. delphifreestuff.com/freeware/files/sm-setup.exe*. For more on Startup Manager, see Chapter 5.

Optimize Your Swap File

First things first: forget every piece of advice you've ever heard or read about virtual memory. There's a lot of correct information about it out there, but there's also a lot of dubious advice. You've probably heard something about multiplying the amount of memory you have by three and using that figure. Forget that. Generic, one-size-fits-all advice about virtual memory doesn't work for your system. The amount of memory (and the amount of virtual memory) you need depends on what you do with your computer—not on what some hotshot computer journalist does with it.

Windows' default method of handling virtual memory works well for exactly two kinds of people: those who have far too little memory in their systems (8 MB or so), and those who run voice recognition programs like Dragon Naturally Speaking or IBM ViaVoice. If you fall into either of these categories, proceed to the next section.

If you're still with me here, you need to figure out how much virtual memory you require. So hit the Web and go to *www.sisoftware.demon.co.uk/sandra*, where you can download an outstanding utility called SiSoft Sandra Standard. This is a free utility that gives a host of invaluable information about your system. Install Sandra.

Now, think for a minute. Picture your computer at its worst—the hourglass sitting there taunting you, the hard drive grinding incessantly, the computer acting like someone poured thick molasses into it. Maybe it's when you have your web mail client, your instant messaging client, and your MP3 player all open and active at once. Maybe there's one game in your library that takes forever to load and then trudges along jerkily. Whatever it is, find that configuration.

Maybe you're lucky and you haven't found that configuration yet. If that's the case, I'll tell you how to make it. If you're a gamer, load a game, then switch back to Windows Explorer and launch another. Switch back again and launch another. Repeat until you've either loaded every game you own or you can't stand your computer's slowness anymore.

If you use your computer for personal productivity, open your web browser and your email client. Open Solitaire or Minesweeper or some other simple game. Run your spreadsheet program and open your biggest, nastiest spreadsheet file. Now open your word processor and load that 25-page paper you had to write last term (or whatever your biggest word processing document happens to be). Open your personal finance program. If you have a desktop publishing program, open it along with its biggest document. Open your photo editing program and load your biggest picture into it.

If your system isn't crawling by now, congratulations. You have absolutely too much memory, and you get to proceed to the next section and ignore everything else I have to say here. And if you're thinking you never have this much stuff open, don't worry about it. Someday you'll strain your computer—we're getting it ready for that day. We're trying to simulate the absolute toughest load you can throw at your computer.

Now that your computer is begging for mercy, launch SiSoft Sandra (Start → Programs → SiSoft Utilities → SiSoft Sandra 99 Standard). Hit OK to clear its startup tip. Double-click the icon labeled Windows Memory Information. Look at the heading labeled Current Swap File, then look at the heading labeled Free Page File. Subtract Free Page File from Current Swap File, and you now know the amount of virtual memory you need. Write down that number because you'll need it in a few minutes. Hit OK, then close Sandra, then close that obnoxious number of programs I had you open. Now that you have a clean system with no programs running, go into Control Panel and open the System applet. Proceed to Performance → Virtual Memory → Disable Virtual Memory. Windows will complain about reduced performance and other assorted paranoia. Ignore it. We need Windows to start without a swap file, because Defrag cannot defragment the swap file, nor can it move it. So we turn off virtual memory in order to get the swap file out of the way. We'll re-create it after we're finished.

After rebooting, run Start → Run → Defrag. Go ahead and defragment all of your hard drives, even if Windows says they are 0% fragmented. Windows' definition of 0% fragmentation is awfully lenient. If the files themselves aren't fragmented, the disk can have gaps in the free space and still be considered 0% fragmented. A disk meeting this definition of zero fragmentation won't stay unfragmented for long. We'll talk a whole lot more about defragging in Chapter 3.

Should Windows fail to start properly, reboot and hit F8 at the "Starting Windows 9x" message. Select Safe Mode from the boot menu. Safe Mode will always run, but defragmentation in Safe Mode is much slower than normal.

Now that your hard drive is defragmented, reenter Control Panel → System → Performance → Virtual Memory → Let me specify my own virtual memory settings. Enter the number you got from running Sandra for the minimum and maximum values.

These settings work very well for the majority of applications. Windows spends less time trying to figure out how much virtual memory it's going to need—it usually does a poor job anyway—and the CPU spends its time instead concentrating on real work.

Optimize Your Disk Cache (and Get a UPS!)

The only reason I can think of for using Windows' default disk cache settings is fear of data loss should the power go out. Windows keeps the last few filenames and directory names it has accessed in memory to improve performance. The default settings use about 16K; the best settings (without registry hacks) use 40K. Unless you have less than 8 MB of RAM, this is just about the best investment of 24K of memory you can make. Admittedly, this change does make the system more vulnerable to power outages, so you should have an Uninterruptible Power Supply (UPS) if you choose to use this setting. This isn't a big deal—a UPS makes your system crash less and last longer by supplying it with consistent power, and UPSs are cheap. I frequently see low-end APC UPSs, which are fine for home use, on sale for $50.

Go to Start → Settings → Control Panel → System → Performance → File System → Typical Role of this Machine → Network Server. Windows will now store the last 2,729 filenames and the last 64 directory names it's used. Of the well-known tips, this one tends to make the most noticeable difference.

The original August 24, 1995 release of Windows 95 and the OEM Service Release 1 (Windows 95A) both contain a bug in this setting that actually causes the network server settings to dramatically slow the machine down.

To find out what version of Windows 95 you are running, go to Control Panel → System → General. Under a heading labeled System, Windows will tell you its version number. If the version is Windows 95 4.00.950 or Windows 95 4.00.950 A, you need the bug fix, presented later in this chapter; it involves changing the Windows registry.

Tune the Hidden Windows Disk Cache Settings

This trick is not as well known. You can force Windows to allocate a fixed amount of memory for disk caching, or to set a floor or ceiling on the amounts it uses. To do this, press Start → Run → SYSEDIT. Click on the window labeled *C:\Windows\ System.ini*. Near the bottom of the file, there is a line containing [vcache]. Under [vcache], add the following lines:

```
MinFileCache=4096
MaxFileCache=4096
```

The values you include for these two settings will vary. If you have a Pentium-class processor, set MinFileCache to $1/8$ of your total memory or 1024, whichever is lower, and set MaxFileCache to $1/4$ of your memory or 16384, whichever is lower. If you have a 386 or 486 processor, set MinFileCache and MaxFileCache to the same value—either $1/4$ of your memory if you have 16 MB or more, or $1/8$ if you have less.

Windows uses its VCACHE to mirror data on your hard drive. It takes only a little bit longer to read 128K off the disk than it takes to read 64K, so when Windows asks for 64K, the VCACHE will go ahead and read more data than Windows asks for. And if Windows asks for the next piece, VCACHE can provide that data from RAM instead of from the disk. Also, if you ask for a piece of data once, there's a decent chance you'll ask for it again, so VCACHE holds whatever data you've loaded last for as long as possible.

To illustrate this principle, try restarting your computer, then loading a large application like Microsoft Word. Count off the seconds before it loads—an unscientific one-one-thousand, two-one-thousand will suffice for this illustration. Now immediately close Word and load it again. This time, it will load much more quickly, because much of Word is loading from RAM rather than from disk.

Long ago, disk caches were a fixed size. You told the system how much memory to use to cache the hard drive, and that memory couldn't be used for any other purpose. Windows 95 introduced dynamic disk caching, which uses however much free memory is available for a disk cache. If you're not using much memory, you get a big disk cache. If you're using a lot of memory, Windows is supposed to use a small disk cache.

On a fast computer with a lot of memory, this is a really good idea. But slow computers may not have enough CPU time to dynamically tune their caches without affecting the other work they have to do. And a computer with 8 MB of RAM can't hold Windows Explorer entirely in RAM, so there's no point in allocating more than $1/4$ of available RAM to caching. And there's no point in letting Windows constantly chew up CPU cycles to come to that conclusion.

Even if you have memory to burn, it makes sense to give Windows a floor and a ceiling, because Windows' dynamic caching often makes imprudent decisions— sometimes allocating as much as 80% of system memory to the disk cache. There are very few situations where you don't want a disk cache, but by the same token, if you are using more than about $1/4$ of your available memory for disk cache, you're improving disk performance at the expense of the rest of your system.

Tune Your CD-ROM Caching

Stop—read this tip even if you don't have a CD-ROM drive. Just because you know you don't have a CD-ROM drive doesn't mean Windows does. Open Control Panel → System → Performance → File System → CD-ROM.

The conventional advice is to set the Supplemental cache size slider all the way to the right, and set Optimize Access Patterns to quad-speed or higher, regardless of the speed of your CD-ROM drive. If you make heavy use of your CD-ROM drive and you have more than 16 MB of memory, you should do this step.

If your system doesn't have a CD-ROM drive, or if you don't use the CD-ROM drive for anything but installing software or listening to music CDs, do the opposite. Slide the supplemental cache size all the way to the left, and set Optimize Access Patterns to "No read-ahead." Now Windows will allocate 64K of precious memory to caching your nonexistent CD-ROM drive. This is wasteful, but could be worse. Sometimes Windows chooses to allocate 1.2 MB to this task. This trick is absolutely essential if you are running Windows 95 or 98 on a system with 4 or 8 MB of RAM. I'll tell you how to recover that 64K of memory later in this chapter, after we talk about Regedit.

Windows' default CD-ROM drive settings don't make a whole lot of sense. Slow and fast drives alike benefit from large amounts of caching. Windows would be better off picking an arbitrary amount of memory to cache any CD-ROM drives present, and pick the amount based on the total amount of system memory, rather than on the speed of the drive. Though Windows doesn't do it automatically and you can't change the memory usage from the Control Panel, you can change it from the registry. If you have plenty of memory and you want the smoothest possible playback from CD-ROM, it's possible to tune the quad-speed settings for today's much faster drives. Since this tip requires digging into the registry, I'll talk about it later in the chapter.

Turn Off CD-ROM Autoplay

Under some circumstances, Windows 9x polls the CD-ROM drive every few seconds to see if a CD has been inserted. Depending on the nature of your system, this can make things noticeably more sluggish. You can turn this off with the Windows 95 PowerToys, but it's best to go to the source. Control Panel → System → Device Manager → CD-ROM → <name of your CD-ROM drive> → Properties → Settings. Clear the box labeled Auto Insert Notification, then click OK. If you have more than one CD or DVD device, repeat this process for each drive in your system.

Unfortunately, a small number of software titles assume you have autoplay turned on. If you turn autoplay off and then a program refuses to install or behaves erratically when you run it, try turning autoplay back on to see if the program will run.

Optimize Your Multimedia Settings

Windows 95 and 98 make some fairly absurd assumptions about the multimedia devices connected to a typical PC. Click Start → Settings → Control Panel → Multimedia → Advanced (in Windows 98, Start → Settings → Control Panel → Multimedia → Devices). Expand the view for Media Control Devices. Among these, you will find entries for VISCA VCR Device and Pioneer LaserDisc Player. If you don't have a laser disc player connected to your computer, click on its entry, hit Properties, hit Remove, and hit OK. If you're like me and 99.9% of all other computer users, and you don't have a VCR connected to your computer, do the same for the VCR device entry.

Windows 9x assumes that you have these devices connected to your computer, yet you don't want to use them. It doesn't make the same assumptions about more common hardware like CD-ROM drives and sound cards. It assumes you have them and want to use them, even if you don't. If you don't have a CD-ROM drive or you don't use it to play audio CDs, go to CD Audio Device → Properties → Do not use this Media Control Device → Remove → OK. If you don't have a sound card, remove the MIDI Sequencer Device and Wave Audio Device in the same fashion. If you're really strapped for memory and are willing to risk incompatibility with some software, you can try doing the same thing for the ActiveMovie MCI Driver and the Motion Video Device. A small number of multimedia titles and older games—especially those that stream full-motion video straight off the CD-ROM—need these features, so there's a small chance you may find you have to add them back in. But most popular game titles today don't use them, and neither do most productivity titles. Should you find yourself needing them back—you'll know you do if a program that used to work suddenly starts giving you error messages—just insert your Windows CD-ROM, then go to Control Panel → Add New

Hardware → Next → No → Next → Sound, video and game controllers → Next → Manufacturer → Microsoft MCI, and select the device you need. If you need multiple devices, repeat this process for each one.

Windows 9x also installs coder/decoders (codecs) for various obsolete audio and video formats. You can remove these on an interim basis, adding them back in if you find your software uses them. Newer software is more likely to use Apple's QuickTime video standard than Intel's older Indeo® standard. You can ditch Indeo® with Control Panel → Multimedia → Advanced → Video Compression Codecs → Indeo® video 5.04 and Intel Indeo® Video Interactive 32-bit Driver → Properties → Remove → Yes → OK → OK. While you're there, you can go into the Audio Compression Codecs, and you can get rid of the Indeo® audio software. Windows 95 also installs an MSN audio codec, which you can eliminate.

If you find you need to replace any of these codecs, it's easy enough—just go to Control Panel → Add New Hardware → Next → No → Next → Sound, video, and game controllers → Next → Manufacturer, then pick the appropriate manufacturer (usually either Microsoft or Intel), and pick the codec you need to reinstall.

Turn Off Power Management

By default, Windows will shut down your hard drive after a period of inactivity. This feature can cause significant slowdowns, because your drive then has to power back up the next time it's accessed. The delay can easily be a second or more. This delay will be noticeable if your disk cache has been working well and your system hasn't had to access the drive for a long period of time, but a sudden change of events makes the system look to the drive.

The wisdom of turning off hard drives in order to save power is questionable anyway. This practice causes them to wear out much more quickly, and the amount of money you save will be pennies per year, if that—the amount of power a modern hard drive consumes is that negligible. Reducing the lifespan of a useful drive that will cost $200 to replace in order to save a dime just doesn't seem like a wise move.

In laptop computers, the situation is a little bit different since your primary concern is battery life, rather than performance or longevity. You have little choice but to use power management on your laptop; however, keep it turned off on your desktop computer.

In Windows 95, go to Start → Settings → Control Panel → Power. Clear the box that reads "Allow Windows to manage power usage on this computer." Then click on the Disk Drives tab and clear the checkbox there as well.

In Windows 98, go to Start → Settings → Control Panel → Power Management → Power Schemes → Home/office desk → Turn off hard disks → Never.

Take Down Your Wallpaper

This is usually an unpopular tip, but on anything but the newest systems, a backdrop on your desktop slows down your system by consuming memory to store it and consuming CPU cycles to redraw it. The simpler your backdrop is, the faster your system will be. And if you have a 486, by all means don't have a fancy backdrop—you have neither the CPU cycles nor the memory to spare.

In all fairness, modern CPUs and fast AGP video cards minimize this effect. The amount of speed you wring out of the typical Pentium II 450 won't be noticeable, but it can make a difference on a marginal system. I'll use wallpaper on my Cyrix MII-PR233 because it has a fast 128-bit STB video card and a boatload of RAM. But I don't even think about wallpaper on my Pentium 90 with its puny 32-bit Trident video card. That system needs all the help it can get.

If you have Windows 98 or have Internet Explorer 4 or 5 installed under Windows 95, Active Desktop permits you to use GIF or JPEG images or web pages as wallpaper. This is a serious performance drain. If you must keep your wallpaper, you can convert it into a resource-saving *.bmp* file and reset it as your wallpaper in one swoop by loading the image into Internet Explorer or Netscape Navigator, then right-clicking it and selecting the Set As Wallpaper option.

Use Hotkeys Instead of Desktop Icons

Many people keep shortcuts to their most frequently used applications on their desktop. In the past, I've recommended that people follow this practice. Unfortunately, having dozens of icons on the desktop slows the system down for the same reason that having desktop wallpaper does, only more so because the system frequently has to load the icons from disk when redrawing the desktop. Keep your desktop simple—if you need fast access to certain key applications and don't want to navigate the Start menu, define hotkeys instead. They're faster than double-clicking an icon, they're always available without having to make the desktop visible again, and they don't slow the system down.

To make a hotkey, right-click on the Start menu and hit Explore. Navigate to your program's icon, then right-click on it and hit Properties. Click the Shortcut tab, and click in the box labeled Shortcut Key. Hit a key that makes sense—I typically use the first letter of the application's name—then hit OK. From then on, hitting Ctrl-Alt and that letter key will launch that application.

I use my word processor to print a list of my computer's hotkeys in ten-point text—just a simple list containing each key and the program it launches—and I cut it out and tape it to my monitor.

Lose the Screen Savers

The need for screen savers evaporated in the early 1990s when monitor refresh rates increased, but people continue to buy them. There is absolutely no compelling reason to use them; from a technical standpoint, they do far more harm than good. The real danger with monitors is not the picture becoming permanently etched onto the screen; it's the phosphors wearing out from being overworked. Many screen savers have nearly as much movement as a fast-paced video game and make the monitor and CPU work about as hard as well. If your system is doing routine maintenance like scanning for viruses, checking hard disks for errors and correcting them, or defragmenting hard disks—things it should be doing automatically, and we'll cover that in Chapter 5—a screen saver interrupting those tasks will make them take much longer. If you're waiting for the computer to finish some time-intensive task like a transform in Photoshop or even a lengthy download from the Internet, the screen saver steals valuable RAM and CPU power from that task. It also creates one more task for the computer to juggle—and one more reason for it to crash. Some screen savers have been known to crash systems.

Using the Blank Screen screen saver that comes with Windows is a good idea; it doesn't use any CPU power, and it gives your monitor's phosphors the opportunity to really rest, saving wear and tear on the monitor and reducing its power consumption. If you want to protect your monitor, use Blank Screen and give it a timeout period of 30 minutes. The use of any other screen saver causes more harm than good.

Some monitors eliminate the need for any screen saver altogether. My Iiyama Vision Master Pro monitor has a power management menu. If your monitor has digital on-screen controls, it may also have its own power management. If that's the case, set your monitor to put itself in power-saving mode after 30 minutes, which allows you to dispense even with the Blank Screen screen saver.

Lose the System Sounds and Desktop Schemes

The Microsoft Plus packs for Windows 95 and 98 contain some gimmicks such as desktop themes than cause icons to spin as they're clicked. Unless you have an extremely high-end computer—as of this writing, that would be a better than 400 MHz computer with more than 64 MB of RAM—turn that stuff off. In many cases, it takes longer for the computer to spin the program's icon than it does to load and launch the program.

You also want to turn off animated cursors and system sounds, as these toys can steal large amounts of memory and CPU time. If you need system sounds to warn you of important things like critical events, program errors, or incoming mail, go ahead and use them, but refrain from assigning sounds to every event. On the majority of systems, I go into the Sounds control panel, select the schemes box, and set it to No Sounds.

I know you lose some personalization by doing these things. I know that setting the Critical Stop event to a *.wav* file of Peter Sellers saying, "Special delivery for you. A bomb. Did you order one?" helps you keep your sense of humor when Windows decides to crash. And I've been known to run down the canonical list of weird band names, making multimedia themes based on the music of Alien Sex Fiend and of Crispy Ambulance (heaven forbid I use a halfway calm and sane-sounding artist like Elvis Costello or Aimee Mann) for my colleagues' systems. I can also tell you that I've never seen a 300 MHz system run as slow as it did with those themes installed. At the time, that was one of the fastest computers money could buy, but it ran like a low-end 486. That's why I never put any of these themes on my own systems—only on other people's.

If you want to express your creativity without dragging down your system or alienating your friends, family, or coworkers, there are other, less expensive ways to customize your system. Try coming up with your own color schemes, or changing Windows' font sets and sizes instead. Right-click on the desktop, select Properties, and click on the Appearance tab. Use those settings to express yourself, rather than CPU-hogging cursors and sounds. You can also try playing around with Lite-Step, a replacement Windows shell (covered in Chapter 6, *Replacement Windows Shells*), which is almost infinitely customizable.

Turn Off the Windows 98 Animations

One of the few noticeable changes between Windows 95 and Windows 98 is the menu animation in Windows 98. That slows the computer down. It might also annoy or distract you. To turn it off, go to Control Panel → Display → Effects → Animate windows, menus, and lists.

Turn Off Windows 98 Tooltips

One of the most maddening things (to me at least) about Windows 98 are the tooltips that pop up right as I'm about to do something. If I didn't know what the close box on the program's title bar did, would I be pointing at it?

To banish the tooltips, install the Windows 98 version of TweakUI, located in *tools**reskit**powertoy* on the Windows 98 CD. Right-click the *tweakui.inf* file and select Install to install it. You can now pick TweakUI from the Control Panel, and choose the General tab. Confusingly, the tooltips are called "Mouse hot tracking effects." Deselect that option, and Windows will assume you know what you're doing and won't annoy you when you reach for that minimize or maximize button.

Find the Fastest Settings for Your Video Card

You may be expecting me to say that the best setting for your video card is 640×480 with 256 colors. That's the classic advice, but unless you have an old, unaccelerated VGA or SVGA video card, that isn't the case anymore. That's good, because 640×480 doesn't provide enough resolution for effective multitasking, and web pages just don't look very good in 256 colors.

Since people generally don't use those low-resolution, 256-color settings anymore, video card manufacturers optimize their cards and drivers for high-resolution, high-color displays. Computer magazine benchmark programs usually test at a minimum of resolution of 1024×768 with 16-bit color, so video card manufacturers frequently optimize their drivers for that resolution in an effort to give the appearance of being the fastest video card. Gaming sites on the Web frequently test at 800×600 with at least 16-bit color, so if the video card manufacturer is targeting the gaming crowd, it may optimize for that resolution.

You can benchmark your system's video performance at various settings to determine the best one to use. But for most people, an unscientific test will suffice. If you have Windows 98, go to Start → Settings → Control Panel → Display → Effects → Show window contents while dragging. This setting gives the video card a good workout. Enable this, then drag the window around and note whether the movement is jumpy or smooth. Try different resolutions and color depths (Control Panel → Display → Settings → Colors, Screen Area), and note which setting gives the best movement.

On Windows 95, go to Start → Settings → Control Panel → Display → Plus! → Show window contents while dragging, which will have the same effect. If you don't have the Plus! Tab, you can download the Windows 95 font smoothing utility from *www.microsoft.com/windows95/downloads* to get that capability. Alternatively, just load a long document into your word processor, and see if the speed of its scrolling changes as resolution and color depth change.

Interestingly enough, I found that on some modern AGP video cards, 16-bit color is fast, 24-bit color is extremely slow, but 32-bit color is nearly as fast as 16-bit color. Your common sense and intuition aren't likely to help you much in finding the fastest video setting. Try them all, even the modes that go against your better judgment.

Enable Your Hard Drive's DMA Setting

If your disk controller is capable of direct memory access (DMA) and has the correct driver installed, you can dramatically reduce the amount of CPU power your drives require. DMA permits the controller chip to write to memory directly, rather than sending it to the CPU and making the CPU write it to memory. This feature alone doesn't do much to improve the speed of the data transfer, but it does permit the CPU to do other work while disk access is taking place, which can increase overall system speed.

Many people know to download the DMA-capable drivers for their disk controllers, but they frequently miss this step, which negates most of the benefit of having the drivers. To enable DMA, go to Start → Control Panel → System → Device Manager → Disk Drives → <any IDE drive present> → Properties → Settings → Options → Enable DMA.

If the drive or controller isn't capable of DMA, or if the installed driver doesn't support DMA, the Enable DMA box won't appear. In addition, this box probably won't appear on SCSI devices, because SCSI controllers generally use DMA by default and don't give the option to turn it off.

Shrink Your Start Menu

If you absolutely must save every last CPU cycle you can, right-click your taskbar, hit Properties, and check the box that says "Show small icons in Start Menu." This gives you a smaller Start menu, which will draw slightly faster, allowing you to cut down the time it takes to launch programs by a few fractions of a second. Or, if you're like me, you may find you like the look of the smaller Start menu better, in which case the few fractions of a second you save are just a bonus.

While you're playing with the Start menu, you might as well organize it, too. Right-click the Start menu, then click Explore. You'll probably find all sorts of things right away that think they're the most important part of your system. Three common items are New Office Document, Open Office Document, and Netscape Smart-Update. Maybe you're like me and you've never clicked on any of those. Delete them if you don't use them. The only item that appears here that you really need is Windows 98's Windows Update, which you should never delete. Now double-click on Programs. You can reorganize these items as well. For example, Netscape browsers create a folder with tons of superfluous icons. Chances are the only icon in the group that you use is Netscape Navigator. Drag it out to the Programs section, then delete the folder.

Come up with an organization scheme that makes sense to you. Maybe you want all of your 3D shooter games grouped together in one folder. Create or rename a folder and drag all of the icons into it, then delete the old ones. We all work a bit differently, so our Start menus should probably reflect that. You want to be able to quickly find the things you use frequently. It makes you work faster, and, yes, the computer spends less time drawing the menu.

A Primer on Regedit and the Registry

Regedit is the tool Microsoft ships to edit the Windows registry, which is a kind of catch-all for system settings. Regedit was intended to replace *autoexec.bat, config. sys*, and the myriad of *.ini* files in the Windows directory. These files didn't completely disappear in Windows 9x, but they are much smaller and much less important than they used to be. The registry itself is a large database consisting of two files named *system.dat* and *user.dat*.

You shouldn't casually poke around inside the registry and change things. A corrupt registry can cause programs to malfunction, or worse, it can render the system unstartable.

Since Regedit is such a powerful and dangerous tool, it doesn't appear anywhere in the Start menu. You can add it to the Start menu or to the desktop by creating a new shortcut, typing Regedit in the command-line field, and clicking OK. Or you can just go to Start → Run → Regedit. Which approach you should use is up to you—if you're technically adept and are the only person who uses your computer, go ahead and add an icon. If other people use your computer, I suggest resisting the temptation to create an icon for it.

When you launch Regedit, its window will look like Figure 2-1. Regedit resembles Windows Explorer somewhat both in feel and in concept. The folders resemble subfolders of a hard drive, so I will refer to them in the same fashion—referring to HKEY_CURRENT_USER\Control Panel\Desktop just as I would *C:\Windows\ System*. When I say to navigate to HKEY_CURRENT_USER\Control Panel\Desktop, I mean double-click on HKEY_CURRENT_USER, then double-click Control Panel, then double-click Desktop.

Just as you can create a new file by right-clicking in an empty area in Explorer and selecting New from the pop-up menu, you can create a new registry key by right-clicking in an empty area in Regedit and selecting New.

The registry's layout is a bit complicated, but some explanation makes it much more logical. The registry is divided into six major subtrees:

HKEY_CLASSES_ROOT (HKCR)
> This part contains user interface information, such as shortcut settings, drag-and-drop operations, and file associations. The settings here define Windows' reaction to mouse clicks, menus, and the other fundamental things that make

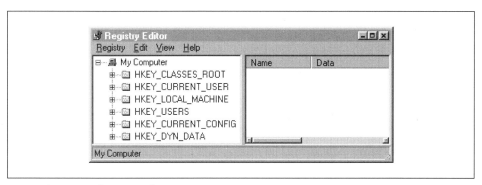

Figure 2-1. Launching Regedit

Windows 9x *feel* like Windows 9x. This branch is a mirror of HKLM\Software\ Classes.

HKEY_CURRENT_USER (HKCU)

This part contains settings or preferences for the currently logged-in user. Many important performance tuning settings are located here. Unfortunately, Windows is inconsistent about which settings should be global and which settings should apply only to the current user, so if you have a networked environment with more than one user logging into a PC, you may have to do some of the optimizations for each user who logs in.

HKEY_LOCAL_MACHINE (HKLM)

This part contains generic, global hardware and software settings that apply to all users of the machine. These settings are stored in \ *Windows\system.dat*. Because of the global nature of this subtree, optimizations performed here only have to take place once.

HKEY_USERS (HKU)

This part contains all of the data for all of the machine's users. Think of this as the permanent storage area for each user's HKCU subtree. Each user of the PC gets a separate subkey here, which is mirrored to HKCU at logon. If the system has only one user, the only subkey here is called .Default.

This branch's values are stored in \ *Windows\user.dat*, and if profiles are enabled, in \ *Windows\Profiles\<login-name>\user.dat*.

HKEY_CURRENT_CONFIG (HKCC)

This part is the source of HKLM. Windows 9x supports multiple hardware configurations, although this ability is seldom used except on laptop computers. Each configuration has a number, and this number is the configuration's subkey under HKCC. When Windows boots and you select a hardware configuration, that configuration is mirrored from HKCC to HKLM.

If you have multiple hardware profiles enabled on your PC—for instance, if you have a laptop with separate profiles for the office and for home—and you want to optimize it, you must perform these optimizations once in each profile.

HKEY_DYN_DATA (HKDD)

As the name suggests, this part contains dynamic data that can change. This subtree exists only in memory, not in either of the registry's files. This contains Plug-and-Play information and performance monitoring statistics.

From the standpoint of performance tuning, the only truly important registry subtrees are HKCU and HKLM. HKCC and HKU are important only because they are the source for HKLM and HKCU, but it is safer and easier to manipulate HKLM and HKCU than it is to manipulate HKCC and HKU directly.

In the following sections, I will explain the various subkeys in HKCU and HKLM, since an overview of these subtrees adds a little bit of clarification to what we are doing in the rest of the chapter. The Windows registry is much like an unfamiliar city. A map is no substitute for a lifetime spent in the city, but it helps you to understand written directions a bit better. What follows is a map of the two most important parts of the city, or registry. The written directions will follow the map.

If you want a more detailed discussion of the registry, there are several books available. *Windows 95 in a Nutshell*, by Tim O'Reilly and Troy Mott (O'Reilly & Associates), and its companion book by O'Reilly, Mott, and Walter Glenn, *Windows 98 in a Nutshell* (O'Reilly & Associates), both dedicate a full chapter to an overview of the registry from the user's standpoint. *Inside the Windows 95 Registry*, by Ron Petrusha (O'Reilly & Associates), goes into much more detail about the registry and how it works, and covers advanced use of Regedit from the perspective of a software developer. Experienced users wanting a more thorough understanding of the registry will benefit from consulting *Inside the Windows 95 Registry*.

Although performance tuning does require some spelunking into the registry, these excursions are limited to a few small areas. The important areas (from a system optimization standpoint) are noted. A brief overview of the less important areas is provided strictly for clarity—for the same reason people will usually describe nearby streets as well as the destination street when giving directions.

HKCU

HKCU contains seven top-level subkeys that define how Windows will behave. Their structure is somewhat inconsistent—merely a repository for the data the authors of Windows and whatever applications you have installed felt necessary to store someplace. This inconsistency, unfortunately, goes all the way down to the capitalization and use of spaces in the subkeys.

HKCU\AppEvents stores the associations between application events and the sounds the system plays when they occur. When you select a sound scheme in the Control Panel (something that is almost always detrimental to performance, as stated earlier), the information contained in the scheme is stored here.

HKCU\Control Panel stores some of the data from the Control Panel applets, though many Control Panel settings are still stored in *.ini* files. Windows 9x's inconsistencies are rarely more evident than they are here: not all changeable control panel settings are stored in HKCU/Control Panel, and not all of the changeable settings stored in HKCU/Control Panel are accessible and changeable from the Control Panel applets. There are several settings that can be changed here to improve performance.

HKCU\InstallLocationsMRU lists the last five locations from which software was installed (MRU stands for Most Recently Used). This subtree has no bearing on system optimization.

HKCU\keyboard layout is used only in multilingual Windows 95 setups, if you have defined multiple keyboard layouts in Control Panel → Keyboard → Language. Again, this subtree has no bearing on system optimization.

HKCU\Network stores network connections you have made. This subtree has no bearing on system optimization.

HKCU\RemoteAccess stores data for Dial-Up Networking, and has no bearing on system optimization.

HKCU\Software contains subkeys for each vendor whose software you have installed, knowingly or unknowingly, on your PC. Each vendor's subkey in turn has subkeys for each installed product. Software settings that change from user to user are stored here; global software settings are stored in HKLM\SOFTWARE.

HKLM

HKLM contains eight top-level subkeys, one of which is not present on all systems. Their structure is not necessarily consistent within HKLM nor within HKCU. HKCU\Software and HKLM\SOFTWARE work together, yet even their name conventions are inconsistent. Inconsistencies such as these are one of the most frustrating and intimidating aspects of the registry.

HKLM\Config is home to hardware profiles. The currently selected profile is mirrored to HKCC. This subtree has no bearing on system optimization.

HKLM\DesktopManagement is not present on all systems. It provides information for Microsoft's Desktop Management Interface (DMI). It has no bearing on system optimization.

HKLM\Enum is a good place to avoid. This subkey contains Plug-and-Play and other hardware-related information. It has no bearing on system optimization.

HKLM\hardware contains more hardware-related information, including serial port information and settings and CPU information. Again, this subkey has no bearing on system optimization.

HKLM\Network contains network settings, used heavily by Dial-Up Networking. This has no relevance to system optimization.

HKLM\Security is used by remote administration. It is poorly documented and is irrelevant to system optimization.

HKLM\SOFTWARE is very important to the system, but all of the Windows settings worth changing are actually stored in its companion section, HKCU\Software.

HKLM\System is the most important section from a system optimization standpoint. System startup, device driver, and operating system information and settings live here. The subkey CurrentControlSet has a number of changeable values.

Backing Up the Registry

Windows 98 automatically keeps five backup copies of the registry; Windows 95 keeps a single backup copy of the registry made after it was first installed. Whichever version you run, you're much better off making a backup copy before you make any changes to the registry.

Before you make any of the registry changes suggested in this chapter, restart your computer in DOS mode (Start → Shutdown → Restart the computer in MS-DOS mode → Yes).

In later chapters, I suggest making a directory called *C:\Windows\backups.xyz* for storing backup copies of various Windows files. We'll do that now, then we'll copy the registry into that directory:

```
c:\>cd c:\windows
c:\windows>md backups.xyz
c:\windows>attrib -h -r -s system.dat
c:\windows>attrib -h -r -s user.dat
c:\windows>copy system.dat backups.xyz
c:\windows>copy user.dat backups.xyz
c:\windows>attrib +h +r +s system.dat
c:\windows>attrib +h +r +s user.dat
```

Now that you have a backup copy, restart your computer normally.

After you've done this, a few simple commands from MS-DOS mode (not from within a DOS box in the Windows GUI!) will restore your registry from the last backup you made:

```
c:\>cd c:\windows
c:\windows>attrib -h -r -s system.dat
c:\windows>attrib -h -r -s user.dat
c:\windows>copy system.dat system.bad
c:\windows>copy user.dat user.bad
c:\windows>copy backups.xyz\user.dat
c:\windows>copy backups.xyz\system.dat
c:\windows>attrib +h +r +s system.dat
c:\windows>attrib +h +r +s user.dat
```

Restarting will restore your computer to its last good state.

Since these last few tips require Regedit unless you are willing to install Microsoft's PowerToys, they are slightly more difficult to implement. The last two cannot be implemented with PowerToys, though various freeware programs can manipulate them. These tips scare liability lawyers more than they should scare you, however. As long as you exercise caution, don't rush, and follow the instructions *exactly*, you will cause no harm to your system. Even if you do make a mistake, a backup copy will get you back up and running. *Do* make sure you make a backup copy, because usually the only way to revive a system with a corrupt registry and no backup copy is to reinstall Windows entirely, or restore from a backup copy as described in Chapter 1.

Turn Off Windows 95's Window Animation

By default, Windows 95 makes its windows explode into and out of the taskbar. This animation eats up CPU time, especially on computers with slow processors and/or slow video cards, and for some people it's distracting. To turn this feature off, launch Regedit. Navigate to HKEY_CURRENT_USER\Control Panel\Desktop\ WindowMetrics. Look for an entry titled MinAnimate. If it's not present, right-click an empty spot in the window and select New\String Value. Type MinAnimate and hit Enter. Now double-click on MinAnimate, delete its default value of 0, and Enter a value of 1. This change requires you to restart the system.

If you're not comfortable playing with the registry, download the Windows 95 PowerToys, which permit changes to this value. This tip is unnecessary in Windows 98, which allows you to turn off animation from the Effects tab of the Display Control Panel, as described earlier in this chapter.

Turn Off Pause in Menus

Unless Internet Explorer 4 or 5 is installed, Windows 95 pauses for an instant before it displays the contents of its menus. The only explanation I can think of for this is dramatic effect, and if I wanted drama, I'd go to the theater. To turn this off, open Regedit, navigate to HKEY_CURRENT_USER\Control Panel\Desktop.

Look for an entry called MenuShowDelay. If it's not there, right-click an empty spot in the window and select New\String Value. Type MenuShowDelay and press Enter. Now double-click MenuShowDelay, and give it a value of 1. The start menu, taskbar, and menus will now be much faster.

Internet Explorer 4 and 5 both disable this key, so changing this key has no positive effect on Windows 98 systems or Windows 95 systems with a recent version of Internet Explorer.

Alternatively, you can change this setting with Microsoft's Windows 95 Power-Toys, if you prefer not to dive into the registry.

Turn Off Click Here to Begin

The pre-Internet Explorer 4 Windows 95 also shoots an animated arrow across the taskbar at bootup, pointing at the Start menu, and telling you to click here to begin. Most of us already know to do this, and those who don't usually figure it out pretty quickly. This is little more than a distraction on newer PCs, but on slower machines, this process can interfere with the launch of your first program if you try to navigate the Start menu while the animation is still playing. You can upgrade your CPU and video card, or you can just turn off the useless fluff. To do that, open Regedit and navigate to HKEY_CURRENT_USER\Software\Microsoft\Windows\CurrentVersion\Policies\Explorer. Look for a value titled NoStartBanner. If it's not present, right-click a blank area and select New\Binary Value. Type NoStartBanner and hit Enter. Double-click NoStartBanner, and change its value to 01. This change requires a reboot to take effect.

Tune Windows 9x to Your Modern CD-ROM Drive

Like the file system settings for the computer profiles, the CD-ROM access patterns are stored in the registry, so we can modify them. (Unfortunately, Windows doesn't dynamically allocate memory to CD-ROM caching like it does to disk caching.) All the control panel's System applet does is write predefined values into the registry. To fine-tune performance, we can just overwrite those values manually with our own values.

Start Regedit (Start → Run → Regedit), and navigate to HKEY_LOCAL_MACHINE\System\CurrentControlSet\control\FileSystem\CDFS. There, you will find two keys named CacheSize and Prefetch. These can be stored as DWORD values or as binary values—the easiest way to tell is to double-click on the entry and look at the resulting dialog box. If it says, "Edit DWORD value," it's a DWORD key, whereas if it says, "Edit Binary value," it's a binary value.

The value you should use for CacheSize depends on how much memory you're willing to dedicate to the CD-ROM cache. This will require some experimentation with your favorite CD-ROM titles, since some titles benefit very little from these settings, while others benefit a great deal. You want to increase your values enough to make a noticeable difference, but unless you have more than 64 MB of RAM, you probably don't want to go dedicating over 4 MB of memory just to a CD-ROM cache.

The CacheSize parameter tells Windows how many 2 KB pages to use for caching the CD-ROM drive. Table 2-1 gives a list of suggested values, containing a page count in decimal, along with the memory usage of each setting, and the binary and DWORD values that implement each setting.

Don't let the binary values confuse you if they don't look like the ones and zeroes you remember from using the binary system in math class. The registry stores its binary values in hexadecimal (base 16, using the numbers 0–9 and the letters a–f) instead of binary. Hexadecimal translates much more quickly and easily into binary than does our decimal (base 10) numbering system, and it's much easier to type than binary.

Table 2-1. CacheSize Parameter Values

Page Count	Memory Usage (in KB)	Binary	DWORD
619	1238	6b,02,00,00	0000026b
1238	2476	d6,04,00,00	000004d6
2476	4952	ac,09,00,00	000009ac

Table 2-2 provides a list of prefetch values. The prefetch value is slightly higher than the amount of memory in kilobytes that Windows will use to cache the CD-ROM drive, but you can make a quick estimate of how much memory Windows will be using by adding the CacheSize and Prefetch.

Table 2-2. Prefetch Parameter Values

CD-ROM Speed	Decimal	Binary	DWORD
4x [Default]	228	e4,00,00,00	000000e4
8x	448	c0,01,00,00	000001c0
16x	896	80,03,00,00	00000380
24x	1344	40,05,00,00	00000540
32x	1792	00,07,00,00	00000700

These are suggested values for the given drive speeds, but feel free to move up or down the scale as available memory permits. Your old 4x drive would benefit from the 32x parameters if you have the extra memory to dedicate to it. The faster drives benefit more, but if you have some games that use the CD-ROM drive extensively, go ahead and use large CacheSize and Prefetch values.

Recover That Wasted CD-ROM Cache Memory

It's possible to use the principles from the previous section to recover the 64K of memory that Windows insists on using to cache your phantom CD-ROM drive on CD-less systems—or to save memory on systems that have CD-ROM drives that are rarely used. Simply open Regedit (Start → Run → Regedit), navigate to HKEY_LOCAL_MACHINE\System\CurrentControlSet\control\FileSystem\CDFS, and zero out the value for Prefetch.

The best way to keep Windows from wasting memory on low-RAM systems is, of course, to never give it the opportunity.

Fix the Windows 95/95A Filesystem Bug

Out of the box, Windows 95 and 95A store the wrong number of paths and files in the Network Server template. This causes greatly reduced performance if you select this template.

To fix this bug, you need to load Regedit by going to Start → Run → Regedit and then hitting Enter. Navigate to HKEY_LOCAL_MACHINE\Software\Microsoft\Windows\CurrentVersion\FS Templates\Server. The values for NameCache and PathCache are reversed. Double-click NameCache, delete the first two numbers, and type A9 0A. Next, double-click PathCache, delete the first two numbers, and type 40 00. Now close Regedit and restart your computer.

Improve the Windows 9x Server Template Even More

If you have an uninterruptible power supply and any version of Windows 95 or 98, go ahead and throw some more memory at the disk speed problem. Follow the same procedure as in the previous section, but instead of typing A9 0A, type 52 15. Instead of typing 40 00, type 80 00. If you have more than 32 MB of RAM and a UPS, enter A4 2A in place of A9 0A, and 00 01 in place of 40 00. As I've said before (but it never hurts to say it again), a UPS is a good investment for reasons other than this—in the event of a power failure, you get a few minutes to gracefully shut your system down, which will prevent data loss. And the UPS will ensure your system gets cleaner power, making it crash less frequently.

Reduce Filesystem Fragmentation

There is a trick commonly passed around online as a way to optimize the filesystem for multimedia applications. The standard advice is to select Start → Run → Regedit, then navigate to HKEY_LOCAL_MACHINE\System\CurrentControlSet\control\FileSystem and go to New → DWORD → ConfigFileAllocSize. Then double-click → Decimal → 512. This trick is more of a placebo than anything else, as the default setting is 500.

This setting simply tells Windows how much free space, in kilobytes, it should look for when writing a new file. If all you do is work with large files, such as audio and video applications, you will want a large setting, such as 1024.

If you work with a lot of small files—for instance, if your primary uses for a computer are word processing, email, and gaming—you might be better served with a smaller number because your typical files will be much smaller than the default 500 KB, and Windows won't waste its time looking for a block of free space larger than your typical file size.

For most purposes, the default setting of 500 KB is fine. But if you want a super-tuned system, here's how to go about finding an appropriate setting for this entry. Go to Start → Run → Command, which will open a command prompt. Enter this single command:

```
c:\>dir c:\ /w /s
```

This command forces Windows to run through and list every file on your hard drive. We're interested in the last statement it makes—the file totals. Divide the total number of bytes used by the total number of files, then divide that number by 1024 to get an average file size in kilobytes. On one of my systems, I get a total of 9,494 files, occupying 4,228,611,074 bytes. That's an average file size of about 435K. On another one of my systems, where my usage habits are different, the average file size is only 137K.

To find a value for this registry entry, divide your average size by 32, round up to the next whole number, then multiply by 32 again. So rather than use a minimum file size of 137K, I would specify a size of at least 160K. On my other system, a size of 448K is theoretically more appropriate.

If your average file size is larger than 500K, you definitely want to adjust the default number upward.

I'm not so sure that I would want to change this setting on either of my systems described here, however, since it's far better for this value to be too large than too small. After all, looking for a 160K block to write a 600K file will result in fragmentation. If there's a large disparity between your average file size and the 500K default—such as there is on my system with an average file size of 137K—you can speed disk writes slightly by adjusting this setting downward, as long as you're defragmenting your drive frequently.

That's it for the classic tips. These are the easiest tricks to implement, since they don't require much digging into the system. A few minutes in the Control Panel can quickly implement the majority of these tricks on any system. But there are still plenty of things you can do to make Windows run faster: they just require a more thorough understanding of the systems at work below the pretty graphical interface.

3

Disk Optimization

Most people know that they need to run ScanDisk and Defrag on their computers every once in a while, and most people have a vague idea that these two programs somehow make their hard drive faster and more reliable.

However, routine use of the disk tools Microsoft included with Windows is neither the first word nor the last word in disk optimization. The hard drive is one of the biggest bottlenecks in your system, so no matter what you do with your system and no matter which hard drive you have in it, you want to do everything you can to help out your hard drive.

The constant theme of this book is working within Windows' limitations. This is always important, but nowhere is it more important than when dealing with hard drives. There are five factors that slow down your drive. They are:

- The number of entries in crucial system directories. Fortunately, this can be fixed without any special tools.

- Fragmentation. This can be corrected with Defrag, the disk optimizer included with Windows, or with a third-party disk optimizer.

- Physical limitations of the disk itself, which cause better performance on the outermost tracks than on the innermost. Defrag can do a little bit to help this, but it takes a third-party disk optimizer to really combat this problem.

- The filesystem. FAT16 is faster than FAT32, period.

- Data compression. It made some sense in the early 1990s, but not on today's supercheap gargantuan hard drives. The performance drain is just too great, and the gain too low.

Once you know the things that slow your disk down, you can take steps to start fixing them.

Directory Optimization

There's a little-known optimization trick that's perhaps even more effective than defragmentation. It has circulated in guru circles for years, but I have only seen it in print once—buried in the old Microsoft MS-DOS 5 manual, where it was mentioned only in passing—and I have never seen a good explanation of why it works. The trick is to limit the number of entries you have in crucial system directories, especially in the root.

The reason why this works is obvious to any second-semester computer science student once he or she thinks about it. The FAT filesystem stores its directories as linked lists, which are very easy to program but notorious for becoming very slow as the number of entries increases.

Optimizing Your Root Directory

For years, programs simply installed themselves in their own dedicated subdirectories hanging off the root. WordPerfect 5.1 installed itself in *C:\WP51*, Lotus 1-2-3 installed itself in *C:\123*, DOS installed itself in *C:\DOS*, and Windows in *C:\Windows*. It wasn't uncommon at all to find dozens and dozens of entries in the root directory of *C*. This didn't seem like a problem to software manufacturers, because the root directory of hard drives could store 512 entries.

Windows 95 forced this to change. Traditionally, FAT filenames have been limited to eight characters plus a three-character extension. Windows 95's VFAT addressed this problem, permitting long filenames by spanning the names across multiple directory entries. But this created another problem: it's difficult to know for certain how many directory entries are actually in use on a Windows 95 computer, since any filename that contains a space, uppercase characters, or more than eight characters is occupying at least two directory entries. With long filenames in the mix now, it didn't take long for that once-large 512-entry limit to become inadequate. The easiest solution was to stop installing programs into the root directory and start installing them by default in *C:\Program Files* instead. This went a long way toward helping to make PCs run faster.

This trick works because FAT directories are also linked lists. Let's take this chapter as an example. For the sake of argument, we'll say it's stored in *C:\My Documents\Books\Optimizing Windows\Chapter 3.doc*. There are 17 entries in my root directory. Windows sorts through them until it finds *My Documents*. That directory has hundreds of entries, because I write a lot and I never throw anything away. I keep the important stuff sorted, but admittedly that's more for my convenience than for my computer's. Finally, Windows finds the entry for *Books*. Since this is the first book I've published, there aren't many entries there. A couple of works in progress, plus this one, so it finds *Optimizing Windows* pretty quickly. Since this book is pretty short, there aren't many entries inside it either. It finds *Chapter 3.doc* pretty quickly as well.

But after stepping through that process, isn't it easy to see how we could have made the document load much faster if I had corralled all those hundreds of loose files in *My Documents* into a directory called, say, *Junk* or *Misc*?

If you partition your drive, you force a pretty efficient root directory structure. If you partition your drive with PartitionMagic and then use the included Magic Mover utility to move your applications directories into one partition and your data directories into another partition, you'll have a pretty efficient disk structure. If you don't have PartitionMagic, you can accomplish much the same thing manually by uninstalling applications before you resize, then reinstalling those applications in the new partition. In most cases you can move data partitions just by dragging their contents from one drive to another.

Whichever method you use, you'll probably have to point your applications towards your data's new home—usually an application will have a Preferences menu buried somewhere in its menu structure, where you can specify the locations of its data files.

Ideally, your drive map should look something like this:

```
Directory of C:\
RECYCLED      <DIR>              04-04-98  4:52p RECYCLED
WINDOWS       <DIR>              04-04-98  4:46p WINDOWS
IO       SYS     214,836        08-24-96 11:11a IO.SYS
SYSTEM   1ST     230,116        01-10-99  3:47p SYSTEM.1ST
COMMAND  COM      93,812        08-24-96 11:11a COMMAND.COM
MSDOS    SYS       1,730        03-27-98  1:36p MSDOS.SYS
CONFIG   SYS         188        03-27-98  1:36p CONFIG.SYS
AUTOEXEC BAT         122        04-01-99  7:40p AUTOEXEC.BAT
AUTOEXEC DOS          92        01-10-99  3:37p AUTOEXEC.DOS
CONFIG   DOS          67        03-28-99  7:54p CONFIG.DOS

Directory of D:\
PROGRA~1      <DIR>              12-02-98 10:41p Program Files

Directory of E:\
MYDOCU~1      <DIR>              12-02-98 10:37p My Documents

Directory of F:\
TEMP          <DIR>              12-02-98 10:57p TEMP
CACHE         <DIR>              12-02-98 10:59p CACHE

Directory of G:\
WIN386   SWP           0        01-27-99 11:38p WIN386.SWP
```

But idealism and reality are rarely the same. Windows normally puts a number of files in the root of *C:* that are of questionable necessity. Just to be on the safe side, I create a directory inside *C:\Windows* called *backups.xyz*. I move all the extraneous files, like *MSDOS.**, and *autoexec.old*, all the *.txt* and *.log* files, and anything else not on the list of files above into this directory.

If you have applications that installed themselves into the root directory on one of your drives, move them into *\Program Files* with PowerQuest's Magic Mover (which comes with PartitionMagic) or with CleanSweep or UnInstaller. If you don't have any of these utilities, you can use Windows' Add/Remove Programs applet to uninstall them and reinstall them, and specify a subdirectory within *\Program Files* when it prompts you for a destination directory. Some older Windows 3.1 applications won't accept *\Program Files* as a valid directory name; in those cases, specify *\progra~1* instead. The vast majority of old 16-bit applications will accept that directory name.

Optimizing Your Data and Applications Drives

Technically, if you dedicate a partition exclusively to data and exclusively to applications and move those files there, you can dispense with the *Program Files* and *My Documents* subdirectories, but since FAT16 drives have a limited number of entries in the root directory, I continue to use these directories anyway. It seems like my applications and data drives always end up temporarily holding non-related data whether I plan it that way or not; keeping permanent stuff in one permanent subdirectory helps me clean things up after the fact.

You will want to sort the contents of your applications and data directories into subdirectories for optimal speed. How you organize your data files is completely up to you: invent a system that makes sense to you. Organizing your applications is a bit trickier. Games will usually sort themselves by manufacturer. Sierra games, for instance, always seem to want to install into *\Program Files\Sierra\[title]*. You may just want to sort the *Program Files* subdirectories by category: put games into *\Program Files\Games*, applications into *\Program Files\Apps*, utilities into *\Program Files\Utilities*, and so on. Try to think of categories that will give you a number of subdirectories with roughly an equal number of entries. But if you don't have more than a couple dozen subdirectories, don't bother. You'll spend more time organizing than you'll save in increased performance.

Try to look for the obvious as you go through this process. For instance, my *\Program Files* directory had 22 entries in it. Of those, six were Internet-related utilities, so I created a subdirectory and moved those applications' subdirectories into it, dropping the number of entries to 17. Another four were graphics utilities, so I created another subdirectory for them, reducing the number of entries to 14. That's quick reduction of the directory size by just over a third. But then I noticed that one of those remaining applications was a music editor, and another was CD-recording software. Why not make the *graphics* directory *multimedia* instead and include those two applications? The key is often not to get too precise in sorting; if a subdirectory only has three entries in it, it's probably not worth having. Shoot for between 6 and 12 entries; sending your PC down a long trail of small subdirectories isn't any better than giving it one huge unsorted directory.

You don't want to mess around much inside your applications directories themselves—the locations of most applications files are hard-coded. The exception to this is your data—if your application can store data elsewhere, say, inside *\My Documents*, move your data there. Some applications default to storing your data in the same directory as the application itself, which hinders performance and confuses file management. There's one other notable exception. Microsoft software has an annoying tendency to create directories called *Mscreate.dir* all over your hard disk. To quickly purge your drive of this space- and performance-hogging menace, go to Start → Find → Files or folders → Named → mscreate.dir → Look in → My Computer → Find Now → Ctrl-A-Shift-Delete → Yes → Yes to all. Repeat this process any time you install any piece of software from Microsoft.

Optimizing Your Windows Directory

There is one directory that's always worth optimizing, and it's probably worth all the time it takes to optimize: *C:\Windows*. It is always a mess. It's not uncommon for this directory to have several hundred files in it. I've managed to whittle it down to about 140 files, and the speedup after doing so is noticeable. You've probably noticed that Windows always seems much faster right after it's been freshly installed, and once you started installing applications, it slows down. That's because your applications are dumping files into *C:\Windows*, and since Windows and just about every application in existence load files from that directory, anything that affects the speed of that directory, either positively or negatively, will have a global effect on system performance.

With that in mind, I make a *Windows* subdirectory inside *C:\Windows\backups. xyz* and start moving files into it. I start with any file with an extension of *.bak* or *.old*. You're not likely to ever need these files, but since they tend to be small, I don't worry about the disk space. I throw them in the backup directory on the off chance I might one day need them, and I do the same for any file with a numeric extension, such as *system.001*. There, they consume a minimal amount of disk space and they're not in the way of anything. There are a few *.doc* and *.txt* files in the Windows directory as well. You can either move those into the backup directory or delete them entirely. Delete any *.tmp* or *.~mp* files you find in the Windows directory. If you use desktop wallpaper, create a directory called *C:\ Windows\wallpaper* (or better yet, *x:\My Documents\Wallpaper*, specifying the drive letter of your data drive for *x*, of course) and move all the *.bmp* files into it. When you go to choose your wallpaper, you'll have to open that subdirectory first—select Control Panel → Display → Wallpaper → Browse → Drives → <drive that contains My Documents> → My Documents → Wallpaper. This adds a few steps to changing your wallpaper, but doing this will keep a large collection of wallpaper from significantly slowing down your system.

You're likely to also find numerous backup copies of critical system configuration files. The crucial files are *system.dat*, *user.dat*, *system.ini*, and *win.ini*. If you find any files by these names with different extensions (a quick look into the Windows directory on one of my machines revealed backup copies with extensions of *.bak*, *.b4*, *.syd*, *.rdb*, *.cor*, *.nu4*, and *.blx*—many of which correspond somewhat to software packages I've either installed or at one time had installed on that PC), move them into *C:\Windows\backups.xyz\Windows*. If you want to always have a pristine system, double-check your *Windows* directory every time you install or uninstall a software package, since these are the operations most likely to generate backup files.

You can automate this process to a degree by adding the following lines to *autoexec.bat*:

```
Move /y c:\windows\win.* c:\windows\backups.xyz\windows
Move /y c:\windows\system.* c:\windows\backups.xyz\windows
Move /y c:\windows\*.bak c:\windows\backups.xyz\windows
Move /y c:\windows\*.txt c:\windows\backups.xyz\windows
Move /y c:\windows\*.old c:\windows\backups.xyz\windows
Move /y c:\windows\*.0?? c:\windows\backups.xyz\windows
Move c:\windows\backups.xyz\windows\*.ini c:\windows
Move c:\windows\backups.xyz\windows\*.dat c:\windows
Move c:\windows\backups.xyz\windows\*.com c:\windows
```

These lines won't catch every file, but they will get the majority of them. This is better than simply deleting the files, because on rare occasions, you will need to refer back to a backup copy of your files. I know I've been stuck needing a backup but not having one far too many times. Since disk space is cheap, we can afford to keep some old backup files lingering around, as long as they're not getting in the way of important work (or play).

If you upgraded from a previous version of Windows, there are undoubtedly some files left over from your previous version, and most of them are unused. Search your Windows tree for files that match the dates of any previous versions of Windows, then move them into the *Backups.xyz* directory. I suggest you recreate the Windows directory structure inside your backup directory, storing any files you find in *C:\Windows\System* into *C:\Windows\Backups.xyz\Windows\System*. If it turns out that you needed a certain file after all, it will be much easier to restore it that way.

These are the file dates that correspond to various versions of Windows:

03/10/92: Windows 3.1
09/30/92: Windows for Workgroups 3.1

11/01/93: Windows for Workgroups 3.11
12/31/93: Windows 3.11
07/11/95: Windows 95
08/10/96: Windows 95 OSR2
05/11/98: Windows 98

If you find a directory called *WIN32S* in your Windows 9x directory structure, delete it as well. There will be references to it in your *system.ini* file, so be sure to remove those after deleting *WIN32S*. *WIN32S* was a 32-bit subsystem that allowed some 32-bit Windows programs to run under Windows 3.x, and it's no longer needed under Windows 9x (Windows 9x has its own 32-bit subsystem). A few programs mistakenly install it.

Windows also puts a number of *.exe* files in its root. I move a good number of these into *C:\Windows\Command*. Windows will still find them there, and system performance will increase.

Generally speaking, you don't want to move applications around by hand, but the *C:\Windows* directory plays by a different set of rules from the rest of the system. Since *C:\Windows*, *C:\Windows\Command*, and *C:\Windows\System* are all in the system path, standard practice is to call just the executable file without specifying its full path. So executable files that are part of Windows can reside in any of these three directories without harming Windows.

It may be tempting to just move all the executable files from *C:\Windows* into *C:\Windows\Command*, see what breaks, and move files back until you fix all of the problems. That's a very ineffective approach to solving this problem—when I tried that approach on a Windows 98 system, it caused so many problems that I ended up reinstalling the whole program. Just moving the files back didn't solve the problem. This kind of optimization calls for a more conservative, one-at-a-time approach. It's better to move too few files than too many.

Many people tend to copy certain ubiquitous small utilities such as PKZIP/UNZIP or Info-ZIP's Zip/UnZip, useful batch files, utilities from the Windows CD-ROM and Microsoft's Resource Kit, and other useful command-line tools into *C:\Windows*. I've done this myself. If you do this, move those files out of there and stop putting things there. If you're a command-line utility junkie like me, instead of putting these utilities in the overcrowded *C:\Windows*, either put them in *C:\Windows\Command* or follow the accepted procedure of creating a utilities directory somewhere (say, *D:\Program Files\Utils*) and adding it to the PATH statement in *autoexec.bat*.

Most Windows installations won't have all of the files listed in this chapter, but on any given machine, you can expect a subset of these files to make up a sizeable percentage of the executable files in the *C:\Windows* and *C:\Windows*

System directories. Most Windows installations have 100 or more executable files in *C:\Windows*, but you shouldn't have any trouble dropping that number below 50; the smallest number of executables I've seen in a functioning Windows installation is 22.

There are no issues to moving the majority of the executable files. Files that have no issues are listed below, followed by files that have minor issues. If a file isn't listed, don't move it.

Files you can move without issues into *C:\Windows\Command*:

Arp.exe	*Cfgback.exe*	*Clipbrd.exe*
Clipbook.exe	*Cmpagent.exe*	*Control.exe*
Drwatson.exe	*Extract.exe*	*Extrac32.exe*
Faxcover.exe	*Faxview.exe*	*Fontview.exe*
FTP.exe	*Grpconv.exe*	*Ipconfig.exe*
Jview.exe	*Logview.exe*	*Mkcompat.exe*
Nbstat.exe	*Net.exe*	*Netdde.exe*
Netstat.exe	*Netwatch.exe*	*Packager.exe*
Ping.exe	*Progman.exe*	*Qfecheck.exe*
Quikview.exe	*Regedit.exe*	*Route.exe*
Scandisk.exe	*Scanregw.exe*	*Shortcut.exe*
Sysedit.exe	*Sysmon.exe*	*Taskman.exe*
Taskmon.exe	*Telnet.exe*	*Tour98.exe*
Tracert.exe	*Tzedit.exe*	*Waitd.exe*
Wangimg.exe	*Welcome.exe*	*Win.com*
Winfile.exe	*Winhelp.exe*	*Winhlp32.exe*
Winipcfg.exe	*Wintop.exe*	*Winver.exe*

Files whose Start menu entries will have to be updated if you move them to *C:\Windows\Command*:

> *Aniedit.exe* (Animated Cursor Editor)
> *Cdplayer.exe* (CD Player)
> *Cleanmgr.exe* (Cleanup Manager)
> *Dialer.exe* (Phone Dialer)
> *Exchng32.exe* (Inbox, on the Windows desktop)
> *Hypertrm.exe* (HyperTerminal)
> *Infinst.exe* (INF Installer)
> *Mshearts.exe* (Hearts)
> *Pbrush.exe* (Paintbrush)
> *Pwledit.exe* (Password List Editor)
> *Scandskw.exe* (ScanDisk)

Sndrec32.exe (Sound Recorder)

Sol.exe (Solitaire)

Tuneup.exe (Maintenance Wizard)

Winmine.exe (Minesweeper)

Calc.exe (Calculator)

Charmap.exe (Character Map)

Defrag.exe (Disk Defragmenter)

Directcc.exe (Direct Cable Connection)

Freecell.exe (FreeCell)

Imagedit.exe (Image Editor)

Mplayer.exe (Media Player)

Notepad.exe (Notepad)

Pinball.exe (Space Cadet Pinball)

Rsrcmtr.exe (Resource Meter)

Scanpst.exe (Inbox Repair Tool)

Sndvol32.exe (Volume Control)

Sysagent.exe (System Agent)

Winchat.exe (Chat)

Write.exe (WordPad)

Files specified in system configuration files whose entries will have to be updated if moved to *C:\Windows\Command*:

EMM386.exe (config.sys)

Mscdex.exe (autoexec.bat)

Setver.exe (config.sys)

Smartdrv.exe (autoexec.bat)

If you're willing to spelunk into the registry, you can move the eight shell folders inside \ *Windows* elsewhere. Move *Copy Desktop, Favorites, Fonts, NetHood, Start Menu, Recent, SendTo,* and *ShellNew* to a new location—one possibility is *C:\ Windows\Shell*—and then launch Regedit. Punch through to HKCU\Software\ Microsoft\Windows\CurrentVersion\Explorer\Shell Folders, export the branch just in case you make a mistake, then change the paths of 10 of the 11 entries to point at their new locations (the *Personal Entry* won't change; *Startup* and *Programs* are subdirectories of *Start Menu*, so they have to change as well). Next, head down to HKCU\Software\Microsoft\Windows\CurrentVersion\Explorer\User Shell Folders and make the changes again for *Favorites* and *Recent*. Restart, and if all is well, delete those subdirectories in *C:\Windows*. One caveat: well-behaved programs should check the registry for the locations of these directories, but some may be hard-coded to write to certain directories, like *C:\Windows\Desktop*. If you don't like programs that clutter your desktop or add new items to the *New* section of Explorer's context menu without your permission, having them malfunction might be a good thing. But be aware that this change is uncommon enough that many software developers are likely to overlook the possibility that these directories could be anywhere else.

Once you've cleaned out *C:\Windows*, defragment your drive to clean up the empty directory entries. The performance increase after completing this process will vary, but it should be noticeable on all systems and dramatic on some.

Taking Care of Fragmentation

The most well-known limiting factor on disk performance is fragmentation. Fragmentation is a by-product of the way that FAT writes files. When told to write a file, FAT takes a look at the segment of clusters, grabs the first cluster available, then the next, then the next, without any thought. On a fresh disk, all these clusters will be next to one another. If you've deleted a number of files, however, the free space on the disk may not be contiguous, causing the disk head to shuffle back and forth as it reads the file. If the file is badly scattered across the disk, it can take considerably longer to read it. If a large number of files are similarly scattered, overall system performance drops. Since FAT has to walk one step at a time down a blind alley every time it writes a file, it lacks the insight to reduce fragmentation. Windows 95's enhancement to the FAT filesystem, called VFAT, added some intelligence to the process. Rather than grab the first available cluster, it looks for a group of clusters larger than 500 kilobytes. This adds some overhead to disk writes, but the reduction in fragmentation is worth the small penalty. However, VFAT doesn't even come close to eliminating fragmentation. VFAT doesn't look for a block of space the size of the file—in some cases, the operating system doesn't know how large the file it's writing is going to be—so the intelligence is limited. If there's a 500 KB block just before a 1 MB block and you're writing a 600K file, the first 500K will go into the first block, and the next 100K will go into the first part of that 1 MB block.

Defragmenting your hard drive will sometimes lead to significant performance improvements, and it also reduces the amount of wear and tear on your drive.

Scan Your Drives for Errors Before Defragmenting

There are two situations when you want to use ScanDisk or a third-party disk repair tool. Any time your system locks up and you have to push the reset button or cycle power without being able to shut down properly, you should run a disk repair tool on all of your hard drives. Windows 95B, 95C, and 98 should prompt you to run ScanDisk after improper shutdowns, but they don't always, and they sometimes scan only drive C. To be safe, scan all of your drives.

You also want to run these tools just before you defragment your drive. Defragmenting a drive with errors on it isn't the end of the world—the defragmentation tool will spot the error, refuse to continue, and tell you to repair the disk. You might as well scan the drive first in order to avoid having to run Defrag twice.

Disk repair tools usually offer to make an undo disk, which stores the information necessary to undo any changes they make to the drive (hence the name). If Scan-Disk or another tool finds a major disk problem, such as mismatched FATs or a bad partition table, make an undo disk. If the problem is lost clusters, don't bother.

A colleague in California likes to tell an undo disk story. Late one evening, he received a frantic phone call from one of the users he supports in his office. She'd been working on a large project in Microsoft Publisher when the computer crashed, but then it wanted to save her work and she ran out of disks. He was confused—what program says, "Hey, I'm about to crash and there's nothing you can do about it, but here, I'll be nice and save your data first," after all?—but he told her he'd come in in the morning, recover whatever he could, and make sure the computer was OK before she came in to get back to work.

When he came in the next morning, he found a stack of 25 disks sitting next to the computer. "What do you mean, *ran out* of disks?" he asked himself. He turned on the monitor and got the answer to his question. The familiar blue ScanDisk screen was up, telling him it had found some 130,000+ lost clusters on the drive and asking for the next disk so it could save its undo file. Evidently, as ScanDisk started asking for disks the night before, she had frantically run from office to office, scooping up every spare disk she could find, and dutifully shoved them into the drive as it asked for them. To add insult to injury, she probably would have only needed another disk or two to complete the tedious but altogether unnecessary task of backing up the lost clusters from this monster MS Publisher document.

There's no need to save an undo file to reverse the creation of lost clusters. Just have it save the collection of lost clusters as a file (they always end up being files with an extension of *.chk* in the root), then inspect the file after ScanDisk finishes. If the file is important, rename it. If it turns out to be gibberish, delete it.

Defragmentation Tools

Windows 95's disk defragmenter is better than nothing, but there's little more to say about it. There are several defragmenters out there that do a better job. Golden Bow's Vopt (*www.goldenbow.com*) is a longtime shareware favorite. It's not much more configurable than the one that comes with Windows 95, but it is much faster, and at about U.S.$20, it's inexpensive. Defrag Plus, part of Mijenix Fix-It 99 (*www.mijenix.com*), is similar to Vopt in speed and configurability, but like Windows 98's defragmenter, it strategically interleaves certain files to speed application loading.

Disk Optimizer, the defragmentation tool that ships with McAfee Nuts & Bolts (*www.mcafee.com*), is faster than the Windows 95 defragmenter, and it also supports advanced features like file reordering and directory sorting. The best overall defragmenter on the market, however, is Norton Speed Disk (*www.symantec.com*), part of Symantec's venerable Norton Utilities. Like McAfee's tool, it can reorder files and sort directories, and while not as fast as Vopt, it is much faster than McAfee's Disk Optimizer. For the best combination of speed and configurability, you'll want to go with Norton Utilities. For more information on the utilities suites that include these tools, see Chapter 5, *Utilities*.

Strategies for Defragmentation

There's little strategy available for the Microsoft-provided defragmenters besides running them regularly. If you use a third-party tool, however, you have a number of options that allow you to super-tune a disk for an extra measure of performance. You want to make the utility reorder files by their last access date, sort directories in some intelligent manner (preferably by cluster number, but if that option's unavailable, by size in descending order), and place subdirectories first.

Here's the reasoning behind these settings. Windows 95, unfortunately, doesn't count the number of times a file has been accessed, but it does track the last time a file was accessed. So every time you run a program, the associated files are marked with the current date. Frequently accessed files are likely to have a fairly recent access date. There will be anomalies—if you have files that you only access once a year and you optimize your disk the day after you just accessed one of those files, they're going to move toward the front of the disk for no good reason. Sorting files by access date works well enough for the majority of circumstances, however. It's certainly better than leaving the files sorted in their default haphazard order.

Sorting directories by cluster number in conjunction with sorting the files by access date causes the directories' file entries to be sorted in order of importance. When Windows searches for a file, it finds its directory, then looks at each entry starting from the first. By sorting the directories by file importance, Windows finds the most important files first. When sorting by cluster number isn't possible, sorting by size gives another indication of importance.

You usually place subdirectories first because they are important. An application will typically store its frequently accessed components in subdirectories, so you want them at the top of the linked list, where Windows will find them rapidly.

For details on how to implement this defragmentation strategy using one of the three major utilities packages on the market today, see Chapter 5.

The Fragmentation Controversy

Some experts question the effectiveness of disk defragmentation on several grounds. Much of what they say is true, but their arguments don't always hold up well under scrutiny.

It is true that many technical support people, when faced with a problem they don't know how to solve, tell the user to run ScanDisk and Defrag, then call back if that doesn't solve the problem. This is a placebo—running this combination of programs solves only a small fraction of computer problems not related to speed.

However, the abuse of ScanDisk and Defrag does not automatically make them useless tools, any more so than a doctor telling a patient to take two aspirin and call in the morning makes aspirin a useless drug. Nor does overuse of aspirin as a placebo invalidate the whole category of drugs known as painkillers. While Defrag is not the best tool to use, if a disk is badly fragmented, running it will still show an undeniable improvement.

Some experts also question defragmentation based on technical merits. They say that unless the drive is very full, defragmenting makes little difference in performance, and that a better way to improve speed is to buy a big, fast, new hard drive.

However, buying a larger hard drive does nothing to solve the problem of fragmentation. It reduces the effects, because frequently a large hard drive will also be a technological improvement over the drive it replaces in other ways—it may have a faster spindle, a larger cache, a lower seek time, and/or higher platter density—but under Windows 9x, this does nothing to solve fragmentation since VFAT just uses the first half-megabyte block of free space it finds, and, failing in that endeavor, uses whatever free space is available. And the slowdown of a drive as it fills up has nothing to do with fragmentation. The two effects can compound each other, but they are unrelated.

Buying a big, fast, new hard drive will improve speed, but hard drive replacement can be costly and time-consuming and only puts off the real problem.

Some experts also point out that the act of defragmenting and file reordering just moves files around so that a program sits on consecutively numbered sectors. However, there is no guarantee on a modern hard drive that consecutively numbered sectors are actually adjacent. They usually will be, but when a sector is bad, the drive's electronics will swap it with a sector from its pool of spares. So two "adjacent" sectors could actually be on opposite ends of the drive.

—Continued—

The non-adjacent "adjacent" sector argument has the most validity of the three, but this argument is a symptom of knowing a lot about how disk drives work but not enough about how FAT works. Consecutively numbered sectors will be physically adjacent enough of the time to make defragmentation generally worthwhile, and consecutively numbered sectors are always adjacent in the FAT tables.

This argument is stronger when used against file reordering, which is what Norton Utilities and Nuts & Bolts do when you tell them to sort files by access date. File reordering is based on the observation that operations on low-numbered sectors near the front of the drive are faster than operations on high-numbered sectors. The thinking goes that if you take recently accessed or frequently accessed files and move them toward the front of the drive, you will increase system performance. Why keep that backup copy of *config.sys* that hasn't been touched since 1996 on valuable fast sectors near the front?

Theoretically, it is impossible to know exactly which sectors on the drive will be the fastest, because it's impossible to know where the clusters are on the disk, and it's also impossible to know how the drive is mapping them. However, the way FAT orders its tables is both known and constant. Being a linked list, entries near the front will always get faster access than entries at the back of the table. If you move a file to the front of the FAT, access will be faster. The file's physical placement on the disk may end up being less than optimal, but what's to say its physical placement on the disk was optimal in the first place? The same experts who argue against file reordering frequently argue that mild fragmentation isn't much of a problem, so their own arguments can be used against them.

These arguments also ignore another benefit of no fragmentation. Due to the way files are stored, once a fragmented file is deleted from the disk (not just stored in the Recycle Bin), it's impossible to recover it. You can recover the first fragment, but you won't get back the whole file. Microsoft no longer ships an undelete utility with Windows 9x (they did with MS-DOS 6.x), but several utilities packages still ship with undelete utilities. When you want a file back, you want it back. If your disks are partitioned with temp files, your swap file is quarantined off, and you defragment your drives regularly, your chances of recovering a deleted file are pretty high. Your chances of cross-linked files— instances where two files claim ownership of the same cluster on the disk— also decrease if your disks are defragmented.

So, while the physical benefits of fragmentation may be questionable, the logical benefits—at least when your disk drive speaks FAT—are not. I will grant the naysayers that prevention is more important, but with prevention measures like strategic partitioning (discussed later in this chapter) in place, optimization performed on a regular basis increases performance without taking forever.

When to Defragment

As mentioned earlier in the book, you should defragment your drive(s) every time you uninstall a program, as well as after you install any program. In addition, you should defragment all of your drives once a month, whether your disk defragmenter says it's necessary or not. An optimized disk is a healthy disk.

Using a Scheduling Program to Automatically Defragment a Drive

The Windows 95 Plus! Pack, Windows 98, and most anti-virus utilities ship with a scheduling program, which allows you to specify certain times for programs or events to occur. This is a real boon for defragmentation programs: just schedule a disk-checking program to run first in order to prevent disk errors from hanging up the defragmenter, then run the disk defragmenter. This approach is better than running both at startup, because you can have them run at off-hours. If you leave your system on all the time, you can schedule it to fix errors and defragment every day at 4 a.m., if you want. It's overkill, but it ensures that your system is always as close to 0% fragmentation as possible. And if it runs every day, it won't take very long and won't cause much wear and tear on your drive either.

There are far too many scheduling programs to give explicit instructions for each of them. But if you already know how to schedule an event, the only additional information you need is the filename of the utility and its command-line arguments. To schedule a disk scanning event, feed your scheduler the command:

```
scandisk /a /n
```

This causes ScanDisk to scan all local hard drives, no questions asked. To schedule a defragmentation event, feed the scheduler the command:

```
defrag /all /f /noprompt
```

This causes full optimization on all drives, again, no questions asked. You can substitute the /u or /q parameters for files only and quick optimization if you wish, but if you're scheduling the optimizations for after-hours, you might as well do a complete optimization. I usually schedule the events about 15 minutes apart to give the disk scanning plenty of time to finish.

If you have the Norton Utilities, you can schedule its components instead of Microsoft's utilities. The commands for Norton Disk Doctor are NDD32 /q to run everything but a surface test, and NDD32 /c to do everything including a surface test. I suggest running the surface test once every six months. It's overkill to do a surface test any more frequently than that, as it takes a long time and causes the drive to work unnecessarily. The command for Norton Speed Disk is:

```
SD32 [drive:] /f
```

If you have multiple drives, you'll unfortunately have to schedule a separate event for each of them. If you want to do a files-only or quick optimization instead, substitute the /u or /q parameters.

Working Within the Physical Limitations of the Disk

Performance is always better on the outside tracks (the logical front of the disk) than on the inner tracks. This is because modern hard disks place more sectors in the outer tracks, a technique known as Zoned Bit Recording (ZBR). The performance difference between the innermost and outermost tracks on the Quantum Fireball™ hard disk, circa 1996, was 47%. This is part of the reason why a system seems much faster when you freshly format its disk and then install Windows. Even a 486SX/25 from 1992 seems reasonably fast with a freshly formatted disk and nothing but Windows 95 installed.

The utilities packages described in the previous section do a great deal to minimize this effect. If for some reason you can't use anything but Windows' built-in tools, you can minimize these effects to a degree by hand, as described in the following section.

Uninstall Rarely Used Applications (Then Reinstall If Necessary)

We all have programs we don't use very often. Ideally, we wouldn't keep them installed, but that's not always an option. Since the Defrag included with Windows doesn't sort files by access date or by anything else besides its own whims, you have to use a workaround. Uninstall any programs you rarely use, then run Defrag. Now, if you decide some of the programs you just uninstalled are important enough to merit reinstalling them, reinstall them, one at a time, *in order of importance*. Be sure to run Defrag after installing *each* program. The result isn't quite as optimal as using the defragmenter from Norton Utilities or Nuts & Bolts, but it's close and doesn't cost anything extra.

Delete Unnecessary Files

Windows tends to create a lot of junk files, from a web browser cache to the notorious temp files that applications open to use as temporary scratch pads, but then never seem to clean up.

Internet Explorer allocates entirely too much disk space—10% of your drive—to browser cache, and while Netscape's fixed cache is a more reasonable size, neither browser seems to be very good about staying within the limits you set and deleting obsolete content. Despite this drawback, I don't agree with people who say you should delete your browser cache regularly. Delete it when you're short on disk space, yes. Though having a ton of ancient *.gif* and HTML files on your drive accomplishes nothing useful, if you're like most people, you frequent a small number of sites, and having a large cache makes visiting those sites much faster. If you're deleting your cache every week, you're spending too much time downloading the same files over and over again—especially if you have a modem connection.

Temp files are another story. Programs dump them everywhere—in your applications directories, in your data directories, in *C:\Windows*, in *C:\Windows\Temp*, and anywhere else imaginable. Programs also tend not to do a very admirable job of cleaning these files up. Creating a quarantine partition for temp files, as described earlier in this chapter, helps. But sometimes applications will ignore Windows' directives and dump temp files in random locations anyway.

The easiest way to clean out temp files with Windows 95 is to restart, then go to Start → Find → Files or Folders → *.tmp. Then, use Explorer to open your temp directory—*C:\Windows\Temp* by default, or if you redirected it with SET statements in *autoexec.bat*, open that directory and delete its contents as well.

If you delete these files before defragmenting your drive, the defragmentation process will go faster and it will be more effective.

Living with FAT

FAT is frequently maligned today, and rightfully so. On disk drives smaller than 200 MB, it's one of the most efficient filesystems possible. Unfortunately, FAT doesn't scale well at all. Under Windows 95 and 98, you have little choice about what filesystem to use: your menu is limited to three flavors of FAT. Since you can't change filesystems, you have to learn to work within FAT's limitations if you want maximum performance.

Why FAT16 Is Faster Than FAT32

Windows 95 OEM Service Release 2, released in late 1996, introduced a new variation of FAT, called FAT32. This greatly extended the number of clusters per disk, which allowed smaller partitions to use smaller cluster sizes, thus wasting less space, and it also allowed disk sizes far in excess of the old FAT16 2 GB limit. FAT32 offers greatly extended storage capacity by upping the maximum number of clusters to nearly 4.3 billion (actually 4,294,967,295, if you're counting). On small drives, this means smaller clusters. That 2 GB drive formatted with FAT32 uses 4K clusters rather than the 32K clusters forced by FAT16. Using 32K clusters, FAT32 can handle partitions of two terrabytes (2048 gigabytes, or just over two trillion bytes) in size.

These new features came at a price, however. FAT32 has significantly more overhead than FAT16, so if you take two identical drives, and format one as FAT16 and the other as FAT32, the FAT16 drive will give better performance. The other problem is the lack of backward compatibility. Disk utilities written for FAT16 will not work properly on a FAT32 drive.

The reason that FAT32 is slower than FAT16 is because of the way FAT stores its tables. FAT stores a list of every cluster on the disk, chaining the clusters together on this map to keep track of the disk's files. The table is implemented as a linked list, which is known for three things:

- Efficiency in terms of the amount of memory it uses

- Ease of implementation

- Very slow execution speed

A linked list is simply the data sitting next to the address of the next piece of data, so it doesn't use much memory. This was a good feature, since FAT was first implemented on 8-bit computers with extremely limited amounts of RAM using disk drives with less than 200K of storage.

Bill Gates demonstrated the ease of implementation by writing the first implementation of FAT in a hotel room in just one night in the mid-1970s. However, the efficiency and ease of implementation come at the price of execution speed. Let's say we have a linked list of four items. In order to get to the fourth item, the computer has to look at the first item to get the address of the second, then look at the second item to get the address of the third, then get the address of the fourth item from the third, and finally look at the data.

The main reason why FAT32 is so much slower than FAT16 is that the size of the linked list increased dramatically. A 2 GB FAT16 drive has 65,536 clusters. A 2 GB FAT32 drive has 524,288 clusters!

Much of Windows 98 is tuned to work optimally on FAT32 drives, but Windows 98 can't do anything to get past this fundamental difference between the two systems. Some operations on FAT32 drives will be faster under Windows 98 than they were under Windows 95B, and some operations under Windows 98 will be faster on FAT32 drives than they would be on FAT16 drives. But FAT16 is always going to be an all-around better performer than FAT32. It's just not possible to completely escape the pitfalls of FAT32's much larger data structures.

The large size of today's hard drives makes it impractical to completely avoid using FAT32. However, you should always install Windows on a FAT16 partition if at all possible.

Disk Partitioning Explained

This chapter talks a lot about disk partitioning, because partitions help to solve a wide variety of performance issues. Although PCs frequently come with their hard drives formatted as one big drive, it doesn't have to be that way. You can split a single physical drive into multiple logical drives. As far as you and your applications software are concerned, there are multiple hard drives in your system.

DOS-derived operating systems, including Windows 95 and 98, permit three types of partitions: primary, extended, and logical. *Primary partitions* are the most common. When you partition a drive as one drive letter, you're using a primary partition. Primary partitions have the advantage of being bootable. You can have up to four primary partitions on a drive, but Windows can see only one primary partition at a time.

Extended partitions are really nothing more than a container for holding logical partitions. When you want to partition a drive into more than one partition, you create a primary partition, and then you create an extended partition that fills the remainder of the drive. You then create *logical partitions* of whatever sizes you desire inside the extended partition. An extended partition can contain up to 20 logical partitions.

Windows gives each partition a drive letter. Drive letter mapping can be confusing, unfortunately. Here's the rule. *C:* is always the primary partition on your first hard drive. The lettering afterward depends on how many drives you have. If you have a second hard drive, its primary partition gets mapped to *D:*. A third hard drive's primary partition gets *E:*. The system runs through your chain of hard drives, from first to last, and maps the primary partitions first. It then goes back to the first drive, maps all of its logical partitions, then maps all of the second drive's logical partitions, and so on. Devices like CD-ROM and Zip drives are mapped last—hard drives of any kind take precedence.

Let's say a system has two hard drives partitioned in the manner described in Figure 3-1. Windows would map the drive letters as shown in Figure 3-2.

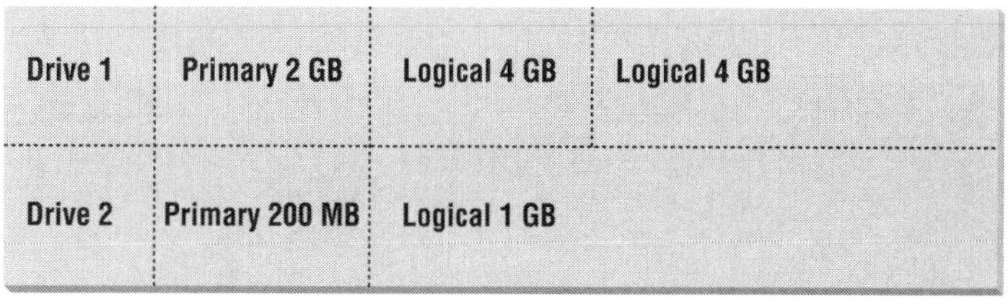

Drive 1	Primary 2 GB	Logical 4 GB	Logical 4 GB
Drive 2	Primary 200 MB	Logical 1 GB	

Figure 3-1. Physical hard drive layout

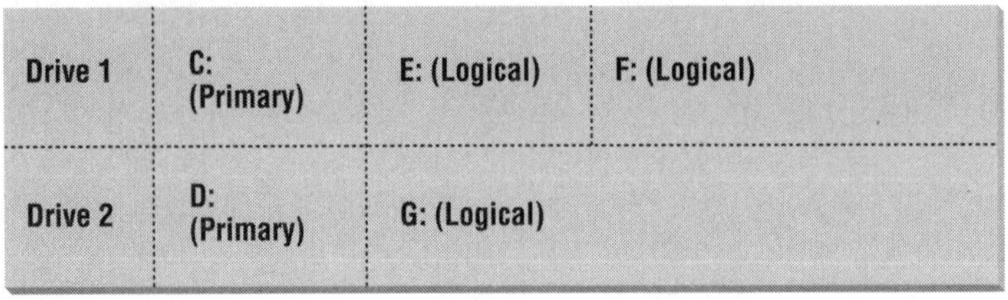

| Drive 1 | C:
(Primary) | E: (Logical) | F: (Logical) |
| Drive 2 | D:
(Primary) | G: (Logical) | |

Figure 3-2. How Windows maps the physical drive layout from Figure 3-1

Since this process can get confusing, people with multiple hard drives frequently will opt not to put a primary partition on any drive but their first drive, and just put logical partitions on subsequent drives. If you do it this way, drive letters always advance from one partition to the next, from one drive to the next, in completely predictable, sequential order.

Why you should partition your drive

Disk partitioning utilities like PowerQuest's PartitionMagic and Quarterdeck's Partition-It used to have very aggressive advertising campaigns, asking users why they stood by idly while FAT's overhead consumed an average of 25% of their expensive 1 GB hard drives' usable space. "Buy our product, regain $70 or $80 worth of disk space, and speed up your system in the process," they urged. Of course, they never said how much you could expect to speed up your system, nor did they tell you why it might speed up your system.

The speed improvement is real—not just marketing hype—but the reason for not giving a concrete estimate is pretty simple. It depends on your system, just like defragmenting your drive. There are a few reasons why partitioning will improve your system's speed. First, if you cut a drive in half, you also cut its partition tables in half. The drive maneuvers more quickly as its partition tables become less complex: suddenly you've doubled the number of sectors you have at the front of a partition. Secondly, if you partition your drive into two equal parts, chances are that half the files will end up in one half and half the files will end up in the other. This setup dramatically speeds up directory searches. These are pure side effects of partitioning, but they work, due to the weaknesses of FAT.

If you plan your partitioning right (or are just plain lucky), a third benefit can also come into play: reduced fragmentation. Let's consider what happens when you launch Microsoft Word and load a document:

1. Windows loads the Word executable.

2. Windows loads the system DLLs that Word requires.

3. Windows allocates virtual memory on disk if needed.

4. Word opens the document.

5. Word writes a variety of temporary files, including backup copies of the document.

6. Ten minutes later, Word re-saves your document.

Writing and deleting files cause fragmentation. Generally speaking, executables and DLLs don't change, so the first two operations won't cause any fragmentation. The allocation of virtual memory could cause fragmentation under some circumstances. The act of opening the document causes no fragmentation, but the writing of temporary files is very likely to. Temporary files by their very nature are constantly changing, eating tiny holes into your free space. Similarly, saving your document can cause fragmentation. Your document and Word's temp files can very easily start interweaving like a tapestry. If your system doesn't have a great deal of physical RAM, there's also the possibility that your virtual memory will get entangled in this mess as well. Virtual memory is slow enough as it is.

Partitioning can minimize the damage, however. If there's a small partition on the drive dedicated to virtual memory, virtual memory will never become fragmented. If your data is stored on another partition, it may become fragmented, but that's less likely, and it won't be nearly as much of a tangled mess. If your temporary files are stored on yet another partition, you're doing damage control. There's very little you can do to keep temporary files from becoming fragmented, but if they're isolated, at least they aren't causing anything else to become fragmented.

Since 10 GB drives are inexpensive and look to become standard equipment very soon, I'll suggest the disk layout shown in Figure 3-3.

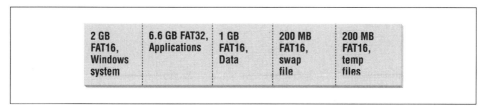

Figure 3-3. Partitioning a 10 GB drive

If you have a smaller drive, scale the partitions accordingly. If you have a larger drive, enlarge the applications and data partitions to fill the drive.

I suggest isolating Windows 95/98 and your applications software largely for performance reasons. The Windows boot drive always has a cluttered root directory because there are so many files that have to be stored in the root and can't be moved elsewhere. Windows will operate faster if it doesn't have application directories cluttering up its drive, and your applications will run faster if they don't have operating system files slowing Windows' search for their crucial files. Having the

Windows system isolated in its own partition also speeds disaster recovery. When a power outage or an errant task causes Windows to trash a drive, it's usually the boot drive that gets trashed. If the boot drive contains nothing but Windows, you'll be able to get back up and running simply by restoring your boot drive.

Your boot drive should include FAT16 for performance reasons. Windows programs tend to rely very heavily on underlying Windows code, loading it in and out of memory, so making Windows files accessible quickly speeds system performance as a whole.

I suggest isolating applications from user data mostly to minimize fragmentation. On a large drive, you have no choice but to use FAT32 for your applications partition. If you have truly speed-intensive applications, you can install them in your system partition for better performance, but I suggest making this the exception rather than the rule.

User data should definitely be isolated. This is the only part of the system you really need to back up, as Windows can be reinstalled from CD and updates re-downloaded from the Internet; applications can be reinstalled from CD or re-downloaded; and swap files, temporary files, and browser cache files are meaningless data. A gigabyte is usually more than enough space for your data, unless you work in publishing or audio/video editing.

Likewise, temporary files should be isolated. These files are the most likely to become fragmented and to cause other files to become fragmented. If you quarantine them, they will fragment only one another and won't hinder overall system performance nearly as much. You can redirect your temporary files with the following lines in *autoexec.bat*:

```
Set temp=x:\temp
Set tmp=x:\temp
```

Substitute *x* for the drive letter of your quarantine partition, and after creating the partition, don't forget to create a directory called *\temp*.

Isolating the swap file prevents it from becoming fragmented. Moving the swap file isn't difficult: open the Control Panel, then go to System → Performance → Virtual Memory → Let me specify my own virtual memory settings → Hard disk, and then select the drive you want to use.

If your system has multiple hard drives, incorporate them into the strategy. Always put the swap file on a different drive from your operating system, unless the second drive is extremely old and slow. If the two drives are of sufficient size that one can hold Windows and the other can hold the applications, that's fine. If you have an old 170 MB drive in a neglected 386 or 486, put that drive in your system and assign your temporary files and web browser cache to it. Remember that a hard drive can do only one thing at a time. So if your system is loading a file into virtual memory, the drive heads are shuffling back and forth between the two files. If you have a second hard drive, however, the drive that's loading the file can be fetching the next piece while the drive that hosts the virtual memory is writing the current piece.

I used to utilize elaborate partitioning schemes across multiple hard drives, mostly in order to get maximum performance for the swap file. Memory prices have collapsed recently, however, making memory so cheap that we don't have to think much about virtual memory anymore.

You can get a slight performance gain by putting two hard drives in a system, and installing the operating system on one drive and applications on the other, but the gain isn't significant enough to deem this setup absolutely essential.

A partition layout for small drives

If you have a small hard drive (say, 2 GB or smaller), you probably can't afford to partition it into three drives—the partition sizes will be too small to be very useful. In the cases of small drives, go ahead and create one large partition (about 75% of the available drive space) to hold Windows and applications, then create a partition with the remaining space to hold temp files, browser cache, and data.

Partitioning your drive with FDISK

When Microsoft released Windows 95 and declared DOS dead, they forgot something. Clunky old FDISK, a DOS remnant that should have been replaced in 1984 with something less cryptic, is still hanging around. FDISK usually does the job if you don't have anything else—as long as that job doesn't include ridding a system of non-DOS partitions. Lack of updates to FDISK is one of the biggest faults I find with Windows 9x.

FDISK is a destructive utility. If you use it to repartition a drive with data already on it, you will lose all of that data. If you decide you want to repartition your drive, back up all of your data before running FDISK, then realize that you will have to reinstall Windows, then restore your data, and in all likelihood you will also have to reinstall a good number of your applications.

To run FDISK, it's best to restart your computer in MS-DOS mode, then type FDISK at the command prompt. If you've just added a second hard drive and want to partition it, you can get away with running FDISK from a command prompt within Windows, but if you're repartitioning the drive that contains Windows, run it from DOS mode (and don't proceed until you also read either Chapter 10, *Clean Windows Installation*, or Chapter 11, *RAM Disks*, whichever is appropriate for your system).

If you have Windows 95B, Windows 95C, or Windows 98 and you have a hard drive larger than about 500 MB, FDISK will ask you if you want to enable large disk support. This is FDISK's cryptic way of asking whether you want to format your drives with FAT16 or FAT32—yes, you select this feature from FDISK, not from FORMAT. If you want to mix FAT16 and FAT32 on the same drive, you have to run FDISK twice: once with large disk support enabled (for FAT32) and once with it disabled (for FAT16).

Let's step through the process of formatting a drive with a single FAT32 partition and a single FAT16 partition—the ideal configuration for an applications/temp file drive described earlier. We will assume the drive has a single primary partition, as most do.

1. Restart in MS-DOS mode, type **FDISK** at the command prompt.

2. Answer yes to the prompt asking whether to enable large disk support.

3. Select 3—Delete partition or logical DOS drive.

4. Select 1—Delete primary DOS partition. Answer all prompts. FDISK will then return you to the main menu.

5. Select 1—Create DOS partition or logical DOS drive.

6. Select 1—Create primary DOS partition.

7. FDISK will ask you if you want to use all available space and make the partition active. Answer no. FDISK will then ask what percentage of the disk you want to dedicate to the primary partition, or what size in MB. Pick an appropriate size—in this case, using all but about 200 MB will do—and enter it.

8. Exit FDISK.

9. Run FDISK again, answering no to the prompt asking whether to enable large disk support.

10. Select 1—Create DOS partition or logical DOS drive.

11. Select 2—Create extended partition. Remember, extended partitions are a wrapper for logical DOS drives. Whether your disk has two partitions on it or 24, you must create an extended partition. FDISK will ask you how much of the drive to use. Go ahead and use whatever's left.

12. FDISK will automatically select the option to create logical drives in the extended DOS partition. FDISK will offer to use all of the available space. Take it up on the offer, since we're creating only one drive.

After you restart, your drive will be partitioned but the partitions won't be formatted yet. Format them with the DOS FORMAT command from a command prompt, or format them from Windows' My Computer window.

All in all, FDISK is a pretty clunky, inconsistent program. If you just want to partition a brand-new drive into two parts, it's adequate, but if you want to get fancy with your partitioning, it's easy to get confused. Except for the initial partitioning of the drive, you're far better off using another tool.

Partitioning your drive with FIPS

FIPS is an open-source disk utility written by Arno Schaefer and released under the GNU GPL. FIPS is an acronym for First Interactive non-destructive Partition Splitting program. Although little known in the Windows world, FIPS is widely used by Linux users to free up disk space on a DOS or Windows PC for Linux installations, and it also has gained some prominence among OS/2 users.

As the name suggests, FIPS can split a partition into two parts without destroying the data contained within it. This is a real boon—it permits you to partition an existing drive without losing any data. However, it is not a complete replacement for a commercial product like PartitionMagic, nor is it intended to be. FIPS will truncate an existing partition, but it won't do cluster resizing. The new, reduced partition will use whatever cluster size it previously used, so FIPS won't save you any disk space. And while FIPS will split a FAT16 or FAT32 partition, it cannot split the larger FAT32X partitions. You should look into FIPS if your primary interest is in partitioning a drive in order to reduce fragmentation. If you want to be able to change a drive's cluster size to free disk space or increase speed, if you want to convert drives between FAT16 and FAT32, or if you have a large drive with FAT32X partitions, you need PartitionMagic.

FIPS is available all over the Internet, but you can download the current version 2.0 (released in May 1998) from the author's web page at *www.igd.fhg.de/ ~aschaefe/fips/*.

Under Windows 9x, FIPS can't completely replace FDISK—it takes a primary partition, truncates it, then creates a second primary partition. DOS and Windows don't officially support multiple primary partitions. The author says he's used multiple primary partitions with DOS versions 5 and up, but it's better to play by the rules and delete the second primary partition with FDISK, then create an extended partition and create a proper logical drive within the extended partition. You'll probably want to do this anyway, since there's a good chance you'll want to mix FAT16 and FAT32 on the drive, and FIPS won't handle that for you.

Before you run FIPS, you need to scan your disk for errors and defragment it. Run ScanDisk and perform a thorough check on the drive, including the surface scan. This is important—a bad cluster might throw FIPS off, and when you're dealing with a low-level disk utility, you want everything to be rock solid. After running ScanDisk, run Defrag. This is important, too. FIPS needs all of the drive's free space to be at the end of the drive so it can truncate it. If you use a utilities package like

Norton Utilities or Mijenix Fit-It 99, be sure to turn off the feature that puts seldom-used files at the end of the drive. It's probably easiest just to use Microsoft's Defrag. If your swap file is on the disk you want to split, disable virtual memory and restart before you run Defrag, because Defrag can't move the swap file.

Finally, back up your data before you run FIPS. FIPS was designed to let you avoid the time-consuming backup followed by partitioning followed by restore, but that's no excuse for not having your data backed up. Always be aware that there's a small risk of FIPS malfunctioning and rendering the drive unreadable. FIPS is a very paranoid program and won't do anything if it finds something unusual about your disk. Thousands of people have used FIPS reliably since 1993—but the risk is always present. Back up any word processing files, spread-sheets, and other data files you've created. Don't bother with your operating system and application directories, because you can reinstall them from their original CD-ROMs if need be.

Once your disk is error-free and defragmented, prepare a boot disk. You must not run FIPS from within Windows! Open a command prompt, insert a disk, type **sys a:**, then copy the FIPS files *restorrb.exe*, *fips.exe*, and *errors.txt* to the disk. Now restart with the boot disk in the drive. Your PC will boot off this disk and present you with a command prompt. Type **FIPS** at the command prompt to launch the program. FIPS asks a lot of questions, but many of them are of the yes/no variety, asking for confirmation before it does anything. This is a good feature, because it's easy to make a mistake with low-level partitioning utilities. It's better to ask too many questions than not enough.

If you have multiple drives, FIPS will ask you which drive you want to split. Select one. FIPS will then display partition information for that drive. If you have multi-ple partitions on the drive, FIPS will ask which partition you want to split. Select one. FIPS will then scan the partition for errors and anomalies, then scan to deter-mine how much free space is in the partition.

Once FIPS is happy there are no errors and knows how much free space is in the partition, it will offer to make a backup copy of your current partition configura-tion. Take it up on the offer. This will allow *restorrb.exe* to undo the split if some-thing goes wrong. FIPS will then offer to split your drive, based on how much space is available. Initially, it will shrink the old partition to its smallest possible size and allocate all available free space to the new partition. You can adjust how much space goes to which partition with the arrow keys. When you get the space allocation you want, hit Enter. FIPS will then run a test and ask if you want to con-tinue. Then it will give you the new partition information. If you want to proceed with writing the new partition data, answer yes.

After FIPS completes, restart your computer, hit F8 and select the command prompt only. When the *C:* prompt appears, run ScanDisk. After ScanDisk completes, it's time to hand the game back over to FDISK. Type FDISK at the command prompt, then select option 3—Delete partition or logical DOS drive. Then select option 1— Delete primary DOS partition. Carefully look at the partition map FDISK prints, and select the partition whose filesystem is UNKNOWN. FDISK will then prompt for the volume label. Unformatted partitions always have no volume label, so hit Enter. FDISK will ask for confirmation; type Y. After FDISK reports the primary DOS partition is deleted, hit Escape. FDISK will take you back to its main menu. Select option 1—Create partition. FDISK will then ask what kind of partition. Select option 2—Create extended partition. FDISK will ask for the size, giving you a default of whatever free space is available on the drive. Accept it. After creating the extended partition, FDISK will automatically begin creating logical drives. It will ask for a size for the logical drive, defaulting to the size of the extended partition. If you just want one more drive, like the example before, hit Enter to accept the default. After FDISK finishes this process, hit Escape twice and reboot, intercepting Windows again with the F8 key to take you to a command prompt.

Before you can use your drive, you have to format it. But you want to be absolutely certain you're formatting the right drive. Type DIR D: at the command prompt. If you get an invalid media type error, you have the right drive. If you don't get an error message, retype the command, proceed down the alphabet, replacing D: with the next letter in sequence until you get an Invalid media type error.

Once you get the error message, type FORMAT x:, replacing x: with the drive letter you just uncovered. Formatting the drive may take a while. Once the drive is formatted, you can reboot into Windows.

Partitioning your drive with PartitionMagic

In comparison to FDISK or even FIPS, PartitionMagic is a far more elegant and intuitive tool. It has a slick graphical interface, and is capable of not only splitting partitions nondestructively, but completely resizing them. It can also convert between FAT16 and FAT32 with ease. It's a commercial utility with a retail price of about $70, but if you do much work with partitions, it quickly pays for itself. Experimenting with different partition layouts isn't very feasible if you just have FDISK and FIPS to work with. PartitionMagic will let you change your partition layout on a whim. PartitionMagic is also far more automatic than either of the other tools. It formats the partitions for you as it creates them, and if you just want to split a partition, it will automatically create the extended partition and logical drive for you.

When you install PartitionMagic 4.0, be sure to install the DOS version rather than the Windows version. The DOS version is completely graphical, you can run it from the Windows Start menu (it restarts the computer in DOS mode), and it looks just like the Windows version (see Figure 3-4), but I find it more reliable than the

Windows version. Also be sure to install Magic Mover, which will automatically move applications between drives for you.

In Figure 3-4, note the graphical representation of the partitions and the partition types. The first three partitions are primary DOS partitions. The large box that surrounds drives *D:* and *E:* represents the extended partition.

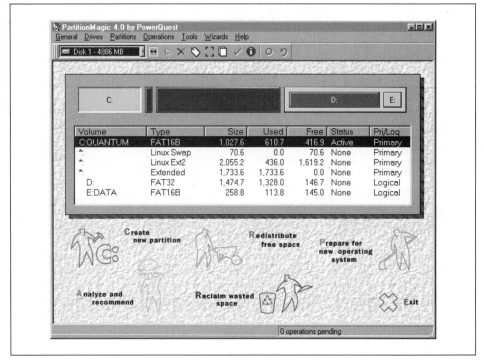

Figure 3-4. The PartitionMagic 4.0 screen

Repartitioning with PartitionMagic is extremely easy. PartitionMagic includes Microsoft-style wizards to walk you through the process and make recommendations, but I don't bother with them. You can just right-click on the drive letter you wish to reduce, select resize, and shrink the partition down. There's no need to defragment beforehand. Then, right-click on the empty space and select Create. By default, PartitionMagic will create a logical partition. Give it the size, and Partition-Magic will automatically create an extended partition to encompass the logical partition for you. When you reboot, the drives will be ready to use. There is no immediately obvious way to select between FAT16 and FAT32; if you select a cluster size within FAT16's range, it will go FAT16, while if you select smaller cluster sizes, it will go FAT32. PartitionMagic will tell you what type of partition you're telling it to create, and it won't let you create partitions that are outside the bounds of FAT's limitations.

PartitionMagic will also let you resize the clusters. Right-click on the drive whose clusters you want to resize, then select Advanced → Resize clusters. PartitionMagic will tell you how much space you will save or waste by changing cluster sizes. If you've created a partition for your swap file, I suggest you use 32K clusters, as this size will speed access to the partition slightly. If you have a partition holding temp files and a browser cache, you might consider doing the same with it as well. This will speed access and reduce fragmentation, though the partition will fill much more quickly. If you're cleaning out your temp directory regularly (as you should be), this won't be a problem, and speed is much more critical than wasted space with the temp directory.

Other Disk Performance Tools

Windows has two more tricks to improve the performance of your hard drive. Both deal specifically with the time it takes for applications to load.

Aligning Your Applications

Windows 98 introduced a utility called WALIGN that takes an application and aligns its program code on 4K boundaries, which speeds up load time due to the architecture of Intel and Intel-compatible x86 CPUs. WALIGN is a cut-down version of the utility WinAlign, which ships with the Windows 98 Resource Kit. Aligning has nothing to do with defragmenting a file: both will make files load faster, but they take completely different and unrelated approaches, and aligning only works with executable files. The results of the two are cumulative.

Windows 98 doesn't automatically align all of your applications, because technically, the modifications WALIGN makes violate the clause in most programs' license agreements against modifying the program's executable. WALIGN is therefore intended to modify only Microsoft Office, and it will execute only if it finds Microsoft Office on your system.

However, there is no need to go buy the Resource Kit—which costs as much as Windows 98 itself—in order to align your programs and gain the benefits of faster application loading. Even if you don't have Microsoft Office, you can add the registry keys that WALIGN looks for, and then WALIGN will function properly. Launch Regedit, then add the following empty key: HKEY_LOCAL_MACHINE\Software\Microsoft\Windows\CurrentVersion\Uninstall\Office8.0. Don't add this key if you do have Office installed, as this will make it impossible to uninstall Office should you need to. On the other hand, if you add this key and later want to install Office, this key won't interfere with it. Office will just overwrite it.

Although the capability isn't advertised, once you add this key to the registry, WALIGN will happily align any Windows program. There is the slight risk that

WALIGN will make a program cease to operate properly. The safest and easiest way to run WALIGN is from a pair of batch files stored in *C:\Windows\Command*. To enter *align.bat*, go to Start → Run → EDIT C:\WINDOWS\COMMAND\ALIGN.BAT, enter the following lines, then go to File → Save, then to File → Exit:

```
::ALIGN.BAT
@MD %1\UNALIGN
@COPY %1\*.EXE UNALIGN
@COPY %1\*.DLL UNALIGN
@WALIGN %1\*.EXE
@WALIGN %1\*.DLL
```

Now here's the corresponding *unalign.bat*. The entry process is similar: Start → Run → EDIT C:\WINDOWS\COMMAND\UNALIGN.BAT, then enter the following lines, then File → Save, then File → Exit:

```
::UNALIGN.BAT
@COPY /Y %1\UNALIGN\*.* .
@DELTREE /Y %1\UNALIGN\*.*
```

After entering and saving this pair of batch files, you can safely align any application from a command prompt. Simply feed the batch file the location of the application you wish to align. For instance, type:

```
ALIGN "D:\Program Files\Real"
```

to align a copy of RealPlayer installed in *D:\Program Files\Real*.

Aligned applications load more quickly than unaligned applications and consume less memory during the load process. This is possibly the most compelling new feature of Windows 98. There are, however, a few disadvantages to aligned programs. They occupy more disk space than their unaligned counterparts—so don't do it if disk space is tight—and program updates from the manufacturer almost certainly won't work properly. So if an update to a program you use is released, unalign it with *unalign.bat* (*unalign.bat* doesn't really unalign a program—it just replaces the aligned versions with backup copies created by *align.bat*), run the program update, then align the program again.

If you're concerned about the disk space these backups consume, it's possible to modify ALIGN/UNALIGN to store the backup copies in a Zip archive. You must have Info-ZIP's Zip and UnZip somewhere in your PATH (I suggest in *C:\Windows\Command*) in order for these batch files to operate. Here's the modified *align.bat*:

```
::ALIGN.BAT
@ZIP -9 A %1\UNALIGN.ZIP %1\*.EXE %1\*.DLL
@WALIGN %1\*.EXE
@WALIGN %1\*.DLL
```

And here's the corresponding *unalign.bat*:

```
::UNALIGN.BAT
@UNZIP -o %1\UNALIGN.ZIP
@DEL %1\UNALIGN.ZIP
```

I use Info-ZIP instead of WinZip because WinZip isn't very useful from a batch file, and Info-ZIP is free. The original PKZip would work for this process, but Info-ZIP does a slightly better job of compressing than PKZip 2.0 does, and Info-ZIP is free for all uses, commercial and noncommercial.

Fast Loaders

This category of software arrived on the scene in late 1996 and early 1997, got some press coverage, then disappeared as quickly as it had come. A fast loader made it into Symantec's Norton Utilities, and Helix Software bundled a fast loader together with a memory compression program and marketed the package as Hurricane, which Network Associates in turn bundled into the first version of McAfee Office Suite (but not in McAfee Office 2000). But nobody really promotes this software category anymore.

Although their effectiveness varies, these programs work essentially the same way, monitoring the way Windows loads applications and reordering their read requests in a more efficient manner. This technique is very similar to the way modern CPUs or modern SCSI controllers gain efficiency, and it was just a matter of time before this hardware technique started to be applied to software. Unfortunately, some flaws in these products hurt system stability. There was no question that the computer loaded the applications more quickly with a fast loader installed. But there was also no question that the computer crashed more frequently.

The revised Defrag program that ships with Windows 98, working in tandem with WALIGN and Windows 98's revised disk cache, compromised these programs' compatibility with Windows 98, yet provided most defragmentation features. Speed Start, the Norton Utilities' fast loader, is incompatible with Windows 98.

There is only one product left in this category that is both easy to find and compatible with Windows 98—Acceleration Software International's Superfassst (which was licensed to Syncronys software and marketed for a time under the name Windrenalin). The original product in this software category, it is still commercially available. Superfassst 98 can be downloaded from *www.accelerationsw.com*. It's now an advertising-based product. The program is free, but in order for it to function, your web browser's home page must point to Acceleration Software's page. If several software companies started to promote their software this way, it's easy to see how this could cause some conflicts. This procedure can also be a problem if you want to run it on a system that isn't connected to the Internet. You may not like the idea of having to keep a web browser that you never use on your computer.

Superfassst 98 is a 1.13 MB download. When you go to install it, it asks permission to change your web browser's home page. If you say no, it gives you several opportunities to change your mind, then exits if you persist. If you let it change your home page, it asks for an installation directory, installs itself, then offers to run ScanDisk and Defrag on your hard drives. Superfassst is most effective on defragmented drives, but if you have a better defragmenter installed, you'll want to decline Superfassst's offer and defragment the drive yourself using the better utility. After defragmentation finishes (or after you decline), Superfassst will restart your computer and give you a bar graph representing the speed increases you can expect from your various drives. On my Pentium 90 with an old non-UDMA Quantum Fireball hard drive, the expected speed increase ranged from 104% on its FAT16 boot partition to 211% on its big FAT32 applications partition.

Superfassst then puts an icon in the system tray to show that it's loaded. Double-clicking on it brings up its configuration settings. You can globally turn Superfassst's acceleration on or off, or you can turn off individual acceleration settings. You can also set Superfassst to automatically defragment your drive every four hours. If you choose to do this, you will definitely want to partition your drive as described earlier in this chapter in order to minimize fragmentation. Superfassst uses Defrag, which can be painfully slow.

The first time you load an application, Superfassst observes it. There might be a delay right after the application launches during which the computer will appear to freeze, not even responding to mouse movements. This is normal; Superfassst is still analyzing. Your system should return momentarily. From the second launch on, Superfassst will step in and accelerate. I tested Superfassst by loading Microsoft Word 97. Unaccelerated, Word takes 11 seconds to load on my Pentium 90 from disk, and 4 seconds from the disk cache. With Superfassst installed, it takes 4 seconds to load from disk and 3 seconds to load from cache. Internet Explorer 4.0 shows similar improvements. I can't complain—we're talking a minimum of a 25% improvement, and that's when loading the application from RAM. Considering some of us are willing to fork over hundreds of dollars for high-end SCSI controllers and drives to get a 25% improvement in disk speed, that's pretty good.

The claimed improvements on my Cyrix MII-PR233 were less dramatic, ranging from 88% to 113%. On that PC, Word 97 loads in 4 seconds unaccelerated, 3 seconds with Norton Speed Start, and 2 seconds with Superfassst. The speed when loading from the disk cache under all three circumstances is about 2 seconds.

Interestingly, Superfassst makes my Pentium 90's vintage 1996 hard drive quite comparable to the 7,200 rpm Maxtor hard drive in my Cyrix. Much of the difference in load time between the two PCs now appears to be due more to CPU speed and the slower PCI bus in the Pentium 90. Superfassst's memory usage is reasonable; it uses about 1.58 MB. You definitely don't want to be running it on a 4 MB system, but on a system with 16 MB or more, it will be worthwhile. You'll have a faster system, and you can steal an equivalent or larger amount of memory from the disk cache and/or the CD cache if memory usage starts to concern you.

If Superfassst turns out to be incompatible with any software you have installed, open your Start menu's Explorer view, locate the program's icon, then right-click and select Unaccelerate. Next, right-click and select Don't Allow Acceleration. If the program starts running again, you know you can keep Superfassst installed so you still have the benefits of fast-loading for the programs Superfassst is compatible with.

Superfassst has had installation issues in the past; if it fails to install, try restarting your system, disabling any utilities packages you might be running (Norton Utilities, First Aid, etc.), installing again, then reenabling those utilities after a successful installation.

Unfortunately, I found that Superfassst made my Windows 95 system too unstable. I typically have to reboot once a week, but with Superfassst installed, I found I was having to reboot about once every two days. It's been okay on my Windows 98 system. Superfassst doesn't yet seem to be stable under all conditions, however.

I wish I could recommend Superfassst without any reservations besides its monopolization of your home page. It's faster than Norton Speed Start, compatible with Windows 98, and improves upon the speed-enhancing features already present in Windows 98. If it works on your system, you'll love it, but don't install it on a mission-critical system just before you get started on a big project. Norton Speed Start is more stable, but it's not compatible with Windows 98 and its speedups aren't as dramatic either. If I had to recommend one over the other, I'd give the nod to the more conservative Norton Speed Start.

How Much Difference Will This Make?

The results of implementing all these tips will vary depending on what programs you run and on your usage habits.

Back when I was in college and all I had was my 66 MHz 486, a neighbor was in the process of upgrading his PC. He put a 66 MHz CPU upgrade and a brand-new 1 GB hard drive in his system. He figured because his computer was a 486DX (with a math coprocessor) and mine was a 486SX (without a math coprocessor), and since he had a newer hard drive, his computer would blow mine away. Imagine his disappointment when my system was still faster!

When I looked at his system, it didn't take long for me to figure out why. Since he had a huge (for its day) 1 GB drive, he figured he could just install every piece of software he'd ever bought or downloaded, and he installed every program in a subdirectory hanging off the root. His root directory had well over 160 entries. I told him that cleaning up his root directory would make a difference. He acted like he didn't believe me, but a week or so later, he dropped in and told me that cleaning up his root directory made a bigger difference in his system performance than either the CPU upgrade or the hard drive upgrade had.

Later in my college career, I took some consulting jobs to make some money on the side to help pay my expenses. I did a lot of work for a professor who had a 66 MHz 486 similar to mine. Windows 95 was taxing the limits of his machine: his 420 MB hard drive was filling up, and his 16 MB of RAM was proving to be inadequate. I added another 8 MB of RAM to his system, and the system ran better. Then I installed Norton Utilities and used it to defragment and reorder his drive. It took Norton Utilities easily half an hour to run, but once it finished, the system showed dramatic improvement—at least as much improvement as adding the memory had delivered.

Rearranging the hard drive shouldn't be seen as a complete substitute for a hardware upgrade, but my experience shows it makes a difference—sometimes a dramatic difference.

Getting Rid of Disk Compression

In the early 1990s, the disk compression business became a small industry. Companies such as AddStor and Stac released products that compressed and decompressed the data on your hard drive transparently, claiming you could double your disk space for $40. These programs worked pretty well, but under some circumstances they hurt system performance. For many people it was worth it, however, because the price difference between a 50 MB drive and a 100 MB drive was several hundred dollars.

It didn't take long for Microsoft to get into the act. Early archrival Digital Research was bundling data compression with their DR-DOS product, so Microsoft released MS-DOS 6.0 with its own disk compression program called DoubleSpace and printed the words "The easy way to double your disk" right on the front of the product box. That was the beginning of the end for the disk compression industry. Why pay $40 for Stacker when a usable disk-doubling program ships with the operating system?

Microsoft's DoubleSpace had three problems. First, it was unreliable and corrupted many users' data. Second, it almost always hurt system performance. Third, it infringed on some of Stac's patents. Microsoft quickly remedied the first and third problem but never did anything about the performance problem. As part of the settlement with Stac, DoubleSpace evolved into DriveSpace, which continues to ship with Windows 9x to this day.

Despite rumors to the contrary, DriveSpace isn't particularly dangerous to your data. It is, however, a drain on performance. There's little point in using DriveSpace to compress a hard drive in this day and age, however. Hard drives are the biggest bottleneck in modern systems today, but they generally can deliver data faster than a modern CPU can decompress it. Data compression therefore is a performance hindrance on hard drives.

Slow devices such as floppy drives and Zip drives can benefit from data compression, since they deliver data more slowly than most CPUs can decompress it. However, data compression is more complicated on removable media—you won't be able to exchange the media between computers running different operating systems, and you can't necessarily count on other Windows 9x computers to have DriveSpace installed. Therefore, it's hard to recommend disk compression even on removable media. (We'll talk about the one circumstance where disk compression makes some sense in Chapter 11.)

If you've compressed any of the drives in your system with DriveSpace, I recommend you uncompress them. Press Start → Programs → Accessories → System Tools → DriveSpace, then highlight your compressed drive, and from the Drive menu, select Uncompress. The process may take some time, but you should find performance will be significantly better afterward.

4

Speeding Up the Boot Process

First impressions matter. It's purely psychological, but a system that boots quickly just seems fast. When a system takes four minutes to load Windows, it's difficult to convince anybody that the computer is fast. In the early 1990s, this was one of the arguments against IBM's OS/2 operating system. OS/2 ran virtually all Windows 3.1 programs, but Windows 3.1 loaded much more quickly than OS/2 did, and Windows 3.1 loaded Windows programs more quickly than OS/2 did. Once the systems were running, the speed difference was usually negligible, and sometimes OS/2 was faster. And OS/2 was unquestionably more stable. But people just couldn't get past those long load times.

Software developers tell me they are aware of this phenomenon, and if they can't make their programs load quickly, they do everything they can to at least make programs look like they load quickly. This is why you see animated splash screens—if the computer is doing something, anything, it appears faster than just a blank screen.

Windows 9x certainly takes longer to load than previous versions did. I've seen bogged-down systems take upwards of five minutes to boot. Of course, it's possible to reduce this time. Once it finishes its power-on self test (POST), my Cyrix MII-PR233 system boots in 26 seconds. My Pentium 90 boots about 40 seconds after POST completes. Neither PC is a state-of-the-art system.

The Boot Process Explained

The boot process for a PC running Windows is long and complex. When you first apply power, the CPU is running in real (8086 compatibility) mode. The CPU loads and executes the ROM BIOS bootstrap, located at address FFFF0h. The BIOS bootstrap does a number of things. At minimum, it executes its POST, where it checks to ensure that the memory, video card, keyboard, and other essential system components work properly. Then it checks the first boot device (usually a floppy drive, but it can also be a CD-ROM or Zip) for the presence of a boot disk. If it finds none, it looks for a hard disk. If a hard disk is found, the bootstrap loader jumps to the operating system loader, also located in ROM. The system then reads the master boot record (MBR) and partition table from the hard disk. If your system is equipped with a Plug-and-Play BIOS (most systems manufactured after 1995 are), the BIOS scans the system for I/O ports, DMA channels, IRQ lines, and other resources needed by system peripherals. The system then disables all Plug-and-Play devices, creates a map of used and unused resources, configures and reenables the devices one at a time. This device information is retained so the Windows 95 Configuration Manager can refer to it later.

The MBR contains the location of the boot partition. This is queried, and then the system loads the boot sector contained in the boot partition. In addition to the disk boot program, the boot sector contains a table of disk characteristics. The boot sector locates the root directory, then loads *io.sys* into memory and executes it.

io.sys first loads a minimal FAT filesystem, and then it looks for a file in the root directory called *winboot.ini*, used by the Windows 9x setup program. When it doesn't find *winboot.ini*, it reads *msdos.sys*. The "Starting Windows 9x" message displays for the amount of time specified in the *msdos.sys* `BootDelay=n` line (the default is two seconds), or until you press a function key. If you enabled multiple hardware profiles in Windows 9x (which you may have done if you have a laptop), it prompts you to select a profile. If the *msdos.sys* `Logo=n` line is set to 1, *io.sys* loads and displays *logo.sys*, the Windows startup logo. You can clear the logo to display the text it hides by hitting Esc at any time during the boot process.

If the *msdos.sys* `DrvSpace=n` or `DblSpace=n` lines are set to 1, *io.sys* looks for the appropriate *.ini* files, and if it finds them, loads the matching driver into memory. *io.sys* then checks to make sure the registry files contain valid data, and attempts to load them. If it doesn't find *system.dat*, it loads the backup *system.da0* file, and if startup is successful, it copies *system.da0* to *system.dat*.

If the *msdos.sys* `DblBuff=n` line is set to 1, or if the registry key HKLM\System\CurrentControlSet\Control\WinBoot\DoubleBuffer is enabled, *io.sys* loads *dblbuff.sys*. Windows then loads the machine's hardware profile before processing *config.sys*.

After processing *config.sys*, *io.sys* reads *msdos.sys* for the `WinBootDir` parameter. From this directory, *io.sys* loads *ifshlp.sys* (a complete FAT filesystem, required for running Windows), *himem.sys* (an extended memory manager, necessary for accessing more than 640 KB of RAM, and also required for Windows), and *setver.exe* (a hack to fool poorly behaved DOS programs into thinking they're running under some specific version of DOS). You can speed up booting somewhat by moving *setver.exe* from *Windows* into *Windows**Command*. If some of your programs respond with the message "Incorrect DOS Version," move the file back or write a batch file that invokes *setver.exe* before launching the program.

io.sys then reserves all upper memory blocks (UMBs), the memory between 640 KB and 1 MB, for its own use, then loads *command.com*, which processes and executes the commands contained in *autoexec.bat*.

After *autoexec.bat*, *command.com* executes *win.com*, the Windows bootstrap loader. *win.com* then searches for *vmm32.vxd*, and if there is enough memory available, loads it into RAM. Otherwise, *vmm32.vxd* is accessed from disk, greatly slowing boot time. *vmm32.vxd* is the core of the Windows system.

The virtual device driver loader in *vmm32.vxd* examines \Windows\System\ Vmm32 and compares it to the device drivers contained in *vmm32.vxd* itself. If duplicates are found, the versions in \Windows\System\Vmm32 load instead. Once the drivers have had a chance to load, *vmm32.vxd* checks to make sure they all loaded successfully. If they didn't, it tries again.

If *msdos.sys* is set to DisableLog=0, the virtual device drivers are logged to \bootlog.txt. *vmm32.vxd* then starts initializing drivers.

Finally, *vmm32.vxd* switches the CPU from real mode into protected (32-bit) mode, and the drivers finish loading, in order of importance. Once all drivers are loaded and initialized, *vmm32.vxd* loads *krnl32.dll*, *gdi.exe*, *user.exe*, and whatever shell is specified in \Windows\system.ini, usually *explorer.exe*.

If the PC is networked, Windows pauses to ask for a network logon. Windows then loads the desktop associated with that user ID, or loads the default desktop. Finally, Windows executes the files specified in the *Startup* folder and in the HKLM\Software\Microsoft\Windows\CurrentVersion\Run and RunOnce keys.

Speeding Up the Boot Process

Most of the boot process's changeable behavior is determined by parameters in *msdos.sys*. The key to optimizing the boot process, therefore, is a matter of altering *msdos.sys*.

To change *msdos.sys*, you first have to give yourself permission. Double-click My Computer, then select C: → View → Options → View → Show all files. Now, look for *msdos.sys*. Select Context menu → Properties. Clear the boxes labeled Read-only, Hidden, and System. Hit OK. Now, hold down the Shift key and right-click (this brings up a different, more option-laden menu than just right-clicking), then select Open with → Notepad → OK.

Alternatively, you could open a DOS window and type:

```
ATTRIB -R -S -H C:\MSDOS.SYS
```

Now hit Enter, then type:

```
NOTEPAD C:\MSDOS.SYS
```

or:

```
EDIT C:\MSDOS.SYS
```

Thanks to a tuned *msdos.sys*, both of my PCs can boot in well under a minute, even without help from the Norton Utilities or another commercial optimization package. Here's a selection from my *msdos.sys* file:

```
;SYS
[Paths]
WinDir=C:\WINDOWS
WinBootDir=C:\WINDOWS
HostWinBootDrv=C

[Options]
BootGUI=1
DrvSpace=0
DblSpace=0
Logo=0
BootDelay=0
DisableLog=1
BootMulti=1
DoubleBuffer=0
AutoScan=2
WinVer=4.10.1998
```

msdos.sys will normally contain several dummy lines to ensure that the file is larger than 1024 bytes. Some programs assume any *msdos.sys* file smaller than that size must be infected by a virus, so these lines keep those programs happy. I edited them out of the text here, but leave them in your copy of the file.

msdos.sys Options

The settings presented earlier generally give excellent performance under a wide variety of configurations. Here's a complete *msdos.sys* reference.

[Paths] Section

HostWinBootDrv=*path*

This optional parameter points to the boot disk. Default: HostWinBootDrv=C.

UninstallDir=*path*

If Windows 9x was installed over a previous version of Windows, this parameter points to the directory used by the uninstall routine. (Optional)

`WinDir=`*path*

> Points to the main Windows directory, as specified during Setup. If you wish to have multiple copies of Windows on your PC, you may switch between them by changing this parameter. (Required)

`WinBootDir=`*path*

> Points to the directory containing files required for starting Windows. Default: `WinBootDir=C:\windows`. (Optional)

[Options] Section

`AutoScan=`*n*

> In Windows 95 OSR2 and higher, and in Windows 98, specifies whether Scan-Disk should run automatically after improper shutdowns. You will normally want the computer to go ahead and run ScanDisk, since there are frequently disk problems in need of correction after an improper shutdown.

> Possible values:

> *0* Never scan.

> *1* Prompt user, scanning automatically if there's no response after 60 seconds. (Default)

> *2* Scan automatically, no prompting. (Recommended)

`BootDelay=`*n*

> Sets initial startup delay to the specified number of seconds. The only purpose of the BootDelay entry is to give you more time to bring up the boot menu. Since when you want the boot menu, you're probably pounding on the F8 key long before the system is ready to respond, there's little need for this delay. In most cases, it spends more time slowing you down than it spends helping you.

> Examples:

> *Set to 2 second delay (default)*
> > `BootDelay=2`

> *Set to no delay (recommended)*
> > `BootDelay=0`

`BootSafe=`*n*

> Forces safe mode startup. This parameter is invoked only when there are major problems that keep Windows from booting properly. You will want Safe Mode to be available for correcting these problems unless you are extremely paranoid about security.

Examples:

Disable
```
BootSafe=0
```

Enable (default)
```
BootSafe=1
```

BootGUI=*n*

Enables/disables automatic load of the Windows GUI. If `BootGUI=0`, Windows 9x boots to the DOS 7 prompt; typing `WIN` at the *C:* prompt starts the GUI. If you wish to use an *autoexec.bat/config.sys* boot menu to choose between DOS 7 and Windows 9x, you must set this parameter to 0.

Examples:

Disable
```
BootGUI=0
```

Enable (default)
```
BootGUI=1
```

BootKeys=*n*

Allows/prevents the functions of F5, F6, and F8 keys during Windows startup. This keeps users from booting into Safe mode or DOS mode, which is useful if you want to prevent users from circumventing other security measures. Normally, you wouldn't want to do this, however, as having Safe mode and DOS mode available are useful diagnostic tools. If `BootKey=0`, the system automatically sets `BootDelay=0` as well.

Examples:

Disable keys
```
BootKeys=0
```

Enable keys (default)
```
BootKeys=1
```

BootMenu=*n*

If enabled, causes Windows to always display the boot menu, which is normally only displayed by pressing F8 at the Starting Windows 9x prompt. This shouldn't be confused with the boot menus you create with statements in *autoexec.bat* and *config.sys.* If you find yourself bringing up the boot menu after just about every restart, you'll probably want to set this parameter to 1.

Examples:

Always display
```
BootMenu=1
```

Display only when F8 is pressed (default)
```
BootMenu=0
```

BootMenuDefault=*n*

Sets the default item on the Windows startup menu. The default is usually 1, or 4 if the last boot was unsuccessful. Under normal circumstances, you shouldn't change this parameter yourself.

Example:

```
BootMenuDefault=3
```

BootMenuDelay=*n*

Specifies the number of seconds Windows will wait before automatically selecting the default boot menu item. There is no point in setting this parameter unless you also set `BootMenu=1`.

Examples:

Three-second delay
```
BootMenuDelay=3
```

No automatic selection (default)
```
BootMenuDelay=0
```

BootMulti=*n*

Enables/disables dual-booting with old versions of DOS. This parameter is normally functional only under Windows 95 and Windows 95A, though there are freeware programs (one is available at *www.tu-chemnitz.de/~jwes/ win95boot.html*—more on that in Chapter 7, *Optimizing DOS*) that reenable this under newer versions of Windows 9x by replacing some of their code with Windows 95A code.

Examples:

Disable (default)
```
BootMulti=0
```

Enable
```
BootMulti=1
```

BootWarn=*n*

Enables/disables Safe Start warning and menu.

Examples:

Disable
```
BootWarn=0
```

Enable (default)
```
BootWarn=1
```

BootWin=*n*

Enables/disables Windows 9x as the default operating system (see `BootMulti` above). Note: pressing F4 will override `BootWin` if `BootMulti=1`.

Examples:

Disabled

    BootWin=0

Enabled (default)

    BootWin=1

DblSpace=*n*

Prevents/allows automatic loading of *dblspace.bin*, if present. Windows 9x is supposed to unload this device driver if it finds no compressed drives on the system. Since data compression slows down hard drives, you shouldn't use it; therefore, you should have no need for this driver. Not loading the driver speeds up boot times, and permits you to delete the file *dblspace.bin*.

Examples:

Prevent (recommended)

    DblSpace=0

Allow (default)

    DblSpace=1

DisableLog=*n*

(Undocumented) Enables/disables automatic creation of *bootlog.txt,* a sometimes useful diagnostic tool. This parameter would be useful in Unix environments, since Unix computers fail and require rebooting very rarely, and hardware problems are frequently the reason for it. Windows 9x PCs fail and require a reboot at least once every two months, sometimes as frequently as once a day, and hardware is rarely the culprit. It's better to just turn off the logging and let the reboot proceed as quickly as possible. If the reboot fails, boot in DOS mode, change this parameter back, then reboot again and look at *bootlog.txt*.

Examples:

Disable (default)

    DisableLog=0

Enable (recommended)

    DisableLog=1

DoubleBuffer=*n*

Enables/disables double-buffering. Double-buffering is sometimes necessary because, in virtual memory environments like Windows, a memory address may not necessarily be in RAM. So if a disk controller tries to write directly to memory, as most disk controllers do in order to save work for the CPU, it may not be able to find the true address. Double-buffering sets up a sort of translation zone, where the data will be sent to memory, then moved to the proper address. This is, of course, a performance hindrance. Newer PCI controllers have ways of working around this problem, but older ISA SCSI cards don't.

A value of 1 enables double-buffering for controllers that need it; a value of 2 enables it for all controllers, regardless of whether they need it. If deemed necessary, Windows loads a 3K driver called *dblbuff.sys* into conventional memory.

It's best to tell Windows whether you need double-buffering. If you run only Windows software, you don't. If you don't have an ISA SCSI controller, you don't need double-buffering. If you do have an ISA SCSI controller and you run DOS protected-mode programs (usually DOS games, and they usually display a message at startup that reads something like "DOS/4GW Protected Mode Run-Time") from within the Windows GUI, you probably need double-buffering. If you only run DOS protected-mode programs in MS-DOS mode, you don't need double-buffering.

Your system will boot more quickly and possibly run a bit more quickly if you disable double-buffering. Your system also will boot more quickly if you specify either 0 or 2 for this parameter, since Windows can skip the step of trying to figure out whether a controller needs it.

Examples:

Disable (recommended)
```
DoubleBuffer=0
```

Enable when needed (default)
```
DoubleBuffer=1
```

Enable always (recommended if you run DOS games within the Windows GUI and have an ISA-based SCSI card)
```
DoubleBuffer=2
```

DrvSpace=*n*

Prevents/allows automatic loading of *drvspace.bin*, if present. Windows 9x is supposed to unload this device driver if it finds no compressed drives on the system. Since data compression slows down hard drives, you shouldn't use it; therefore, you should have no need for this driver. Not loading the driver speeds up boot times and permits you to delete the file *drvspace.bin*.

Examples:

Prevent (recommended)
```
DrvSpace=0
```

Allow (default)
```
DrvSpace=1
```

LoadTop=*n*

Enables/disables loading of *command.com* and/or *drvspace.bin* and/or *dblspace.bin* at the top of conventional memory. If you have problems with software that makes certain assumptions about memory availability, try setting this to 0. The only place I know of where this feature is necessary is in Novell NetWare network environments.

Examples:

Disable

LoadTop=0

Enable (default)
LoadTop=1

Logo=*n*

Hides/shows the animated Windows logo that displays at boot time. Some of the files Windows uses to display the logo can cause compatibility problems under rare circumstances; setting this parameter to 0 prevents these problems. On all machines, setting this parameter to 0 speeds up boot time: if you want your computer to boot in under a minute, do this.

Examples:

Disable (recommended)

Logo=0

Enable (default)

Logo=1

Network=*n*

Specifies whether Windows 95 networking components are loaded, enabling the "Safe mode with network support" option on the boot menu. This parameter may be set to 1 if you have a dial-up Internet account, even if you aren't on a LAN. I usually leave this setting alone.

Examples:

Off (default for non-network)

Network=0

On (default for networked station)

Network=1

SystemReg=*n*

(Undocumented) Enables/disables scanning the registry for hardware profiles. The description "Don't load Registry" found in most English-language Windows texts suggests this setting creates a sort of pseudo-safe mode, where the registry is ignored. This appears not to be the case. A number of German web pages say setting SystemReg=0 disables the search for hardware profiles at bootup. On a 200 MHz Cyrix MII-PR233, I measure a slight decrease in system boot time and no loss of system functionality by changing this setting. I find that setting this parameter to 0 can cause some systems to hang at bootup. Reboot, hit F8, select Command Prompt Only and change this setting back to 1 if this happens to you.

Examples:

Scan Registry (default)
```
SystemReg=1
```

Don't scan Registry
```
SystemReg=0
```

`WinVer=`*s*

Sets Windows version (Windows 98). This key determines what version Windows will report itself as.

Example:
```
WinVer=4.10.1998
```

Wringing That Last Ounce of Speed from msdos.sys

winboot.ini is a surrogate for *msdos.sys*, intended to be used as a temporary stand-in the first time Windows 9x boots after installation. The boot process looks for *winboot.ini* before it looks for *msdos.sys*. I suppose the most obvious use of this would be to more easily toggle between two copies of Windows 9x on the same system, a technique described in Chapters 9 and 10. However, since *winboot.ini* is scanned earlier in the boot process, your system boots faster if you copy *msdos.sys* to *winboot.ini*. The other advantage of *winboot.ini* is that it need not be 1024 bytes in length or longer. The 16-line *msdos.sys* file shown earlier in this chapter, standing alone, is a perfectly valid *winboot.ini* file. Eliminating the dummy lines also eliminates the need to process them.

Once you move your configuration data into *winboot.ini*, you may be tempted to delete *msdos.sys*—after all, it seems to be occupying a precious root directory entry needlessly. Don't do it! Even if it's not used, a 1K or larger *msdos.sys* is required in order for the system to be bootable.

However, unless you have a very, very slow system, you're not likely to notice any difference after doing this. On my Cyrix MII-PR233, I observed no difference with a stopwatch test.

Speeding Up autoexec.bat

There's very little you can do to speed up *autoexec.bat* processing, especially if your system has no *autoexec.bat* file. Mine is minimal; it redirects temp directories and little else. The less you have *autoexec.bat* do, of course, the faster it processes.

If you don't need to watch the commands scroll by, you can turn off echoing. Frequently the first command in *autoexec.bat* is either **echo off** or **@echo off**, which turns off the printing of the commands to the screen as they are processed. The **@** sign at the front of the latter command prevents **echo off** itself from being echoed to the screen.

Rather than using the **echo off** command, however, you can simply precede each command with the **@** sign. This is slightly faster. So, if you have a minimalist *autoexec.bat* that looks like this:

```
echo off
set temp=f:\temp
set tmp=f:\temp
```

You can speed it up by replacing it with this:

```
@set temp=f:\temp
@set tmp=f:\temp
```

The **echo off** command won't turn off a program's screen output, however. To do this, you have to redirect the program's output. For instance, let's say you run **doskey** in *autoexec.bat.* To turn off the "DOSKey installed" message, add **> nul** to the end of the command, like this:

```
@doskey > nul
```

The slower your computer, the more noticeable the speed gain from turning off output will be. Don't expect any miracles; the time saved will be minimal—along the lines of the amount of time saved by creating *winboot.ini.*

Getting By with Less in Your Startup Group

It seems as if every program wants to put something in your Startup group. Sometimes these tools are necessary for the program to run, but sometimes they're just in the way, consuming memory and slowing down your boot time. Why not make them slow down that program's boot time, rather than your system's boot time? After all, if you don't use that application every time you turn on the computer, there's no point in having pieces of it sitting there in memory unused, right? And if you're using the program, what difference does it make whether the delay from loading some startup module is during boot, or during the launch of the program?

The practice of one program altering the system configuration to make itself run well at the expense of every other program isn't new at all. DOS and OS/2 programs would frequently rewrite the PATH statement in *autoexec.bat* (or *config.sys* in OS/2's case), putting their own directories up front to make the executable files they wanted to call run fast, but slowing down everything else. A program might even put a terminate-and-stay-resident module (TSR) into memory, helping itself when it was running, but sitting there idle the rest of the time. This practice wasn't limited just to PCs.

DOS and OS/2 power users would outsmart these programs by writing batch files—they'd take the statements these programs wanted in *autoexec.bat* and add them to a batch file that contained these statements, executed the program, then changed the statements back.

Not everyone seems to know it, but Windows 9x (and Windows NT, for that matter) still supports batch files. And this old trick still works under Windows 9x. For instance, Microsoft Office adds an item called Office Startup to the Startup group. Office loads a little bit better with this in place, but when you're not running Office applications, it just sits there, taking up memory. Since Office runs properly without Office Startup, I just leave it out. But if I want Office Startup to launch when I run Word, I can do it with a batch file.

First, I need to know the names of my suspects. Right-click the Start menu, then select Explore → Startup → Office Startup. Right-click Office Startup, then select Properties → Shortcut. From the field labeled Target, I learn that Office Startup's filename is *D:\Program Files\msoffice\msoffice.exe*. I close the Properties window and return to the Explorer window, where I navigate back until I find Word's icon. Then, I right-click Word and select Properties → Shortcut. From its Target field, I learn that Word's executable is called *D:\Program Files\msoffice\winword\winword.exe*.

Once I make note of this, I can create my batch file. Click Start → Run → notepad and type the following lines:

```
"d:\program files\msoffice\msoffice.exe"
"d:\program files\msoffice\winword\winword.exe"
```

Remember, when you use long filenames in a batch file, you have to enclose them in quotation marks. Now, select File → Save As → *D:\Program Files\msoffice\winword\winword.bat*. Substitute your application's path for *D:\Program Files\msoffice*, of course.

Now all I need to do is point Word's icon to the batch file, rather than to its executable. Right-click Start and select Explore. I punch through to Word's icon, bring up its Properties menu, and proceed to its Target tab. I replace the line *D:\Program Files\msoffice\winword\winword.exe* with the name of my batch file—in this case, *D:\Program Files\msoffice\winword\winword.bat*. At first, it will look like nothing has changed. Click Apply, then OK, and still it will look like nothing has changed. Bring up its context menu again, and all the properties associated with a DOS program will appear. Now, select Program → Run → Minimized → Close on exit. This prevents the batch file's window from lingering where you don't want it. Now, hit the Change Icon button. Type in the name of the executable. Every icon contained in the executable file (there may be more than one, to your surprise) will appear. Pick the one you want to use, then hit OK.

Word will now take just slightly longer to load, but I've reduced my boot time by not having to load Office Startup at boot. I've saved a little bit of memory, too, though the memory savings goes away the first time I run Word.

Microsoft Office certainly isn't the only party guilty of adding to your *Startup* group. WordPerfect 7 put something called PerfectPrint in my *Startup* folder as well. Using a batch file, I can get rid of that, too.

Speeding Up POST

My Cyrix MII-PR233 actually spends more time executing its Power On Self Test (POST) routine than it spends booting Windows. Part of this is because of its highly optimized *msdos.sys*, part of it is due to the fast hard drive, and part of it is because POST takes an inordinate length of time. Still, I can't complain—when I turn on the power, I see the Windows desktop in less than a minute.

Depending on your system, there may not be much you can do to speed up POST. The CMOS setup program in many brand-name systems, notably IBM and Compaq PCs, doesn't leave much room for configuration.

If your system has an AMI, Award, or Phoenix BIOS, there may be some things you can do to speed things up—particularly if you have a Pentium-class system. I can't walk you through every type of system, since computer manufacturers tend to make changes to the BIOSs in their systems. But I can walk you through the changes I made to speed up POST on my Pentium 90, which has an AMI BIOS, and on my Cyrix MII-PR233, which has an Award BIOS. This will at least give you an indication of what to look for.

The way you enter your the setup program in your BIOS varies, so check your manual. Frequently, you enter by hitting DEL, F1, F8, F10, or F12 at the BIOS startup screen.

There are several time-consuming processes that take place during POST: the memory test, the initial floppy drive seek, the attempt to boot off the floppy drive, the autodetection of IDE hard drives, and if your PC has a SCSI card, the scan for

SCSI devices. The more of these processes you can disable, the faster your system will boot.

Turning off the memory test does little harm; usually, memory will be so bad that it prevents the system from even booting, or good enough to slip past the memory test but still fail. Passing this minimal POST memory test is no more of an indication of good memory than passing most states' driving test is an indication of a good driver. Some systems don't give you a provision to disable the memory test, while others give you the option to test only the first 640K, and others give you the option to either test or count the memory.

The initial floppy drive seek is useless; the original IBM PC did this in order to determine what drives were present. Modern PCs set the presence of floppy drives in the CMOS, so this once-useful feature is now just meaningless tradition. Many BIOSs will have a "floppy seek at boot" or "initial floppy seek" or similarly worded function in their setup program. Some BIOSs just don't do this anymore—thankfully—and don't even give you the option to turn it on.

The option to eliminate the floppy drive from the boot order speeds up the boot process—the system just looks to the hard drive, which should always be bootable—along with other benefits. I get phone calls all the time from people panicking that they received the dreaded "Non-system disk or disk error" message when they rebooted. This is almost always due to having a non-bootable floppy disk in the drive. Taking the floppy drive out of the boot order eliminates this error, and also protects you from the spread of boot-sector viruses. Sometimes you do need to boot off a floppy drive, but you can always enter CMOS Setup again, change it, restart, and boot from the floppy.

By default, modern systems usually detect only what IDE devices are connected to the system, rather than forcing you to manually enter the number of heads, cylinders, and sectors of each drive as they did in the bad old days. Modern IDE drives will give their vital statistics upon request, and modern computers take advantage of this feature. However, it takes time to issue the command to get a drive's parameters. Most systems are set to autodetect the drives at boot time, but most modern systems also have an IDE autodetect feature in their CMOS Setup program. Selecting this option enters your drives' parameters in your CMOS so that your system doesn't have to detect them at bootup, speeding up your boot times.

SCSI controllers, by default, wait ten seconds for all SCSI devices to come online. This is an industry standard, and on many systems it isn't changeable. Consult your SCSI controller's documentation.

As I said before, systems vary, but they tend to be similar. Note the similarities below on my two primary systems. Your system probably won't be identical to either of these, but it will most likely be similar enough that the two processes will give you some guidance.

Here are the changes I made on my AMI-based system:

1. Turn off memory test: Advanced → Above 1 MB memory test → Disabled

2. Turn off floppy seek: Advanced → Floppy drive seek at boot → Disabled

3. Make hard drive the first boot device: Advanced → System bootup sequence → C:\, A:\

4. Automatically enter hard drive parameters in CMOS: Utility → IDE Setup

Here are the changes on my Award-based system:

1. Turn off memory test: BIOS features setup → Quick Power-On Self Test → Enabled

2. Make hard drive the first boot device: BIOS features setup → Boot Sequence → C, A, SCSI

3. Automatically enter hard drive parameters in CMOS: IDE HDD auto-detection

Compacting the Registry

The Windows registry grows as data is added to it, but it never shrinks when data is removed. A bloated registry with a lot of empty space in it can slow down boot time as well as Windows performance as a whole. All three major Windows utilities suites—Mijenix's Fix-it 99, Symantec's Norton Utilities 4.0, and Network Associates' McAfee Nuts & Bolts 98—have registry compaction tools. Note that Microsoft's popular RegClean tool does not eliminate empty space from the registry—it just removes invalid keys. This, too, can speed up the boot process slightly, but those invalid keys become empty space after RegClean removes them. To reap the full benefits of RegClean, you have to compact the registry as well.

If you don't have any of the major utilities suites, you can still compact your registry with a few commands from MS-DOS mode. Note that these commands *must* be entered from MS-DOS mode—they will not work properly from within Windows. Before you enter these commands, be sure to Start → Shut down → Restart the computer in MS-DOS mode. You can either enter these commands by hand, or enter them into a batch file and execute the batch file:

```
md c:\windows\backups.xyz
del c:\windows\backups.xyz\registry.reg
del c:\windows\backups.xyz\system.dat
del c:\windows\backups.xyz\user.dat
regedit /e c:\windows\backups.xyz\registry.reg
attrib -r -s -h c:\windows\system.dat
attrib -r -s -h c:\windows\user.dat
```

```
move c:\windows\system.dat c:\windows\backups.xyz
move c:\windows\user.dat c:\windows\backups.xyz
regedit /c c:\windows\backups.xyz\registry.reg
```

These commands make a backup copy of your registry in *C:\Windows\Backups.xyz* before they pack it. If an old backup exists, it is deleted. If the directory *C:\Windows\Backups.xyz* doesn't exist, it is created. Be patient, as these commands take some time to execute.

Should the process fail and your system lose its ability to start Windows, boot into DOS mode and issue these commands, which will back up the bad registry and replace it with the backup copy that the previous commands just made:

```
attrib -r -s -h c:\windows\system.dat
attrib -r -s -h c:\windows\user.dat
ren c:\windows\system.dat c:\windows\system.bad
ren c:\windows\user.dat c:\windows\user.bad
move c:\windows\system.bad c:\windows\backups.xyz
move c:\windows\user.bad c:\windows\backups.xyz
move c:\windows\backups.xyz\system.dat c:\windows
move c:\windows\backups.xyz\user.dat c:\windows
attrib +r +s +h c:\windows\system.dat
attrib +r +s +h c:\windows\user.dat
```

5

Utilities

Each new Microsoft operating system incorporates more utilities than the previous release, but the utilities Microsoft includes with the operating system aren't always as good as those available separately from other vendors. This is an extreme example, but there are numerous reports on Usenet of Windows 98's Defrag utility taking 16 hours to defragment 20 GB drives. A third-party defragmentation tool should do the job in 45 minutes or less.

There are a lot of good free utilities out there to help improve a system, and Windows' utilities are certainly better and more numerous than the utilities that come with MacOS, but if you want a pristine system, you'll need at least one utilities package.

What Tools You Need and How to Use Them

The tools available today are, unfortunately, imperfect. Over the course of the next few years, they will hopefully improve. While detailed descriptions of how to use this year's model is valuable information, there's always the possibility that next year's model will be closer to ideal, or act so differently that this year's instructions just won't apply. So I want to start with a thumbnail sketch of how you should use the utilities available to you to improve your system's performance and keep it running like a high-performance machine.

Disk Utilities

Since disk drives remain the biggest bottleneck in the computer, disk optimization is crucial. Chapter 3, *Disk Optimization*, discusses how hard drives work and how

Windows relates to them. Ideally, your disk utility should permit you to arrange your data strategically, as in Table 5-1.

Table 5-1. Ideal Disk Optimization Layout

Frequently used applications
Frequently modified files
Free space
Rarely used files

This layout places important files at the front of the disk, where access is fastest, while placing frequently modified files next to the free space, which helps reduce fragmentation. Placing rarely used files at the end of the disk helps conserve the drive's speed for disk writes.

Another nice feature is the ability to interleave executable files and the DLLs they load so that the code the program is loading is in order, even if it's contained in different files. This is how Windows 98's Defrag works, and it can improve load times. Both Mijenix Fix-It 99 (*www.mijenix.com*) and Norton Utilities 4 and 2000 (*www.symantec.com*) include this feature, as well.

Ideally, your disk utility should also sort directory entries, sorting files by some measure of importance (access date would be best, but none of the current utilities do this; frequently we have to settle for sorting by size) and eliminating the entries for deleted files.

Registry Utilities

You should clean your registry once a month. All three utilities suites on the market today have tools for cleaning and optimizing the registry, and both major uninstallation programs have tools for cleaning the registry as well. You should run your utilities suite's registry cleaner, then run your uninstallation program's registry cleaner if it has one (since one will frequently pick up on things the other missed), then run your utilities suite's registry optimizer.

Should I Upgrade to Windows 98?

This is the big question. Windows 98 adds five significant features that the August 24, 1995 release of Windows 95 lacked: some bug fixes, FAT32, Internet Explorer 4.0 integration, improved disk caching, and an improved defragmentation utility. Internet Explorer 4.0 is obsolete, can be downloaded separately free of charge, and its shell integration slows down the system tremendously. While some people report Windows 98 is more stable than Windows 95, others report it is less stable. Windows 98 fixed some bugs but added some new ones, unfortunately.

Windows 98 Second Edition, in addition to fixing some bugs, adds a proxy server for sharing a dialup Internet connection among networked PCs. It's not a free upgrade for Windows 98 users, though Windows 98 users can get the upgrade for $19, rather than paying $99 or $109 like Windows 95 users.

The trend in Windows 9x operating systems ever since Windows 95's initial release has been to release a new version every year and a half or so, include about $25 worth of new features, throw in a handful of bug fixes, and charge anywhere from $25 to $120 for it.

These incremental improvements aren't really worth paying for. If you buy a new system, get the current version because it's far more likely to have support for whatever new hardware the system might have, but it's rarely worth the cost and hassle to make sure an old system has the latest and greatest incarnation of Windows 9x. If you need a proxy server, WinGate costs $40, or if you're technically inclined, you can install Linux on a cast-off 386 or 486, and configure its free proxy server. You can get an improved disk defragmenter by buying one of the big three utilities suites, which cost $50 or less and do more to improve your system speed.

The Big Three Utilities Suites

For many years, the biggest names in utilities suites were Norton Utilities and PC Tools. Symantec bought out Central Point Software, makers of PC Tools, right around the time Windows 3.1 really caught fire, and the Norton Utilities had a stranglehold on this software category until 1996, when Helix Software (now part of Network Associates) released its Nuts & Bolts utility suite. In 1999, Mijenix released its own offering, Mijenix Fix-It 99. Fix-It 99 is receiving tremendous reviews and quickly moved past Nuts & Bolts in retail sales. But each of these packages has certain strengths and weaknesses, and if you're interested in system optimization, there are pieces of each that you don't really need to concern yourself with.

Although many reviewers have been saying Mijenix Fix-It 99 is as good as or better than Norton Utilities, I tend to disagree. The Norton Utilities' disk optimization program is far more configurable. This makes it harder to use, so I can see why a reviewer who's looking for ease of use would prefer Fix-It. But if you're into performance, Fix-It's automatic transmission approach will aggravate you. Fix-It is far more integrated than Norton Utilities, which looks nice from a user's perspective, but again, this causes a problem for performance-minded users. Without separate modules that accept command-line arguments, you can't schedule system events. Fix-It 99 includes its own scheduler, but the scheduler unfortunately can't schedule disk scanning, which is a major oversight. It's not absolutely necessary to scan a disk for errors before defragmenting it, but if the defragmenter finds errors, it will halt and the disk won't get optimized that night.

By the same token, Norton Utilities doesn't come with a scheduler at all, and its registry optimization tools are far inferior to Fix-It 99's. However, disk performance is more crucial to system performance than registry optimization, so I have to give Norton Utilities the nod. If you can afford to buy both, however, use Norton Utilities to optimize your disk and Fix-It 99 to optimize your registry.

Nuts & Bolts 98 is the dark horse. Its disk optimizer is the most complicated and slowest of the three, but if you can deal with the complexity, it will give you the most optimal disk layout. Unfortunately, the lack of documented command-line switches makes it difficult to use Nuts & Bolts' disk tools with a program scheduler, and it's by far the slowest of the three. Its registry tools are more complete than those in Norton Utilities and very similar to those in Fix-It 99. Since the other two tools are easier to automate, I prefer them, though if you already have Nuts & Bolts there's no point in throwing it away.

Table 5-2 shows comparisons of these utilities suites, with each feature ranked 1–3, best to worst.

Table 5-2. A Comparison of the Big Three Utilities Suites

	Norton Utilities	**Nuts & Bolts**	**Fix-It 99**
Ease of disk optimization	2. Respectable.	2. Respectable.	1. My dog could use it
Speed of disk optimization process	1. Excellent.	2. Optimize before you go to bed, because you won't get any more gaming done that night.	1. Excellent.
Effectiveness of disk optimization	2. Good.	1. Outstanding.	3. Respectable.
Registry tools	2. Anemic.	1. Excellent.	1. Excellent.
Ease of automation	2. Decent—no scheduler is built in, but the utilities will work from another scheduler.	3. Extremely difficult.	1. Built-in scheduler is easy to use, but low on options.
Application launch speedup	1. Good.	3. Primitive and unstable.	2. None outside of features in defragmenter.
Cleanness of installation	2. Okay.	3. Terrible—pieces will linger if you ever uninstall it.	1. Good.

Table 5-2. A Comparison of the Big Three Utilities Suites (continued)

	Norton Utilities	Nuts & Bolts	Fix-It 99
User interface	2. Good—pretty consistent, but more closely resembles a collection of separate utilities than a single package.	3. Fair—like Norton Utilites, resembles a collection rather than a single, unified suite.	1. Excellent—clean and consistent.
Overall	1. In essence, Norton Utilities compromises its way to the top. It works in politics, and all too often in computers as well.	3. Slow disk optimizer and lack of automation are big holes.	2. If Mijenix adds a configuration tab to its disk optimizer and lets you automate disk repair, Fix-It will beat Norton Utilities senseless.

All suites have shortcomings, some of them aggravating, but it's hard to go wrong with any of them. Any one of them will give you tools that significantly improve performance over a system that lacks a utilities suite.

Optimizing Your System with Norton Utilities 4.0 or Norton Utilities 2000

The venerable Norton Utilities remains a valuable tool in the PC speed shop. Of the three major utilities suites, Norton Utilities is the oldest. Many of its features are dubious, but Norton Disk Doctor is far superior to Windows' built-in ScanDisk, and Norton Speed Disk is a tremendous improvement over Windows' Defrag. (Microsoft licensed technology from Symantec, the makers of Norton Utilities, for Defrag.)

You never want to accept Norton Utilities' default installation. Run the installation software, then, when asked, tell it you want a custom installation. Unfortunately, utility suites are beginning to suffer from the same kind of bloatware mentality that killed the office suites. If one suite adds a certain feature, you can expect that the next version of the other utilities suites will also have that feature, whether the feature is truly useful or not.

Deselect Norton CrashGuard. CrashGuard takes up excessive amounts of memory and causes about as many system and application crashes as it prevents. Norton System Doctor will warn you when it thinks it's time to maintain your system, but it will slow it down in the process. Leave it out, too. The Norton Utilities Integrator is superfluous—integration seems to be in vogue right now, but it's fine for tools to be standalone programs. You're better off just running the tool you need directly, so leave Integrator out as well.

Norton File Compare is small, but rarely useful. Norton Registry Editor is a bit easier to use than Windows' built-in registry editor, but the examples in this book use the standard Microsoft tool. If you spend a lot of time in the registry (you probably shouldn't), go ahead and install it. The Norton Utilities Demos aren't all that useful. Norton Space Wizard will try to dig up extraneous files for you to free some disk space, but its advice isn't always all that good. I prefer to delete my temp files myself and save disk space by leaving superfluous components like Space Wizard out. I also like to leave out Explorer Shell Extensions—I don't need to run Norton Utilities from Explorer's context menu.

If you want to do an absolutely minimalist Norton Utilities installation, here are the bare essentials: Disk Doctor, Optimization Wizard, Basefiles, WinDoctor, and Speed Disk.

After you select your components, Norton Utilities will ask you how tightly you want to integrate with Windows. Personally, I choose to replace ScanDisk with Disk Doctor, but I don't enable the Norton Protected Recycle Bin or WipeInfo on the desktop. Norton Utilities will then ask what components to run at startup. I don't run any of them. And, of course, when installation completes, you want to let Norton Utilities run LiveUpdate to see if there are any patches to the suite—there frequently will be minor bug fixes and enhancements.

Once the components of Norton Utilities finish installing and updating, you want to put them to work immediately. Be sure to close any running applications before you optimize your system with Norton Utilities. It will do its best to stay out of your applications' way, but a running application accessing your drives or the system registry can get in the way of Norton Utilities, making it complete the job more slowly, or, even worse, less effectively.

You also want to turn off your screen saver and your power management. Both of these features can dramatically interrupt Disk Doctor and Speed Disk, forcing them to start their work over from the beginning. A job that should have taken 15 minutes can stretch out over an hour with too many interruptions. Disk Doctor can run in the background, but I can't imagine wanting to do this—if you're running Disk Doctor, you suspect there's something wrong with your hard drive. If there's something wrong with your hard drive, you risk losing work or crashing your game prematurely. Sick hard drives aren't very good for gaming performance either.

Before optimizing the disk, make sure it doesn't have any major problems. If the disk has lost clusters, you can't optimize it, and if the disk has even worse problems, you want to fix them before optimizing the disk.

Before you run Speed Disk for the first time, you want to run Optimization Wizard. Optimization Wizard by default will do three things: move your swap file to your fastest drive and set it to three times your physical RAM, install and configure SpeedStart to speed up application load times (if you're running Windows 95), and optimize your registry. Save the registry optimization for later—just let it move your swap file, and if you have Windows 95, install SpeedStart.

Now that you have a game plan, select Start → Programs → Norton Utilities → Norton Optimization Wizard. Click Next. If you have multiple hard drives or partitions, Optimization Wizard wants to figure out which one is fastest so that it can recommend you put your swap file there. Make sure the box labeled "Test my drives for speed" is checked, and click Next. Check the box labeled "Configure swap file for optimal performance" and click Next. Check the two Norton Speed-Start boxes and click Next. Finally, Optimization Wizard will offer to optimize your registry. Clear that checkbox and click Next. You want to optimize your registry after you check it for errors—that step comes later.

Optimizing your disk with Speed Disk

Of all the tools in the Norton Utilities, Speed Disk is far and away the most valuable. Your hard drive is your system's biggest bottleneck, and with the right settings, Speed Disk can dramatically improve your hard disk speed, and therefore, the speed of your entire system. To launch Speed Disk, select Start → Programs → Norton Utilites → Speed Disk.

The first time you run Speed Disk, you might be shocked at the amount of fragmentation it reports. For instance, when I installed NU4 on my Cyrix MII-PR233, Defrag reported my drive as 1% fragmented and didn't want to run. Speed Disk reported the same drive as 4% fragmented and wanted to run a full optimization. Speed Disk is far more aggressive than Defrag. That's fine; the less tolerant your disk utilities are of fragmentation, the faster your system will run. Don't just run it with the defaults though. Cancel the dialog box, then select Properties → Options → Customize → Folders → Move Folders to Front → By Date → Sort Files by Last Access Date → Group files by → Month → Sort Entries → Sort folder entries → Sort files by → Size → Sort order → Descending.

This procedure moves your commonly used files up to the front of your drive, where access time is generally faster. Junk files will move to the very back, leaving free space near the moderately fast center of the drive. It also optimizes your subdirectories, moving them up to the front, and sorting the files by size. This way, your most important files will (hopefully) be found first. Size isn't necessarily the best indication of importance—last access date would be ideal—but unfortunately, Speed Disk won't sort directory entries by access date. The only options are name (worthless), date (worthless), time (worthless), extension (OK), and size (slightly better). A list sorted by extension, alphabetically, won't necessarily put the DLL and EXE files at the very top, but the EXE and DLL files that form the core of the application will usually be among the largest files. The largest files are almost always the most important, though the largest file may not be the most important. Sorting the files this way is more optimal than leaving them in a haphazard order.

Now, click OK → Save → OK → Start. The first time you run Speed Disk, it will take a while, because it will probably end up having to move nearly every file on your disk. Be patient—the improvement in system performance is worth the time it takes for Speed Disk to sort things out initially.

After running Speed Disk for the first time on the system, my boot time dropped from 24 seconds to 20 seconds. Four seconds isn't much time, but consider that's almost a 17% improvement. While system boot time isn't the best measure of system performance, it is one of the more disk-intensive tasks you can ask a computer to do. Your mileage will vary, of course, but the more marginal your system, the more you will notice the difference.

Optimizing your registry

The registry tends to grow with time, and even if you remove information from the registry, the file doesn't shrink, and Windows doesn't scan it any more quickly than before. Because the registry is so central to Windows 9x's operations, a streamlined registry will improve performance systemwide. The registry optimization tools in the Norton Utilities can't be accessed directly, and they're hidden in two modules—Norton WinDoctor and Norton Optimization Wizard—that wouldn't seem to have much to do with one another. That's unfortunate, because it makes it easy to run them in the wrong order. This won't damage your system, but it will give you less-than-optimal results. I don't like less-than-optimal results. If there's one thing I hate, it's an underachieving computer.

Before optimizing the registry, you want it to be as error-free as possible. Frequently, there will be references to invalid or deleted files, invalid ActiveX components, and other anomalies. These are most frequently the result of installing and uninstalling applications—the uninstall programs frequently do a sloppy job and leave the registry entries behind after they delete the corresponding files. They can also be the result of deleting files without properly uninstalling them. This is a bad practice, but that doesn't make it uncommon.

To correct the errors in your registry, select Start → Programs → Norton Utilities → Norton WinDoctor. By default, WinDoctor will do more than just scan your registry, but that's OK. The disk tests don't take long. Hit Continue from the introductory screen, then Perform all Norton WinDoctor Tests (recommended) → Next. WinDoctor will scan your registry for various problems. The process takes a few minutes, and it may find a large number of problems. Don't be alarmed. I frequently see systems with dozens of problems reported by WinDoctor. Normal use of the system will cause errors. These probably aren't making your computer any less reliable than it could be, but they probably are contributing to registry bloat. When WinDoctor reports that it's finished scanning, hit Next. It will tell you how many problems it found, and how many rough categories it lumped those problems into. You can scroll through the gory details, or you can just hit the Repair All button. WinDoctor may not be able to solve all of the problems, or the solutions to some problems may depend on the resolution of some other problem. Don't fret if it says there are a handful of problems it can't fix. Fix what you can, then close the program and run it again. Chances are there will be fewer problems than the number of unfixable problems the previous run indicated. If not, let it try once again to fix them. A few problems, particularly of low or medium severity, aren't the end of the world. As my Dad was fond of saying, it wasn't a big deal and didn't cause any problems until you found out about it.

Now that your system has a healthy registry, you can slim it down. To optimize your registry, select Start → Programs → Norton Utilities → Norton Optimization Wizard. Optimization Wizard will tell you that you already have your swap file configured for optimal performance, and suggest you leave it that way. Clear the checkbox that says "Configure swap file for optimal performance," and click Next. If you have Windows 95, Optimization Wizard will then ask if you want Speed-Start enabled. If you're like me, once you have SpeedStart enabled, you don't want to live without it. Leave the two checkboxes alone and click Next. Finally, Optimization Wizard will offer to optimize your registry. Click Next.

Optimization Wizard will tell you it recommends closing all running applications. Take this precaution seriously, especially in this case. Registry optimization is delicate work. Hit Reboot, and Optimization Wizard will optimize your registry before it restarts your system. The amount of time this takes will depend on your system's complexity.

Speeding application launches with Speed Start

Speed Start is pretty straightforward. If you have Windows 95, run it, and it installs itself and speeds up application load times. The improvement isn't as dramatic as Superfassst, mentioned earlier in the book, but it's more stable.

Optimizing Your System with Mijenix Fix-It 99

Installing Fix-It 99 is easy because there aren't any options. Just install and go. Fortunately, Mijenix can get away with this approach because Fix-It isn't very invasive. It doesn't launch anything at startup and it doesn't ask any questions. Symantec would do well to learn from that tendency—Norton Utilities does far too much at system startup by default.

Optimizing your disk with Defrag Plus

I find it amusing that Mijenix is claiming the name Defrag Plus, seeing as Microsoft's Defrag originated at Symantec. Naming conventions aside, I can see why most reviewers like Defrag Plus better than Norton Speed Disk, because Defrag Plus' defaults give better results than Speed Disk's. The only options it gives have to do with frequently modified and rarely accessed files, and those options are less cryptic than Speed Disk's—you can just tell it that a rarely accessed file is a file that hasn't been touched in 60 days, and a frequently modified file is one that's been modified within the last 30 days.

However, I greatly prefer Norton Speed Disk's method of optimization. Defrag Plus sorts the disk contents in frequently used/rarely used/frequently modified/free space order, which is less than optimal. Putting rarely used files at the very end of the drive will yield better performance.

There is one more thing to like about Defrag Plus. It rearranges files to speed up their load time like Windows 98's Defrag does. This feature can help your programs load faster, and if you have Windows 95, this gives you the biggest benefit that Windows 98 adds, for about half the price of Windows 98.

To launch Defrag Plus, just launch Fix-It Utilities 99, then Disk and Files → Defrag Plus. Select the checkboxes next to the drives you want to optimize, then hit Next. The defaults will do the job for you.

Optimizing your registry

This is where Fix-It 99 shines. All of its registry tools are collected in one place, and arranged on the screen almost in the order you should run them. The exception is the placement of the Registry Editor—this part just launches Microsoft's Registry Editor, included with Windows.

Registry Fixer will scan your registry for problems and offer to fix them. If it finds problems that it can't automatically fix (like references to files that have been moved), it will ask you for the new file location. Registry Fixer found 107 problems with my registry, even though I'd previously run Norton WinDoctor. After running Registry Fixer, have it fix any items labeled in white, then run it again. Frequently, fixing one set of problems will lead to another set of problems surfacing. You should rerun Registry Fixer until it no longer turns up any items labeled in white.

It's a good idea to run through the Registry Fixer process once a month.

WinCustomizer contains all of the customizations in TweakUI, plus a few more. Many of the things it changes—like menu speed—can also be done with registry hacks presented in Chapter 2, *First Steps*, but WinCustomizer's GUI is easier. Be sure to check your *msdos.sys* settings after running WinCustomizer, however, because it will change some of them. If you've optimized *msdos.sys* as described in Chapter 4, *Speeding Up the Boot Process*, you will want to back it up before you run WinCustomizer.

WinCustomizer allows you to easily move eight of Windows' shell folders (it calls them special folders: *Fonts, Desktop, Start Menu, Favorites, NetHood, Recent, SendTo*, and *ShellNew (Templates)*), out of the *C:\Windows* directory. This trick is described in Chapter 3. It won't do the directory copying for you, so you'll still have to copy the directories into their new locations, but WinCustomizer will make the registry changes for you. This is the most significant trick up WinCustomizer's sleeve. You really need to run WinCustomizer only once.

Registry Cleaner pulls unnecessary registry entries from your system. By default, this just pulls out the Recent documents list, Find Computer list, Find Documents list, Run list, and Tips of the Day. In the Advanced section, you can also pull out keyboard layouts and time zones you don't use. You should only remove the keyboard layouts and time zones if you're sure you won't use them. You only need to run the Advanced portion of Registry Cleaner once, and you only need to run the rest of Registry Cleaner as a prelude to running Registry Defrag.

Registry Defrag is an excellent utility. It searches your registry for empty space and fragmentation, and eliminates it. This, too, is superior to the registry tools in Norton Utilities. You should run Registry Defrag once a month.

Optimizing Your System with Nuts & Bolts 98

Nuts & Bolts, like Norton Utilities, includes a lot of fluff. If you need Personal PGP, then install it, but chances are you don't. Insert the CDs, select Install Nuts & Bolts. When it asks you whether you want a custom or express install, choose custom. You'll notice about half of the installation options are grayed out. Deselect everything that you can; the unselectable options will become selectable as the components that require them go away. Now, choose Disk Minder, McAfee Image, Cleanup Wizard, Disk Tune, Registry Wizard, and whatever else you want. If you don't think you want or need it, you probably don't. Don't install Launch Rocket on a Windows 98 system.

Hit Next, and installation will continue. If you're like me, you don't want McAfee Zip Manager on your desktop and you don't want McAfee Image running every time you restart your system. Deselect those. Having Zip Manager on the SendTo menu might be useful; choose it if you want it. I'm not as comfortable with Disk-Manager as with Windows' default scanner (the one it uses during bootup if it detects disk errors). Microsoft's minimalist ScanDisk does the job. If you ever uninstall Nuts & Bolts, DiskManager will stay behind, and that's one of my pet peeves.

Create a rescue disk if you don't have one, then finally, tell Nuts & Bolts Setup where you want Nuts & Bolts to appear on the Start menu. Now that you've won at 20 Questions, installation will begin.

Optimizing your disk with Disk Tune

Disk Tune's options are even more complex than Norton Speed Disk's options. Launch Disk Tune with Start → Programs → Nuts & Bolts → Disk Tune, select a drive, and hit Next. Click Advanced. Be sure the "Remove deleted directory" options box is checked. Click the Directory Sort tab. Under Sort Criteria, click "Files after <DIR>s," then click Add, then click Cluster number, then click Add. This will give you the best directory order possible. Click on the File Placement tab. Nuts & Bolts by default doesn't look for files that are rarely touched, so we have to make it do that. Click User Specified 1 → Specify. In the first box in Last Access Date Range, enter 1/1/80. In the second box, enter a date from two months ago. For example, if today happens to be December 8, 1999, enter 10/8/99. Hit OK. Now click on the User Specified 1 field in the Placement Strategy box, then click on the down arrow until it's moved to the very bottom. Now click on Free Space, and move it up between User Specified 1 and Recently Modified Files. I also uncheck Windows Components; that way, crucial Windows components get lumped in with recently accessed programs and move to the top, while rarely used Windows components migrate to the bottom.

All of these configuration options make Disk Tune far and away the most versatile disk optimizer on the market. It has no equal under Windows 95, and if it were revised for application launch speedup like the tools in competing suites, it would be the best one for Windows 98 as well. However, it's also considerably slower than anything other than Windows Defrag.

Optimizing your registry

Nuts & Bolts' Registry Wizard is similar to the one in Fix-It 99. It offers to automate backup and restore of the registry—a feature that can save you a lot of hassle, since the only way to recover from a corrupted registry is often to reinstall Windows—as well as clean up unnecessary entries, repair, and optimize. The two packages are almost interchangeable.

Run the Registry Repair Wizard, which will scan for problems for you. You can repair them one at a time, but it's better to click the Repair All button. After running the wizard once, you should rerun it to see if it turns up any additional problems. Continue this process until it turns up no problems, or until it turns up the same set of problems repeatedly.

After you run the Registry Repair Wizard, you should run the Registry Tune-Up Wizard, which will create a new, optimal copy of your registry.

You should back up your registry once a month, and you should also do registry cleanup, repair, and optimization once a month to keep your system running at peak performance.

Speed your application load times with Launch Rocket

Launch Rocket is similar to Norton Speed Start, but it's less automatic. It tracks what applications you've run since installation, then offers to improve acceleration. This is similar to the way earlier versions of Superfassst operated. Although more stable than Superfassst, it's a generation behind Superfassst and Speed Start in usability. While it doesn't seem to hurt stability as much as Superfassst does, it's not as stable as Norton Speed Start.

Give Launch Rocket a try if you are running Windows 95, but don't use it under Windows 98, as the two aren't compatible.

Uninstallation Programs

I probably don't have to tell you that Windows programs frequently don't uninstall cleanly. They might just leave empty subdirectories hanging around, or they might leave DLLs in your Windows directory and a bunch of junk entries in your registry. Installation programs like InstallShield have made it much less important to have an uninstallation program than in the past—they were absolutely necessary in the days of Windows 3.1—but if you want a clean system, it's best to have an uninstallation program on your shelf.

If you do a lot of gaming, there's a decent chance that you're installing and uninstalling games pretty frequently. An uninstallation program will do that job more cleanly than Windows' built-in Add/Remove Programs applet. There's also a very good chance that you have a large number of DLLs duplicated throughout your hard drive, since many games, especially 3D shooters, are based on one another. By deleting these duplicate files, you can save a large amount of disk space and directory entries, thus speeding up your system.

Many programs install online registration programs and never delete them, even after you've registered the program. An uninstallation program will allow you to safely delete those registration programs, again saving precious disk space and directory entries.

If you're looking to move executable files from your *Windows* or *Windows*\\ *System* directories as described in Chapter 3, an uninstallation program provides a safer way of doing so, automatically updating your Start menu in the process.

Most importantly, you can use either of the major uninstallation programs to automate the process of cleaning up temp files and other junk files that are safe to delete. This will free up space, speeding up your disk optimizer (you do have one scheduled, don't you?) and allowing it to do a better job.

Like the utilities suites business, the uninstallation program business is dominated by two companies, Network Associates (UnInstaller) and Symantec (CleanSweep), and neither utility originated at either company.

UnInstaller

UnInstaller was the first popular program of this type, and remains popular today. When you first install it, it scans your hard drive to find how the various files relate to one another, then it asks you what kinds of files you want to protect from deletion, such as word processing files or MP3 files. It will then flag directories that contain such files, and will let you add or remove programs from the list. UnInstaller will allow you to schedule computer cleanings for removing temp files, orphan shortcuts, and orphan registry entries automatically on a regular basis. This can be an excellent companion to regular automatic disk optimization—UnInstaller clears out poorly utilized disk space, then your utilities package can optimize the use of the newly freed space. UnInstaller also includes a program that monitors applications and the changes they make, so that when you uninstall them, you truly get rid of them and return your system to its previous state. This option, called Installation Monitor, isn't enabled by default, but you get the option to enable it at installation time. I suggest you enable it.

Rather than group them into distinct modules, UnInstaller offers two sets of options: Quick Clean, which removes junk like temp files, and Power Clean, which digs deeper. You should run both programs every month, before you defragment your drive or optimize your registry with your utilities package.

Power Clean has some especially nice features that CleanSweep lacks. The nicest of these features searches out Windows 3.1 components and offers to delete them for you. If you upgraded your system from Windows 3.1, this feature can dramatically improve your system efficiency. UnInstaller is most effective at uninstalling programs that it was able to watch install, but it can uninstall previously installed applications as well.

UnInstaller also includes some other useful features, like the ability to move an application elsewhere on the hard drive. This is useful if you repartition your drive with FIPS—PartitionMagic contains its own applications mover—or add a second hard drive and need to move applications to a newly created applications drive. But if you want to safely move Windows components out of *C:\Windows* and into *C:\Windows\Command*, UnInstaller, like PartitionMagic's Magic Mover, won't do it. UnInstaller can also archive an application so you can reinstall it later, and package an application so you can duplicate its settings and installation on another computer.

CleanSweep is easier to use, but UnInstaller is less expensive. I've seen it on sale occasionally for as little as $19. CleanSweep is better, but it isn't three times better. If you see UnInstaller priced at $19 and CleanSweep priced at $49, you might as well save your money and opt for the less-expensive choice. And if you upgraded from Windows 3.1, UnInstaller is the better choice anyway.

CleanSweep

Of the two packages, CleanSweep is easier to use. Like UnInstaller, it will monitor program installations and move, archive, and package applications for you, and its Fast & Safe Cleanup module allows you to schedule cleanups. However, Clean-Sweep does a better job of searching for orphan programs, DLLs, and registry entries. And, importantly, CleanSweep will move Windows components out of *C:\ Windows* and into *C:\Windows\Command*, like the procedure described in Chapter 3, if you instruct it to.

Like UnInstaller, CleanSweep works best if you let it monitor program installs, although it can also uninstall applications installed previously.

There are several CleanSweep modules that you should run regularly. Run Duplicate File Finder once a month and follow its advice. Run Redundant DLL Finder and follow its advice every time you install a new piece of software. You probably will need to run Orphan Finder only once, immediately after installing Clean Sweep. You should run Cookie Cleanup, Plug-in Cleanup, and ActiveX Cleanup once a month before defragmenting your drives, and run Registry Sweep once a month before optimizing your registry.

Like UnInstaller, CleanSweep contains a module that moves an application program from one drive or directory to another. This is mostly useful if you've partitioned your drive with FIPS or added a second hard drive and need to move programs into the new drive.

Anti-Virus Software

Viruses are an unfortunate fact of life these days. Viruses, as you may know, are small programs written with two objectives in mind: to replicate as much as possible, and to cause as much damage as possible. A successful virus will strike a balance between these objectives. If the virus causes too much damage too quickly, it will cripple the system before it can spread to another system. But if the virus doesn't cause any damage, by definition it isn't a virus, but a worm. (The distinction is subtle, and worms can indirectly be destructive by consuming disk space and CPU cycles.) A destructive program that doesn't make any effort to replicate itself is called a Trojan Horse. Both the Melissa virus, which replicated itself through Microsoft Outlook, and the Chernobyl virus, which was an especially destructive executable program, caused much-publicized outbreaks in 1999. Melissa is now infamous for the speed at which it spread, while Chernobyl is notorious for the sheer amount of destruction it wrought.

Categorizing these programs is more academic than anything else; you don't want any of them on your system. The only time you can get by without anti-virus software is when you operate your computer in total isolation, never installing software of any kind and never exchanging documents with anybody. The people at the highest risk of virus infection are those with Microsoft Office installed (the great majority of new viruses today utilize one of the macro languages present in Office) and software pirates. However, even if you buy your software legitimately and don't have Office, you're not immune. Viruses sometimes creep into software while it's being developed. Microsoft has unknowingly shipped CDs containing infected Word documents many times.

There's no particular advantage to one anti-virus package over another, as long as you download the program updates at least once a month so that you're protected against all of the latest viruses.

The default settings for most anti-virus packages cause a noticeable degradation of performance, however. Anti-virus software frequently scans every file as it is accessed, which is a great way to make a Pentium II feel like a 486 and make a 486 completely unusable. Since the majority of viruses in the wild today operate within Microsoft Office, you will want your anti-virus software to scan all Office files. Scanning all executable programs is overkill, but that option can't always be turned off. In lieu of scanning each program as it's executed, it's better to scan your hard drive at least once a day. You can schedule a virus scan at off-hours, if you wish. You should also scan for viruses immediately before and immediately after installing software.

If you can't set your anti-virus program to automatically scan Office documents without automatically scanning executable files, be sure to manually scan any Office documents before you open them.

I like Norton AntiVirus' ability to plug into Netscape browsers and scan programs as you download them. This is an especially valuable feature, since the Internet is an excellent conduit for transmitting viruses. Norton AntiVirus is available in a bundle called Norton SystemWorks, which includes Norton Utilities and Norton CleanSweep at a discounted price. This gives you a good anti-virus package, an outstanding uninstallation program, and a serviceable utilities suite for less than Norton Utilities alone cost five years ago. If you don't have all three, SystemWorks will plug three big holes in your system at a fair price.

Freeware and Shareware Utilities

The commercial offerings don't do it all. Some freeware and shareware components don't cost much money, but they're nearly as valuable as the components in the commercial offerings.

Memory Utilities

A few years ago when memory prices were still high, RAM doubling programs were the rage. These programs generally didn't work well, when they did anything at all. Today's memory utilities don't try to double your RAM; they just recover underutilized memory. Windows frequently allocates more memory to programs than they need; programs like the freeware Freemem (*www.meikel.com*), by German programmer Meikel Weber, and the $20 shareware MemTurbo (*www.memturbo.com*), by Silicon Prairie Software, reclaim that memory and return it back to the available memory pool. One or the other of these packages should be installed on every Windows 9x system.

MemTurbo has several advantages. It runs automatically when it senses memory is low, causing the system to slow down for a second or two as it goes to work, then returning the system to full speed. It also defragments your available memory, which is an additional benefit. Consolidating your available memory into the largest possible chunks can prevent additional swap file access—after all, if a program wants a 6 MB chunk but the biggest fragment your system has is 4 MB, the system has no choice but to use the swap file to juggle. Be sure to disable MemTurbo's automatic memory recovery (it's on MemTurbo's Options tab) during those intensive games, however. A memory recovery during the game can cause annoying pauses in gameplay. Instead, defragment your memory immediately before and after the game.

In the Freemem documentation, Weber recommends setting the program to try to recover half of your physical memory. I find I get good results (with both Freemem and MemTurbo) by trying to keep $1/3$ or $1/4$ of my memory available; trying to recover half of it tends to force heavier use of virtual memory than I like.

You should definitely have one or the other of these programs in your toolkit. Having lots of memory available improves both the speed and the reliability of Windows 9x systems.

A CPU Utility

Software utilities to overclock certain motherboard/CPU combinations are rumored to exist, but they are far from universal, so it's safe to say that with few exceptions, you can't make your CPU run faster through software.

What you can do is judiciously allocate the CPU cycles you already have, which is what BinaryWork CPU Controller (*binarywork.hypermart.net/*) does. Windows implements priorities for running processes, but it doesn't make much use of them. A process set to high priority gets more CPU time than a process with normal or minimum priority. CPU Controller is popular in the MP3 community because it permits you to encode MP3 files more quickly. However, it is a useful general-purpose utility, as well. Microsoft Word, for instance, is much snappier at high priority.

CPU Controller 1.0 is available for evaluation but features a very clunky interface. In order to control a task's priority, CPU Controller itself has to launch it. This makes program launching a tedious process at best—you have to launch CPU Controller, then navigate your disk directories in search of the program you want to run, then launch the program, then switch back to CPU Controller and set your processor usage.

Version 1.2, available to registered users, permits you to create shortcuts that call CPU Controller and set a priority, which makes the program much easier to work with. Once you set up a program, you can launch it just as you normally would. Version 1.5, which should be available by the time you read this book, promises the ability to change the priority of running tasks, which will increase the program's usefulness immensely. For example, some games launch a configuration program, then launch the game's executable itself. CPU Controller can't control games that do this.

CPU Controller is a boon on marginal systems, especially when you're running a CPU-intensive task like game playing and you don't *want* the background tasks stealing attention from what you're doing. However, CPU Controller won't do much for you in multitasking situations. Run two tasks at high priority, and your system tasks and the other tasks you have running won't get much CPU attention. BinaryWork also warns against using the maximum priority setting. With this setting, the program gets all available CPU time. This would be a tremendous gift to gaming, but if the program crashes, the operating system may not regain control of the CPU. Be aware of the pitfalls if you use this setting.

CPU Controller is shareware; a registration fee of $36.90 is required to use it beyond a 30-day evaluation period.

If your motherboard will take an inexpensive AMD K6-2 or Cyrix processor (many models of this CPU sell in the $35–$40 range), you would probably be better served by a low-cost CPU upgrade. However, if you already have the fastest CPU your motherboard can take, or if it will cost more than $40 to step up to the next CPU grade, CPU Controller is a good way to squeeze next-level performance out of your existing hardware. For most purposes, a 500 MHz Celeron running CPU Controller will be faster than a 550 MHz Pentium III and cost hundreds of dollars less.

RAM Disks

A RAM disk is the opposite of virtual memory. Rather than using disk space to emulate RAM, RAM disks use RAM to emulate a disk. As a result, RAM disks are lightning fast. The disadvantage is that their contents disappear when you power down or reboot.

Ten years ago, RAM disks were popular under DOS because there wasn't a whole lot of other use for large amounts of memory. But it's been a long time since using a RAM disk has been a good idea, because memory prices have always been too high to make it affordable to keep a good-sized RAM disk and still have enough memory for Windows to work effectively. But with memory prices currently hovering at around a dollar per megabyte, it's prudent to put 128 MB of memory in a system, then create a 16 or 32 MB RAM disk for speed-intensive tasks. This still leaves plenty of room for Windows to operate.

Windows 9x comes with a RAM disk driver called *ramdrive.sys*, but it has problems. *ramdrive.sys* allocates memory at the bottom of extended memory, but under most circumstances, Windows needs at least 1 MB of the first 16 MB of available memory, which limits you to a 15 MB RAM disk. I've also had difficulty using *ramdrive.sys* on systems with 128 MB of RAM, and I've had problems with Microsoft Office applications locking up during autosave when I had my temp files redirected to a RAM disk created with *ramdrive.sys*.

XMSDISK

The freeware XMSDISK, by French programmer Franck Uberto (available at *www. opus.co.tt/dave/index.htm*) is a smaller, more versatile, and more reliable substitute that exhibits none of these problems. It loads from *autoexec.bat* and is capable of allocating its memory from the top of the available memory pool. This allows it to work with Windows 9x without restriction, and on certain motherboards, makes it beneficial to add more memory. Many older Pentium motherboards, such as those with the Intel 430TX chipset, can only cache a limited amount of memory. Adding more memory beyond the cacheable limit works, but access to that memory will be much slower than usual, so it can actually hurt system performance. But if you allocate that slower, non-cached memory to a RAM disk, you force the system to use cached memory for critical operations. The non-cached memory still makes for a lightning-fast disk drive, but since programs aren't running from it, it no longer hinders system performance.

To install XMSDISK, copy *xmsdsk.exe* to *C:\Windows\Command*, then add to *autoexec.bat* the line:

```
XMSDSK [size in kilobytes] [drive letter:] /t /y
```

The best use for XMSDISK is as a repository for temp files. Microsoft Office and other applications generate tons of temp files, and sending them to a RAM disk greatly speeds operations. The slower your hard drive, the greater the improvement. To redirect your temp files, add the following lines to the end of *autoexec. bat*, replacing the emphasized type with the letter you assigned your RAM disk:

```
Md ram disk letter:\temp
Set temp=ram disk letter:\temp
Set tmp=ram disk letter:\temp
```

To be at all effective, a RAM disk needs to be at least 1.5 MB in size, and I sometimes find I have more than 4 MB of temp files at any given time. If you have 32 MB of RAM, I'm inclined to suggest you create at least a 1.5 MB RAM disk. Even if you have less, you'll probably want one—Windows wastes far more memory than that on excessive disk caching and CD-ROM caching. If you've recovered memory from those functions, try reinvesting 1.5 MB of your savings in a RAM disk to hold your temp files, and see if it improves system performance.

If you use the Windows desktop as a temporary work area and would like to speed it up, you can redirect the desktop to the RAM disk as well. Add the following lines to *autoexec.bat*, substituting your RAM disk's drive letter for the italicized text:

```
md ram disk letter:\desktop
copy c:\windows\desktop\*.* ram disk letter:\desktop
```

To make Windows use the new lightning-fast desktop, open Regedit, navigate to HKCU\Software\Microsoft\Windows\CurrentVersion\Explorer\Shell Folders, and change the location of the Desktop entry to the subdirectory in your RAM disk. If there are shortcuts you want to always have available on the desktop, copy them to another directory, then add a line to *autoexec.bat* to copy them to the desktop subdirectory in your RAM disk.

You can by all means use the RAM disk as a temporary work area as well.

Compressing your XMSDISK RAM disk with DriveSpace 3

When hard drive prices started dropping from the sky around 1997, people stopped talking about data compression, and with good reason. Data compression has a reputation for being extremely risky—brought about by the extremely buggy DoubleSpace data compression that was present in Microsoft's MS-DOS 6.0—and that's not really fair. Data compression has been around a lot longer than DoubleSpace; it was safe before DoubleSpace came around, and DoubleSpace didn't do anything to change that. The big problem with data compression is that it gives the CPU yet another task to juggle, and hard drive speed is so crucial to system performance that it's not wise to throw that extra factor into the equation.

Because of this extra overhead, I really hate to talk about data compression in regards to RAM disks. Suddenly we have this lightning-fast disk drive, so why would we want to slow it down? Disk compression made sense back when it allowed you to do things you couldn't do without it. It was painful, but it was better than not being able to install your software. Once hard drives the size of the Grand Canyon became available for a hundred bucks, it stopped making sense to compress hard drives.

RAM prices are at historic lows as of this writing, but it's still going to be a while before systems with a gigabyte of RAM become commonplace. In the meantime, if you need to have 24 MB of data at hand on your RAM disk but can only spare 16 MB of RAM, you can run DriveSpace on the RAM disk to give yourself some more space. A compressed RAM disk is still faster than a physical hard disk. RAM disk compression requires DriveSpace 3, which shipped with the Windows 95 Plus! pack and with Windows 98.

To compress your RAM disk, install DriveSpace from Windows 98 Setup or from the Plus! pack setup, if you haven't already. Since the RAM disk has to be created from scratch every time you boot your system, you need to run DriveSpace at startup. Right-click your Start Menu and select Explore. Double-click Programs, then double-click Startup, then right-click in the right pane of the window and select New → Shortcut. When prompted for a command line, type:

```
DRVSPACE /COMPRESS D:
```

replacing D with your RAM disk's drive letter. Click Next, then Finish.

If you like to be able to save and restore the contents of your RAM disk, DriveSpace unwittingly provides a fast and easy way to do it. Look at your RAM disk's host drive (usually *H:*). You should find two files: a readme file, and a very large file with a name like *DRVSPACE.000* or *DRVSPACE.CVF.* Copy that file to your hard drive (say, to *C:\Windows\Command*), then add the following line to *autoexec.bat*:

```
COPY C:\WINDOWS\COMMAND\DRVSPACE.CVF D:\
```

Substitute your RAM disk's drive letter for the drive letter at the end of the file. Windows probably won't automatically mount the drive, so right-click your Start Menu and select Explore. Double-click Programs, then double-click Startup, then right-click in the right pane of the window and select New → Shortcut. When prompted for a command line, type:

```
DRVSPACE /MOUNT D:\drvspace.cvf
```

replacing *D:\drvspace.cvf* with the path and filename of your DriveSpace file. Click Next, then Finish.

These two techniques for compressing a RAM disk are mutually exclusive. Choose the first technique if you don't need to preserve your RAM disk's contents; choose the second technique if you do.

VRAMDIR

An alternative RAM disk is the controversial VRAMDIR by Virtual Software (*www. virtusoft.com*). The source of this controversy is Virtual Software's choice of benchmarks to demonstrate their $10 shareware program. They simply illustrate how much faster their RAM disk is than a physical disk. This is a worthless benchmark because it doesn't give any indication of the program's improvement on real-world performance. VRAMDIR may perform hundreds or thousands of times faster than a hard disk, but a system with VRAMDIR won't perform hundreds of times faster. This has caused some wrangling on Usenet between representatives of Virtual Software and end users.

The nice thing about VRAMDIR is that it uses a combination RAM disk/hard disk approach that's completely transparent. You just tell it what directories to shadow, and VRAMDIR redirects those requests to RAM until available memory fills up, then it uses disk space. As available system memory increases, VRAMDIR grabs up more memory for its RAM disk. As system memory becomes scarce, VRAMDIR releases memory.

VRAMDIR's approach is nice, but the shareware version of the program is limited to 30-minute sessions, so it can be hard to gauge how much it improves your system. You can use it to shadow your temp directories (there's no need to redirect them if you don't want to), your desktop, *C:\Windows\Spool* to speed up printing, your Start menu—any directory where speed is more important than permanence. Just be sure to work fast if you want to determine what it can do for you.

Cleanup Utilities

Australian programmer Kevin Solway wrote a program that's an excellent complement to uninstallation programs. Clean System Directory, available from *www. ozemail.com.au/~kevsol/sware.html* scans all of the executable programs and DLLs on your system to see what DLLs they call upon, compares it to the list of DLLs in your system directory, and moves any orphans elsewhere. Windows installs a good number of DLLs on the assumption that something you install later might need them; until that day arrives, they're just slowing the system down. Clean System Directory will move them out of the way. Programs that need DLLs they don't find in the system directory will usually install them, but if a program malfunctions after installation, try moving all of the DLL files out of Clean System Directory's hold directory back into *C:\Windows\System*, then run Clean System Directory again. It should detect what DLLs your newly installed program is using and leave those alone, while moving the orphans back out of the way again.

Under some bizarre circumstances, Clean System Directory can move a DLL that's in use. If a program's code is compressed or encrypted, Clean System Directory won't be able to determine what DLLs it uses. Fortunately, not many programs do this anymore, since it hurts performance. If you run Clean System Directory and a program that used to work suddenly starts complaining about a missing DLL, look for it in Clean System Directory's directory of junk DLLs and copy it back into *C:\Windows\System.*

Microsoft's RegClean is a must-have if you don't have Fix-It 99 or Nuts & Bolts. The registry cleaners in these programs are more powerful, but Microsoft's offering is free. Download it from *support.microsoft.com/support/downloads/DP3049. ASP.* It's completely automatic—run it, and it scans for invalid registry entries, then asks permission to clean them up. It's best to run RegClean after installing or uninstalling any new piece of software, and you should run it multiple times until it says it can't find any entries to clean up. RegClean has some issues with certain development packages (some of them, ironically, from Microsoft), but it's safe on gaming systems.

Another good cleanup program is EasyCleaner, a freeware offering from Finnish programmer Toni Helenius. EasyCleaner will scan the registry for invalid entries and remove them for you, as well as scanning for duplicate files and junk files like an uninstallation program would. It's not automatic—you have to select the registry entries or files you wish to discard—and the duplicate file finder is a bit slow, but the program works well, the price is right and it does have a Select All button to quickly eliminate junk in large quantities. EasyCleaner is available at *www. saunalahti.fi/tonihele.* I suggest running EasyCleaner once a month if you don't have an uninstallation program or utilities suite to clean your system up.

Last but not least is Brad Stowers' Startup Manager, available at *www.delphifreestuff. com.* This program allows you to toggle on or off any program that loads at system startup. This is useful, for example, for getting rid of AOL Instant Messenger after Netscape browsers install it. You don't need AOL Instant Messenger unless you're online, so why keep it loaded all the time? And if you don't use AOL Instant Messenger, why load it at all? You can also use it to quickly and effectively get rid of the installation nags some commercial programs install.

Additional Utilities That Come with Windows 98

Windows 98 comes with a number of additional utilities that are fairly simple and generally used only when your system develops problems. Neither of these tools is reason enough on their own to upgrade to Windows 98, but if you have them and need them, you might as well use them.

System Configuration Utility

The System Configuration Utility is a slightly updated tool similar to the old undocumented SYSEDIT utility that's been shipping since Windows 3.1 days. It provides a clumsy GUI interface for changing system configuration files, making the editing of *.ini* files, *config.sys*, and *autoexec.bat* more like editing the registry. You can run the System Configuration Utility by pressing Start → Run → MSCONFIG and pressing Enter.

The most noteworthy features in the System Configuration Utility, as usual, are buried behind a button labeled Advanced. You should only change these settings if you're having problems, and then only after running the Troubleshooting section of Windows Help, but the most important setting is the one labeled "Disable Scan-Disk after bad shutdown." On some systems with very large (greater than 8 GB) FAT32X partitions, the text-mode version of ScanDisk can cause serious disk corruption problems. You should always run ScanDisk or a third-party disk repair tool after an improper shutdown, but disable this setting and instead run the tool after Windows starts.

Depending on your system, you may also find you want to disable fast shutdown (if it turns out to be incompatible with your hardware), or the Pentium F0 workaround if you have an Intel Pentium or Pentium MMX processor (this fixes an obscure bug in these chips that can crash the system).

Most programs keep their hands off the text-based configuration files these days, but not all do. If you are about to evaluate a piece of software but think there's a good chance you'll immediately want to uninstall it, you can back up your current configuration (run MSCONFIG and press the button labeled Create Backup), then restore it after you uninstall the program (run MSCONFIG and press the button labeled Restore Backup). This trick only works if you haven't installed any other programs since installing and uninstalling the program, but in a pinch this trio of utilities can give you some of the capabilities of a full-blown uninstallation program.

System File Checker

System File Checker (SFC) examines the files in the *C:\Windows* hierarchy and tracks changes to the files there. A number of things can corrupt these files, including errant programs, improper shutdowns, and viruses. Installing and uninstalling programs can sometimes also make undesirable changes to these files. SFC is no substitute for an anti-virus program (if some other program on your system is infected, it the virus will quickly spread back into your Windows directory), but as a quick fix for a system that's past its prime, it's invaluable, capable of fixing problems that previously could only be fixed by reinstalling Windows.

To run SFC, Start → Run → type SFC and press Enter. SFC offers two options: "Scan for altered files" and "Extract one file from installation disk." Normally you'll want to run the former option. Hit OK, then hit Start, and SFC will look for files, replacing anything it doesn't like and storing backup copies of the files it replaces.

The default settings are pretty conservative and won't catch every problem, so if your problem persists, you should press the Settings button and check the box labeled "Check for deleted files," then run SFC again. You should only go back into settings and check the box labeled "Check for changed files" if the first and second passes fail to correct the problem, since there are both legitimate and illegitimate reasons why a system file could be changed. Some programs will occasionally install updated versions of the Windows system files they use.

If SFC fails to fix the problem or makes it worse, just copy the files from *C:\Windows\HelpDesk\SFC* back into their appropriate locations.

Running SFC three times is a bit of a pain, but it's far better than reinstalling Windows in the blind hope that it will repair the system. I don't recommend running it on such a regular basis as utilities like Defrag or your registry tools because you really shouldn't need it very often. Unless you're running a lot of pre-release software or have a serious problem with exposure to viruses, you shouldn't need to run it more than once every three months.

The exception to this (there's always an exception) is if you don't have an uninstallation program. If you want to keep your system in pristine condition, always run SFC before installing a program. Click Settings → Log File → Overwrite existing Log → OK, hit Start to run SFC's analysis, then click Settings → View Log → File → Print. Store this hardcopy with the program's documentation. Exit Notepad (the program SFC uses to view the log), then exit SFC. Install the program, then run SFC again the same way. You now have a record of every change the program made to the system.

If you later decide to uninstall the program, run SFC again before and after the uninstallation and compare the logs to the set you created when you installed the program. If some of the files the installation program added still remain, it could mean some other program is using them, or it could be an indication of a sloppy uninstallation routine. You should run Kevin Solway's Clean System Directory to determine if the file is still needed.

SFC won't track the changes to the registry, so it's an incomplete substitute for an uninstallation program, but it's far better than no tracking tool at all. In conjunction with a good set of tools like an uninstallation program and a utilities suite, SFC should make it possible to completely eliminate the phenomenon of OS rot described in Chapter 1, *System Optimization Theory*.

Windows Registry Checker

Windows 98 automatically keeps five backup copies of the registry, creating a new backup every time you successfully boot. You can also manually back up the registry, fix minor problems with the registry, or restore a backup with the Windows Registry Checker.

The Windows Registry Checker runs only from within DOS mode. Boot to a command prompt by holding down the Control key at boot, then type SCANREG at the *C:* prompt.

To back up your registry, type SCANREG /BACKUP, restore a previous backup with SCANREG /RESTORE, and attempt to repair a faulty registry with SCANREG /FIX.

If you are about to evaluate a piece of software but think there's a good chance you'll immediately want to uninstall it, you can boot into DOS mode after uninstalling the program and restore your previous backup with SCANREG /RESTORE. This trick will only work if you haven't made any other changes to the registry since installing and uninstalling the program, but in a pinch it can work along with SFC to give you some of the capabilities of a full-blown uninstallation program.

6

Replacement Windows Shells

One of the biggest reasons Windows 9x requires so much more memory than Windows 3.1 is the Explorer shell itself. In Windows 95, the Explorer shell requires nearly 4 MB of memory on its own. Thanks to the shell integration with recent versions of Internet Explorer, that requirement balloons to closer to 16 MB under Windows 98. Consider that the underlying Windows subsystems themselves occupy about 16 MB of memory, and you start to see why 32 MB is the bare minimum requirement for running Windows 98.

The large size of Explorer makes some software developers wonder just what they're getting for their 4 MB, as should you. In many ways, Explorer makes Windows 9x what it is—Explorer provides the familiar Start menu, manages the desktop, and serves as Windows 9x's file manager. But should all of these elements really be integrated into a single program, always loaded in memory? Do you really need a file manager in memory if you're running a word processor and it's the only task running? What about a full-blown, fourth-generation web browser?

If your goal is ease of use and you have buckets and buckets of memory, then maybe you want that stuff. But if your goal is performance and you don't make a lot of changes to your Windows environment—and most people don't—then you're probably better suited with something else. There are a surprising number of alternatives to using Explorer as your shell, and they can be configured to use considerably less memory than Explorer uses.

Replacing Explorer is pretty easy to do: Start → Run → `sysedit` → System.ini. Scroll down to the section labeled [`boot`], which is usually the first section in the file, then look for a line that reads `shell=Explorer.exe` (it's usually about halfway through the section). You can replace Explorer with just about anything you like, as I describe later in Chapter 12, *Hardware Upgrades*, where I present the idea of using a 486 as a dedicated kiosk. Under most circumstances, however, you will probably want to replace Explorer with something designed to launch other programs.

One potential fear with using anything that replaces Explorer is what happens to Explorer elements like the desktop and Start menu. These programs don't tamper with either of those elements; if you decide to try another shell and decide to revert back to Explorer, Explorer will find its data undisturbed and will never realize it was replaced.

Program Manager

Yes, Program Manager—the venerable Windows 3.x shell—still runs under Windows 9x. It's even included. During the Windows 95 setup, it asks you if you want to use the Windows 95 user interface (Explorer) or the old Windows 3.1 interface (Program Manager). Most people never notice that option or change it. But if you select the Windows 3.1 interface, you're presented with a Program Manager screen at the end of the installation. It looks a little different—the Program Manager title is off to the left; the window gadget on the left-hand side is the program's icon rather than a generic box; and the minimize, maximize, and close gadgets are on the right-hand side. Picture a slightly modernized Windows 3.1, and that's what you get (see Figure 6-1). But aside from the look of the title bar, it looks and acts just like Windows 3.1. Windows 98 doesn't give you the option to use Program Manager as your user interface, but the executable is still included, so you can add it manually.

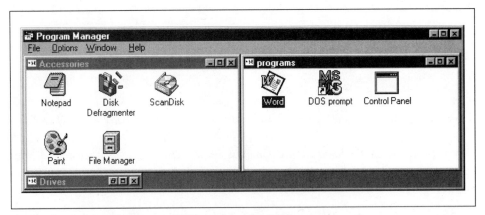

Figure 6-1. Program Manager, slightly updated for 1999

Advantages of Program Manager

Program Manager's memory footprint is a fraction of Explorer's—about 1.6 MB—making it a suitable choice for low-memory systems. And although Program

Manager development ceased in 1994, it was at the time a proven and stable shell, if frequently maligned. Plus, Program Manager is still tightly hooked into Windows—when you install software, any program knows how to create program groups for it. This feature gives it a usability edge over some other alternative shells, which require at least one additional step to add programs to their menus after installation.

The biggest advantage Program Manager has over other shells, however, is its familiarity and ubiquity. This was, after all, the interface for Windows 3.x, which was the most common operating environment in the world for nearly half a decade. There are hundreds of freeware and shareware programs that extend the capabilities of Program Manager, and hundreds of articles in back issues of computer magazines offer tips for its effective use.

Disadvantages of Program Manager

The bad news is that Program Manager was the shell that spawned a thousand replacements. In the Windows 3.1 days, it seemed like every utility company on the planet was making and selling a Windows 3.1 shell. Program Manager doesn't use a folder/subfolder structure like Explorer does—it stores its icons in program groups, and you can't nest groups. Easy access to your drives and network resources is history. There's just not a whole lot to like about Program Manager, besides its reduced memory footprint. I suspect the Program Manager interface sold more than a few Macintoshes the first half of this decade.

Another disadvantage to Program Manager is that it won't import Explorer's Start menu. If you've added software, you'll have to add it back in yourself. You can get the details for any program with Start → Context Menu → Explore → Programs. Next, open the program's group, then select Properties from the program's context menu. Now, go to Start → Run → progman, then File → New → Program Item → Description → <description> → Command Line → <path and filename>.

Perhaps most importantly, Program Manager is still a 16-bit application. While 16-bit programs tend to be smaller than their 32-bit counterparts, they also tend to be less stable, and the extra overhead of switching into and out of protected mode hurts performance slightly. The less time your Windows 9x system spends in real mode, the faster and more stable it will be, and, chances are, the happier you'll be.

Tips for Improving Program Manager

That said, you can dress up the Program Manager interface and make it tolerable. To get a My Computer-like view, select File → New → Program Group → My Computer → OK. Now, to add your C drive to the group, select File → New → Program Item → Description → Drive C → Command Line → C:\. Repeat this for every drive you'd like to be able to access. To add a Control Panel to it, select File → New → Program Item → Description → Control Panel → Command Line → control.exe.

Now, open all of the program groups you use most frequently. Expand the Program Manager window so that it fills the screen. Then select Window → Tile. Now your most frequently used programs are just a double-click away, and your rarely used programs are a click and a double-click away. Your Program Manager screen will somewhat resemble Figure 6-1. This configuration mimics the convenience of having all of your most common program icons out on the Explorer desktop, but without causing the performance hit.

It's fine to use program groups to sort your programs into logical categories. However, you should try to avoid having a large number of groups. The more Program Manager groups you have, the slower Program Manager runs, because it has to keep track of all of them. This was a much more serious consideration back in 1992, when people were trying to run Windows 3.1 on 25-MHz PCs that didn't have any memory or CPU cycles to spare. However, Program Manager does store its groups in files in the *Windows* directory, so a large number of groups can contribute significantly to system overhead, even on modern PCs.

Recommendations

Program Manager uses more memory than either EVWM or LiteStep, but it is easier to customize. If you have to optimize a low-memory PC that doesn't have an Internet connection (and thus no easy means to download another shell), Program Manager may be your only choice. In situations where you've replaced Windows 3.x with Windows 9x, Program Manager is also a good choice, since it's already familiar. Of all the options currently available, Program Manager strikes the best balance between memory usage and ease of customization.

I've used Program Manager under two circumstances. When I've set up a new Windows 9x-based computer for someone who's been using a Windows 3.1-based computer for the past several years, and he has no interest in learning how to use a new interface, I've set up Program Manager. This makes the computer less alien, and has the advantage of making it run a little bit faster.

Program Manager is also good for special-purpose computers. Many people want a computer for word processing, email, and web browsing, but nothing else. I have a number of relatives in this category. When this happens, I'll take an old PC, install Windows, then install a suitable word processing package, then install a Netscape browser and a friendly email client like Qualcomm's Eudora Light, set up the ISP, and then install Program Manager, create a new program group, and set up icons for the word processor, web browser, and email client. There's little need for File Manager or Explorer, since modern word processors contain adequate file management capabilities like creating folders and moving files. I'll go ahead and put tools like Defrag and ScanDisk in another group in case I need them. Then I open the group that contains the word processor, browser, and email client and restart Windows to make sure the group stays open the next time the computer gets started. While Explorer's Start menu is pretty intuitive, it's hard to get any more intuitive than this. After all, when you want to email, you just double-click that icon. When you want a word processor, double-click that icon. What could be better? You made the computer easier to use, and you reduced the amount of horsepower necessary to run it.

EVWM

EVWM, by Eliot Gillum, is a freeware replacement shell that resembles the FVWM window manager that was once the most popular GUI for the *XFree86* X Window system for Linux and FreeBSD. (Window managers under Linux are roughly equivalent to program shells under Windows 9x.) If you were using Linux before it became trendy, you'll probably be right at home with EVWM.

If you're not acquainted with EVWM, its capabilities are somewhere between that of Explorer and Program Manager. It's a design that saves a lot of screen space by dispensing with the Start button, and making the system tray a transparent, movable item that floats over whatever applications might be running behind it. This increase in usable screen space will be welcome at low resolutions. Rather than use a Start menu, a pop-up menu appears any time you left-click on the backdrop. A context menu appears when you right-click, but it, too, is minimal. It shows the running tasks and little else.

Like Program Manager, there are no icons on the backdrop. The desktop is a separate window, accessible from the main menu.

Advantages of EVWM

EVWM's biggest advantage is probably its ease of installation. You simply download and run it—there's no installation routine, and no need to mess around with *system.ini.* Just run it, and it will see that Explorer is running and offer to set itself up as the default shell. If you accept its offer, it diligently imports your Start menu, brings up a configuration screen to let you customize it (you can get by with just closing it for now). EVWM is also very small, requiring about 1.2 MB. On low-memory systems, EVWM is an excellent choice.

Although FVWM never was the most common user interface and probably never will be (KDE and GNOME eclipsed it in the Linux world soon after Linux's explosive growth in 1998), it was modeled after Windows 9x's interface. Whether the designers were successful in improving on the Windows interface is a matter of personal opinion, but it's similar enough that most Windows 9x users should be able to adapt to it fairly easily. The main menu has all the functionality of Windows' Start menu and a little bit extra to boot. It provides instant access to the Control Panel, which is nice. This feature compensates somewhat for the lack of any kind of functional context menu.

Finally, unlike Program Manager, EVWM is a 32-bit program.

Disadvantages of EVWM

Unfortunately, EVWM is a much less mature program than either Explorer or Program Manager. Since it's still very much in development, it tends to crash more frequently than either of Microsoft's alternatives. This condition should improve with time, but be aware that version 1.0 still has some stability issues.

If you install software after installing EVWM, it won't appear instantly on your main menu—you'll have to reimport the Windows Start menu. This is fairly easy to do—Main menu → Special → Configure EVWM → Import. But remembering to do this and making it a habit may take some time.

EVWM's context menu is pretty vacant as well. Since it puts most of its functionality in the main menu, you can certainly argue that it doesn't make any sense to put much in the context menu. Since Explorer is so context menu–intensive, experienced Windows 9x users may be lost without it. When you open up Explorer windows, however, the standard context menu, including the beloved Send To command, is available. (EVWM still uses Explorer windows to display drive contents.)

Installation and Configuration of EVWM

You can always download the newest version of EVWM from *www.evwm.com*. Its installation is the easiest of any Windows shell I've found—just unzip it to an appropriate target directory, such as *D:\Program Files\evwm*, and run it. It will do the rest.

The appearance of EVWM's menus is customizable—EVWM calls its menu backdrops *cloaks*. Not all distributions of EVWM come with cloaks, however. You may wish to download a couple of cloaks from *www.evwm.com* at the same time you download EVWM, just to be on the safe side. Unzip them into a subdirectory off the main EVWM directory—for example, *D:\Program Files\evwm\cloaks*. The distribution I downloaded came with no cloaks, but was configured by default to use them. If you want to save memory and CPU cycles by not using cloaks, select Main menu → Special → Configure EVWM → Options → uncheck Use custom menus (cloaks). If you want to dress up EVWM with a cloak, select Main menu → Special → Configure EVWM → Options → Cloak Directory → <location of your cloaks> → check Use custom menus (cloaks) → Cloak Chooser.

EVWM will honor any wallpaper you choose using the Display Control Panel.

As stated before, you must reimport your Windows Start menu any time you add programs.

Recommendations

I noticed improved performance when using EVWM even on a 32 MB machine, so EVWM is a good choice for low-memory systems. Some people may have difficulty getting used to EVWM's sparse desktop and accessing the Start menu from a right-click. But if that change doesn't bother you, EVWM has plenty to offer.

EVWM definitely isn't as flashy as Explorer or LiteStep, and, arguably, it's not even as flashy as Program Manager. It's the four-door family sedan of the group: reliable, simple, and easy to set up and use. It launches programs without getting in the way, which is certainly good enough.

If you want a smaller memory footprint than Explorer and a smaller download than LiteStep, EVWM is your best choice. If you don't want to spend a whole Saturday configuring your new shell interface, EVWM is your best choice. If you want glitz, look elsewhere.

StarOffice

StarOffice, a productivity suite from Sun Microsystems (the company found itself in the news when it bought StarOffice's original producer, German software manufacturer Star Division) is an unusual choice for a replacement shell. StarOffice is an extremely integrated package consisting of a word processor, spreadsheet, database, drawing program, PIM, email client, HTML editor, and web browser, tied together by an Explorer-like interface that even imports the Windows Start menu. It's the only program many people will ever need (though whether it's the best tool for any given task may be open to question). If you can tolerate a 63 MB download, it's available free of charge from *www.sun.com*. If you prefer not to tie up your phone line for hours on end, it's available on CD with a printed manual for $39.

StarOffice's design suggests it might have had ambitions as a replacement shell, but the implementation falls short. StarOffice doesn't offer to make itself your shell; it just masquerades as your shell, covering up Explorer (which means you have two shells loaded, in effect). If you want StarOffice to truly be your shell, you must manually specify its executable (*soffice.exe*) in *system.ini*. Scroll down to the section labeled [boot], which is usually the first section in the file, then look for a line that reads shell=Explorer.exe.

Advantages of StarOffice

If you have enough memory for it, everything you need is always right there in memory. The other advantage is the automatic importing of the Start menu.

Disadvantages of StarOffice

Unfortunately, those who have enough memory to be able to afford to use Star-Office as a shell are also most likely to be those who won't be satisfied with its power and will want a full-blown office suite for daily use.

When StarOffice is used as a shell, there's no obvious way to exit Windows; you must bring up the Task Manager by hitting Ctrl-Esc, then select Shutdown Windows from the File menu.

StarOffice's biggest weakness as a shell is its hefty memory footprint. It occupies about 35 MB of memory when used as the shell, which suggests it's keeping a sizeable part of the full suite in memory. Packing a shell and a full suite of productivity applications into an application that uses about 35 MB of memory is a commendable achievement in this age of bloatware, but unless StarOffice really is the only program you ever use (besides a few utilities), I can't imagine wanting to have a full applications suite loaded in memory all the time. It takes the Microsoft idea of a totally integrated system to an unnecessary extreme, and it's hard enough for me to justify always having a web browser in memory. The main reason for using a replacement shell is to gain performance; StarOffice fails here.

Recommendations

As an applications suite, StarOffice falls somewhere between Microsoft Works and the full-blown applications suites like Microsoft Office, Lotus SmartSuite, and WordPerfect Office. Since 90% of users need and use only about 10% of the functionality the large office suites offer, StarOffice is more than adequate for typical home use and even for a large percentage of business use, and the price is right. But it's best to let StarOffice stick to what it does best and was designed to do in the first place—juggling household data—and leave general program shell duties to something smaller and nimbler.

LiteStep

LiteStep, like EVWM, is based on a popular *XFree86* window manager. LiteStep's predecessor, OpenStep, was based on Steve Jobs' NeXTStep environment. Now that NeXT has been absorbed by Apple and what was left of NeXTStep evolved into the next generation Mac OS, NeXTStep is pretty much an orphan, but its look and feel still have a rabid following. In a way, it's a sort of poetic justice to see a

NeXTStep clone appear on the Windows desktop, since many of the "innovations" in Windows Explorer were lifted straight from NeXTStep.

LiteStep is the fruit of many programmers' labor, as it is released under the GNU Public License.

Advantages of LiteStep

LiteStep has a cult following, and it didn't take long for me to see why. Though it's not yet quite as stable as Explorer under all circumstances, it has some very definite advantages.

The first advantage is just that its model, NeXTStep, is a very good, effective user interface. I hadn't used a NeXT machine since college, so I'd forgotten that—and, chances are, a lot of people never had a chance to see a NeXT, let alone use one. One of LiteStep's features is virtual desktops. I like this feature much better than the virtual screens modern video cards offer, where your monitor is just a section of a much larger virtual screen. I find it distracting to scroll around and have the screen move on me, especially since I tend to overshoot when I'm moving the mouse toward the edges. LiteStep can function in this manner, or in the manner I prefer—giving you four virtual desktops, where you select the desktop you want by right-clicking on it. Later revisions of the AmigaOS supported a feature like this—Amiga called them "public screens"—and I came to like them, but I like this implementation even better. Linux users will feel right at home with this. If you want an application out of your way but don't want to minimize it, just click its likeness on the virtual desktop and shove it off into one of the other quadrants. Then, when you need to check on it, you can just right-click on that quadrant, then switch back. No more endless Alt-Tabbing through the task list, and no more desktop clutter!

The center of the Windows user interface, of course, is the Start menu. The center of the NeXT user interface was the Dock window. Dock windows were similar to the Office toolbar, though they could contain pop-out menus containing sets of icons. LiteStep includes a Dock-like interface called the Wharf bar. Besides pop-out menus, the Wharf bar can also contain the virtual desktop manager, date and time, and computer resource statistics. Adjusting from a Start menu–centric interface to a Dock-centric interface could take a little getting used to, but if you use the Office toolbar much, you'll be right at home with Wharf pretty quickly.

LiteStep also has support for the Windows Start menu. The standard distribution doesn't have it by default and the documentation doesn't come right out and say how to add it, but the hooks are there, and at least one of the LiteStep configuration programs (lce) will add it automatically.

Another nicety is LiteStep's customizability. There are themes that mimic NeXT, MacOS 8, BeOS, and AmigaOS. If you covet these foreign user interfaces but want the ability to run Windows software, these themes make a good compromise. The customizations go beyond just trying to mimic foreign computers. There are LiteStep themes that invoke all sorts of different moods—from otherworldly atmospheres to tributes to popular games. LiteStep goes way beyond just letting you change your wallpaper—you can customize virtually every aspect of your computer.

LiteStep's memory requirements surprised me—about 1.5 MB. These requirements are higher than that of EVWM, but not by a whole lot. Being able to dispense with the Office toolbar and having resource meters available all the time makes it worth the extra 300K. Like EVWM, LiteStep is a 32-bit environment, but it is more stable.

Of all the shells available for Windows, LiteStep is my personal favorite.

Disadvantages of LiteStep

For all of its advantages, LiteStep does have some disadvantages. Its tremendous capacity for customization could prove to be a problem—some of the LiteStep themes available go overboard on memory and CPU usage. The question arises where to draw the line—once you throw a glitzy user interface on the screen, the temptation arises to add memory-hogging backgrounds, system sounds, screen savers, and other glitz to match. If you have a powerful computer, you might be able to get away with this, but I've seen my share of 350 MHz Pentium IIs that felt more sluggish than my 90 MHz Pentium. I downloaded a transparent-background command prompt—they're the rage in the Linux world—to see if I liked it. I could have gotten used to it, but I didn't like how my CPU usage shot up from 30% to 100% when I had a command prompt open. Making matters worse, this fancy command prompt was eating so much CPU time that it actually fell behind my typing and transposed characters. I'm a fairly quick typist, but the idea of a 200 MHz computer being unable to keep up with any human being's typing is ridiculous, especially seeing as that same computer does a fine job with voice recognition.

LiteStep's biggest weakness, compared to Explorer, is ease of setup. LiteStep is no harder to use than Explorer—in an ease-of-use comparison, I might even give the edge to LiteStep—but when it comes to configuring and customizing it, Explorer has LiteStep beat, hands down. There's no dragging and dropping icons onto the desktop, the Wharf bar, or the pop-up menu. Any customizations you wish to do require breaking out a text editor and hacking a file called *step.rc*. Personally, I don't mind doing this—I have used a variety of Dock clones in the past, and they generally required customization through text files as well. Adding drag-and-drop capability to LiteStep would make it much larger, so I'd rather use a configuration utility or tweak a text configuration file. If you've spent much time in Linux, or if you hacked the Windows 3.1 *.ini* files to customize Windows, LiteStep's configuration file probably won't put you off. If you rely on drag-and-drop, you probably won't care much for LiteStep.

The other disadvantage of LiteStep is the way it uses screen space. It will force you to work differently. If you're used to keeping all of your windows maximized, you may not like LiteStep because the Wharf toolbar occupies about four times the screen space of the Office toolbar. You can make Wharf autohide, but then you lose the CPU meter and the clock unless you move the mouse over to it. To be fair, the virtual desktops more than make up for the extra space. I find multiple screens is a lot like multitasking in that it takes some time to get used to it, but once you do get used to having the ability, it makes it really hard to go back to using computers that don't have it.

Finally, LiteStep's stability is still a question. I find that while I'm in the process of configuring it, LiteStep dies more frequently than Explorer does. I can recover with Ctrl-Esc → Run → `c:\progra~1\litestep\litestep.exe` and get back to work, but the inconvenience is aggravating. As LiteStep continues to develop, this should become less of an issue. It tends to be pretty stable when you're not messing with it—as it should be, seeing as it does little more than launch programs—but if you're the tinkering type, you'll be rebooting a lot.

Installation and Configuration

You can always download the current version of LiteStep from *www.litestep.net*, along with a good selection of themes and utilities. Be sure to get the current version and any patches that may exist for it, as revisions to LiteStep seem to occur almost as frequently as with Linux.

After unzipping LiteStep, you need to run its installation program. It will prompt you for a destination directory; for the sake of clean directory structure, I suggest someplace other than the default *C:\Litestep*. I use *\Progra~1\Litestep*. (If you put it in a directory with a long filename, you have to use the short filename, or Windows won't find it the next time you boot.) After you click the Install button, it will ask you if you want it to make Litestep your default shell. I suggest you answer yes.

Unless you ever wondered why Linux didn't become really popular until 1998 and want to find out firsthand, you'll want to download a LiteStep configuration program as well. The LiteStep documentation mentions a program called LSCP, but I found one called ICE in the utilities section of *litestep.net* that I liked. I don't mind hacking a text file to customize a user environment, but creating one essentially from scratch using nothing but a text editor isn't exactly my game. I'd much rather use a configuration tool to get me going, then make adjustments by hand, if necessary.

Resist the temptation to reboot immediately after installing LiteStep to get a quick look at it. The default configuration file is unusable and you'll get a blank screen. Instead, run ICE. It'll immediately do some nice things for you, like add the Start menu to LiteStep's pop-up menu.

If you prefer a leaner and more efficient configuration file than the one ICE automatically generates for you, here's one to get you started:

```
PixmapPath C:\PROGRA~1\LITESTEP\IMAGES\

AutoHideDelay 0
HideApplication
FolderBackPix b24_folderpic.bmp
NoTaskBar
VWMNoAuto
VWMNoGathering
VWMForeColor BABCBA
VWMBackColor 707770
VWMSelBackColor A3A5A3
VWMBorderColor 707770
UsClock

HotListName "HotList"
PopupTitlePix b24_bartitles.bmp
PopupEntryPix b24_barnorms.bmp
PopupSelEntryPix b24_barsels.bmp
PopupEntryColor D3D3D3
PopupSelEntryColor D3D3D3
PopupFontFace "Verdana"
PopupFontHeight 14
NoPopupBevel
PopupSubMenuHeight 20
minpopupwidth 208

WharfTitlebarPix b24_wcap.bmp
WharfAutoUnpress
WharfNoAnim
AutoHideWharf
WharfBevelWidth 0
WharfPressOffset 1
LSTimeThemeFile C:\PROGRA~1\LITESTEP\tinclock.thm

LoadModule C:\PROGRA~1\LITESTEP\desktop.dll
LoadModule C:\PROGRA~1\LITESTEP\wharf.dll
LoadModule C:\PROGRA~1\LITESTEP\shortcut.dll
LoadModule C:\PROGRA~1\LITESTEP\hotkey.dll
LoadModule C:\PROGRA~1\LITESTEP\popup.dll

; Wharf Bar config
*Wharf Tasks b24_tasks.bmp !WharfTasks
*Wharf "Date & Time" b24_lstime.bmp @C:\PROGRA~1\LITESTEP\lstime.dll
*Wharf "VWM Top" b24_vwmtop2.bmp !None
*Wharf VWM b24_vwmbg.bmp @C:\PROGRA~1\LITESTEP\lsvwm.dll
*Wharf "VWM Bottom" b24_vwmbot.bmp !None
```

```
; Popup Menu config.
*Popup Start 17 default.bmp "!PopupFolder:C:\WINDOWS\Start Menu\Programs"
*Popup Step.rc notepad c:\PROGRA~1\litestep\step.rc
*Popup &Run !Run
*Popup Shutdown !Shutdown
*Popup Recycle LiteStep !Recycle
```

This setup doesn't do a whole lot. It sets the look and feel, gives you a Wharf bar with a clock, virtual desktop, and task list, and gives you a Start menu when you right-click on the desktop. It's begging for improvement. This example as written is designed for easy experimentation. It deliberately adds little more than a Start menu to the pop-up menu (which you get from right-clicking on the desktop). There's the *step.rc* option, which gives you the configuration file; the Run menu, in case you find yourself in need of running something not in the Start menu; a shutdown menu; and finally, a Recycle option, which reloads LiteStep so you can see the results of any configuration changes you make.

Add the lines you desire from the collection in the examples to follow, then see their effects by selecting Recycle from the pop-up menu.

Let's start by improving the pop-up menu. These lines add most of the features present in both Explorer's context menu and in Explorer's Start button. For the sake of clarity, add them after the line labeled `; Wharf Bar Config`:

```
*Popup "Display Properties" control.exe desk.cpl
*Popup System Folder
    *Popup "My Computer" explorer /root,,::{20D04FE0-3AEA-1069-A2D8-08002B30309D}
    *Popup "Control Panel" explorer /root,,::{20D04FE0-3AEA-1069-A2D8-
            08002B30309D}\::{21EC2020-3AEA-1069-A2DD-08002B30309D}
    *Popup Desktop c:\windows\desktop
*Popup ~Folder
*Popup Shutdown Folder
    *Popup Recycle !Recycle
    *Popup Logoff !Logoff
    *Popup "Shutdown Menu" !Shutdown
    *Popup Quit !Quit
*Popup ~Folder
```

The syntax of LiteStep's configuration is fairly simple, if not immediately obvious. A configuration line begins with an asterisk, followed by the type of item it defines (pop-up, Wharf, shortcut, hotkey), followed by its name (surrounded by quotation marks if it contains spaces), then the command-line arguments or the LiteStep internal command. To put a group of icons into a folder, frame them with lines that read `*Popup [folder name] Folder` and `*Popup ~folder`. The first line creates and names the folder, while the last indicates the end of the folder list.

Next, let's add more to the Wharf bar. Insert the desired lines from the next example immediately after the line labeled `; Wharf Bar Config`. The function of each line is pretty self-explanatory. If the line makes reference to Network Neighborhood, it adds Network Neighborhood. If you never used Network Neighborhood in Explorer, you won't use it in LiteStep either, so omit it. Pick what you want—LiteStep is all about taking control of your system and making it act as you want.

If you have other programs you want to add, simply copy the Notepad or Word-Pad line and use it as a template. Find or make a bitmap file to serve as an icon for the program, then substitute its name, icon, and path for the ones provided. Your possibilities are only limited by your imagination and your willingness to type. For example:

```
*Wharf "System Folder" b24_sys.bmp Folder
    *Wharf Recycle b24_recycle.bmp !Recycle
    *Wharf "Control Panel" b24_cntrlpanel.bmp explorer /root,,::{20D04FE0-3AEA-
            1069-A2D8-08002B30309D}\::{21EC2020-3AEA-1069-A2DD-08002B30309D}
    *Wharf MS-DOS b24_dos.bmp command.com
    *Wharf Explorer b24_explorer.bmp explorer.exe
    *Wharf Logoff b24_logout3.bmp !Logoff
    *Wharf "Shutdown Windows" b24_shutdown.bmp !Shutdown
*Wharf ~Folder
*Wharf "Apps Folder" b24_apps.bmp Folder
    *Wharf "Network Neighborhood" b24_netneigh2.bmp explorer /root,::{208D2C60-
            3AEA-1069-A2D7-08002B30309D}
    *Wharf Notepad b24_notepad.bmp notepad.exe
    *Wharf WordPad b24_wordpad.bmp "C:\Program Files\Accessories\WORDPAD.EXE"
*Wharf ~Folder
```

LiteStep can do shortcuts too. It's not drag-and-drop like Explorer, but it is more customizable. You can add shortcuts at will, and if My Computer and Network Neighborhood annoy you, don't type them in. Add these lines to the end of the file:

```
; Shortcuts
*Shortcut "My Computer" explorer /root,,::{20D04FE0-3AEA-1069-A2D8-08002B30309D}
*Shortcut "Network Neighborhood" b24_netneigh2.bmp explorer /root,::{208D2C60-
    3AEA-1069-A2D7-08002B30309D}
*Shortcut "Explorer" -64 -64 b24_sc_filecab1.bmp b24_sc_filecab2.bmp .none
explorer.exe
*Shortcut "DOS" -128 -64 b24_scdos1.bmp b24_scdos2.bmp .none command.com
```

LiteStep also does hotkeys. Hotkeys have always been my favorite Windows feature—in the Windows 3.1 days, it was the *only* thing I liked about Windows—so I'm glad this feature's present. If you're a command-line junkie, you probably use Explorer's Windows-R hotkey a lot to get instant access to the Run menu. I also add Windows-D to open a DOS prompt, plus a few more key combinations I find useful. If your keyboards don't have a Windows key, you can substitute other key combinations. I like to use Ctrl-Function Key combinations for hotkeys, since the only Ctrl-Function Key combination I use that's implemented by the system is Ctrl-F4 (close window). For instance, the line `*Hotkey Ctrl F3 command.com` makes Ctrl-F3 open a DOS prompt. Add these lines to the end of the file:

```
; Hotkeys
*Hotkey Win R !Run
```

```
*Hotkey Win C !Recycle
*Hotkey Win D command.com
*Hotkey Win E explorer
*Hotkey Win S !Shutdown
*Hotkey Win L !Logoff
```

Recommendations

Of all the shells available for Windows 9x, I tend to think LiteStep is the best over-all. It's nimble, configurable, and easy to use once you manage to set it up. On systems with less than 16 MB of memory, I favor EVWM. If LiteStep's configuration file doesn't scare you off, I suggest replacing Explorer with LiteStep whether you have 32 MB of RAM or 512 MB.

Of course, if none of these shells works for you, there's always Microsoft Bob. Or maybe not.

7

Optimizing DOS

Although it's somewhat hidden, DOS is still very much a part of Windows 9x, and Windows 9x depends very heavily on it, although not quite in the same manner or to the same degree as in previous versions.

Windows handles much of its own I/O, such as keyboard and mouse input as well as output to the screen. Windows still only partially handles disk I/O, however. The processes of file handling are still DOS based. Windows is also partially dependent on DOS for memory management, so Windows doesn't have complete reign over all of your system's memory. DOS gets first dibs on available memory and also handles the most fundamental pieces of memory management. Windows isn't (and never has been) a true operating system. It's safe to say that Windows does about 90% of the things an operating system does, but for the remaining 10%, Windows relies on DOS, which still represents the foundation of the Windows system. While a strong foundation doesn't necessarily ensure a strong building, a weak foundation does ensure a weak building. Windows 9x runs better when its DOS is configured correctly. The more marginal your system, the more vital this element becomes.

But by the same token, Windows programs will pretty much run no matter what we do—we can take a live-and-let-live attitude towards DOS if that's our only concern. It's when we try to run those pesky DOS games that the old DOS configuration nightmares come to bite us. What DOS games? Come on. I still get a kick out of the old, original EGA Railroad Tycoon, and I have the original Civilization as well. After the computer mops up the place with me in Alpha Centauri, I like to go back to the game that started it all and remember how good I was when artificial intelligence was predictable. And just try to find an adventure game of today that's as funny as the Secret of Monkey Island series. Those games are old and out of print, but I still like them. Giving those up makes as much sense as giving up my

Cars records just because the group broke up in 1987. I like some newer DOS games too. I think Redneck Rampage and Carmageddon are good games. I know I'm not the only one who still plays the occasional DOS game. I see them next to the video rentals section of my supermarket, priced from $4.95 on up. Somebody's still buying them, but I suspect more people are buying them than playing them. The most challenging part of many DOS games is just getting them to run.

I can help you get those DOS programs running, and Windows will run better in the process. Sound like a good deal? Good. Then let's just dive right into the three major strategies for getting DOS games to run: trying it, running the program in DOS mode, and running the program under an earlier version of DOS. (The process is the same for other DOS programs as well, but the majority of people don't care about any DOS software besides games anymore, and games tend to be the most difficult programs to get running.)

Try It

Microsoft's plan was for most DOS programs to just run under Windows 9x without any special tricks. This works more often than it seems—the overwhelming majority of DOS programs will run without any difficulties. The problem is 90% of the people want to run the 10% of DOS games that push the system and cause problems, and they couldn't care less about WordStar 1.0 (they care about it even less than they care about Atarisoft's 1984 port of Donkey Kong that ran in CGA), so there's a perception that Windows 9x doesn't run DOS programs well.

So the first step is to insert that crusty old disk or CD and install the software (if you haven't already), then open the program's directory in Explorer, find the executable, double-click on it, and see what happens. You might actually find that Microsoft's promise that DOS games will run more smoothly than ever before is true.

"Insufficient Memory?" I Have 64 Megs!

There are few things more frustrating and perplexing than having some punk game from 1992 tell you that your fire-breathing 550 MHz Pentium III with 256 MB of RAM doesn't have enough memory for it to run. Try telling the game that when it was written, your PC would have been classified a supercomputer. It doesn't care.

It doesn't care because the only thing it cares about is the first 640K of memory, and if it wants 619K of that memory and you only have 584K of it free, the game won't run. It doesn't care if you have a grand total of 192 MB free. That's like going to the computer store wanting to buy a $499 eMachines PC/monitor/printer bundle, only to find out they've sold out of those, but they've got 52 tangerine-colored iMacs in stock.

The process of building optimal *autoexec.bat* and *config.sys* files is a gradual one. The files most manufacturers deliver with their PCs are worse than no file at all, which is why in Chapter 2, *First Steps*, I suggest renaming the two files so your system stops using them. Starting with Chapter 3, *Disk Optimization*, we start building new replacement files from scratch, starting with two SET statements in *autoexec.bat*. In this chapter, we conclude the process.

An optimal *config.sys* file starts with three lines that form the basis of DOS memory management (whether you have anything more than that depends on your system). So, fire up Notepad, then enter the following lines:

```
Device=c:\windows\himem.sys
Device=c:\windows\command\emm386.exe noems
DOS=high,umb
```

The second line assumes you followed Chapter 3's advice and moved various Windows executables into *C:\Windows\Command*. If you didn't, substitute the line:

```
Device=c:\windows\emm386.exe noems
```

for the line above. Now, to save the file, select File → Save As → c:\config.sys.

You're not quite done optimizing yet. In the [386Enh] section of *system.ini*, add the line LocalLoadHigh=1. This change will make Windows make more use of upper memory.

A Windows 9x PC with no *autoexec.bat* or *config.sys* typically has a little over 580K of conventional memory (the PC's first 640K of memory) available for running programs. A Windows 9x PC with the settings presented in this section will have anywhere from 603K to 619K of conventional memory available.

Different Types of Memory

Due to the peculiarities of PC architecture, PCs actually have seven types of memory: conventional, expanded (EMS), extended (XMS), upper, high, DOS protected (DPMI), and Virtual Control Program Interface (VCPI) memory.

Conventional memory

These different types of memory are a direct result of the PC's history and the perceived need for backward compatibility. The Intel 8088 CPU, used in the original IBM PC in 1981, was a pseudo 16-bit processor (internally, it was a 16-bit CPU, but it had an 8-bit data bus to cut costs), capable of addressing a single megabyte of memory. IBM tried several different memory configurations, but eventually decided to reserve the first 640K for system RAM, and to map other necessary things such as system ROM, and the ROM and RAM on expansion cards, into the upper 384K of memory. This decision is the source of Bill Gates' infamous quote, "640K ought to be enough memory for anybody."

Expanded memory specification (EMS)

Gates was right, for a time. But when Lotus introduced its revolutionary spreadsheet Lotus 1-2-3, accountants began to create worksheets that taxed this 640K limit. So Lotus teamed up with Intel and Microsoft to invent a convoluted scheme to put more memory in a PC. They couldn't move the 640K boundary up any, so they mapped off a 64K area in that upper 384K of memory. They then used that 64K area as a window into a block of memory up to 32 MB in size. Lotus modified 1-2-3 to use this new type of memory, which eventually came to be known as *expanded memory*, or EMS, to hold data. Other developers soon followed suit. It's been nearly a decade since PCs shipped with physical expanded memory; in the early 1990s, software developers started to emulate expanded memory by using extended memory, which is explained next.

Extended memory specification (XMS)

The advent of the Intel 80286 processor added some more types of memory. The 286 was a fully 16-bit processor, capable of addressing up to 4 MB of RAM. It introduced a new mode of operation called *protected mode*, in which it could address its full amount of memory. Intel knew that backward compatibility would be a must if they were to sell this chip to IBM, however—they learned their lesson with the ill-fated Intel 80186, which really does exist, but never caught on because it wasn't completely compatible with its predecessor. So the 286 was capable of running in another mode, where it was nothing more than a fast 8088. This mode came to be known as *real mode*. Real mode was to be used to run DOS, while protected mode was intended to open the door to more powerful operating systems like Unix. Microsoft even produced and marketed an operating system called Xenix, which was a version of Unix for the 286. Software developers eventually found a way to switch the 286 between real mode and protected mode, gaining access to a full 4 MB of memory all at once. Memory accessed by switching into and out of protected mode came to be known as *extended memory*, or XMS.

Upper memory blocks (UMBs)

The Intel 80386 added some more tricks, including the ability to remap memory. DOS was getting bigger, and DOS programs were getting bigger, and it was getting impossible to keep everything you needed within DOS's 640K limit. But even a fully loaded system didn't come close to using all of the 384K chunk of memory IBM had reserved, so software developers began to use the 386's ability to map RAM into unused blocks of that area and move pieces of DOS into that area. The memory between 640K and 1 MB became known as *upper memory*.

High memory area (HMA)

California software developer Quarterdeck (now part of Symantec) soon came up with another trick. They found a bug in the 286 chip, also present in the 386, that allowed them to address the first 64K of extended memory in the same fashion as conventional or upper memory. This 64K area came to be known as the HMA, or *high memory area.*

DOS Protected Mode Interface (DPMI) memory

Addressing large amounts of memory via EMS or XMS proved cumbersome, however, so game developers started switching the processor into protected mode and leaving it there. This was unusual at the time; protected mode had previously been the exclusive realm of Windows and operating systems like Xenix or OS/2. Memory addressed in this fashion came to be known as DOS Protected Mode Interface (DPMI) memory.

Virtual Control Program Interface (VCPI) memory

VCPI is another method, not as commonly used, that allocates memory as either EMS or XMS memory. Windows 9x doesn't support VCPI; so programs that use it must run in DOS mode.

Memory usage

DOS programs generally run in conventional memory. However, upper memory and high memory operate in the same fashion as conventional memory; a program intended for conventional memory will run in one of these other two types without special tricks. Windows 9x by default loads parts of its DOS into high memory. Upper memory is most useful for things like device drivers and terminate-and-stay-resident programs—in other words, the stuff you load in *config. sys* and *autoexec.bat.* (*autoexec.bat* is related to the *autoexec* files used by games like Quake II and SiN in naming convention only; they're not interchangeable.)

When a DOS program needs more than 640K of memory, it uses one of the other schemes. A program will use only one other type of memory, however.

An Alternative to Using EMM386

The second line of the *config.sys* files presented in this chapter loads a file called EMM386, which manages upper memory and expanded memory for DOS and Windows systems.

EMM386 creates a messy situation. Windows runs a bit better when it has some upper memory to work with, and some DOS programs won't run at all without upper memory freeing up some valuable conventional memory. EMM386 has some drawbacks, however. It works by turning blocks of extended memory into upper memory, so you lose a block of extended memory in the process. EMM386 also has a decent-sized footprint. You'll consume about 300K worth of conventional and extended memory in order to create about 150K of upper memory.

That's not very efficient, but we put up with it since DOS games only need a fraction of the total amount of memory available anyway. But Windows needs every byte of memory it can get.

Modern PCs actually do have RAM in the zone between 640K and 1 MB. Some BIOSs remap this memory, but the majority of them just mark it as reserved. They use some of it to shadow your PC's ROM chips (RAM is much faster than ROM, so this speeds the system up when it's accessing ROM routines) and let the rest of it go to waste.

In late 1995, the technically oriented German computer magazine *c't* published a memory manager called UMBPCI that took advantage of this waste, implementing UMBs by switching this unused memory back on. The magazine's published version had problems and it supported a very limited number of systems, but German programmer Uwe Sieber took the source code, cleaned it up, added support for most Pentium-compatible chipsets, and re-released it. You can download the revised version (not supported by *c't*) from *www.uwe-sieber.de/umbpci_e.html*.

If your system supports UMBPCI, it has several significant advantages over EMM386. It uses a scant 240 bytes of memory, leaves all of your extended memory alone, and doesn't have to switch between real mode and protected mode to access upper memory. This configuration makes your system run faster than it would with EMM386, yet gives you nearly all of EMM386's benefits.

The easiest way to determine whether your system supports UMBPCI is to just try it. Download it, copy 'the file *umbpci.sys* into *C:\Windows\Command*, then, if present, pull the line `Device=c:\windows\command\emm386.exe` from *config.sys* and add the following three lines to the beginning of the file:

```
DOS=high,umb
Device=c:\windows\himem.sys
Device=c:\windows\command\umbpci.sys
```

Then restart. If UMBPCI doesn't support your chipset, you'll get an error message saying so. If UMBPCI does support your chipset (chances are it will if your system is a Pentium-class PC or better), you've just gained yourself some memory. The amount will vary from system to system—one of my PCs gives me 84K of additional memory, while another gives me 160K. Every little bit counts.

If you have DOS games that use EMS memory (check your documentation), you need to enable EMS. UMBPCI doesn't provide EMS services (that's one of the reasons why it's small and fast). That's fine, because Windows does, so long as you add a line to *C:\Windows\system.ini* and you exclude the EMS page frame (C800-D7FF) from the *umbpci.sys* line in *config.sys*. For instance, if I were to use this line in *config.sys*:

```
Device=c:\windows\command\umbpci.sys /i=d800-efff
```

and then add this line to *system.ini* in the section labeled [386enh]:

```
EMMPageFrame=c800
```

Windows would then be able to provide EMS services to any DOS programs that need it.

When DOS Programs Are Sluggish

If one or more of your DOS programs execute without error messages, but so slowly that you don't feel it's appropriate to say the program is "running," you need to play around with their individual settings.

For example, Redneck Rampage plays decently in Windows 95 on my PCs, but it could be better. I have it installed in *F:\Program Files\Games\Redneck*, so I open that directory. The executable is called *Rr.exe*. I right-click on *Rr.exe* and select Create Shortcut. Having a shortcut allows me to play around with the memory settings and other things. After creating the shortcut, right-click on it and select Properties. This will bring up a tabbed window with settings galore.

The first thing you want to do is select the Program tab. There's a checkbox labeled "Close on exit." Check that; you don't need extra empty windows hanging around. While you're there, click the Advanced tab. If the game complains about running inside Windows, check the box labeled "Prevent MS-DOS–based programs from detecting Windows."

Now select the Memory tab. In the conventional memory field, you'll want the total set to Auto. Set the initial environment low: 256 should be sufficient. Checking the Protected box can make the game more reliable, isolating it somewhat from the rest of the system. It sometimes hinders performance, however, so experiment with the setting.

The other types of memory will vary from game to game. As I said before, a game will use a maximum of two types of memory: conventional and something else. Check your game's documentation to figure out what kinds of memory it uses. In the case of Redneck Rampage, it's like most first-person 3D shooters, using DPMI memory. So I set EMS and XMS to None, and I set DPMI to 16384. Specifying the correct amount of memory considerably decreases the amount of disk thrashing that takes place during a game.

Finally, proceed to the Screen tab. Some DOS games can run in a window, but most run more quickly when run full-screen. Running DOS games in a window on the desktop is more of a novelty than anything else anyway—who wants to run a game in a small 640×480 window occupying a little piece of the desktop when you can run it full-screen? You'll also want to take a look at the Performance settings. Fast ROM emulation can actually slow down some games; turn it off if the game is still sluggish after switching it to full-screen mode. The same goes for Dynamic memory allocation.

Once you get settings that work, you can drag the shortcut to the Start menu to facilitate easier program launching. Most DOS programs will run much better after tuning these settings. The default behavior of autodetecting memory makes Windows 9x more user-friendly, but it comes at the price of reduced performance.

Running DOS Programs in DOS Mode

Sometimes a stubborn DOS program just won't run right within Windows 9x, no matter how you tune the settings. Some programs just don't like to share memory space and CPU time, especially with a big hog like Windows. Strangely, I have more problems with this with older programs than I do with newer ones. Redneck Rampage complains about running inside Windows, but it will run, and it runs reasonably well (though admittedly, it is better in DOS mode). The original Jeopardy! from Sharedata, copyrighted 1987, is a different story. I can always win at Jeopardy! because the countdown timer, which is supposed to be 10 seconds, is closer to 30 seconds when I run it in Windows. So I get plenty of time to decide whether there's any chance at all of me being able to come up with an answer. Then I get forever and a day to enter it. Problem is, a standard game with as many questions as the half-hour TV game show takes closer to an hour and 15 minutes to plow through. The only explanation I can think of is that Jeopardy! was designed in the day when the 4.77 MHz 8088 CPU was the norm and an 8 MHz 80286 was fast; Jeopardy! is seeing my PC's faster processor and trying to compensate for the speed, but Windows is taking up some of the CPU time, so Jeopardy! ends up overcompensating.

The trick is to return to the program's shortcut, right-click, hit Properties, then go to the Program tab and hit Advanced. This time, we check the box labeled MS-DOS mode.

Since we blew away the computer's original MS-DOS configuration, you need to click the radio button labeled "Specify a new MS-DOS configuration." If your computer had *config.sys* and *autoexec.bat* files that worked well for DOS programs, you can just copy and paste them into the appropriate text fields. If you didn't, you'll have to generate your own. Fortunately, that isn't very difficult.

config.sys

Every *config.sys* file should start with the following three lines:

```
Device=c:\windows\himem.sys
Device=c:\windows\command\emm386.exe ram hiscan
Dos=high,umb
```

This sets up upper memory and instructs DOS to use it. You may substitute *umbpci.sys* for *emm386.exe* if you wish, provided your game doesn't need EMS. If your game uses the CD-ROM or DVD-ROM drive, you need to add a driver for that. Follow the instructions that came with your drive. Here's a typical line:

```
Devicehigh=c:\windows\command\atapicd.sys /d:cdrom00
```

You may put the CD-ROM drivers anywhere you like, so long as you specify the path. The key is getting the filename right, and using the same /d parameter on both the CD-ROM driver in *config.sys* and the *mscdex.exe* program line in *autoexec.bat*.

If your sound card requires a device driver in *config.sys*, add it as well. Consult your documentation.

autoexec.bat

An *autoexec.bat* for games tends to be pretty simple. It just needs to load sound drivers, set sound parameters, load CD-ROM extensions and possibly a mouse driver.

The sound drivers vary; consult your sound card's documentation. Some sound cards don't require anything besides a **SET** parameter, while others may require you to launch an executable file. Check your documentation.

Mouse drivers are usually very easy; most mice come with a disk containing an executable file, usually called *mouse.exe*. Copy it to *C:\Windows\Command* and add it to the *autoexec.bat* file.

The CD-ROM extension is completely standardized; at least in *autoexec.bat*. You launch a program called *mscdex.exe* (which is part of Windows), and pass it the same /d parameter you passed the device driver in *config.sys*.

The only other thing you have to remember is to precede each executable file with **LH**, to load it into upper memory.

There's one more thing you'll probably want to consider. In DOS, there is no disk cache unless you load it yourself, and performance will suffer. For optimal performance, you need to load *smartdrv.exe*, and give it a 2 MB disk cache (the maximum amount it permits).

Here's a typical *autoexec.bat*:

```
Lh mscdex.exe /d:cdrom00
Lh mouse.exe
Set blaster=a220 i7 d1 t2
Lh smartdrv.exe 2048
```

When you launch a program that's configured to operate this way, Windows closes all other programs, unloads itself except for a 4K stub, kicks into DOS mode with the configuration you specified, then launches the program. When the program exits, Windows reloads.

If You've Lost Your Drivers and/or Documentation

Don't despair if you can't find drivers or documentation for your mouse, sound card, and CD-ROM drive. A number of web sites provide links to drivers and manuals for these peripherals, including those whose manufacturers have gone out of business. Check out these sites:

www.geocities.com/SiliconValley/4421/drivers.html
   CD-ROM drivers

www.drivershq.com
   CD-ROM, mouse, and sound card drivers

www.windrivers.com
   CD-ROM, mouse, and sound card drivers

A Pseudo-Dual Boot

As long as you're using UMBPCI as an upper memory manager, I can't imagine that you'll run short of conventional memory for running programs in DOS mode (on my PCs, I get a maximum executable program size of 620K and the largest DOS programs use 619K). This number jumps to 628K if I select Command Prompt Only from the Windows boot menu. But there might be reasons why you wouldn't want Windows to load. Maybe there are DOS programs you find yourself using almost as frequently as you use Windows and you have no need to run them in a multitasking environment.

Whatever your reasons might be, Windows 9x retains the capability of inserting boot menus into *config.sys* that was introduced in MS-DOS 6.0. Since Microsoft never documented the technique very well, this practice never became very common, and as a result, DOS gamers tended to shuffle a never-ending pile of boot disks optimized for each game. Running the games from icons in the Windows GUI is one effective method of freeing yourself from that stack of disks; implementing a boot menu is another.

If you've looked at *system.ini* or *win.ini*, you've probably noticed the files are divided into sections, with each section having a header. *config.sys* also has different sections, though most people never bother to put anything but the main section into it.

Here's the structure for a boot menu–enabled *config.sys*:

```
[menu]
menuitem=Win95, Windows 95
```

```
menuitem=DOS, DOS with XMS
menuitem=EMS, DOS with EMS

[common]
device=c:\windows\himem.sys

[Win95]
device=c:\windows\command\umbpci.sys /I=c800-efff
dos=high,umb
buffers=13
files=99

[DOS]
device=c:\windows\command\umbpci.sys /I=c800-efff
dos=high,umb
devicehigh=c:\windows\command\atapicd.sys /d:cdrom00
files=30

[EMS]
device=c:\windows\command\emm386.exe ram
dos=high,umb
devicehigh=c:\windows\command\atapicd.sys /d:cdrom00
files=30
```

The section names are completely determined by your boot menu items. The first menuitem parameter is the name of the item's section, while the second parameter is the menu text. If you have *config.sys* settings that work for certain games, nothing stops you from creating game-specific boot menus.

The [common] section is always executed. Since all of these configurations need *himem.sys*, I put it in the [common] section to reduce repetition.

A boot menu–enabled *autoexec.bat* is a bit trickier. *config.sys* sets an environment variable based on the boot selection. There are a number of ways to act upon that variable, but by far the easiest is to simply use a goto statement. Put any statements you want part of all the configurations at the beginning before the goto statement. Then, you can just add section names, preceding them with a colon (:) like this:

```
@echo off
Set temp=f:\temp
Set tmp=f:\temp
Goto %config%

:Win95
win
goto end

:DOS
lh mscdex.exe /d:cdrom00
lh mouse.exe
Set blaster=a220 i7 d1 t2
```

```
Lh smartdrv.exe 2048
Goto end

:EMS
lh mscdex.exe /d:cdrom00
lh mouse.exe
Set blaster=a220 i7 d1 t2
Lh smartdrv.exe 2048
Goto end

:end
```

Of course, if you're comfortable with the concepts of program flow, you can get fancy with your goto statements. If you're not comfortable, don't worry about it. Just plug your *autoexec.bat* sections into the file, framing them with a label at the beginning and a goto end statement at the end.

Since *autoexec.bat* is just a batch file, if your sections are game-specific, they can even include the commands to launch the game. A PC with several DOS games installed and a well-thought-out boot menu can be every bit as easy to use as a game console—and with a lot of the games, you won't even have to worry about changing CDs. Just reboot and choose another game.

There is one more thing you'll have to do to enable the boot menus. By default, Windows will go ahead and load no matter what. You'll have to edit *msdos.sys* to change this behavior. Add (or modify) the line BootGUI=0 to disable the automatic loading of Windows. Remember, you have to make the file editable with the command:

```
attrib -r -s -h msdos.sys
```

before editing, and change it back with the command:

```
attrib +r +s +h msdos.sys
```

before restarting.

Dual-Booting Windows 9x and True DOS

Some programs just refuse to run properly under Windows 9x, even in DOS mode. Usually such programs rely, for whatever reason, on quirks like undocumented system calls or bugs that happen to be present in specific versions of DOS but aren't present in Windows 9x's DOS. When this happens, you have no choice but to run the program under an honest-to-goodness DOS. You can go about this a couple of ways. You can make bootable DOS disks or CDs, but then you have to keep track of them and remember to use them. If your *C:* drive is formatted FAT16, you can actually run DOS.

Dual-Booting Caldera DR-DOS

DR-DOS was a popular alternative DOS among power users during the late 1980s and early 1990s because it was fast, stable, and always a step ahead of Microsoft when it came to included features. It was also highly compatible—DR-DOS would run some obscure DOS programs that newer versions of MS-DOS wouldn't run.

With a small modification, DR-DOS is even compatible with Windows 9x. Caldera has written a small TSR that allows Windows 9x to run on top of DR-DOS rather than atop the included MS-DOS 7. Caldera claims Windows 9x is about 10% faster when run in this fashion. However, there is no word on when or if this TSR will be released to the public.

DR-DOS is a fascinating product. It started life at Digital Research (the DR in DR-DOS), which was the company that produced the popular 1970s operating system CP/M and an early Windows competitor called GEM that was popular in the mid-1980s. MS-DOS itself started off as a close CP/M clone, so it wasn't much of a stretch for CP/M to evolve into an MS-DOS clone. It's because of this CP/M legacy that DR-DOS bears a 1976 copyright date.

In the early 1990s, network operating system maker Novell (of NetWare fame) was looking to expand its business into other areas and challenge Microsoft in size and prominence, so they bought out Digital Research, continued development of DR-DOS, and eventually released their efforts as Novell DOS 7. The offering was revolutionary—it added multitasking and peer-to-peer networking to DOS—but it gained little market share. Novell eventually divested itself of DR-DOS and other acquisitions it made during this time frame and returned back to its core business. Linux vendor Caldera, with backing from Novell founder Ray Noorda, acquired the rights to DR-DOS in late 1996 and resumed its development. Since then, DR-DOS has gained acceptance in embedded systems and refurbished PCs. You can download it from *www.lineo.com* to evaluate it for your purposes; after 90 days you must either delete it or pay a registration of $29 for the version without networking or $39 for the version with it.

Dual-booting DR-DOS with Windows 9x is extremely easy: simply install it, then issue the command LOADER at the command prompt, and it will implement a boot menu that allows you to choose between DR-DOS and Windows at bootup.

Unfortunately, though DR-DOS is an easy choice, it may not be the best one. Many of the undocumented system calls and bugs that aren't present in Windows 9x aren't likely to be in DR-DOS either. DR-DOS always had a high degree of compatibility with utilities and productivity applications, but its games compatibility wasn't quite as high. If you want to be able to multitask DOS applications without Windows' overhead, DR-DOS is for you, but if you just want to get a stubborn game working, DR-DOS may not do the job any better than what you already own.

Dual-Booting MS-DOS or PC DOS 5.x or 6.x

Windows 95, 95A and 98 will happily dual-boot with MS-DOS versions 5 and up, as well as with PC DOS versions 5 and up (IBM's PC DOS is derived from MS-DOS and offers an extremely high degree of compatibility). By design, DOS should be installed before you install Windows. But if you didn't know you needed DOS when you installed Windows 9x, this could be a problem. The workaround isn't well documented, but it's pretty easy.

Make a backup copy of your DOS installation disk, then open a command prompt and enter the following lines:

```
Attrib -r -s -h a:\msdos.sys
Attrib -r -s -h a:\io.sys
Attrib -r -s -h a:\command.com
Copy a:\msdos.sys c:\msdos.dos
Copy a:\io.sys c:\io.dos
Copy a:\command.com c:\command.dos
Attrib +r +s +h a:\msdos.sys
Attrib +r +s +h a:\io.sys
Attrib +r +s a:\command.com
Attrib +r +s +h c:\msdos.dos
Attrib +r +s +h c:\io.dos
Attrib +r +s +h c:\command.dos
```

Create a usable *autoexec.bat* and *config.sys* (the DOS utilities in *C:\Windows\ Command* will work with earlier versions of DOS, so there's no need to install the full DOS 5.x or DOS 6.x package), and name them *autoexec.dos* and *config.dos*. Finally, add (or modify) the line **BootMulti=1** to *msdos.sys* to enable dual-boot. Remember, you have to make the file editable with the command:

```
attrib -r -s -h msdos.sys
```

before editing, and change it back with the command:

```
attrib +r +s +h msdos.sys
```

before restarting.

Windows 95 OSR2 (and its variants) disabled dual booting because they were intended for OEM distribution—I suppose Microsoft assumed people who bought new PCs wouldn't want to run any DOS programs that were incompatible with Windows 95—so if you have this version of Windows, you'll have to head to *www. tu-chemnitz.de/~jwes/win95boot.html* to download a small utility by Jörg Weske that replaces the OSR2.x boot code with code that is capable of dual-booting.

Windows 9x uses the same boot menu commands as DOS 6.x, so if you dual-boot with one of these versions of DOS, you can put a boot menu in *config.dos* and *autoexec.dos*.

Tweaks You'll Want Even If You Never Run DOS Software

Even if you never run DOS software, you'll want to download *umbpci.sys* and add it to your *config.sys*. It will increase your available memory slightly, because Windows by default wants to load certain parameters into upper memory. UMBPCI allows it to do this without the slowdowns associated with *emm386.exe* and other memory managers that emulate upper memory blocks by using XMS memory.

There are two lines you can add to *config.sys* that tend to make Windows a bit more stable. They are:

```
Files=99
Buffers=13
```

Windows 9x's disk caching makes the buffers largely obsolete. A buffer count of 13 tends to solve some obscure memory configuration problems, so it's a good habit to use that count. The buffers serve no other useful purpose, and a count of 13 uses very little memory (Windows 9x's default count is 20).

The line `Files=99` refers to the number of files Windows can have open at once. The default setting of 30 is far too low for a multitasking operating system. Windows is more stable with a count of 99; if you have *umbpci.sys* installed, go ahead and crank the count up to 255. This uses 14K of memory from a pool that you wouldn't normally use anyway. That's a small price to pay for fewer crashes.

The default of 30 is more than adequate for DOS games.

What to Do When DOS Games Run Too Fast

What could be more frustrating than spending an hour configuring your system to run some DOS game, only to find it runs so fast on your system as to be unplayable? Some DOS games, unfortunately, are written for specific-speed systems, and if the game was designed for a 16 MHz 386SX, it's just not going to be playable on a newer 400 MHz system.

I remember when a good friend bought his first PC in November 1996. We spent a good part of the weekend running around, shopping for the best deals on the best components, and we ended up building a pretty nice system for the time: a 100 MHz AMD K5 processor on a nice Asus motherboard with a 1.2 GB hard drive and 16 MBs of RAM. We installed it to dual-boot Windows 95 and OS/2 4.0, and we spent some time optimizing both operating systems. For the cost of a Pentium 75, he was getting the performance of a typical Pentium 133. So, what programs did he want me to install first on this smokin' new system? Adobe Photoshop? No.

He pulled out a small pile of disks he'd been saving for just this occasion, once he got a PC of his own: the original Railroad Tycoon, and an old DOS shareware multiplayer game called Tank Wars.

Getting Railroad Tycoon to run was no problem, but Tank Wars was another story. It ran too well. Tank Wars was an updated version of the old, old game Artillery, where you entered an angle and the amount of power behind your shot and tried to blow up your opponent. You adjusted the angle of your shot with the arrow keys on the keyboard. The problem was, at 100 MHz, a super-brief tap of the key could adjust the angle of your shot by 90 degrees or more. In a valiant effort to slow the game down, we launched every program on the system and tried to involve each of them in some time-consuming task to chew up CPU cycles. Even that didn't help much. It's funny how it's sometimes easier to get the computer to run faster than it is to get it to run slower.

Fortunately, there are a variety of slowdown programs available that all work pretty much the same way. Usually you execute the slowdown program before you execute your game, and the slowdown program grabs one of your PC's timing loops and executes meaningless code designed just to waste your CPU's time. Not all slowdown programs work equally well on all systems, so you may need to try different programs to make a specific game work correctly. Using one of these programs allows you to run misbehaving games in something more closely resembling the environment they were designed for, without crippling your system the rest of the time:

Slowdown

A freeware program by U.S. programmer Bret Johnson; available at *oak. oakland.edu/pub/simtelnet/msdos/sysutl/slodn101.zip.*

Bremze

A $10 shareware program by Latvian programmer Ansis Ataols Berzins; available from *ansis.folklora.lv/bremze/* or *oak.oakland.edu/pub/simtelnet/msdos/ sysutl/bremz500.zip.*

Mo'Slo

A $15 shareware program by U.S. programmer David Perrell; available from *www.hpaa.com/moslo/moslotry.asp.*

The caveat to these programs is they tend to make your entire system sluggish. So if you're playing an old game inside a DOS box within Windows, rather than in DOS mode, your entire system will slow down. I suggest you quit most or all other programs while running a DOS game with a slowdown program.

Putting It into Practice

Theory is nice, but there's nothing more useful than a real-world example. Even if you don't own or have any desire to own any of the five games I use as examples, it's much easier to adapt existing settings than it is to create new ones.

With that in mind, I dug out five DOS games (Chuck Yeager's Air Combat, Seven Cities of Gold, Redneck Rampage, Populous II, and Ultima VII) and installed them. These games represent a wide variety of system requirements. Yeager is a very old game that uses nothing but conventional memory. Seven Cities of Gold uses XMS, Redneck Rampage uses DPMI, Populous II uses EMS, and Ultima VII uses a proprietary memory management scheme called Voodoo (not to be confused with 3Dfx's line of 3D accelerators) that isn't compatible with EMM386.

On my system, Seven Cities of Gold ran pretty well without any special hocus-pocus. Redneck Rampage has always been acceptable from within Windows 9x even though it complains—the biggest annoyance with Rampage is that accidentally hitting the Windows key on your keyboard in the middle of gameplay kills the game. Yeager acted like it was going to play, but always crashed eventually. Populous II complained that it couldn't find any EMS memory even after I enabled EMS in *system.ini*. Ultima VII just wanted to go straight into DOS mode, no questions asked—it didn't even try to run inside Windows.

The key to making DOS games run, whether it's by specifying *config.sys* and *autoexec.bat* settings in program icons or building a boot menu, is to study the program's system requirements.

Chuck Yeager's Air Combat (and Other Conventional-Memory Games)

Very old DOS games that just use conventional memory may be among the most problematic under Windows, but they don't take much work to get running properly. To be on the safe side, you want to use memory management software to make as much conventional memory available as possible, and if your sound card uses a device driver or TSR to provide Sound Blaster emulation you will need to load that (check your sound card's documentation). If the game uses a CD-ROM driver, load it, but most games of this vintage don't. If the game needs a mouse (Yeager doesn't), add your mouse driver to *autoexec.bat*.

Here are *config.sys* settings that worked for me on this game:

```
Device=c:\windows\himem.sys
Device=c:\windows\command\umbpci.sys /I=c800-efff
DOS=high,umb
```

And here are the corresponding *autoexec.bat* settings:

```
Set temp=f:\temp
Set tmp=f:\temp
Set blaster=a220 i7 d1 t2
Lh smartdrv.exe 4096
```

Substitute the following for the second line in *config.sys* if your system is incompatible with UMBPCI:

```
device=c:\windows\command\emm386.exe noems
```

A disk cache probably isn't really necessary with this game, but I load it anyway because it isn't doing any harm.

Seven Cities of Gold (and Other XMS Games)

Games that use XMS memory are very easy to configure—no different, really, from conventional-memory games.

Here are *config.sys* settings that worked for me on this game:

```
Device=c:\windows\himem.sys
Device=c:\windows\command\umbpci.sys /I=c800-efff
DOS=high,umb
```

And here are the corresponding *autoexec.bat* settings:

```
Set temp=f:\temp
Set tmp=f:\temp
Set blaster=a220 i7 d1 t2
Lh smartdrv.exe 4096
```

Substitute the following for the second line in *config.sys* if your system is incompatible with UMBPCI:

```
device=c:\windows\command\emm386.exe noems
```

Populous II (and Other EMS Games)

Games that use EMS require a different bag of tricks. It's possible to configure UMBPCI to provide upper-memory services and EMM386 to provide EMS services, but it's easier to just use EMM386 for everything. You would theoretically get better performance from UMBPCI, but most DOS games won't benefit from the extra performance. If the DOS game requirements are less than a 486DX4-100, don't bother—the game already has to use compensation to slow the computer down. You don't need to make the slowdown engine work any harder. (I know, normally this is blasphemy, but running seven-year-old games requires a different mentality than running the very newest stuff.)

Here are *config.sys* settings that worked for me on this game:

```
Device=c:\windows\himem.sys
Device=c:\windows\command\emm386.exe ram
DOS=high,umb
```

And here are the corresponding *autoexec.bat* settings:

```
Set temp=f:\temp
Set tmp=f:\temp
Set blaster=a220 i7 d1 t2
Lh smartdrv.exe 4096
```

Redneck Rampage (and Other DPMI Games)

Of all the games here, Redneck Rampage is the only one that even comes close to pushing a modern system. This game actually uses the mouse and CD-ROM drive, unlike the others listed here, but its configuration really isn't very complicated. This configuration assumes your CD-ROM and mouse drivers are located in *C:\ Windows\Command.*

Here are *config.sys* settings that worked for me on this game:

```
Device=c:\windows\himem.sys
Device=c:\windows\command\umbpci.sys /I=c800-efff
DOS=high,umb
Devicehigh=c:\windows\command\atapicd.sys /d:cdrom00
```

And here are the corresponding *autoexec.bat* settings:

```
Set temp=f:\temp
Set tmp=f:\temp
Set blaster=a220 i7 d1 t2
Lh mouse.exe
Lh mscdex.exe /d:cdrom00
Lh smartdrv.exe 4096
```

If you need to be able to network your computers for a multiplayer game, add the command NET START NWLINK to *autoexec.bat.*

Ultima VII (and Other Anomalies)

Ultima VII is the kind of game that frustrates users, prompts people to take software back to the store demanding a refund, and sells lots of books. It's part of an acclaimed series that's sold truckload after truckload of copies since the early 1980s, and once you get it up and running it's terribly addictive, but it's extremely difficult to install and run under Windows 95.

Here are *config.sys* settings that worked for me on this game:

```
Device=c:\windows\himem.sys
DOS=high
```

And here are the corresponding *autoexec.bat* settings:

```
Set temp=f:\temp
Set tmp=f:\temp
Mouse.exe
```

Ultima VII handles most things on its own, which is the reason for the minimalist *autoexec.bat* and *config.sys*. In fact, the game functions with an empty *config.sys* and an *autoexec.bat* that does nothing but load a mouse driver. These settings are slightly more optimal. With these settings, Ultima VII will operate, but since it was designed for 386-class CPUs, the graphics run far too fast. To run Ultima VII properly on a modern PC, you will have to use a slowdown program like one of those mentioned earlier in this chapter.

The best thing to do when you find a game that just doesn't want to run well or at all is to hit the Web, type the game's name into your favorite search engine, and see what you find. Most popular games have web pages dedicated to them, and most of them will include instructions on getting them to run with Windows 9x.

A Boot Menu for These Games

You can either enter these settings directly into the program icons' Advanced Program Settings windows, or you can use the known good settings to create a boot menu for them. Simply use this example as a pattern, plugging your games' settings into each file under their own headings.

Here's a *config.sys* boot menu for these five games:

```
[menu]
menuitem=yeager, Chuck Yeager's Air Combat
menuitem=7cog, Seven Cities of Gold
menuitem=populous2, Populous II
menuitem=redneck, Redneck Rampage
menuitem=ultima7, Ultima VII
menuitem=Win95, Windows 95

[yeager]
Device=c:\windows\himem.sys
Device=c:\windows\command\umbpci.sys /I=c800-efff
DOS=high,umb

[7cog]
Device=c:\windows\himem.sys
Device=c:\windows\command\umbpci.sys /I=c800-efff
DOS=high,umb

[populous2]
Device=c:\windows\himem.sys
Device=c:\windows\command\emm386.exe ram
DOS=high,umb
```

```
[redneck]
Device=c:\windows\himem.sys
Device=c:\windows\command\umbpci.sys /I=c800-efff
DOS=high,umb
Devicehigh=c:\windows\command\atapicd.sys /d:cdrom00

[ultima7]
Device=c:\windows\himem.sys
DOS=high

[Win95]
Device=c:\windows\himem.sys
Device=c:\windows\command\umbpci.sys /I=c800-efff
DOS=high,umb
Files=99
Buffers=13
```

And here's the corresponding *autoexec.bat*. Note the sequence of commands after each code block. These load the game automatically. If you wish to make the games on your particular system do this, substitute the commands to switch to the game's directory and run the game's executable for the ones I included. These commands will be present in the game's documentation.

```
@echo off
Goto %config%

:yeager
Set temp=f:\temp
Set tmp=f:\temp
Set blaster=a220 i7 d1 t2
Lh smartdrv.exe 4096

F:
Cd\progra~1\games\yeager
Yeager.exe

Goto end

:7cog
Set temp=f:\temp
Set tmp=f:\temp
Set blaster=a220 i7 d1 t2
Lh smartdrv.exe 4096

F:
Cd\progra~1\games\7cities
7cities.exe

Goto end

:populous2
Set temp=f:\temp
Set tmp=f:\temp
```

```
Set blaster=a220 i7 d1 t2
Lh smartdrv.exe 4096

F:
Cd\progra~1\games\pop2
Go.bat

Goto end

:redneck
Set temp=f:\temp
Set tmp=f:\temp
Set blaster=a220 i7 d1 t2
Lh smartdrv.exe 4096

F:
Cd\progra~1\games\redneck
rr.exe

Goto end

:ultima7
Set temp=f:\temp
Set tmp=f:\temp
Set blaster=a220 i7 d1 t2

F:
Cd\progra~1\games\ultima7
Slowdown /350 Ultima7

Goto end

:win95
win

:end
```

Running DOS Games from a RAM Disk

If you have sufficient RAM, you might want to consider using a RAM disk rather than a disk cache to speed up loading. A RAM disk is the opposite of virtual memory: rather than using disk space to emulate RAM, RAM disks use RAM to emulate disk space. As a result, RAM disks are lightning fast. Loads that take seconds from disk occur instantly. Disk-intensive games operating from a RAM disk will be much more fluid, and will give your hard drive a rest.

Windows comes with a RAM disk driver called *ramdrive.sys*. There are problems with this driver when running Windows, so you should only use it in DOS mode. The freeware RAM disk called XMSDISK (available from *ftp://ftp.simtel.net/pub/ simtelnet/msdos/ramdisk/fu_rd19i.zip*), introduced in Chapter 5, *Utilities*, is more efficient and more versatile, so I'll use XMSDISK in this example rather than *ramdrive.sys.* This example assumes *xmsdsk.exe* is somewhere in your path (I recommend *C:\Windows\Command*).

You have to be careful to make sure you have enough memory to hold the entire game, as well as to run it. Look at the program's requirements. If the program's RAM requirements plus its disk space requirements are less than the amount of memory you have, you can run it from a RAM disk. For instance, Populous II requires 603K of conventional memory and 1040K of EMS when run at 640×480 16-color mode with Sound Blaster sound, and its directory is 10.3 MB in size. Round the disk requirements up to the next megabyte to account for slack space, then add a couple of megabytes to hold saved game files, and the total requirements to do this end up being about 15 MB.

Here's a modified *config.sys* to run Populous II from a RAM disk:

```
Device=c:\windows\himem.sys
Device=c:\windows\command\emm386.exe ram
DOS=high,umb
```

Assuming that Populous II is stored in *F:\Program Files\Games\Pop2*, here's a modified *autoexec.bat* that copies Populous II into the RAM disk and executes it:

```
@echo off
Xmsdsk 13312 z: /t
Md z:\temp
Set temp=z:\temp
Set tmp=z:\temp
Set blaster=a220 i7 d1 t2

Md z:\pop2
Xcopy /s f:\progra~1\games\pop2\*.* z:\pop2

z:
CD pop2
Go.bat

Xcopy /s /y /u z:\pop2\*.* f:\progra~1\games\pop2
```

The first code block creates a 13,312K RAM disk and assigns it drive letter *Z:*. The /t parameter tells it to use the top of memory. This is for Windows 9x compatibility; it's a good habit to just use this parameter all the time. The code block then does some fairly standard housekeeping chores: redirecting temp files to the RAM disk and setting up Sound Blaster parameters. The second block copies Populous II from the hard drive to the RAM disk. The third code block executes Populous II. The last code block copies the game back from the RAM disk to the hard drive. Since Populous II stores its saved game files in its installation directory, this is necessary to preserve the saved game files.

8

Modems and the Internet

The second biggest deficiency in modern computers, after lack of adequate RAM, is the speed of the Internet connection. Not having enough RAM is solvable by reducing your system's memory requirements and/or by throwing money at the problem. If you're willing to spend $500—not an unreasonable amount, considering that $500 was a great deal on 16 MB of RAM in 1996—you can kiss your memory shortage problems goodbye for a few years. I'm not about to say 256 MB will last you forever, because it wasn't all that long ago that Bill Gates said 640K of memory should be enough for anyone, but I think it's pretty safe to say that it'll be at least 2005 before we start seeing a lot of software listing a minimum system requirement of 256 MB. And that $500 figure is extremist. Most people will be happy with 64 or 128 MB of RAM, which will cost roughly $100 or $200, respectively.

The cost of solving your Internet speed problems makes memory pricing look downright reasonable. I don't suggest messing around with ISDN or satellite uplink. The installation fee plus a year's usage of either might buy you a gigabyte of RAM. I'm not talking disk space—I'm talking *RAM*. If you can get a cable modem, it's a bargain. Here in St. Louis, a local cable company offers service for $39 monthly. That sounds high at first, but consider that a dial-up ISP costs $20 a month and a second phone line would cost about $10 a month. The extra speed would be more than worth the $9 a month to me. Unfortunately, the only St. Louis area cable company offering cable modem service doesn't serve my area. ADSL's price is similar, but it's not available in my area yet either.

Maybe you're like me, willing and able to pay for cable modem service or ADSL, but no one's willing to offer it in your area. Or maybe you just can't justify the expense. In either case, you're stuck with a modem: a 56K, 33.6K, 28.8K, or 14.4K connection to the Internet. It makes sense to make the most of what you have.

There are three things you can do to improve your modem's performance. The first thing you need to do is to make sure your PC is receiving the data as fast as the modem can send it—you don't want your modem waiting on your PC. Secondly, once your PC and your modem are communicating efficiently, you want to make sure your modem is communicating with the modem on the other end as efficiently as possible. You want your modem to be using as much of its bandwidth as possible for the transmission of real data, as opposed to overhead. Finally, you want your modem to spend as little time sitting idle as possible. Maximizing your modem really isn't all that different from optimizing the rest of your system—like anything else, you do everything you can to ensure it spends the majority of its time doing real work.

Idealistic General Principles

Ideally, you'll find out what type of modem your ISP has and buy the same brand. Modems of like brand tend to connect more quickly and give better throughput. Of course, mismatched modems can still communicate—that's why we have standards for modems, after all—but their connect rate may be reduced, or even if they do connect at full speed, their throughput rate can be reduced.

This approach isn't always practical, unfortunately. You probably already have a modem, and you probably already have an ISP. However, if you decide to replace your modem—something you should try to avoid doing, seeing as alternatives to modems are becoming faster, more affordable, and more widespread—call your ISP's customer service line and ask what brand of modems they use, and buy the same brand.

Finding Your Modem and Optimizing Your Port Speed

Before you can optimize your modem, you need to know what COM port it's on. Open Control Panel, then select System → Device Manager → Modem → <name of your modem> → Properties → Modem. Look at the section labeled Port.

While you're here, double-check your maximum speed. There's a good chance this setting may be incorrect. Virtually all modern modems talk to the computer at a faster speed than they talk to the modem on the other end. For the past few years, modems have been using hardware data compression to try to squeeze more speed out of a phone line's limited bandwidth. Although data compression is a bad thing when you're dealing with your hard drive, data compression is a good thing with your modem. Since the connection between modems and PCs is a low-bandwidth connection, data compression permits more data to fit in that limited space, which makes everything run faster. Some Internet content, like graphics files and RealAudio sound, is already highly compressed and doesn't benefit much from this. But HTML text, which makes up a large proportion of online content, compresses extremely well. Most modem manufacturers tell you to set your port speed at four times your modem speed. Go ahead and set it at four times your modem speed, unless you have a 56K (actually a 53K) modem. Most systems are limited to 115K port speeds, so set it as high as you can go.

Optimizing Your Port

Now that you know what port your modem is on, go ahead and optimize it as well. While you're in Device Manager, go to Ports → <your modem's port> → Properties → Port Settings. Your modem settings should override these, but it doesn't hurt to go ahead and set them. Set "Bits per second" to the same speed as you set on your modem properties. Then select Flow control → Hardware. Now, click Advanced. There will be a checkbox labeled "Use FIFO buffers (requires 16550 compatible UART)." Virtually all internal modems use a 16550-compatible UART. If you have an external modem, virtually all COM ports built into Pentium motherboards used 16550-compatible UARTs, as did an awful lot of 486s.

To find out what kind of UART you have, download the shareware CTS Serial Port Utilities suite from *www.troubleshooters.com/ttools.htm* or from *www.comminfo. com.* The CTS utilities include a program called PortMaster that will identify your UART. Download them, install them, close all programs, and press Start → Programs → CTS Serial Port Utilities → PortMaster (Reboot to DOS mode) → Agree → Test Com Ports and Identify Modems → Start Test. If you run the program in DOS mode, the line on the summary screen labeled "Type of Port" will give you the model number of your UART.

If you have a 16550 or higher UART, restart Windows, then open the Control Panel and go to System → Device Manager → Ports → <your modem's port> → Properties → Port Settings → Advanced. Check the "Use FIFO buffers" box, then move the Receive Buffer and Transmit Buffer sliders all the way to the right. If you have difficulty connecting with your ISP afterwards, you can move them back a bit.

So What's This UART Business?

A Universal Asynchronous Receiver-Transmitter (UART) is a chip that handles serial input and output. These days two of them are usually integrated along with a bunch of other circuitry into one larger chip. The 8250 UART employed in the original IBM PC wasn't capable of communicating much faster than 2400 bps effectively. The 16450 used in the IBM PC/AT was more efficient, but once 9600 bps modems started using data compression, the chip's 19,200 bps limit became a liability. The 16550 came into favor when 9600 bps modems became popular, because it improved performance of these then-high-speed modems, and was virtually necessary for 14,400 and beyond. The 16550 tops out at about 115,200, so a replacement UART would be nice for use with a 56K modem. You can get 230,400 bps with a 16650-based serial card and thus improve the speed of your external 56K modem for certain types of web browsing at a cost of about $50.

The 16550 improved upon the 16450 by adding a 16-byte buffer to the chip. That way, the CPU didn't have to immediately drop everything and read the port—the CPU had a little bit of time, and the port could keep cranking in characters until the buffer filled up. Besides being more efficient, the newer 16650 doubles the size of the buffer, making it suitable for serial devices of up to about 900 Kbps.

If you have an external 56K modem, you should consider a 16650 card if you don't have one. It will allow you to set your port speed to 230,400 bps and get better throughput. If you use ISDN with an external ISDN terminal adapter (ISDN devices aren't really modems), you definitely need a 16650 card.

A Bit of Low-Tech: Your Phone Connection

A very common yet oft-overlooked source of modem bandwidth problems is the phone connection. The U.S. phone system is modern enough that it can handle communications of 14.4K without much difficulty in most areas. However, speeds of 28.8K and above can be pretty sensitive. It's not terribly uncommon for 28.8K modems to connect at 26.4K and for 33.6K modems to step down to 31.2K or 28.8K or even lower, and a 56K modem's speed can be unpredictable.

Much of this has to do with the quality of the phone lines. If you live in a rural area, you're lucky to connect at 28.8K, let alone any faster. However, even in urban areas with supposedly modern phone systems, it's possible to get stuck with low speeds.

Before you blame the phone company, however, make sure the problem isn't the wiring coming out of your modem. If you have a phone plugged into your modem's auxiliary jack, take it out. Your connection speed may improve. If you're using a long telephone cord, temporarily move your computer closer to the phone jack and connect it with the shortest cord you can find, then try connecting. Your connect speed may improve.

Telephone cords are like any other wire that conducts electricity. The longer they are, the more susceptible they are to signal degradation and interference. Many computer cables, however, are shielded in order to minimize this effect. This is usually not the case with phone cords. If you were forward-thinking enough to get an external modem, you have the option of using a longer serial cable to move the modem closer to a distant phone jack so you can use a short phone cord. If you need your phone jack to share a phone and a modem, you're better off using a Y-splitter, available for a couple of dollars at any discount store.

Download the Newest Drivers for Your Modem

Having your modem's newest drivers can be important. Be sure to visit your modem manufacturer's web site to see about new and updated drivers. If you don't know who made your modem—frequently the case if your system came with an internal modem—you can either check your computer manufacturer's site, or register your copy of PortMaster. PortMaster can query modems to get a manufacturer's name, and knowing your modem's manufacturer and speed, you can probably locate a driver. Or, if you open your system's case, you can take a look at the modem. Frequently the manufacturer's name is silk-screened onto the modem's printed circuit board. If not, try to find the modem's FCC ID, which you can cross-reference with the FCC's web site at *www.fcc.gov* to find the manufacturer.

Tune Your Connection via Software

Windows 95 came out at a time when 14.4 modems were the most common speed out there and 28.8 was slowly gaining acceptance. Its TCP/IP settings were tuned for cable modems and local-area networks. By the time Windows 98 came out, it was possible to get cable modems and other high-speed connections, and LAN connections in the office were finally commonplace, but Windows 98's default TCP/IP settings are tuned for modems. Figure that one out.

Trumpet Winsock's TCP/IP settings are out in the open, where they can be adjusted. There's no pretty control panel interface on them, but they're well documented, with a good number of web sites talking about how to adjust the settings. Many web pioneers improved their throughput by modifying these settings. Windows 95 and 98, apparently taking a cue from the Macintosh, bury TCP/IP settings in poorly documented registry keys that aren't even present by default.

These hidden settings are known as MTU, MSS, RWIN, and TTL. MTU stands for *Maximum Transmission Unit.* When data is transferred over the modem, it's broken into pieces, or *packets.* The MTU determines the size of the packet. If the computers on either end are each expecting packets of different sizes, they have to disassemble and reassemble the packets, which slows down the transmission.

MSS stands for *Maximum Segment Size,* and is always set to MTU-40. MSS is the portion of the packet that actually contains usable data, without the 20-byte headers and footers.

RWIN stands for *Receive Window,* which is a small collection of packets. This setting tells the other end how many packets can build up without acknowledgment. The smaller this setting, the faster your system recovers from transmission errors. If you have relatively clean phone lines—if you're not connecting consistently at the full speed of your modem, you don't—set this to 8*MSS. Otherwise, set it to 4*MSS, then experiment with different settings.

TTL stands for *Time to Live,* which determines how long a packet should be kept before it is discarded. The Windows default is 32; most experts suggest a setting of 128.

You can adjust these hidden settings yourself by adding registry keys, but determining where to find them is tedious—a good job for the computer to do. Fortunately, there are dozens of MTU-tuning programs out there, some shareware, some freeware, and some part of commercial programs. Two freeware MTU-adjustment programs that I like are EasyMTU, by Rob Vonk (available at *members.tripod.com/~EasyMTU*), and iSpeed, by High Mountain Software (available at *www.hms.com/ispeed.htm*). I like EasyMTU because it's small, fast, and nonintrusive—there's no installation routine and it doesn't dump any files into your *Windows* hierarchy. You just unzip it and run it. However, there is one advantage to iSpeed. It keeps a history of its benchmarks, which is useful if you want to make some adjustments and measure the improvement.

Both programs are intuitive, and both are smart enough to figure out the MTU size your ISP uses. The most common setting is 576, but many ISPs deviate from that, so it's not safe to assume an MTU of 576.

Veterans of telecommunications may be disappointed to see such a small packet size—private BBSs were using protocols with much larger packet sizes to transfer files in the late 1980s and early 1990s, even though the modems of that time were far slower than the modems of today. It's true that larger packet sizes are more efficient. However, you have to use the same packet size as the system on the other end for optimal performance, and you have to remember that the Internet was designed more for reliability than for performance.

The other thing to remember is that on a noisy phone line, a smaller packet size is better. To use another example from the BBS era, Jmodem should theoretically have been a faster protocol than Zmodem, because of its larger packet size. But Zmodem was more consistent on noisy phone lines, and in those days, everyone had a noisy line.

Since EasyMTU is the smaller download and intrudes less (I really wish more programs were self-contained like EasyMTU) I'll walk through running EasyMTU.

After unzipping, launch *EasyMTU.exe.* The first thing you will want to do is click on the FindMTU tab and click Start. EasyMTU will determine your ISP's MTU size by executing ping commands using different packet sizes. After it gives you a result, click the Windows 95 tab, then click the Suggested button. If the suggested settings don't match the MTU size that FindMTU discovered, correct them. Make sure the Auto Calculate box is checked to make life easier. A multiplier of 4 will usually be optimal, but you can change it to 8 if you have a fast modem that consistently connects at high speeds. The EasyMTU DefaultTTL of 64 may be a bit low; I suggest setting it to 128. MaxMSS and DefaultRcvWindow shouldn't be changed directly, since they are calculated from other values. Once you have settings that you're satisfied with, push the Save button. The changes don't take effect until you restart.

To get an idea of the improvement, go to the Benchmark tab and press the button labeled Start. Do this a couple of times, since speed will vary a bit. Make note of the throughput and total time. After you restart, launch EasyMTU again and repeat the process. You should see some improvement. Under Windows 95, the improvement may be dramatic. The improvement is likely to be less dramatic under Windows 98, since Windows 98 is tuned for analog modems, but since your ISP may vary from the de facto standards, EasyMTU should be able to give you some improvement under Windows 98, as well.

Speed Up DNS Lookups

When I first saw the description for Giuseppe Criaco's FastNet99, at *members. xoom.com/gcriaco/*, I hung my head. This program is so ingenious, yet so obvious, I couldn't figure out why I didn't think of it myself. Then I wondered why someone else hadn't thought of it way back in August 1995.

Web addresses, such as *www.oreilly.com*, are meaningless to your computer. It has to translate that alphanumeric name into a numeric address—in this case, 204.148. 40.9. The computer has to go to a *Domain Name System* (DNS) server to do the translation. Your ISP's DNS won't list every address on the Internet, however. So if your ISP doesn't know the address, it has to refer your browser to a bigger DNS. This process may repeat several times for a distant address, which explains the sometimes excruciating delays when your web browser is just sitting there with a "Looking up host . . ." message.

Windows maintains a file called *Hosts* that matches names to IP addresses. If you use a web site a lot, you can enter its IP address, followed by its name, and your web browser will look for the address in *Hosts* before it queries the DNS. Sometimes this can lead to a dramatic speedup—after all, sometimes it takes longer to find the server than to display the content it holds. Having your most common addresses in *Hosts* also improves your reliability, in the event that your ISP's DNS is having problems. The sites entered in your *Hosts* file will still work, even without a DNS.

The problem is that finding the IP addresses for all of your favorite sites is a pain. You have to ping the name, then make note of the address, then type the name and address into *Hosts*. It may not be worth the trouble for all of your favorite sites. That's where FastNet comes in. FastNet can take your browser bookmarks (it understands Netscape, Internet Explorer, and Opera), then get the IP addresses for each one and enter them into *Hosts* for you.

FastNet requires Microsoft's Visual Basic 6.0 libraries in order to run, and is downloadable from *http://members.xoom.com/gcriaco*. On my system, FastNet also required Microsoft's Visual Basic 5.0 libraries as well, available at *ftp://ftp.microsoft. com/Softlib/MSLFILES/MSVBVM50.EXE*. Install both of these library sets before you install FastNet.

Before you install FastNet, I suggest that you delete your *Hosts* file. If FastNet finds no *Hosts* file, it offers to copy its own file into place. This file contains the addresses for more than 17,000 web sites, which is probably an improvement over what you have. To delete *Hosts*, select Start → Find → Files or folders → Hosts. If you find a file called *Hosts* (no extension), right-click it and select `Delete`. By default, Windows 9x usually has no *Hosts* file, only *Hosts.sam*—an example file. Go ahead and delete that file—Windows doesn't use it, and it takes up valuable space in your Windows directory.

Now let FastNet launch, then click Bookmarks → Search the registry. This is a nice feature, when it works: it searches the registry for the locations of all your bookmarks. Verify that the locations are correct—they aren't always—and correct them if necessary. Once you're sure they're correct, go online if you aren't already and hit Scan. FastNet will start examining the URLs and collect IP addresses for them to add to *Hosts*. When it finishes (and it will probably take a while), hit Save.

If you want a faster overall browsing experience, you need to catch the sites that aren't necessarily in your bookmarks. Fortunately, all three browsers maintain a list of every URL you've visited online, and FastNet can take advantage of this. Select History → Search the registry. Once again, verify the locations of the files, then when you're sure they're correct, hit Scan. FastNet will then scan your browser history for URLs. Be aware that this operation will take a while. I'm a pretty heavy web user, and FastNet found references to about 2,000 URLs on a PC I'd been using for about four months. It took about an hour for FastNet to sort through the list, identify the unique names, filter out the corrupted names, and get IP addresses for the 100 or so that were in my history but not in Criaco's *Hosts* file. When it finishes, hit Save.

After doing this, every site you've visited frequently, and perhaps every site you've *ever* visited, will have its IP address stored in *Hosts* for faster visits in the future. As long as you keep FastNet running, it will add sites as you visit them.

IP addresses have a way of changing with time (such as when a web site gets new servers), so you need to verify your IP addresses occasionally. You can do this by launching FastNet 99, then clicking on the Edit tab and clicking the Verify All button. Do this once a month or when a web site that used to load no longer loads, whichever is more frequent.

The improvement FastNet yields will vary. If you visit ad-heavy sites, it can be very significant, because every ad could potentially be causing the system to look to the DNS. If you visit a lot of text-heavy sites, the speedup will also be significant, because text sites tend to load very quickly, so the DNS lookup could well take nearly as long as loading the page. Whatever the nature of your web browsing habits, however, FastNet is worth the effort. The difference will almost certainly be noticeable.

Keep in mind that FastNet and tools like iSpeed or EasyMTU aren't mutually exclusive—in fact, they're perfect complements to one another.

FastNet is charityware. If you like the program, the author asks you to make a donation to an organization that preserves nature.

Lose the Ads Altogether

Personally, I don't take issue with ads. I know some people who take an extremely strong anti-advertising stance, and I also know some people who would use ads on the back of athletic jerseys instead of numbers to identify players. But I admit that Internet advertising sometimes borders on the obnoxious. The brightest blinking element on any given web page is usually an ad. And the part that takes the longest to download could well be an ad—after all, ads are usually held on an external server, and ads are frequently animated GIFs. It takes time to look up that server, and it takes time to load the ad. So, while advertising can be informative, and advertising keeps alive some web sites that I frequent, they can also get in my way. Blinking animated ads are distracting—it's human nature to pay more attention to things that move than to things that stand still. And when a web page doesn't display because there's a problem with the server that the ad resides on, and my browser hangs, it's aggravating.

For these reasons, I understand the desire to block advertising at least under some circumstances. I can see why there are a number of $30 ad-blocking programs out there and why people buy them. But I can tell you that you may not need one. You can probably block the majority of advertising on your own.

A FastNet-generated *Hosts* file provides a brute-force method of blocking that sometimes works. I loaded my *Hosts* file into a word processor (Notepad can't handle it if you have 17,000+ entries in it, and for a file that large, I want a program with better performance than WordPad). Then I scrolled through the file. I found entries with names like *ad.doubleclick.net* and *ads1.zdnet.com*. Gee, I wonder what those servers might contain? To block those servers, just change the IP address in front of their names to 127.0.0.1. That's always the IP address of the PC you're using. So, if you make that change and then visit a web page that makes reference to a file called *obnoxious_half-meg_ad.gif* stored at *ad.doubleclick.net*, your web browser will look up the address for *ad.doubleclick.net*, say, "Hey, that's me!" and go look for that file. It will quickly realize the file doesn't exist and just display a broken link where the ad would have been.

The problem is, many servers with "ad" in their name are just ad counters and don't actually store the ads. At least when it's serving the web sites I visit most, *ad.doubleclick.net* appears to be more of a counter than a storage house. Ads are frequently stored on the same server as the rest of the site's content. They may be stored in a subdirectory called */ads*, but you can't use your *Hosts* file to block just parts of a server. That's an all-or-nothing deal. Intelligent blocking requires a little bit more work with a proxy server.

Although the name sounds intimidating, setting up a proxy server is pretty easy, and it doesn't require any additional hardware. A server isn't always a computer or a piece of hardware—in this case, it's just a process running on your PC. A good source of a small proxy server is *www.junkbusters.com*. Their free product, Internet Junkbuster, is a simple cross-platform proxy server. The Windows version is just over 200K to download. It's not a ready-to-go product—there's no pretty graphical installation routine, and by default it doesn't do much more than block cookies. But installation and configuration isn't difficult.

The first thing you need to do is download Internet Junkbuster and unzip it. Go ahead and unzip it into your *\Program Files* directory. The program comes with source code, so if you're not a C programmer, you can safely delete all but the *.ini*, *.exe*, and HTML files. This process cuts the initial footprint down to a fairly svelte 294K.

Next, you need to execute Junkbuster and configure your web browser(s) to use it. Double-click on *junkbustr.exe* to launch it—you can add a shortcut to the file to your Startup group, or, later in the chapter, I'll show you how to set Junkbuster to run only while you're online. Now launch your web browser.

The configuration method varies between browsers, and even from version to version of the same browser:

For Netscape Navigator 2.x and 3.x

> Options → Network Preferences → Manual Proxy Configuration → View → HTTP Proxy → localhost → Port → 8000 → Security Proxy → localhost → Port → 8000 → OK → OK

For Netscape Navigator/Communicator 4.x

> Edit → Preferences → Advanced → Cache, Proxies, and Disk Space → Proxies → Configure proxies to access the Internet → Manual proxy configuration → View → HTTP Proxy → localhost → Port → 8000 → Security Proxy → localhost → Port → 8000 → OK → OK

For Internet Explorer 3.x or 4.x

> View → Internet Options → Connections → Connect through proxy server → Settings → HTTP → localhost → Port → 8000 → Secure → localhost → Port → 8000 → OK

For Internet Explorer 5.x

> Tools → Internet Options → Connections → Settings → Use proxy server → Settings → HTTP → localhost → Port → 8000 → Secure → localhost → Port → 8000 → OK

For Opera

> Preferences → Proxy servers → HTTP → localhost → Port → 8000 → OK

Next, visit *internet.junkbuster.com/cgi-bin/show-proxy-args* to verify that Junkbuster is working. To test to make sure Junkbuster can indeed talk to the rest of the world, visit *www.junkbusters.com/ht/en/ijbwin.html#connect*, then reload to make sure the page is not coming from your browser cache.

If you visit an ad-heavy site now, you won't see any difference yet. You need to download a blockfile—a list of patterns for Junkbuster to look for and filter out of web content—in order to see any difference. A number of web sites have blockfiles. I downloaded one from Charles Coffing's web site at *www.home.unix-ag.org/sfx/junkbuster/blockfile* that worked reasonably well for me, but you'll probably find several by visiting your favorite search engine and entering the words *junkbuster* and *blockfile*. Size matters: the bigger the blockfile is, the more comprehensive it is likely to be. Look for the biggest and/or most recent link, then visit it. You're likely to be presented with a plain text file. Select File → Save As, and save it into your Junkbuster directory. Junkbuster's default blockfile is called *sblock.ini*. You might wish to rename your old *sblock.ini* rather than overwriting it, though you can always extract it from the Junkbuster Zip file if you find you need it again.

After pointing my web browser to the Junkbuster proxy and downloading Coffing's blockfile, I visited a few of my favorite ad-heavy sites. They loaded more quickly, and most, though not all, of the ads were blocked. Some of the ads were still lingering in my browser cache and disappeared in time; a very small number had clever enough names that they managed to slip past Junkbuster.

There are commercial ad-blocking programs available, but Junkbuster does a good job free of charge. The commercial offerings will be more automatic, but Junkbuster installation and configuration is easier than many of the other tasks described in this book. Ad blocking is just one of Junkbuster's many capabilities. You can also configure it to lie about what kind of web browser you are using, to block cookies, to manipulate cookies, and other things. These tricks and others are described in Junkbuster's online documentation at *www.junkbusters.com*.

If you don't mind a larger installation footprint to get an easier-to-use GUI interface, download Proxomitron from *members.tripod.com/Proxomitron*. Compared to Junkbuster, Proxomitron is pretty automatic—just download it, install it, launch it, and point your web browser's proxy services to it. Configuring a web browser to use Proxomitron is just like configuring it to use Junkbuster, with the exception that Proxomitron uses port 8080 instead of port 8000.

Proxomitron has some other nice features as well, such as the ability to detect animated GIFs and just load and display the first frame. This is good for preserving the designer's intended page layout while making the page load faster and making it less distracting.

Preloading and Caching Utilities

Although you spend a lot of time waiting on the modem, once the page is finally loaded, your modem spends a lot of time waiting for you to click a link while you read the page. Preloading utilities make use of this downtime by prefetching the links on the page and storing them in a cache. Frequently they also replace your web browser's caching with their more aggressive caching. Loading web pages from disk is much faster than retrieving them over the phone line, so these utilities can dramatically speed up your web browsing experience.

There are a number of preloading/caching utilities available, but I like Web3000's free NetSonic. NetSonic works by caching more aggressively than Netscape or Internet Explorer—when you visit a previously visited page, NetSonic displays the page's previous contents immediately while it waits for the page's current content to load. If it detects changes in content, it prompts you by beeping at you and changing the shape of your mouse cursor. You can then hit your browser's reload button to display the changed content.

You can download NetSonic from *www.web3000.com*. After you install, an icon resembling a jet will appear in your system tray. Click this icon to bring up Net-Sonic's configuration screen.

For best results, go to SonicCache and select Maximum Acceleration and go to SonicFetch and select Pre-load All Links. Maximum Acceleration reduces the amount of time NetSonic spends checking graphics files for changes, which is a nice setting since much of a web site's graphical content never (or rarely) changes. Preloading all links is a very useful feature. You may be more likely to follow links that you've already visited—that depends more on your personal web browsing habits. NetSonic only preloads the text from those links, and it only loads links stored on the same server as the current page, so preloading all links isn't a major drain.

Under General Preferences, I disable the Help Tips because I find them annoying. If you like to get feedback from NetSonic, go ahead and leave Help Tips on.

By clicking the Advanced button, you can configure how much disk space Net-Sonic uses for cache. The default of 30 MB should be adequate, though you can give it more if you like. NetSonic disables your Navigator and Internet Explorer cache, so you don't have to worry about filling your hard drive with double-cached data.

The more you use programs like NetSonic, the better they work. ISPs don't like these programs because under some circumstances they pretty much ensure that your Internet connection is never idle, which increases traffic if too many people are using them. But I would argue that their more aggressive caching means pages don't get reloaded from the Internet connection as often. If there are only a hand-ful of sites you visit regularly, NetSonic can actually reduce the amount of traffic you generate. Since NetSonic only preloads text, leaving the space-heavy multime-dia and graphics content behind until you actually visit the page, NetSonic won't dramatically increase the amount of traffic you generate.

Web3000 makes a commercial version of NetSonic, called NetSonic Pro. NetSonic Pro adds MTU optimization—EasyMTU takes care of that for you—and automatic refresh, freeing you from having to hit the reload button, as well as offline brows-ing and a few other features. NetSonic Pro sells for $39.95, though Web3000 often puts it on sale for less.

Taking Full Control of Your Internet Connection

Maybe I'm nitpicky, but I really dislike Microsoft's implementation of Dial-Up Net-working. I ran Windows 3.1 for about two months after I bought my first PC, and unlike Microsoft's offering, Trumpet Winsock would redial the phone for me when the line was busy. When I upgraded to OS/2, its dialer would redial for me as well.

This might be even more nitpicky, but I didn't like the idea of having a NetSonic 572K executable launching every time I start my computer, and I don't like having Internet-related applications in memory when I'm not online. But once I started using NetSonic, I found I really didn't want to live without it. Enter yet another freeware program—NetLaunch.

NetLaunch, by Robert Simpson, is a versatile public domain Internet utility. It auto-mates Dial-Up Networking for you, redialing if the line is busy, and it reconnects you if you disconnect. This is useful if you have an ISP that likes to live beyond its means. If you get a really poor connection, it will disconnect and redial, which is useful if you have poor phone lines. And, optionally, upon connecting, it will launch a set of programs for you. It can also shut those programs down for you when you disconnect.

By all means, go to *www.blackcastlesoft.com* and download NetLaunch, then install and launch it. I'll walk through the configuration/optimization process.

The NetLaunch window has three tabs, and we'll use all three of them. NetLaunch has a directory similar to the Windows' *Windows**Start Menu* directory, where it stores shortcuts to programs that it launches automatically. Go ahead and open that directory—you can find it by going to Programs → Launch List. Now, right-click Windows' Start button, then click Explore → Programs → Startup. Drag the NetSonic icon from your Startup group into the Launch List window. Now, go back to NetLaunch and select Launch → Configure programs independently → Net-Sonic. Next, select Launch → Connect → Only One Instance → No Focus → 0 sec. delay → Close → Disconnect → Close window → All → Destroy window → All → Quit program.

The next time you go online, verify that NetSonic's settings are still the same as you set earlier. I had to reset them after I started using NetLaunch to control it.

The same process also works just fine for *junkbstr.exe*, to ensure that Junkbuster is running while you are online but not consuming any memory or CPU cycles when you're not. You can use this feature to make NetLaunch start and close other pro-grams as well, such as AOL Instant Messenger and ICQ, which seem to like to stay in memory all the time, and NetLaunch can even start your web browser and email client for you automatically. Personally, I prefer to launch my browser and mail client manually, since I rarely use the same group of programs online, but if automatic launching of everything would be useful for you, go ahead.

If you want NetLaunch to ensure that you always connect at a certain minimum speed, select Connections → Minimum connect speed → <your minimum accept-able speed>. Be realistic in your expectations: NetLaunch doesn't do anything to improve the quality of your phone line. If you connect at a lower speed than the minimum, it hangs up and tries again. So if you find yourself connecting at a vari-ety of speeds, decide what the minimum speed you're willing to live with is, and enter that as the minimum connect speed. NetLaunch will do its best to get it for you.

By default, NetLaunch puts itself in the Startup folder and launches itself when the system starts, putting an icon in the system tray. You can use this tray icon to launch your ISP or to change your NetLaunch preferences. You might like this option, and you'll probably find the 100K or so that NetLaunch needs isn't a big deal—after all, it's now occupying just a fraction of the memory that AOL Instant Messenger and ICQ and NetSonic were occupying all the time.

If you want that 100K back, however, it's possible to get it. Pull NetLaunch out of your Startup folder. Then start NetLaunch, hit the Programs tab, and clear the box labeled "Automatically run NetLaunch at startup." Next, hit the Connections tab. Now, click Start → Run → Notepad. Type in the following batch file (note that the quotes are part of the syntax):

```
"C:\program files\netlaunch\launch.exe"
"c:\program files\netlaunch\launch.exe" <enter the name of your ISP, exactly as it
                                         appears in NetLaunch options>
```

Now, save the batch file. From either your Desktop or your Start Menu's Explorer view, right-click and select New → Shortcut. Point the shortcut to your batch file. Punch through the remaining options. Now, right-click the shortcut and select Properties → Program → Run → Minimized. Also check the "Close on exit" box. If you like, assign a shortcut key to it as well. When you're satisfied with the settings, click OK.

This new icon will automatically start NetLaunch, which will then do its thing. If you define the hotkey, it's every bit as automatic as NetLaunch would be if it were in memory. The batch file adds a little bit of time to the connect time, but it's not enough to worry about. The memory you save may be worth more to you.

To exit NetLaunch, simply bring up its context menu from its tray icon, and select Exit.

The Value of Free Software

As you can see, there are a large number of very useful free utilities out there for making the most of your modem. There are commercial programs that will speed up your Internet connection, but they'd be hard-pressed to beat the combination of FastNet99, EasyMTU, NetSonic, Internet Junkbuster or Proxomitron, and Net-Launch. These programs aren't always quite as polished as commercial software, but if the workarounds are documented, they are certainly tolerable, and you can't beat the price.

Which Web Browser Should I Use?

This is an incendiary issue for many people, but frankly, much of that is due to nontechnical issues.

There is no doubt that Internet Explorer 4.x rendered pages more quickly than Netscape Navigator or Communicator 4.0 or even 4.5. Then Internet Explorer 5.0 raised the bar, before Netscape fired back with Communicator 4.6, which closed the speed gap. The early builds of Gecko, the browser that will give rise to the next generation of Netscape browsers, also show great promise.

Unless you're making your system into a web kiosk, there are more issues at stake than just browser speed, however. Internet Explorer has always been much more invasive than Netscape's browsers. The price of Microsoft's highly publicized browser-OS integration is much higher operating system overhead. This was even the case years ago with the third-generation browsers—installing Internet Explorer 3.0 caused a slight but noticeable slowdown systemwide. Internet Explorer 5 has less effect than IE 4 did, but it is still likely to be noticeable. Under some circumstances, IE will give you slightly faster web browsing (it's very hard to tell much difference between Communicator 4.6 and IE 5.0), but Netscape will give you a faster overall system—assuming that you uninstall Internet Explorer, of course.

If you need a low-overhead, non-invasive browser that renders faster than Netscape on low-end systems and takes less disk space, take a look at Opera (*www.operasoftware.com*). Opera doesn't support every feature that IE and Netscape do, although Sun's Java plug-in works with Opera and adds Java support.

Tune Your Web Browser

Just as you can tune your operating system for speed, you can also tune your web browser for speed. Fortunately, web browsers are far simpler to tune than operating systems.

People frequently ask me how they can automatically delete their web browser cache. While it's true that neither browser handles caching as well as it should, browser cache isn't a bad thing. If your browser is loading pages (or parts of the pages) from cache, it's not loading them from the modem, and therefore your browsing is faster. If your web browser seems slower right after you empty its cache, it's not your imagination.

That said, I suggest you download and install NetSonic to handle your browser cache duties, because NetSonic does a far better job than either of the two big-name browsers. If you find yourself running short of disk space, your browser cache should be the second thing to go—after the contents of your *Temp* or *Windows**Temp* directory—but you shouldn't routinely delete your cache.

The other things you can do to tune your browser are both more routine and far easier to undo. You might wish to disable Java, JavaScript, and ActiveX. These features add overhead, and having them turned off will make your browser render the pages that don't need them more quickly. The pages that need them on in order to work right will complain, but you can always turn these features back on for them.

To turn off Java and JavaScript in Netscape Navigator 3.x, select Options → Preferences → Languages, and clear the appropriate checkboxes. In Netscape Navigator/ Communicator 4.x, select Edit → Preferences → Advanced → Enable Java and Enable JavaScript. In Internet Explorer 3.x, select View → Options → Security, and clear all checkboxes under Active Content. In Internet Explorer 4, select View → Internet Options → Security → High.

You can significantly speed up your browsing by turning off the automatic loading of graphics. Junkbuster's ad blocking helps considerably, but sometimes it isn't enough. Graphics tend to be very large, and, as stated before, they don't compress well. It's not uncommon for the text of a web page to come in at speeds of 115K on your 56K modem, but the graphics will be much slower. Well-designed web pages will have text tags that display when images are turned off (primarily to facilitate screen-reading programs employed by the visually impaired, but there's no reason why the sighted can't make use of them as well) so a text-only Web shouldn't be unusable. With Netscape browsers, you can browse with images turned off, then click the Images button on the navigation toolbar if it turns out the page needs them. On days when the Internet is particularly congested, I turn images off to improve my browsing speed. During low-traffic times, I turn them back on.

In Navigator 3.x, you can toggle the loading of images by going to Options → Auto-load images. In Navigator or Communicator 4.x, select Edit → Preferences → Advanced → Automatically load pictures. In Internet Explorer, select View → Options → General → Multimedia → Show pictures.

Sometimes this tuning may not be enough: nothing will give a 14.4K modem the speed of a cable modem or ISDN connection. But the programs described in this section will definitely speed up any modem. NetSpeed and Junkbuster even made a noticeable improvement on the T1 connection I have at the office. MaxMTU and NetLaunch aren't terribly useful if you have a perpetual connection to the Internet, but the rest of these utilities will speed up any Internet connection. So even if you're seriously considering replacing your modem, try these utilities first. You may find you don't need to upgrade. If the speed still isn't good enough and you decide to upgrade your modem, the optimizations will improve the speed of your upgraded connection.

9

Home Networking

If your household has more than one PC, or if your living quarters puts you in close proximity to other people who own PCs—for instance, in a college dormitory—I suggest you network them. Pooling some of your PCs' resources will make all of them more capable. It will facilitate file sharing without endless swapping of floppy disks and other removable media, ease disk space requirements, and allow PCs to share valuable resources such as printers and CD-ROM drives. It can also make a computer that's no longer useful for running large applications useful again—a 386 or 486, even with a small hard drive, can store data and serve it up to more capable PCs. A PC in this role is great for quick-and-dirty backups. Or you can connect your printer to it and let it spool your print jobs to the printer, freeing your more capable PC more quickly to do less mundane work.

Requirements

Networking a pair (or more) of PCs is no longer difficult nor expensive. Windows 95 included for the first time the capability to connect two PCs via a serial or parallel cable. Previously, such capability was only available by purchasing third-party tools such as LapLink. Windows 95 also included networking capabilities via dedicated network interface cards (NICs).

The physical connection of two PCs via a serial or parallel cable is easy and fairly cheap. If you're interested in multiplayer gaming, a serial link is the most useful. Multiplayer games can use a serial connection without any special support from the underlying OS, something they've been doing for more than 20 years—the pre-PC Commodore PET and Apple II computers featured multicomputer, multiplayer games via serial link. PC architecture is better suited for serial links as well, seeing as they usually have a spare serial port but only a single parallel port that's usually overburdened by printers, external high-capacity removable drives, scanners, and other peripherals. A serial connection is also more appropriate for networking, since a serial cable can be 50 feet long or longer; parallel connections should be no more than 15 feet long, and 10-foot connections are more reliable.

Unfortunately, serial connections are painfully slow. Their maximum speed is 115 Kbps, or about 10 KB per second—just over twice as fast as your 56K modem, and 100 times slower than a cheap Ethernet connection. Under some circumstances, a 56K modem will be just as fast as the direct serial connection, since the modem has the benefit of data compression. A serial connection is therefore only good for gaming (since the games don't transmit large amounts of data), barely adequate for sharing a printer, and intolerable for sharing anything but the smallest of files. To be perfectly honest, the only time I resort to doing file transfer over a serial connection is in an emergency. It's almost always faster to find some other way to transfer the file.

A parallel connection between two PCs is far faster than a serial connection, typically four to eight times faster. The theoretical maximum speed of the PC parallel port is much higher than this, but you won't reach these speeds via direct cable connection. These speeds are fine for sharing a printer between two PCs and OK even for light-duty file sharing. The drawback to this approach is that most PCs only have a single parallel port, which is usually occupied by far too many peripherals already. Plus, the PCs have to be very close to one another.

If you happen to have two PCs and a spare parallel port card, you can use a parallel direct-connect cable to allow the PCs to share a printer and small files. Or if you have both a desktop and a laptop PC, you can use a parallel connection to dump files to the laptop to take on the road, then copy the changed files back to the host PC. But with quality parallel direct-connect cables selling for about $20 apiece, and good quality parallel cards also selling for about $20 apiece, the parallel port is not a cost-effective way to network two PCs, and if you find yourself having to pop the hood and install parallel cards, it's no easier either.

Another disadvantage to both parallel and serial connections is that they limit you to connecting to other Windows 9x PCs. If you have a PC running Windows NT and another PC running Windows 9x, it's possible (but difficult) to connect them via serial cable. So if you want to connect dissimilar computers or think you might someday want to, NICs are the only game in town.

You can walk into virtually any computer store and buy a kit for under $100 that contains all you need to network two PCs, and most kits allow you to easily add more items. I recently purchased a kit that included two PCI Ethernet NICs, a five-port hub, and two 50-foot cables for $80. You can add more computers by buying additional cards and cabling—expect to pay $15–$30 per card and about $10 per cable.

Two types of Ethernet cabling are commonly available new today. The older 10-Base-2 standard uses coax cable, which bears a slight resemblance to that used for cable television, and must be terminated on each end. The computers are connected in series, with no hub. The newer 10-Base-T (10-megabit) and 100-Base-T (100-megabit) standards uses Category 5 (CAT5) cable, which resembles telephone wire and runs from each PC into a central hub. No termination is required. This newer standard is more robust, in that a problem with one machine's connection won't take down the entire network. A problem with one computer on 10-Base-2 can sever the network connection for every PC behind it. In most cases, CAT5-based networks are also faster, since the signal only has to go through one set of wires to the hub, then through another set to the destination, rather than all the way up and down a chain.

While 10-Base-2 used to enjoy a significant cost advantage over 10-Base-T, that's no longer the case. Coax cable is significantly more expensive than CAT5, and the T-connectors that must run between the computers and the terminators that must go on each end add some more expense. And frequently, cards that use CAT5 cabling cost less than 10-Base-2–capable cards. If you're networking more than four computers, 10-Base-T definitely comes out ahead. Even if you're only networking two computers, 10-Base-T's added robustness and ease of expansion is worth the small additional cost. The shopping list is also simpler: a NIC for each PC, a cable for each PC, and a hub, as opposed to a NIC for each PC, a cable for each PC, a T-connector for each PC, and two terminators.

The easiest way to get started is simply to buy a kit that has everything (or almost everything) you need. A kit with two cards, cables, and a hub will almost always cost less than the elements would separately. If you need to add more computers, buy additional cards and cables—just be sure not to buy more than the hub in your kit supports. It's not necessary to buy the additional cards from the same manufacturer who made the kit, but it helps for simplicity's sake to be able to use the same network card driver on all of your PCs.

If you're only connecting two computers, you can save some money by getting two NICs with CAT5 connectors and what's known as a *crossover cable*. A crossover cable looks like a regular CAT5 cable, but it crosses the send and receive lines, eliminating the need for a hub. A crossover cable is much less expensive than a hub and two regular cables, but more expensive than regular CAT5 cable. You're also likely to have far less selection as far as sizes go—you can order a crossover cable of whatever length you want, but your local computer store probably won't stock a 100-footer as a regular item. If the computers are in the same room, you can get by with a crossover cable, but if there's much distance between them, you may need to just bite the bullet and get a hub and regular cables.

What to Look for in Your Kit

Most network kits today come with PCI cards, so you need to make sure all of the PCs you want to network have available PCI slots. ISA cards will work, but PCI cards require less attention from the CPU. If you're wanting to network an ISA computer to a PCI computer (such as when networking a 486 to a Pentium), you might want to consider just getting a PCI kit, adding an ISA card, and holding the extra PCI card in reserve in case you replace the ISA computer with one capable of using the PCI card.

You might also want to make sure your NICs can run at either 10 or 100 megabits per second. This capability adds very little cost to the NICs—it's the high-speed hub that tends to be the expensive component. As 100-megabit Ethernet becomes more and more common, prices will come down; the ability to upgrade your network to the faster standard just by replacing the hub and not having to bother with the time or expense of replacing NICs is a nice luxury.

Whether you should go ahead and buy a 100-megabit kit now is another question. A large 10-megabit network is quickly saturated, but 10 megabits per second is enough speed for most home networking. Prices can vary—sometimes the price difference between a 10-megabit kit and a 100-megabit kit is very small. In that case, you should go ahead and get the extra speed. If you're interested in sharing programs between two computers in order to save disk space, get a 100-megabit kit. Remember, though, that if you're putting 486s on your network, you'll probably be limited to 10 megabits, because 100-megabit cards come only in PCI varieties.

You also want to make sure the hub in your kit will leave you enough room for future expansion. Will you have a port or two free? Can the hub be chained to another hub sometime in the future to add more PCs? You should also take a look at the kit's warranty. Many network cards come with lifetime warranties. The peace of mind is worth the extra cost. I've seen some cards sell for as little as $6, but they usually sell for closer to $15. I've seen Kingston cards with lifetime warranties sell for $19.

Many businesses stick with 3Com or Intel cards and hubs. If you want to be really safe, sticking with big-name components provides an added measure of insurance. Whether that extra security is worth the extra cost is up to you. Sometimes an Intel or 3Com card sells for $70 alone—the cost of an entire kit from a lesser-known manufacturer. Personally, I prefer second-tier manufacturers like Bay Networks or Kingston. Their price is much lower than Intel or 3Com, and just slightly higher than the bargain-basement kits. I got burned by a consumer-oriented kit from a lesser-known manufacturer, ironically, while in the course of writing this chapter. I was using my network one Saturday afternoon, and all seemed fine. I went out that night, and when I came home, I noticed the lights on the hub were all dim. I checked the connections to the cards. They were fine. I checked the hub's power connection on both ends. It was fine. I checked the outlet. It was fine. I tried a different outlet anyway. No joy. I couldn't get the hub to maintain power for more than a half-second. The hub was two months old, and had been in continuous service for about six weeks. Of course it's under warranty—it has a lifetime warranty—but that lifetime warranty doesn't speed up the delivery. That'll be the last time I drop down to the third tier.

Software Requirements

From a software standpoint, all of these types of networks look the same. Whether you use a serial or parallel connection, and whatever type of network card you use, the computers use the same kind of topology to communicate. A NIC requires a driver just like any other peripheral, of course, but the serial and parallel cards require an extra layer of software to make themselves look like NICs to the networking software, so there's little difference in the memory requirements of the various approaches.

If you want to use Direct Cable Connection via a serial or parallel port, you must first install its software components. Push Start → Settings → Control Panel → Add/ Remove Programs → Windows setup → Communications → Details → <check Dial-Up Networking and Direct Cable Connection> → OK → OK. If you're prompted for the Windows 9x setup disks or CD, provide them. You'll then have to set up clients and protocols, which is described in the next section.

Building Your Network

The installation of network cards is pretty simple: Power down your PC, open the case, locate a free slot of the appropriate type (PCI for a PCI card, ISA for an ISA card), remove the bracket, and install the card. Your kit will almost assuredly come with instructions and diagrams. Find a central location with a nearby power outlet to plug in the hub, then run your CAT5 cables from the cards to the hub. Power your computers on. Windows 9x should see the new network cards and ask you for a driver disk. Provide the disk or CD that came with the kit. Windows may also ask for the setup disks or CDs. Do whatever it asks. Windows will then ask for network settings. Your Network control panel will now probably resemble Figure 9-1.

If the Client for NetWare Networks is present, remove it. Click Client for Netware Networks → Remove. If there's an extra Dial-Up Adapter in your setup, it was probably installed by your ISP. Leave it. Of the three protocols that remain—TCP/IP, IPX/SPX, NetBEUI—what you want to keep depends on your environment.

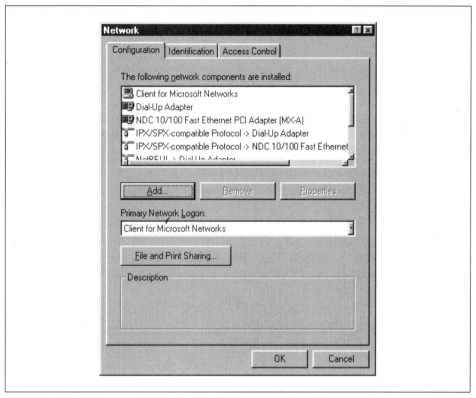

Figure 9-1. A typical Network control panel

TCP/IP

I recommend using TCP/IP as your network protocol, since it's probably already installed on your machines for Internet access. The TCP/IP subnet 168.192.0.x is always local, so you can assign your machines' IP addresses within that subnet without fear of colliding with Internet TCP/IP addresses. Click TCP/IP → <name of your network card—if you're using DCC, the Dial-Up Adapter is your network card> → Properties. Click IP Address → Specify an IP Address → 192.168.0.<unique number between 1 and 254> → Subnet Mask → 255.255.255.0. If you're running a small LAN, leave the rest of the settings alone. If you're interested in large LANs, refer to *Windows NT TCP/IP Network Administration,* by Craig Hunt and Robert Bruce Thompson (O'Reilly & Associates), for more guidance. Their book deals specifically with Windows NT, but Windows NT networking and Windows 9x networking are very similar—Windows 9x was designed to integrate into Windows NT networks.

Of all the protocols that come with Windows 9x, TCP/IP is the most cleanly implemented.

IPX/SPX

This protocol (more properly called a suite of protocols) is commonly used in Novell NetWare environments. Many multiplayer games use this protocol to communicate between computers, so if you're interested in multiplayer gaming and your games can't communicate via TCP/IP, you have no choice but to use IPX/SPX. Remove it otherwise, as it's just consuming memory unnecessarily. If you see IPX/SPX bound to your Dial-Up Adapter, as shown above, remove it. If you want to waste a ton of memory and CPU cycles, installing extra network components is a great way to do it. If you're like me and want to conserve memory and CPU cycles and keep your computers and network running as quickly and smoothly as possible, you'll remove extraneous components. Each installed component chews up memory, and whenever you have more than one protocol installed, Windows has to try to decide which protocol to use whenever you hit the network. This process can result in excess network traffic (which is, admittedly, a more significant problem on large networks than on a small home network), and more importantly, wasted CPU cycles.

NetBEUI

This protocol is installed by default, but it normally shouldn't be used. It's nice for small networks in that it's easy to implement: no need to bother with IP addresses or anything else, just install NetBEUI, tell the computer to go on the network, and you're done. But Microsoft's implementation of the protocol isn't very efficient, so it causes congestion on large networks. Theoretically, it's the fastest protocol on small networks, but you're not likely to notice any difference between NetBEUI, IPX/SPX, and TCP/IP. Any increase you see in network performance will be negated by the memory and CPU cycles NetBEUI consumes, so you're better off removing it. Once again, having unused network components installed is a great way to waste memory.

NetBEUI is another example of a once-promising technology that fell by the wayside—in this case, overtaken by the less proprietary and more versatile TCP/IP juggernaut.

There is one condition under which I would choose NetBEUI. I would use it if I had a small network whose computers weren't connected to the Internet—not even through a dial-up connection—and never would be, and I was interested in using the network solely for sharing files between computers. In other words, no Internet and no multiplayer gaming. That pretty much rules out most home networks, I suspect. Under those circumstances, NetBEUI would be the fastest way to connect the computers. But as soon as I needed to introduce another protocol, I'd be better off dumping NetBEUI. I'm inclined to save myself the trouble and use local TCP/IP, even if Internet access isn't planned or desired. Plans have a funny way of changing, especially when computers are involved.

What to add

Chances are you will want to add File and Printer Sharing for Microsoft Networks, so that your computers can access one another's hard drives, CD-ROM drives, and printers. Go to Add → Service → Microsoft → File and Printer Sharing for Microsoft Networks. Now click File and Printer Sharing and check the appropriate boxes. Chances are you want to share files: check that box. If you have a printer and want to share it, check that box as well.

Setting Up the LAN

Now we need to turn the two wired computers into a network. Click the Identification tab. My Identification settings are shown in Figure 9-2; yours will be similar.

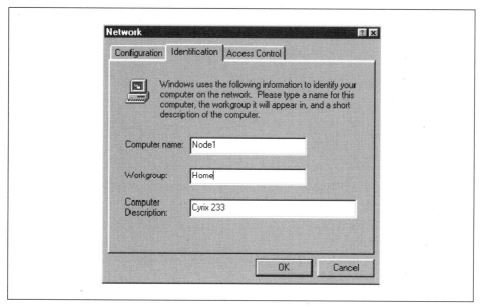

Figure 9-2. Network identification

You can use more creative names than I've chosen for the computer name and the workgroup, of course. Just avoid using spaces, slashes, quotes, and the @ sign in names.

The computer name must be unique, as it identifies the computer on the network. The workgroup defines groups of computers. In a home network, you want to put all of the computers in the same workgroup.

The computer description isn't very important on a small network. I key one in mostly out of habit.

Before the computers can do anything on the network, however, they have to have some other means of identifying themselves—some security. Click Access Control → Share-level Access Control. This allows you to assign passwords to each shared drive and printer. This would be tedious on large networks, but on a small Windows 9x network, it's the quickest and easiest option. Most of us have no interest in running a Windows NT domain at home.

From here, click OK, and Windows will want to restart your computer. Allow it to restart. The next time you restart, Windows will prompt you for a username and a password. Your network connections are bound to your username and password, so type in a username, and type in the password you want to use. When you use this name, Windows will retrieve all of your network drives and printers for you automatically—you won't have to remap them each time.

At home, where I'm not worried about security, I just use the same username and password on all my PCs. You won't get top-notch security on PCs anyway unless you run some flavor of Unix, and if someone for some unimaginable reason wants my data, they can just steal the machines and hire any teenager to recover what they want. So I make no pretension of security: the security on my home PCs stops at the lock on my door. I just use a single username and a quickly entered password, and I use the same one on each machine. In a network like this, there is no central authority on usernames and passwords. If you mistype your password, Windows 9x will set up a new profile for you—and it won't remember any of your network connections. So it's best just to make sure your password is easy to type and easy to remember, in order to avoid having to ask yourself questions like why you suddenly cannot print anymore.

You will need to perform these steps on each computer in your network.

Setting up network drives and printers

If you were to double-click on Network Neighborhood right now, it would be empty. That's because none of your computers are sharing any files or printers yet. Sharing files is easy. Go to My Computer → <drive letter of your CD-ROM drive> → Context Menu → Sharing → Sharing → Shared As → <enter a name that makes sense>. This brings up a window that will resemble Figure 9-3. On small networks, I usually make all of my shares full access, even though you can't write to a CD-ROM. It makes life simpler. Enter a password for full access, then click OK. Windows will ask you to confirm your password. Enter it again, then click OK.

Now go to your other PC. Double-click on Network Neighborhood. The PC whose drive you just shared should appear in the window. Double-click its name. A list of its shared drives will come up. Double-click on the share you just created. Windows will prompt you for a password. Enter the password you just typed on the other PC, and be sure to check the box labeled "Save this password" in your

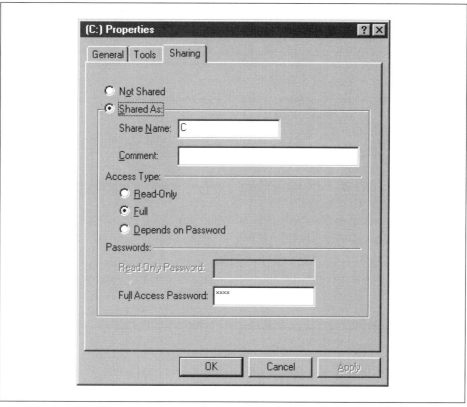

Figure 9-3. Sharing a drive

password list. When you click OK, a window displaying the contents of the other computer's drive will come up.

The standard practice for using drives on another computer is to map them to drive letters, just like local drives. This works when you leave all of your computers on all the time, but Windows has to double-check to make sure the drives are still out there when you boot and every time you open My Computer from the desktop or an application. This delay can sometimes be significant. Most applications will permit you to save and open files from Network Neighborhood, so it's best to access the drives that way.

If you decide you do want to map those drives, double-click Network Neighborhood → <computer name> → <share name>, then right-click and select Map Network Drive. Select a drive letter, then check the "Reconnect at logon box" if you want to always have the drive available. Click OK, and you'll be able to access that drive by its drive letter, just like any other drive.

Setting up a network printer is similar. Go to My Computer → Printers → <printer name> → *Context menu* → Sharing → Shared As: → Share name → <type something identifiable> → Password → <enter a password> → OK → <reenter password> → OK.

Connecting to the network printer from your other PC is a little bit more complicated than connecting to a networked drive, because Windows has to set up a printer driver. Go to Network Neighborhood → <computer name> → <printer name>. Windows will ask if you want to set up that printer for operation. Answer yes. Windows will ask if you print from MS-DOS programs. Answer accordingly, then hit Next. Windows will ask what type of printer it is. Setup is now just like setting up a local printer—feed Windows the disk or CD-ROM that came with the printer, or if the Windows 9x CD had a driver for the printer, pick it from the list. Once the driver is selected, Windows will ask you if you would like to print a test page. I recommend doing so.

It's also possible to map drives and printers from the command line. Just type the command:

```
NET USE x: \\machine_name\share_name
```

For instance:

```
NET USE g: \\node2\c
```

You can map a printer in this manner as well, but Windows applications won't be able to print to it, since Windows won't associate a printer driver or a print queue with it. To disconnect from the network drive or printer from the command line, just type NET USE <letter> /d (e.g., NET USE g: /d).

Normally, I go ahead and share all of a computer's drives and printers. That way it doesn't matter where I've stored a file—I can get to it from any computer on my network.

Using Networks to Save Disk Space

Nothing stops you from pointing your word processors on every computer on your network to the same network drive, so they use one central place as a repository for data files. This practice saves disk space and keeps you from wondering which computer you saved your files on. It also ensures that you can get to your work, no matter which computer you happen to be using.

You can also install programs to network drives to save space—two computers can share a single copy of any given program. You will need to double-check the program's license agreement to make sure this is legal, but if your program permits you to install it on multiple computers so long as you're only running it on one computer at a time, and if the program isn't disk-intensive, you can save quite a bit of disk space with this method. Remember that network drives aren't as fast as local drives—a fast network drive on a 10-megabit Ethernet network will serve up data about as fast as an 8X CD-ROM drive—so you need to keep in mind that you're sacrificing some speed to save some disk space. The convenience and being free from the need to upgrade a system's hard drive may be worth the speed penalty.

All you have to do is install the program twice—install it on the host machine, referring to the drive by its local name. Be sure to install it to a drive that's being shared, and that the other computer has the drive mapped. Now go to the other computer and install it to that drive. Be aware that it will have a different drive letter on the second PC. You can repeat this for every computer on your network if you wish.

Some programs may object to this—particularly if they keep configuration data in *.ini* files in their local directory. Most programs keep their configuration data in *.ini* files in the *Windows* directory or in the registry, however, so this trick works well for many programs. I use this trick to share freeware utilities that I use only occasionally between my PCs.

Some Networking Tips

You can access network drives by mapping them to local drive letters, but you can also access them via their Universal Naming Convention (UNC) names. The first element of a UNC is the machine name, and the second element is the share name. For instance, if I have a share named C on a computer named Node2, I can access it as *Node2**C.* I can also tack on directory and filenames if I wish—Word 97 accepts *Node2**C**My Documents**Books**Essential Windows 9x Optimization**Chapter 8.doc* as a perfectly valid filename.

If you want to launch a share to see its contents, the fastest way might be to press Start → Run → \\<PC name>\<share name>\<path>.

If you want to quickly bring up the Network control panel, either press Start → Run → `control netcpl.cpl`, or right-click Network Neighborhood → Properties.

And, of course, there's one more thing to say about network speed. If you install File and Printer Sharing for Microsoft Networks, Windows 9x gains the ability to serve as a *Browse Master.* The Browse Master is a sort of referee, keeping track of what computers with network shares are available. When you open Network Neighborhood, your computer first looks to the Browse Master for a list of available computers rather than gathering the list itself.

Depending on the nature of your network, you might want to control which computer acts as the Browse Master. I'll give you an example by describing my personal network as it stands at the moment. I own four PCs: a Pentium 90, a Cyrix MII-233, a 486SX2/66, and a 486SX/25. As a young single guy living alone, the only legitimate use I have for four PCs is to allow me to have all four major versions of Windows 9x (Windows 95, Windows 95A, Windows 95B, and Windows 98) running side by side so I can compare the behavior of various versions as I write this book. When they're not displaying screens, the 486s act as file and print servers. I'm not going to use one of them to write this book when I have the Cyrix available. But I can effortlessly dump important files to both 486s' hard drives to ensure that I instantly have two more backup copies of an important file. The Cyrix can certainly handle spooling a chapter to the printer as I work on writing the next, but it's nice to let the 486 handle that duty. But for the most part, those 486s sit there not doing much. When Windows chooses a Browse Master, it usually tries to choose the most powerful machine there, based on the CPU type and amount of memory. The choices don't always make much sense—I know some Windows NT administrators who get a laugh by watching their system logs whenever they have to reboot their servers and watching who wins the Browse Master elections.

But in my case, I'd rather have my two rarely used 486s handle Browse Master chores. So I go to the Pentium and to the Cyrix and right-click Network Neighborhood → Properties → Configuration → File and printer sharing for Microsoft networks → Properties → Browse Master → Disable. I set the 486s to automatic.

But maybe you're not like me. Take my church's sister congregation. They have a small computer lab with three 486DX2/66s, two Pentiums, and some junkers kept strictly for parts. At any given time, any of these computers can be at work doing word processing or some other task. I want those 486s giving the task at hand their full attention, so I don't want the 486s to even be considered in Browse Master elections. So I disable Browse Master on the 486s, and leave the Pentiums set to automatic.

If you have only two computers on your network, disable Browse Master on one of them. Maybe you want your more powerful machine to save its power for important work, or maybe you want it to cover your weaker PC. Make your decision and set it up. On a three-computer network, you need two set to automatic in order to have failover, but in a two-computer network, you don't need any failover, since there is no network when one of the computers is powered down or restarting.

I expect home networking to become more and more common as multi-PC households become common. While first-time buyers consume a lot of the low-cost PCs on the market today, I expect the ever-lower prices will also lure more and more power users needing extra PCs for menial tasks while their main PCs do the hard work. PC prices have fallen to an all-time low—a couple of times this year, vendors have offered $249 PCs including a modem or network card and a monitor, which after adjusting for inflation is far less than the king of inexpensive computers, the Commodore 64, cost in its heyday. While these inexpensive PCs won't give a $2500 Pentium III a run for the money, after some optimization they will be adequate performers, and a network will permit them to share essential peripherals—many sub-$300 PCs get to that price point by sacrificing the CD-ROM drive, and of course, at that price you won't get a bundled printer. If you have a computer-loving family, a network allows you to add a lot of functionality to these minimalist low-cost systems, making them viable computers for not much money. And if you have multiple computers connected to the Internet, a network will pay for itself in less than a year by allowing all of your computers to share a dial-up Internet connection with a program like WinGate (*www.wingate.com*) or with Windows 98SE's Internet Connection Sharing. If you're not networking now, you probably soon will be.

10

Clean Windows
Installation

If you installed Windows 95 as an upgrade to Windows 3.1, or Windows 98 as an upgrade to any earlier version of Windows, your Windows setup is carrying lots of extra baggage. If you've upgraded many of your peripherals since first installing Windows 95, your Windows setup is probably carrying extra baggage. Unless your PC has been spending its days since 1995 or 1996 in the closet, chances are there's plenty of extra stuff hanging around that doesn't need to be there. You can whip your system into better shape with a heavy dose of utilities, but the best way to get your system running its best is probably to do a clean installation.

First Steps with Windows 95

Reinstalling Windows 9x doesn't have to be (and shouldn't be) as difficult as installing it the first time. The hard drive is formatted and makes a fine repository for data, so we might as well make use of it.

The first thing to do is copy the Win95 directory of your Windows 95 CD to the hard drive. We'll be making modifications to the files in that directory, so you don't want to skip this step. It's much faster to install from the hard drive than from CD anyway. Obvious locations to copy to are *C:\Win95* or *C:\Win98* (keeping with the structure of the CD) and *C:\Windows\Options\Cabs* (which is the standard location OEMs use). *C:\Win95* or *C:\Win98* is better, since we'll be moving the existing Windows installation later in the process.

You'll also want to copy the device drivers for your various peripherals (sound card, modem, video card, motherboard) into that directory. I typically just make a directory called *drivers* inside the directory to which I copy the Windows files, then copy the contents of the disk or CD that came with each peripheral into appropriately named directories (*sound* for the sound card, *video* for the video card, *network* for the network card, and so on). Better yet, get the newest drivers for your equipment. If you don't know who made all of your peripherals, download, install, and run SiSoft Sandra, from *www.sisoftware.demon.co.uk*, to get a detailed list of the hardware in your PC. Visit the hardware manufacturers' web sites to get the most recent drivers, then download and extract them into appropriate directories.

I can't stress enough the importance of getting all of the device drivers. Remember, Windows 95 is old technology. It's older today than Windows 3.1 was when Windows 95 came out. Remember that the most advanced PC available when Windows 95 came out was a 120 MHz Pentium. PCI was something new and novel. Arguably, the PC industry has changed more in the five years since Windows 95's release than it did in the five years before it.

A PC is only as fast and stable as the device drivers installed on it. So for optimal performance and stability, get the newest stuff, and don't forget your motherboard. Chances are your motherboard has drivers that enable DMA mode for your hard drive. (DMA is direct memory access, where the disk controller can bypass the CPU and dump data directly into memory, enhancing performance.) And if it's a recent motherboard with a non-Intel chipset, it probably has AGP drivers as well. (AGP is advanced graphics port, which enhances the speed and stability of video cards.) Acquire and install the AGP drivers! Your system will appear to work just fine without them, but it won't be nearly as stable as it would be with them. Many of the reports of Socket 7 instability floating around on the Web are due to people neglecting to install AGP drivers.

If you play many games, chances are you need DirectX and other post-release Windows 95 enhancements that have come from Microsoft over the years. If your games mention any of these enhancements during their installation, abort the install and go to *www.microsoft.com* to look for newer versions of any of those enhancements. If it turns out your game has the current release, go ahead and install what you have, but otherwise, download the newest release and install it instead.

Finally, if you don't already have one, make a boot disk. You don't want to boot off the same hard drive you install Windows to, because we're going to rename the *Windows* directory before installing and that'll mess things up. To make a boot disk, insert a disk, open a command prompt, and type **sys a:**. Now copy the crucial DOS utilities *format.com, extract.exe, sys.com, fdisk.exe*, and *edit.com* to that disk. Here's the sequence of commands, in case you need it:

```
Copy c:\windows\command\format.* a:\
Copy c:\windows\extract.* a:\
Copy c:\windows\command\sys.* a:\
Copy c:\windows\command\fdisk.* a:\
```

```
Copy c:\windows\command\format.* a:\
Copy c:\windows\command\edit.* a:\
```

It doesn't hurt to add ScanDisk to the list either. You may have moved ScanDisk as per my recommendations back in Chapter 3, *Disk Optimization*. To find it, go to Start → Find → scandisk.exe, then right-click on *scandisk.exe*, select Send To, then select 3.5" floppy.

You won't use the majority of these tools for installation (you'll need Edit and possibly Extract), but the rest of these tools are invaluable for repairing a hard drive that won't boot. The command sequence SCANDISK C: followed by FDISK /MBR followed by SYS C: will repair the vast majority of hard drive problems and get most systems booting again.

Hacking Out MSN and the Exchange Client

How does a minimum installation footprint of 18 MB for the August 24, 1995 release of Windows 95 sound? It's possible. The original Windows 95 was joined at the hip to Exchange and MSN, but both of these products are hopelessly obsolete today, and chances are you don't use either one of them. Even if you are an MSN subscriber, you probably have a CD with the newest version of MSN on it, which you should install instead. Windows is faster and more svelte without this old software.

Microsoft didn't intend for these components to be removed. It's easier than removing Internet Explorer from Windows 98, but you'll have to jump through a few hoops. This trick requires a working installation of Windows 95, so don't boot off that floppy yet.

The biggest hurdle we face is the setup program's compression routine. To save space on floppies and CD-ROMs, the Windows installation routine stores the installation files in compressed archives called *cabinets*, also known as cabs for short, because they have the extension *.cab*. Cab files are similar in concept to (but of course incompatible with) the Zip files we're used to seeing online.

Open a command line and use CD commands to navigate to your installation directory. Now issue the following series of commands:

```
MD PRECOPY
CD PRECOPY
EXTRACT ..\PRECOPY1.CAB
EXTRACT ..\PRECOPY2.CAB
DEL ..\PRECOPY1.CAB
DEL ..\PRECOPY2.CAB
EDIT SETUPPP.INF
```

Now use Edit's Find function (it's in the Search menu) to find the lines referring to *mos.inf* and *msmail.inf.* Remove the line *mos.inf* to remove MSN, and remove the line *msmail.inf* to remove the Exchange client. Save the file and exit.

Most versions of Windows 95 and 95A seem to leave *setuppp.inf* alone if they find it during setup. If you want to be really safe, you can put the file back in its cabinet. Unfortunately, the only utility I could find that's capable of creating the *.cab* archives used by Windows 95's setup routine runs within Windows. You can download CabPack, by Lars Hederer, from *ftp://ftp.simtel.net/pub/simtelnet/win95/compress/cabpack14.zip.*

If you want to be absolutely, positively certain that you're rid of the baggage, launch CabPack. CabPack's defaults don't work with the original version of the Windows 95 setup program, so change the compression type to MSZIP. You should set CabPack's source directory to the location of your extracted files. The destination directory doesn't matter, since you'll have to move the files anyway. Use a cabinet name template of *Precopy*.cab*, and a maximum size of 1.44 MB. Hit OK, and CabPack will create two directories, one called Disk 1 and a second called Disk 2. Disk 1 will contain *Precopy1.cab*; Disk 2, predictably, will contain *Precopy2.cab.* Copy these two files into your Windows installation directory, and skip the next section, which is specific to later versions of Windows 95.

OSR2.x's Excess Baggage

The OEM Service Release versions of Windows 95 contain even more stuff to hack out—adding Internet Explorer 3.0 or 4.0, the ICW Internet Connection Wizard, and competing online services to an already crowded lineup. Fortunately, these versions of Windows 95 make cleanup easier—there's no need to create *.cab* files. This software, too, is all obsolete, so you want to remove it. There's no need to have potential orphan DLLs installed, slowing down the system.

First, extract *setuppp.inf* from *Precopy2.cab* using the command:

```
EXTRACT PRECOPY2.CAB SETUPPP.INF
```

Now open *layout.inf* in Edit, Notepad, or your preferred text editor. Search for a line that reads `SETUPPP.INF=2,,4550`. Change the 2 to a 0. This keeps us from having to generate new *.cab* files the original Windows 95 requires. Save the file, then open *setuppp.inf* in your text editor. To remove MSN, take out the line `mos.inf`. To remove Exchange and Internet Mail, take out the line `inetmail.inf`. To remove Internet Explorer, take out the line `ohare.inf`. To remove the competing online services and the ICW Internet Connection Wizard, take out the lines `athena.inf` and `msinfo.inf`. To get rid of ActiveMovie (made obsolete by the new version of Windows Media Player), remove the line `QUARTZ.INF`.

If you use Windows 95 OSR2.5 or later, you'll also have to delete the following files from your installation directory:*

> *\Contents*
> *ch*.**
> *ie*.**
> *aol*.**
> *pro*.**
> *icw*.**
> *jav*.**
> *actsetup.cab*
> *amov4ie.cab*
> *axa.cab*
> *cs3kit.exe*
> *mailnews.cab*
> *mos.inf*
> *mschat2.cab*
> *msinfo.inf*
> *msn251.exe*
> *nm21.cab*
> *nsie4.cab*
> *ohare.inf*
> *pcvkit.exe*
> *swinst4.exe*
> *vdolive.exe*

Installing Windows 98

In most regards, installing Windows 98 is a less complex affair than installing Windows 95. At the very least, it requires less preparation time. Since many more of the peripherals on the market today existed when Windows 98 was released than at the time of Windows 95's release, Windows 98 installation doesn't require nearly as much time and effort digging up device drivers and product updates.

Windows 98 also asks far fewer questions. This is an advantage when everything works the way it's supposed to. When things don't work as they should, Windows 98 presents some challenges.

In addition, Windows 98 presents the mother of all installation challenges: removal of the Internet Explorer 4.0 browser. Browser-agnostic people may not mind the Internet Explorer integration, but seeing Windows 98's performance with Internet

---

* From Sean Erwin's Windows 95 OSR2 FAQ at *www.compuclinic.com/osr2faq.*

Explorer removed could be enough to convince someone to switch to a Netscape or Opera browser.

The tricks presented at the end of the previous chapter for installing multiple copies of Windows and installing Windows to a RAM disk work for Windows 98 as well.

Why Not Install over My Existing Installation?

I'm pretty free about dispensing the advice to reinstall Windows. There are some people who suggest reinstalling every three months. I think this is extreme, but I expect a lot of people would benefit from reinstalling once a year. It doesn't take long for Windows to pick up a lot of baggage, and even if you're religious about running utility programs to keep your registry and system directories clean, there's only so much this can do to prevent the much-publicized "OS rot" that characterizes microcomputer operating systems like Windows 9x, Windows NT, and MacOS.

Unfortunately, when you install over an old installation, you inherit most of the problems the previous installation had, and sometimes you make them worse. The new installation will repair certain kinds of registry damage, but it is by no means a foolproof way to fix an ailing system.

If it's any consolation, a clean install followed by an uninstallation program's constant monitoring and regular use of a utilities suite should reduce, if not totally eliminate, the need for reinstallations on a regular basis.

Disaster Prevention

I've installed Windows 95 and 98 so many times I've lost count by now, and I've installed it on a lot of strange equipment, including computers that really had no business running Windows 9x. I've seen a lot of things go wrong. But Microsoft deserves very little of the blame, because most of these problems aren't bug-related. There are thousands upon thousands of so-called IBM-compatible or PC-compatible peripherals out there, most of which have never been tested for compatibility with one another. They *should* work, but that's mostly theory. In 1991, I heard an IBM engineer quip, "Even IBM computers aren't 100% IBM-compatible." He was right—it's impossible to make a computer that will work with every peripheral and every piece of software manufactured for IBM and IBM-compatible PCs. I hope that engineer didn't think the situation would get any better. The market is many times larger today than it was then.

You would have to be absolutely crazy to sit down at a working PC, reformat the hard drive, pop in the Windows 98 CD, and install from scratch. This approach usually works—eventually—but there are circumstances where a clean Windows installation, especially when very old or obscure hardware is involved, just won't work, and there's nothing you can do about it. If you have an installation that works, no matter how badly, you should preserve it. I'd venture to say this is unnecessary 99 times out of 100, but if your computer turns out to be that rare case that won't install, you don't want to be stranded without a working backup installation.

Before you do anything else, you want to have a boot floppy so you can restore the current bootable operating system to the PC. This is extremely important—if you're upgrading an old PC to Windows 98 and it fails, you won't be able to revert back to the working system without the boot floppy. Open a command prompt, insert the disk, then type the following commands:

```
FORMAT A: /Q /S
```
This formats the disk and makes it bootable.
```
COPY C:\WINDOWS\COMMAND\SYS.* A:\
```
This copies the SYS utility to the floppy—if your hard drive suddenly stops booting,
the command SYS C: will make it bootable again.
```
COPY C:\WINDOWS\COMMAND\DELTREE.* A:\
```
This copies the DELTREE utility to the floppy. Deltree deletes files and
directories the standard DOS DEL command won't.

Now, if you already have Windows installed on your computer and have a couple hundred MB of free disk space, you can save some time and effort by copying the \WIN98 subdirectory of the Windows 98 installation disk to your hard drive, then copying any device driver CDs you might have into subdirectories on your hard drive as well. This is cheap insurance: Windows 98 will sometimes install components that require access to the CD-ROM drive before it installs the device drivers that give it access to the CD-ROM, and this chicken-and-egg scenario can hang a Windows installation. This wasn't a big deal with Windows 95, since Windows 95 will install on a fast system in 15 minutes. Windows 98 usually takes much longer, however, and if you're like me, you don't want the 45-minute installation to hang 30 minutes into the process.

The traditional location to copy these files to is *C:\Windows\Options\Cabs*. We don't want to do that, because the current *Windows* directory is about to cease to exist (this is a clean installation, after all). So instead, copy them into *C:\Win98*, or if you want them to be in the traditional location, *C:\Cabs*.

Once you've copied the Windows CD and have a working boot disk, restart your computer in MS-DOS mode. Once there, we're going to rename the *Windows* directory. If something goes horribly wrong, we can very easily revert back to the old Windows installation with the boot disk, so long as we rename the old

Windows directory rather than overwriting it. So type the following command to do the deed:

```
REN C:\WINDOWS C:\WINOLD
```

Now, if you want your Windows 98 installation files to be in the traditional location, type the following lines:

```
MD C:\WINDOWS
MD C:\WINDOWS\OPTIONS
C:\WINOLD\COMMAND\MOVE CABS C:\WINDOWS\OPTIONS
```

Finally, to commence Windows 98 setup, type the following lines:

```
CD \WINDOWS\OPTIONS\CABS
SETUP
```

Windows 98 setup will begin. As with Windows 95 installation, I suggest doing a custom installation, removing all of the optional components, getting Windows up and running, installing an uninstallation program like UnInstaller or CleanSweep, then going back into Control Panel → Add/Remove Programs → Windows Setup to add any optional components you want or need. You can then reinstall the rest of your software.

Installing Windows 98 Without Internet Explorer

The possibility of installing Windows 98 without Internet Explorer was one of the main arguments in the Microsoft–U.S. Department of Justice antitrust trial. Department of Justice witness Edward Felten, a computer science professor from Princeton University, said he had written a program to do it, though Microsoft tried to demonstrate that the program didn't always do what its author said it did.

In the meantime, an Australian biologist named Shane Brooks, working on his own, figured out how to remove Internet Explorer 4. By replacing the Windows 98 shell with the older Windows 95 shell, he was able to achieve speed improvements of up to 35%. Brooks' program, which he calls 98lite, is available from *www.98lite.net*.

To run 98lite, you need to copy the \ *Win98* directory from your Windows 98 CD to your hard drive, then copy the files *explorer.exe*, *shell32.dll*, *comdlg32.dll*, *wordpad.exe*, and *notepad.exe* from either a Windows 95 CD or an existing Windows 95 installation into \ *Win98*\ *98lite*. Then copy the 98lite files *98lite.exe*, *98option.exe*, and *98logo.sys* into the directory. To install, run *98lite.exe*.

98lite gives you far more installation options than Microsoft's installation program. If you have the Norton Utilities, you have no need for MSInfo, so you can opt not to install it. ActiveMovie is obsolete and has been replaced by the new version of

Microsoft Media Player, so you should opt not to install it. If you don't share your computer with anyone else, you can leave the Multiple Users option deselected. Your system will run faster if you don't install the Windows bitmaps (they consume precious directory entries in *C:\Windows*, after all). By default, 98lite moves all of the Internet Explorer–related directories to your system's temp directory. 98lite gives you the option to turn this off, but I recommend leaving the option on, because it reduces the amount of clutter in the directory, which speeds up your system.

After 98lite finishes generating setup files (a process that takes a few minutes, so be patient), it runs the standard Microsoft-provided Setup program. When Setup asks for a directory to install to, it will default to your old Windows directory. Type in a new directory name, because we don't want to upgrade. Fresh installations run much more quickly and tend to be more stable.

Always select the Custom installation and remove any components you don't use. I prefer to deselect all of the components, get Windows up and running, install an uninstallation program like UnInstaller or CleanSweep, then go back into Control Panel → Add/Remove Programs → Windows Setup to add any optional components I want or need. Once Windows and its optional components are installed, install the rest of your software.

Besides running faster, a Windows 98 installation using 98lite also has more lenient system requirements. Without the components 98lite removes, Windows 98 requires about 70 MB of disk space, a reduction of about 30 MB.

Issues with 98lite

There are some minor compatibility issues with 98lite. The best way to keep abreast of them is to visit the 98lite web site at *www.98lite.net*. Problems tend to be dealt with quickly as they are discovered.

Using the Registered Version of 98lite

The installation process is much easier with the registered version of 98lite than with the freeware version. You simply download the registered version, extract the archive, then run *98lite.exe*. The program will ask for your Windows 98 CD if it can't find the installation cab files on your hard drive, then copy the installation files into a directory you specify. It asks what type of installation you want (the difference being varying degrees of Internet Explorer presence, ranging from none at all to full presence without integration), and it will ask for your Windows 95 CD if the installation type you chose requires it. It will then copy the Windows 95 versions of *explorer.exe*, *shell32.dll*, and *comdlg32.dll* to the installation directory. To install a new, clean, and slimmed-down version of Windows 98, exit to DOS mode, change to the directory into which 98lite copied its files, then run *98lite.exe*. You will then be presented with a hacked version of Windows Setup that has considerably more options than Microsoft's version.

The most aggressive setting for 98lite Professional 2.0, which Shane Brooks calls 98micro, cuts the minimum space required by Windows 98 and 98SE down to about 50 MB. He also claims that 98micro runs approximately 15% faster than the unaltered Windows 98. This is a very reasonable claim, as 98micro has a much smaller installation footprint, a much smaller registry, and about 20% fewer files in its *Windows* hierarchy. On some systems, the speed difference will be even greater.

Installing Windows 98SE Without Internet Explorer

The original freeware 98lite doesn't fully support Windows 98SE, which ships with Internet Explorer 5. However, 98lite Professional 2.0 works equally well with Windows 98 and Windows 98SE.

Removing Internet Explorer from an Existing Windows 98 Installation

Shane Brooks has also written a script to remove Internet Explorer from existing installations. This script, called IE-Remove, is also available from *www.98lite.net*. The script works well, and if you want to quickly give a Windows 98 PC a speed boost, this is a good way to do it. It's better to reinstall, but that's just not always practical.

Although Windows 98SE uses Internet Explorer 5.0 instead of version 4.0, the IE-Remove script appears to work with Windows 98SE as well.

Installing Device Drivers

If you copied your device drivers somewhere to your hard drive before installing (a practice I'm hesitant to recommend unless all of your peripherals have Windows 98–specific drivers), Windows may have found them and gone ahead and installed them. But if it didn't find them, chances are it didn't ask for them either. For example, after I install Windows 98, my network card just doesn't work. Windows 98 knows I have a network card, it knows it doesn't have a device driver for the card, but it didn't ask for one.

You can install most device drivers with the Add New Hardware Wizard after Windows is installed. To run the wizard, go to Control Panel → Add New Hardware. Windows will present a list of devices it can see but lacks proper drivers to use. Highlight the device, click Next, then follow the special instructions (if any) in the documentation that came with the peripheral.

If the peripheral doesn't show up, consult the documentation for instructions on how to install it. If your system doesn't use an Intel chipset, there's also the possibility that Windows 98 won't add your motherboard's AGP and busmaster support. If your motherboard supports these functions, it will come with a disk or CD containing the appropriate device drivers. Be sure to install these drivers. Your system will be far faster and more stable with them installed.

Do Windows 95 Drivers Work with Windows 98?

Generally speaking, Windows 95 drivers will work with Windows 98. This makes sense, because Windows 95 and Windows 98 are both derived from the same kernel. Windows 98 isn't the evolutionary leap from its predecessors that Windows 95 was—it's very easy to trace the improvements from Windows 95 to Windows 95A to Windows 95B to Windows 95C to Windows 98. However, that's not to say there are no differences. The differences between Windows 95 and Windows 95B were significant enough that some peripherals had to ship with different driver sets for the two versions. The jump from Windows 95B to Windows 98 is bigger than the jump from Windows 95 to 95B. It's always best to look for Windows 98–specific drivers on your peripherals' installation disks and CDs, and if you find none there, check the manufacturer's web site.

Backward compatibility has always been one of Windows' goals, but sometimes it's just not possible. You shouldn't just blindly assume that the Windows 95 drivers will work perfectly with Windows 98.

Performing the Installation

Now that the setup files are appropriately modified to cut out some of the bloat, we're ready to proceed. Before you boot off the floppy you created earlier, run ScanDisk or a third-party disk repair tool from within Windows. You want your drive to be error-free when you install, and these tools do a better job than the DOS-based ScanDisk that Windows setup runs. After you finish checking your hard disk for errors, boot from the bootable floppy you created earlier. Now, issue the command:

```
REN C:\WINDOWS C:\WINOLD
```

I never delete a working Windows installation until I manage to produce an installation that works better. If something goes horribly wrong and you just can't get the new installation to work right, you can always revert back to the old installation by deleting or renaming the failed installation and renaming the original installation back to its original state.

That said, I've only had a Windows 9x reinstallation go bad twice. Both times, it worked, but the machine was a whole lot more sluggish than it had been previously. I've installed Windows 95 hundreds of times, so it's pretty safe to say it installs cleanly and relatively easily most of the time. But one of my rules is to always have at least one more backup than I think I need. That way, if you turn out to be that one in two hundred that doesn't work right, you have a safe way out.

You might ask why we rename the Windows directory rather than installing on top of the existing installation. There are two reasons. First, if you install on top of what's there, you've lost your backup copy. It's much harder to revert back to your previous state if you install over an existing installation. Second, an installation over an existing installation inherits most of the characteristics, good and bad, of the existing installation. If MSN was installed on the existing installation (chances are it was), it will be in the new one. The only way to get a clean start is to start fresh.

Start the Windows 95 installation process by changing into your installation directory (I suggest *C:\Win95*) and typing SETUP. I usually feed Setup some command switches: SETUP /is /id /iq /d gives the kind of behavior I like (don't run Scan-Disk, don't check free space, don't check for cross-linked files, and ignore whatever existing configuration files Setup or its spies happen to find). This gives me the fastest, cleanest install possible, assuming you ran a disk repair tool previously. Windows will ask if you accept the license agreement. Hope it hasn't changed since the last time you installed, say yes, then click Next.

Setup will default to upgrading the existing installation in *C:\Winold*. Click Other Directory, specify a different path (probably *C:\Windows*) and click Next. Setup will complain, saying that you'll lose whatever programs are installed in that configuration and you'll have to reinstall them. Tell it you don't care. This is, after all, precisely what we want. Sometimes it seems as if the easiest way to get a clean house is to build it from scratch, and that's definitely the case with computers (and that's true of Windows 9x PCs, Windows NT PCs, Macintoshes, and several other types of computers).

Setup will now present you with setup options: I always choose custom. And as for Microsoft's warning with this option, as far as I'm concerned, if you've gotten this far in this book, you qualify as an advanced user or system administrator. Setup will then ask if you want to look for all hardware devices. Usually you will want to say yes. If you have a very slow computer and know what's in it, say no and uncheck any equipment you know you don't have. If you have an IDE or SCSI CD-ROM drive (if your drive is faster than 2X it probably is), you can uncheck CD-ROM drive. If you don't have a laptop, uncheck PCMCIA. If you're not on a network, uncheck Network Adapter. If you don't have a SCSI card, uncheck SCSI controllers. If you feel like drilling deeper into the list, you can narrow it down even more.

What to Do if Setup Appears to Hang

On some Windows 95 systems, Windows will hang on installation no matter what you do. If this happens on your system, it's probably the hardware detection that's causing the problem. If this happens, uncheck any hardware devices you know you don't have. If that fails, you need extreme measures. Restart the installation and uncheck everything you don't have, as well as everything you think you might not have. All Windows 95 really needs in order to get through installation is the right keyboard and mouse drivers, along with generic VGA video. The right disk controller is nice to have (it significantly increases performance) but not absolutely essential. Go ahead and search for a standard IDE controller, because that's what most systems have. Once installation finishes successfully, you should be able to get the hardware configuration right by running the Add New Hardware wizard from Control Panel.

Hangs seem to be more common with Windows 98. On some systems, Setup will appear to hang as it prepares the Windows 98 Setup Wizard. It will reach 100% and just sit there. For example, Windows 98 tends to hesitate for about five to seven minutes on systems without floppy drives—it's waiting for the nonexistent floppy drive to respond. Other unusual configurations can cause similar delays. If the installation seems to be just sitting there, let it be. Run some errands or something while it sits.

A good test to see whether your system is truly hung or just taking a really long time is to hit the Caps Lock key. If the Caps Lock light on the keyboard won't light up, the system is hung. If the Caps Lock key will light up, there's hope. Give it some time.

If Setup does hang at this point (or at any other point in the installation for that matter), it could be that Setup doesn't like something about your hardware combination. You can still recover. Power down your computer, then open your case, remove any cards except for the video card, and try again, running installation with a bare system. More than likely it will install. After Windows finishes installing, shut down, turn your computer off, put the cards back in, and turn your computer back on. Windows should detect the cards one at a time and either add the device drivers or prompt you for the appropriate disks.

After searching for hardware, Windows will ask what components you want to install. I always clear all of the boxes. No, I don't actually use Windows in super-stripped-down econo-mode configuration. But it's much easier to optimize a minimalist configuration (there will be files you'll want to move to *C:\Windows\Command*). Plus, Windows will never run any faster than it does in this minimalist configuration. It's good to see the system in this state in order to keep your performance goals realistic.

If Windows senses a network card or a modem, or if it has reason to believe you have one, it will ask you for a network configuration. Windows 95 is obsessed with networks. Resist the temptation to configure the network at this stage. Remove all of the components and set your Primary Network Logon to Windows Logon. Adding network components adds overhead, and at this stage we want the lowest overhead possible.

Click Next, and Windows will give you a configuration screen. The most interesting option here is buried at the very end. You can change from the Explorer-based Windows 95 interface to the Program Manager–based Windows 3.1 interface. If your system is short on memory, you might want to do this (and thus have ready-made Program Manager groups from the very start). Make whatever changes, if any, you might want, then hit Next. Windows will ask if you want a Startup disk. You probably don't; the disk you made earlier in this chapter will suffice for emergency use. Hit Next twice, and Windows will install files, then restart a couple of times, and you'll have a nice, minimalist, close-to-optimal Windows installation to work with.

Post-Installation Magic

Once Windows finishes its marathon of reboots, I close the Welcome screen (clearing the box that says Show on Startup), change the background color to black, and install an uninstallation program, followed by a utilities suite (or two). Then I run the uninstallation program, followed by the utilities suite. The more these programs know about my system, the better they work, and this is the earliest stage possible to introduce them. The first two things I do are optional. Technically, the uninstallation program and utilities suite are as well, but your system will run better if you go ahead and use them.

After optimizing the system by moving things around and installing any device drivers that Setup may have missed, I go ahead and configure the network (if need be) and install the optional components I want by going into Control Panel → Add/Remove Programs → Windows Components.

Once the optional components are in place, I go ahead and do another round of optimization (moving what I can from *C:\Windows* and *C:\Windows\System* into *C:\Windows\Command*, as described in Chapter 3).

At this stage, I suggest making a backup copy of your entire Windows configuration. The GPLed Info-ZIP is excellent for this. Download your copy of the DOS version of Info-ZIP's Zip and UnZip command-line utilities from *www.cdrom.com/pub/infozip*. You want the DOS version because you'll have to create your archives from DOS mode—Windows won't let Zip touch the registry while it's running. Copy the

Zip and Unzip executables to *C:\Windows\Command*, then issue the following command:

```
Zip -9 -R -S [c:\windows.zip] c:\windows\*.*
```

You want to specify your own path, outside of the Windows directory, for your archive. You don't want something like that hanging out in your root directory. Once you have a backup, if you ever get into trouble, you can at least get back to this stage within a few minutes with the following commands:

```
COPY C:\WINDOWS\COMMAND\UNZIP.EXE C:\
CD\
DELTREE WINDOWS
MD WINDOWS
CD WINDOWS
UNZIP [C:\WINDOWS.ZIP]
```

Substitute the location of your archive in the last line.

Once I'm satisfied that I have a good backup, I install the rest of the programs I use.

Stupid Installation Tricks

Windows has more tricks up its sleeve. Although it's not exactly pretty, it's possible to have multiple copies of Windows installed on one PC—for instance, one tweaked out for games and another tweaked out for personal productivity—and if you don't mind occasionally shuffling a pair of floppies, you can run Windows 95 and 98 on the same system.

Installing Multiple Copies of Windows

The fewer programs you install, the faster Windows runs. But what about those programs that only get run every once in a while? Maybe you have a program you have to run once every month or two. Constantly installing and uninstalling it is a waste of time, but the program is wasting your time by occupying valuable directory space in your Windows directories.

The solution: install multiple copies of Windows. Microsoft didn't make it easy— they may have intended to make it impossible—but with a batch file for every configuration, you can do it. If more than one person uses your computer, you can set up a configuration for each person. Or you might have a configuration for typical everyday use and a stripped-down configuration (you know, no Office 97, no scanner stuff, not even a printer) for down-in-the-trenches gaming where every cycle counts.

To multiboot Windows, create a directory somewhere (say, *C:\Windows\Command\Multiboot*), then open a command prompt and type these commands:

```
ATTRIB -R -S -H C:\MSDOS.SYS
```
This makes msdos.sys visible so we can manipulate it.
```
COPY C:\MSDOS.SYS C:\WINDOWS\COMMAND\MULTIBOOT\1.SYS
```
This makes a copy of msdos.sys that we can swap in later.
```
COPY C:\AUTOEXEC.BAT  C:\WINDOWS\COMMAND\MULTIBOOT\1.BAT
```
This makes a copy of autoexec.bat for future swapping.
```
COPY C:\CONFIG.SYS C:\WINDOWS\COMMAND\MULTIBOOT\1C.SYS
```
This makes a copy of config.sys for future swapping.
```
ATTRIB +R +S +H C:\MSDOS.SYS
```
This makes msdos.sys invisible again to make it more difficult to accidentally damage it.
```
EXIT
```
This returns you to Windows.

Now install Windows. When it asks for a target directory, point it to a directory other than *C:\Windows*. Don't bother configuring it yet; let's just prove the concept before doing anything serious. Don't worry about losing your previous configuration, because we've archived it.

Once Windows is installed, open a command prompt and type these commands:

```
ATTRIB -R -S -H C:\MSDOS.SYS
```
This makes msdos.sys visible so we can manipulate it.
```
COPY C:\MSDOS.SYS C:\WINDOWS\COMMAND\MULTIBOOT\2.SYS
```
This makes a second msdos.sys we can swap with the old one.
```
COPY C:\AUTOEXEC.BAT  C:\WINDOWS\COMMAND\MULTIBOOT\2.BAT
```
This does the same for autoexec.bat.
```
COPY C:\CONFIG.SYS C:\WINDOWS\COMMAND\MULTIBOOT\2C.SYS
```
and this the same for config.sys.
```
ATTRIB +R +S +H C:\MSDOS.SYS
```
This makes msdos.sys invisible again to make it more difficult to accidentally damage it.
```
EXIT
```
This returns you to Windows.

Now, open your favorite text editor and type in the two batch files shown in Example 10-1 and Example 10-2, saving the first one as *C:\Windows\Command\Boot1.bat* and the second one as *C:\Windows\Command\Boot2.bat*. These batch files automate the swapping process.

Example 10-1. Boot1.bat

```
DELTREE /Y C:\MSDOS.SYS
COPY C:\WINDOWS\COMMAND\MULTIBOOT\1.SYS C:\MSDOS.SYS
COPY C:\WINDOWS\COMMAND\MULTIBOOT\1C.SYS C:\CONFIG.SYS
COPY C:\WINDOWS\COMMAND\MULTIBOOT\1.BAT C:\AUTOEXEC.BAT
ATTRIB +R +S +H C:\MSDOS.SYS
```

Example 10-2. Boot2.bat

```
DELTREE /Y C:\MSDOS.SYS
COPY C:\WINDOWS\COMMAND\MULTIBOOT\2.SYS C:\MSDOS.SYS
COPY C:\WINDOWS\COMMAND\MULTIBOOT\2C.SYS C:\CONFIG.SYS
COPY C:\WINDOWS\COMMAND\MULTIBOOT\2.BAT C:\AUTOEXEC.BAT
ATTRIB +R +S +H C:\MSDOS.SYS
```

To boot the first copy of Windows, just go to Start → Run → BOOT1, then Start → Shut down → Restart the computer. Similarly, to boot the second copy, go to Start → Run → BOOT2, then Start → Shut down → Restart the computer.

If you look closely at the sequence of commands above and at the code in the batch files, you'll see that the only thing that changes is the numbers. You can have as many installations as you want (at least until you run out of disk space) by incrementing the numbers. When you save the batch files, you can give them more meaningful names as well, like *Productivity.bat* and *Games.bat*. The names don't matter.

Chances are there are some pieces of software you'll want to share between Windows installations. That's no problem. Just install the piece of software, then boot into another copy of Windows and install the piece of software in the same directory. Repeat as necessary. The application will then be available to multiple installations.

This technique would be especially useful in families with small children, since a large number of educational titles for children are very finicky. Many of those programs just don't work right unless you go into the System control panel, click on the Performance tab, hit the Graphics button, and slow down the system's hardware acceleration. This lets your educational titles run, but it kills the performance of your other applications. If you create a dedicated installation for educational titles, however, you can turn the hardware acceleration down in that installation, but leave it at maximum performance on your productivity installation.

You can also use this technique to solve DLL conflicts. Sometimes programs will install differing versions of DLLs—the subject of many a Brian Livingston column in *InfoWorld* over the past few years—and the application may crash the system if it finds a DLL it doesn't like. If you're having major problems with one or two programs on your system, try isolating one of them in its own copy of Windows to see if that clears up the problem.

There was a time when this technique was hopelessly wasteful, but with mainstream hard disk sizes doubling every year, we don't have to worry about that problem anymore. The disk space occupied by a 100 MB Windows directory currently costs about $1.20, and heaven knows what it will cost by the time you read this. Since it's easier to drop a bigger hard drive into a PC than it is to drop a new, more efficient file system into Windows, this presents a way to keep a large number of applications loaded on a PC without hopelessly slowing down the system.

Multi-Booting Windows 95 and 98

It would be nice if Windows 98 could use the above method to multi-boot with Windows 95 for the purpose of running games that aren't compatible with

Windows 98. (Windows 98 has compatibility problems with Win-G, used by some older Windows 95 games such as Civilization II or This Means War.)

Unfortunately, if you back up Windows 95 as described in the previous chapter, then install Windows 98 and then point *msdos.sys* to the previous installation, Windows 95 hangs with the infamous Incorrect DOS Version error. Some hocus-pocus with *setver.exe* can get you past that, but then the even more infamous Out of Memory error gets you.

The easiest way to run Windows 95 and 98 on the same PC without a utility like System Commander is to keep a set of boot floppies. Boot Windows 95, then insert a blank floppy disk and open a command prompt. Enter the following lines (comments in italic follow each code line):

```
FORMAT A: /s
```
This formats the floppy disk and installs system files.
```
ATTRIB -R -S -H C:\MSDOS.SYS
```
This makes msdos.sys visible.
```
COPY C:\MSDOS.SYS A:\
```
This copies msdos.sys to the floppy.
```
ATTRIB +R +S +H C:\MSDOS.SYS
```
This makes msdos.sys invisible again.
```
COPY C:\WINDOWS\COMMAND\SYS.COM A:\
```
This copies the SYS command to the floppy.
```
COPY C:\WINDOWS\COMMAND\DELTREE.EXE A:\
```
This copies the DELTREE command to the floppy.

Substitute the path to your Windows 95 directory in the last two lines.

Next, enter the batch file in Example 10-3, and save it to the disk as well.

Example 10-3. autoexec.bat
```
SYS C:
DELTREE C:\MSDOS.SYS
COPY A:\MSDOS.SYS C:\
ECHO Remove disk and restart to boot Windows 95.
```

After installing Windows 98 (to a different directory, of course), insert the second floppy disk, and repeat the process above, substituting the words "Windows 98" for the reference to Windows 95 in the last line of the batch file.

Keep the two disks in a safe place near your PC, and you can switch between Windows 95 and 98 by booting off the appropriate floppy disk.

11

RAM Disks

During the Persian Gulf War of 1990, Iraqi leader Saddam Hussein threatened the United States and its allies with the mother of all battles. He was hoping, I assume, to conjure up images of an apocalyptic battle. For a time after the war, the phrase "Mother of all . . ." circulated in the vernacular, used whenever the speaker wanted to conjure up images of great magnitude.

Somehow, calling RAM disks the mother of all performance tuning tricks seems like an understatement. I put 256 MB of RAM in an old 266 MHz computer, coaxed Windows into running entirely from the RAM disk, and the computer blew away any and all expectations I would have of a 700 MHz screamer. Typical programs loaded instantly. Adobe Photoshop 5, which usually takes longer to load than Windows itself does, loaded in nine seconds.

Not only did these programs exhibit load times that made my head spin, but they also ran faster. The speed improvement depended on how much they accessed the disk, ranging from noticeable to mind-blowing. Applications generally showed the greatest improvement; games improved a bit less since many of them are CPU-intensive rather than disk-intensive. Even still, most of us would be better served by a $499 Celeron or K6 system with 256 or 384 megs of RAM (cost: an additional $200 or $300) than by the typical $2,500 Pentium III system.

Advantages of RAM Disks

RAM disks have a number of advantages over hard drives. First of all, they are lightning fast—hundreds of times faster than even the fastest hard drive. Since the hard drive is far and away the biggest bottleneck in your system, a RAM disk will usually have a dramatic effect on system performance. Finally, there's a storage medium that can almost keep up with your CPU's insatiable appetite for data.

Although a RAM disk can get fragmented, it's less prone than a hard drive to the adverse effects of fragmentation. Since its contents disappear at reboot, the RAM disk has to be rebuilt every time you boot. This eliminates fragmentation. If you don't have to reboot your system very often, of course, you can defragment your RAM disk, and the process is lightning fast. A badly fragmented RAM disk should defragment in less than a minute—though RAM disks are much less susceptible to the detrimental effects of fragmentation.

Finally, since your operating system is contained within RAM and gets rebuilt every time you reboot, you in essence are reinstalling Windows fresh with every reboot. If you install a program and decide you don't like it and don't want to keep it, reboot without updating your configuration. It's gone. And the phenomenon of OS rot—where Windows performance deteriorates over time—is greatly reduced.

Some Background and System Requirements for RAM Disks

RAM disks are the opposite of virtual memory—they take a chunk of memory from the system and use it to emulate a lightning-fast disk drive. RAM disks are a throwback to an earlier era, a time when memory suddenly became cheap and there wasn't much better use for it—a time that sounds an awful lot like today. The memory prices of 1999 are about a quarter that of 1998, so 256 megs of RAM sells for about what 64 megs sold for a year ago, yet Windows 9x doesn't really know what to do with more than 64 megs of RAM.

We can expect RAM prices to fluctuate from month to month or even from week to week for the foreseeable future, but prices aren't likely to rise back to 1997 or 1998 levels. Today's prices make RAM disks extremely practical.

Microsoft didn't make it nearly that easy, but if you have a lot of RAM and even more determination, you can run Windows 95 from a RAM disk. By a lot of RAM, I mean a *lot*—at the very least, 192 MB. On a 64 or 128 MB system, available memory limits you to RAM disks of meaningless sizes, because you want 40–64 MB of RAM left over for Windows itself. (You don't want your system using much hard drive space for memory when it's using RAM for disk space, after all—it totally defeats the purpose.) A 256 MB system will permit a RAM disk of 192 MB, enough to hold Windows and a couple of applications.

Memory prices tend to fluctuate wildly like gasoline prices, but RAM disks make sense when memory is cheap. In the late spring of 1999, 128 MB DIMMs sold for as little as $80, and smaller-capacity DIMMs were priced like party favors—so it makes sense to take advantage of this pricing. But the optimal amount of memory for Windows 9x is somewhere between 40 and 64 MB. A RAM disk is the best use for memory beyond 64 megs, and the best use for a large RAM disk is holding the most speed-intensive piece of software on your PC: the operating system.

The Windows installation routine restarts the computer several times, which of course erases the contents of your RAM disk. Getting Windows into a RAM disk takes a lot of craftiness.

Before you try the RAM disk trick, you need to download Info-ZIP's Zip and UnZip from *www.cdrom.com/pub/infozip*, and XMSDISK, introduced in Chapter 5, *Utilities*, from *www.opus.co.tt/dave/index.htm*. Download both the DOS version and the 32-bit Windows version of XMSDISK. Copy the 32-bit versions of *Zip.exe* and *Unzip.exe* to *C:\Windows\Command*. You also need to back up your current set of configuration files as described in Chapter 10, *Clean Windows Installation*. You want to be sure you save your working installation, since the RAM disk requires significant changes to both *config.sys* and *autoexec.bat*.

Setting up a surrogate drive

Since the reboot erases the RAM disk and there's no way to prevent Windows from rebooting during installation, we have to create a surrogate.

This is easier under Windows 95B or C or Windows 98. There is an old DOS command called **subst** that allows you to treat a disk directory as a separate drive. Early versions of Windows 95 were incompatible with **subst** (the installation program can hang if **subst** is running), but newer versions of Windows will grudgingly coexist with it. Create a directory (for instance, *C:\W*), then add the following line to *autoexec.bat*:

```
C:\windows\command\subst r: c:\w
```

Substitute the drive letter you want to use for your RAM disk and then substitute the path to the directory you created. Windows Setup will complain that **subst** is running, but it will allow you to continue.

If you're using either the original August 24, 1995 release of Windows 95, or even the newer Windows 95A, the easiest way to set up a surrogate is to create a small disk partition. Using PartitionMagic, create a small partition the size of your desired RAM disk (a good rule of thumb is available memory minus 64), then install a minimal Windows 95 to that partition. Then install your crucial applications to the same partition. Only install absolutely critical stuff here—modern applications fill up half a gigabyte faster than you can say "bloatware," and chances are you have at most a couple hundred megabytes to work with. Leave at least 8 MB free in the drive, because Windows frequently needs to write files into its directory temporarily while you work. If the drive fills up, the system won't crash, but whatever program is running will probably malfunction.

Once you have your surrogate drive set up, you need to do one last thing before installing Windows to the surrogate drive. Go into *C:\Windows* and rename your *system.dat* and *user.dat* files to *system.xyz* and *user.xyz*, respectively. Windows has a tendency while booting to go looking for a registry if it can't find one where it expects, and Windows Setup has a tendency to do the same. Your RAM disk can malfunction if Windows finds these registries.

Be sure to rename the two registry files if you decide to boot your disk-based copy of Windows.

What Does PartitionMagic Have to Do with RAM Disks?

PartitionMagic is useful for creating the surrogate partition that temporarily takes the place of the RAM disk. You could also accomplish the task using the freeware partition-splitting utility FIPS, but since disk partitions get first dibs on drive letters, the only way to hand the drive letter over to the RAM disk is to destroy the partition. Without having PartitionMagic to reassign the partition's space to an adjacent partition, you lose use of that disk space.

Admittedly, with disk prices currently at about 2.3 cents per megabyte, the loss of a couple hundred megabytes isn't a tragedy, even though it leaves a bad taste in the mouth of those of us who remember like it was yesterday a time when a couple hundred megabytes of disk space cost $600 or more.

The most obvious alternative to using a partition as a surrogate is an external storage device, such as a Jaz or Zip drive. Load its DOS driver in *autoexec.bat*, then install Windows to the drive. You can then archive the installation, unplug the drive from the system when you're ready to boot from the RAM disk for the first time, then add the drive back to the system once the RAM-based installation is working. The storage capacity and speed (or lack of both) inherent in parallel-port Zip drives will make this a painful proposition, however, and not one that I'm inclined to recommend.

Note that internal IDE Zip drives lack DOS-compatible device drivers, which makes them useless for this exercise, although an internal SCSI Zip or Jaz drive will work.

The layout of your RAM disk

Since RAM is non-permanent, you probably don't want to store absolutely everything in RAM. Windows stores the location of its critical directories in the registry at HKCU\Software\Microsoft\Windows\CurrentVersion\Explorer\Shell Folders, so you can open Regedit and navigate there. For instance, the *NetHood* folder isn't terribly speed-intensive because so few people use the Network Neighborhood icon, so you can redirect it to *C:\ramdisk\nethood* if you like. If you want your Start menu to remain constant, move it to *C:\ramdisk\start menu*. You'll probably want the *Startup* folder to remain RAM-based to speed boot time. The *Favorites* and *Recent* directories are also good candidates for moving.

You also don't have to install all of your applications to the RAM disk. If you can only afford a 128 MB RAM disk, install Windows to it and install your applications to the hard drive. The applications will still benefit, since they frequently use Windows DLLs and other DLLs in the Windows directory. I found that having Windows entirely in RAM shaved at least a couple of seconds off the load time of every application, even those I had installed to the hard disk.

You definitely want to make sure you optimize your RAM disk's directory structure. With the hard drive out of the way, the CPU is now the biggest bottleneck in your system. You want to make life as easy on it as possible.

Once you've installed Windows, be sure to copy the 32-bit *Unzip.exe* to *\Windows\Command*. Windows will need it when it constructs the RAM disk at bootup. You also need to right-click the Start menu → Programs → Startup, then right-click an empty part of the right pane and select New → Shortcut. Type:

```
e:\windows\command\unzip c:\ramdisk\programs.zip -d e:\,
```

substituting your RAM disk's drive letter for `e:\`.

There's one last thing you have to do. By default, Windows puts the swap file on the same drive it boots from. But unless it has 64 MB or more free, putting the swap file on a RAM disk is pointless—you're emulating memory with a disk drive that's in turn being emulated by memory. When Windows runs out of space for virtual memory, system performance slows to a crawl, so under most circumstances, you don't want to use your RAM disk for virtual memory. Go into Control Panel → System → Performance → Virtual Memory → "Let me specify my own virtual memory settings," and specify the hard drive you use in your other Windows setup. If you've left more than 40 MB of memory available for the system, you won't be using virtual memory very much (unless you're using your system for software or multimedia development), so you don't have to worry about the performance hit.

Once you have a satisfactory configuration, save your new configuration using the set of batch files described in the "Installing Multiple Copies of Windows" section of Chapter 10, then boot into your previous Windows configuration. This is where things start to get tricky. We have to set up a directory on drive *C:* that can hold the contents of the RAM disk and enough system software to create the RAM disk in the first place. Make a directory called *C:\ramdisk*, then move the files *himem. sys*, *setver.exe*, and *ifshlp.sys* from your surrogate drive's Windows directory into

C:\ramdisk. Also add *xmsdsk.exe* (the RAM disk driver), the 16-bit DOS version of Info-ZIP's *unzip.exe*, and, if you use them, either *emm386.exe* or *umbpci.sys* to *C: \ramdisk.*

Windows' default behavior is to try to load *himem.sys, setver.exe,* and *ifshlp.sys* from your Windows directory at boot time. It can't do this, since they don't exist yet, so we have to load them manually in *config.sys.* Add the following three lines:

```
Device=c:\ramdisk\himem.sys
Device=c:\ramdisk\umbpci.sys ;substitute Device=c:\ramdisk\emm386.exe if needed
Devicehigh=c:\ramdisk\ifshlp.sys
Devicehigh=c:\ramdisk\setver.exe
```

It's necessary to archive the Windows configuration you just created, because a simple copy or xcopy command won't preserve the file attributes necessary for a valid bootable Windows directory. The 16-bit version of Info-ZIP is likely to be overwhelmed by your configuration, so you need to use the 32-bit command-line version, which is capable of creating larger archives. Copy Info-ZIP's 32-bit *Zip.exe* to your *C:\Windows\Command* directory, then issue the following commands:

```
Zip -R -S c:\ramdisk\windows.zip d:\windows\*.*
Zip -R -S c:\ramdisk\programs.zip d:\progra~1\*.*
Zip -R -S c:\ramdisk\windows.zip d:\windows\startm~1\*.*
```

Replace your surrogate drive's letter for *d.* We need two archives in order to preserve Windows 9x's long filenames.

You'll probably want to create a batch file similar to the one above, which you can then run any time you make changes to your RAM disk configuration (such as after installing software). I call mine *update.bat* (see Example 11-1), and I store it in the *\Windows\command* directory in my RAM disk.

Example 11-1. update.bat

```
Del c:\ramdisk\windows2.zip
Del c:\ramdisk\programs2.zip
Ren c:\ramdisk\windows1.zip c:\ramdisk\windows2.zip
Ren c:\ramdisk\windows.zip c:\ramdisk\windows1.zip
Ren c:\ramdisk\programs1.zip c:\ramdisk\programs2.zip
Ren c:\ramdisk\programs.zip c:\ramdisk\programs1.zip
Zip -R -S C:\ramdisk\windows.zip d:\windows\*.*
Zip -R -S C:\ramdisk\programs.zip d:\progra~1\*.*
Zip -R -S C:\ramdisk\programs.zip d:\windows\startm~1\*.*
```

This file maintains backups of my last two configurations. If my configuration doesn't work right, I can revert to a previous configuration by deleting *c:\ramdisk\ windows.zip* and renaming one of the other archives.

Making the system boot from the RAM disk requires substantial changes to *msdos. sys* and *autoexec.bat.* Assuming you are using the batch files from the last section of Chapter 10, your RAM disk configuration's *msdos.sys* is stored in *C:\Windows*

Command\Multiboot\2.sys and your RAM disk configuration's *autoexec.bat* is stored in *C:\Windows\Command\Multiboot\2.bat.* Load *C:\Windows\Command\ Multiboot\2.sys* into a text editor. Near the top of the file, you'll find a section labeled [Paths]. On my system, my RAM disk is drive *E:*. Substitute your RAM disk's letter for mine in the second line of the file. Here's the [Paths] section of my *msdos.sys*:

```
[Paths]
WinDir=E:\Windows
WinBootDir=C:\ramdisk
HostWinBootDrv=C
```

I also suggest you scroll down to [Options] and set Logo=0 so you can monitor the progress of the boot process. When boot time is measured in minutes, it's good to have some reassurance that the system is actually doing something. Save the file, then load *C:\Windows\Command\Multiboot\3.bat.* Here's what my file looks like:

```
@echo off

REM Set up RAMdisk. Syntax: xmsdsk.exe [size] [drive letter:] /t /y
REM /t specifies use top of memory (required with Win9x)
REM /y confirms the "are you sure?" prompt.
Xmsdsk.exe 196605 e: /t /y

REM Set path; required because we switcheroo so much on the OS.
Path e:\Windows;e:\Windows\Command;e:\Windows\System;C:\ramdisk

REM Extract contents of RAM disk.
REM Syntax: unzip [archive] -d [destination]
REM sub in your RAM disk's drive letter for [destination], of course.
Unzip c:\ramdisk\windows.zip -d e:\
```

To boot from the RAM disk, you must destroy the surrogate drive. Under Windows 95B/C/98, this process is easy—just remove the subst command from *autoexec.bat.* Under Windows 95/95A, you must destroy the surrogate partition. If you have PartitionMagic, you can delete the partition and let the adjacent partition absorb it; otherwise, use FDISK to delete the partition, but you will then lose use of that disk space. If you then set these files as the active system using the batch file from the last section of Chapter 10, Windows will boot from the RAM disk.

Loading up a system with a ton of RAM and running Windows from a RAM disk once seemed like a waste of money, but with memory prices at historic lows now, it makes sense. You can spend $800 on a 10,000 rpm SCSI hard drive and $250 on a disk controller that will do it justice, or you can spend $300 to get enough memory to hold your operating system and your most often-used applications. No hard drive can even dream of approaching the speed of RAM. Or you can look at it another way. Intel's fastest CPU frequently costs $300 more than a more mainstream CPU, but probably at best improves system performance by only 15%. But

Strategies for RAM Disk Preparation

Remember that a well thought out RAM disk makes disk caching almost a moot point. You'll probably still save your data to disk, but the majority of your applications will run straight from RAM and never touch your disk except when saving data. So you can significantly lower your disk cache settings. With a RAM disk, you should easily be able to get by with a disk cache of 1 MB or possibly even less. There's no reason to feel bad about allocating all but 40 MB of system RAM to a RAM disk.

It's entirely possible that you have far more memory available to the system than you thought. The tricks presented in Chapter 2, *First Steps*, can recover a considerable amount of memory for system use.

Since RAM disks are extremely puny compared to the cavernous sizes of modern hard drives, you need to be prudent about what files you keep in your RAM disk. In order to fit Windows and your important applications into the RAM disk, you might have to get rid of a few things. Here are some candidates for deletion to save space:

\Sysbckup

> This hidden directory contains backup copies of critical system files. By their very nature, RAM disks force backups of critical system files. Since your RAM disk–based system effectively rebuilds itself every time you do a hard reboot, this directory is redundant. Lose it.

\Inf

> This hidden directory contains device driver information for Windows' Add New Hardware Wizard. It's huge—on one of my systems, this directory occupies 6.5 MB. Shove it off into *c:\ramdisk* and copy it back into place if and when you add hardware to the system or have to change your configuration. About 99% of the time, this directory is just eating up megabytes of space that would be better used for temporary storage or running programs.

\Media

> Windows *.wav* files consume buckets of disk space. When forced to deal with limited disk space, you'll probably want to lose them.

\Cursors

> Custom cursors are pretty much the same story as *\Media*.

\Help

> Admittedly, this directory's contents can be useful, but few of us use it on a regular basis. I suggest shoving it off to *c:\ramdisk* and copying it into place only when you need it, since it's another one of those things you probably only need once every two to three months at the most.

—Continued—

\Command

>Most of these files should stay, but rarely used DOS commands like *fc.exe* and *diskcopy.com* from this directory, as well as from *\Windows* and *\Windows\System*, can move to *c:\ramdisk* without harming the system and save your valuable RAM disk space for other purposes.

Welcome.exe

>Unless you like Windows' tips on startup, get rid of this and save a couple hundred kilobytes.

Don't forget to optimize your RAM disk–based system using the tips throughout the rest of this book. A big RAM disk eliminates the biggest bottleneck in your system, making molehill-sized waste start to look mountainous.

$300 worth of RAM disk will do much more to improve system performance because programs load almost instantly and run unencumbered by disk bottlenecks.

The additional prep time makes setup more difficult than usual, and the boot time for a system with a RAM disk will be measured in minutes as opposed to seconds, but the performance boost can be unbelievable. Try a minimalist installation with the memory you have before you load up on memory—I stuffed the minimal installations of Windows 95 and Word 97 into a 38 MB RAM disk to test RAM disks on a 64 MB system; the result wasn't suitable for general use but it was fine for experimentation. Chances are if you start with a minimalist install, you'll like what you see and you'll soon be in line for more memory.

I'd love to see someone design and release a battery-backed hardware RAM disk for PCs, as this would eliminate the limitations inherent in XMSDISK. Such devices existed in the early 1990s for the Commodore 64/128 and the Apple IIGS and permitted these systems to boot their graphical operating systems before the PCs of their day had managed to bring up a C:\ prompt. A similar device for today's PCs would do more to boost system performance than any other innovation I see coming down the pipeline any time soon.

Special Considerations for Windows 98 and RAM Disks

Windows 98's only issue with running in a RAM disk as described in the previous section is its size. Whereas the original Windows 95 can shrink down below 17 MB in size, a minimal Windows 98 install, even after the efforts of 98lite, is closer to 70 MB. 53 MB of disk space costs less than a hamburger, so the difference in size is

---

Day-to-Day Work with RAM Disks

Since systems set up to boot from a RAM disk take a few minutes to start, you're probably not looking forward to having to restart the computer or start the computer every day. If you use a RAM disk, leave the system on all the time. Computers use about as much power as light bulbs, and like night lights, they last longer if you leave them on all the time.

A RAM disk probably won't make Windows any more reliable, but you don't always have to do a complete reboot to clear up problems. If you press Start → Shut down → Restart the computer, then hold down the Shift key while you press OK, Windows simply exits to DOS mode, then reloads. From a RAM disk, the whole process takes about four seconds.

---

hardly worth worrying about on a modern system—unless you're trying to use a RAM disk. RAM prices are falling, but 53 MB of RAM is still a significant expense.

If you want to run your operating system from a RAM disk, Windows 95 is the better choice—it allows you to either get by with a smaller RAM disk or install an additional application or two—but, unfortunately, some systems just won't run well under Windows 95. Some newer peripherals lack Windows 95 drivers, and some hardware, such as USB, just isn't compatible with early revisions of Windows 95.

The *INF* and *HELP* directories in my installation of Windows 98 are 6.5 and 11 MB, respectively. Offloading those to disk and pulling them back in on an as-needed basis is an option.

Creating a Compressed RAM Disk

As far as I can figure out, you can't create a compressed RAM disk and then boot from it, because DriveSpace refuses to compress a drive that contains files that are in use. (I won't say it's impossible, because people told me that booting from even a regular RAM disk is impossible.) You can, however, create an applications RAM disk and compress it if need be to get more usable space. A compressed RAM disk will be considerably slower than an uncompressed RAM disk and will consume more CPU cycles, but it will still be much faster than a physical hard drive. (On a Pentium 90, it seems to be about half as fast as an uncompressed RAM disk would be, which is still much faster than any hard drive currently available.)

Creating a compressed RAM disk is much easier than creating a boot RAM disk. Copy *xmsdsk.exe* to *C:\Windows\Command*, then add an appropriate line to *autoexec.bat* to create the RAM disk. For instance:

```
xmsdsk.exe 65535 z: /t /y
```

Restart your computer, then once Windows loads, press Start → Run → **drvspace /compress z:**. DriveSpace will compress your RAM disk. Now, either use a mover application like those included with PowerQuest PartitionMagic, Norton CleanSweep, or McAfee UnInstaller to move applications to your newly created drive *z:*, or install fresh copies of your applications to the new drive.

After you install the programs you want on your compressed drive, open a command prompt and type the following commands:

```
H:
```
This changes you to DriveSpace's hidden drive.
```
Attrib -r -s -h drvspace.000
```
Make the file that makes up the compressed volume visible...
```
Copy drvspace.000 c:\windows\command
```
and back it up for later use.

To activate the compressed RAM disk, enter the following batch file, save it to *C: \Windows\Command*, then right-click Start → Explore → Programs → Startup, then right-click a blank area in the right pane and select New → Shortcut. In the Command Line field, enter *ramdisk.bat* (see Example 11-2).

Example 11-2. ramdisk.bat

```
Copy c:\windows\command\drvspace.000 z:\
Attrib +r +s +h z:\drvspace.000
Drvspace /mount z:
```

The next time you restart Windows, your compressed RAM disk will be available for use. If you have more than 64 MB of RAM but not enough for a boot RAM disk, consider making a compressed RAM disk to hold one or more crucial applications. You'll improve that application's performance dramatically, with little or no impact on the speed of the rest of your system.

12

Hardware Upgrades

This book focuses primarily on software optimization, mostly because Windows leaves so much room open for increasing system performance strictly through software optimization. However, no amount of software optimization will turn an old 386 or 486 into a Pentium II, and there is no substitute for good hardw8are. The only thing software optimization can do is make the definition of good hardware a bit more lenient.

The stated minimum system requirements for Windows 9x vary widely. Few people took the original claims of a 16 MHz 386SX processor and 4 MB of memory seriously—this was the technical minimum, but systems of this caliber were inadequate for running Windows 3.1, let alone Windows 95. When Windows 95 was first released, the general consensus was that the minimal usable system would have a 33 MHz 486SX or DX processor and 8 MB of RAM, with more of each being better. Serious users generally bought 16 MB of RAM and dreamed of 24 or 32—unfortunately, memory cost about $50 a megabyte in 1995, so 32 MB of RAM wasn't exactly realistic.

Those minimums rose with the passage of time. Soon you wanted at least a 66 MHz 486, then you wanted a 100 MHz 486; today, people generally won't consider installing Windows 98 on anything less than a 166 MHz Pentium with 32 MB of RAM.

The true minimum requirements truly depend on your expectations. If a system will run Windows 3.1 adequately, it can probably run a cut-down Windows 95 adequately and it may even see a slight improvement. At the very least, the system will be more stable. There are people who have installed and used (I'll refrain from saying *run*) Windows 95 on a 25 MHz 486SX with 4 MB of RAM.

If you're in that situation, all I can say is follow absolutely every single piece of software advice in this book, then start scavenging for some memory and a second hard drive while saving some money to get something better.

The majority of people are in a somewhat better situation: Windows 95 does operate on their machine, to varying degrees of speed and satisfaction. I can talk until I'm blue in the face about software requirements, but there are limits. The question is, when does it become futile to mess around with software fixes and necessary to buy some hardware?

Prudence in Hardware Upgrades

Common sense dictates that it should be less expensive to upgrade an existing computer than it is to buy a new one. This is true—at the very least, a keyboard, mouse, and floppy drive purchased with a computer from the late 1980s could still be perfectly usable today. So you can upgrade a clunker AT clone from 1987 and save about $40 from the cost of a new computer. Of course, this upgrade scenario is extreme.

If a computer is only a year or two old, it makes good sense to upgrade it by adding whatever you need to it: if it's short on memory, add some memory; if it's short on disk space, add a second hard drive. There comes a time, however, when upgrading gets complicated, and a costlier-sounding upgrade route may actually end up costing less. For instance, it's sometimes less expensive to buy a new motherboard and new memory (but reuse your old CPU) than it is to buy antiquated memory for an aging system. Newer components are manufactured in large quantities and priced like commodities. Older components that are no longer produced in quantity are rarely cost-effective to buy.

People frequently forget one other thing when buying new hardware. They rarely take into consideration the effects the peripheral might have on the rest of the system. Will that modem or printer use some of my CPU cycles to operate? How much memory does that sound card need, and how much CPU time does it consume? These factors are rarely measured, but they can have a dramatic effect on overall system performance, for the same reason that optimizing your Windows settings does.

Realistic Memory Requirements

First and foremost, Windows 9x craves RAM, and lots of it. Realistically, you want a minimum of 32 MB of RAM if you're going to do serious work with Windows 95. You can get by with less, but it will be a serious productivity drain. Intel's advertising campaigns pretty much have people convinced that only having the fastest new CPU matters. But given the choice between a Pentium with 8 MB of RAM and a 486 with 32 MB, I'd choose to work with the higher-memory 486.

Trouble is, memory upgrades are not always practical. Most older 486s used 8-bit 30-pin SIMMs, installed in banks of four (the 486 was a 32-bit processor). The majority of these 486s had eight SIMM slots (two banks), and they were usually occupied by four or eight 1 MB SIMMs. Unless you're one of the lucky people who have 4 MB SIMMs in one of those two banks, you'll be looking at discarding all of your memory to upgrade to 32 MB of RAM. Since 30-pin SIMMs are no longer produced in any kind of substantial quantity (and the chips they use aren't produced in great quantities anymore either), they tend to be very expensive. You can expect to pay $25 for a 4 MB 30-pin SIMM.

You may still be able to find so-called "SIMM trees," which allow you to put more than one SIMM in a slot. With a SIMM tree, you can turn four 1 MB SIMMs into a 4 MB SIMM. So, if your 486 has 8 MB of RAM, you could buy six 4 MB SIMMs and two trees. SIMM trees can cause unreliable operation, however. If you choose to buy some, be sure to check that they're buffered. The easy way to tell is to look at the tree's circuit board. If it just contains four SIMM slots and no other electronics, it's unbuffered and likely to cause timing problems. If you see a small number of chips on the board, chances are it's buffered and will work satisfactorily.

Late-model 486s, especially brand-name models, used 32-bit 72-pin SIMMs. Early Pentiums also used this form of memory, though Pentiums required 72-pin SIMMs to be installed in pairs because Pentiums have a 64-bit data bus. These came in a wider range of sizes than 30-pin SIMMs did, and were easier to install. However, there's plenty of room for confusion with 72-pin SIMMs. They came in parity and non-parity flavors, and they used either fast page mode (FPM) memory or faster EDO memory. Generally speaking, 486s and Pentiums below 75 MHz can't use EDO memory. If you want to be safe, buy your memory from a specialist like Crucial Technology (*www.crucial.com*), who can guarantee their memory will work with your system, and remember as a general rule that very few Pentiums below 100 MHz can use EDO memory.

These days, 72-pin memory is on the verge of going the way of its 30-pin brethren. A 72-pin SIMM generally costs 50–100% more than its modern counterpart.

New systems use 168-pin DIMMs, which are the easiest to install and come in the widest variety of sizes. They're also the most economical form factor to buy. As I write, brand-name DIMMs cost about $1.50 a megabyte, and if you shop really carefully, you can get them for under $1.00 a megabyte—though I don't recommend cheap memory. Today's fast systems require much more precise timing than past systems did, and this makes memory more expensive to manufacture. Cheap memory can harm system stability.

The reason I bring up memory pricing is that sometimes it's more economical to upgrade your system's motherboard in order to buy cheaper, modern memory than it is to buy memory for an existing system. You can pay $200 for 32 MB worth of 30-pin SIMMs, but a decent Pentium-class motherboard usually costs about $65. An IDT WinChip or a Cyrix MII processor for the board can be had for as little as $30. A 32 MB DIMM for the board will cost another $50.

If you have a name-brand system, it may not take a standard AT or ATX motherboard. In those cases, the most economical way to upgrade is to purchase a micro-ATX case and motherboard. They're harder to find, but a micro-ATX board with built-in video can cost as little as $55, and the cases usually cost $50 or less. They use the same CPU and memory as their full-sized counterparts.

It may seem wasteful to discard a still-functioning motherboard and CPU, but when you can get the same amount of memory along with a faster motherboard and CPU, it makes sense to do so. Few people will mistake a $30 IDT or Cyrix CPU for a Pentium III, but these CPUs will outperform any 486, and a new motherboard will give you a more future-proof system—you can always drop in another DIMM or two somewhere down the road. Most modern motherboards will accommodate 384 MB of RAM, and many can take up to 768 MB.

Of course, all of this changes with time. It's impossible to stay completely up to date, due to book production schedules. As of this writing, the most economical memory to buy is PC100 SDRAM. PC133 SDRAM costs just slightly more—manufacturers are still putting a small price premium on enhanced performance. I expect the price difference to eventually reverse itself, as it has in the past. PC66 SDRAM now costs slightly more than PC100 SDRAM. EDO memory costs a bit less than the older FPM memory, even though EDO memory is faster and slightly harder to manufacture. There's now far more demand for EDO memory, so it's produced in larger quantities. Higher demand for one type of memory over another only means higher prices for as long as supplies of the older memory stay high. Once the supply of the older memory dwindles, you can expect the premium pricing for the newer technology to disappear.

Although the specifics change with time, the same set of principles has remained constant throughout the 1990s. When buying memory, be sure to price the memory for your machine, but if your machine is capable of using more than one type of memory, price every type it is capable of using. Also price other types of memory for comparison.

For instance, in November 1998, I was pricing memory upgrades for a friend's PC. His PC had both SIMM and DIMM sockets, and was capable of using 72-pin EDO and FPM SIMMs, 168-pin PC66 SDRAM DIMMs, and 168-pin PC100 SDRAM DIMMs. I found some 64 MB EDO SIMMs on closeout for $59 each. SDRAM would have given better performance, but PC100 SDRAM cost about $2 per megabyte at the time. So we opted for the soon-to-be-obsolete 64 MB SIMMs. Benchmarks indicated a speed difference of about 15% between this older memory and the newer technology, but having double the memory for the money more than made up for the difference.

By February 1999, the situation was different. I was pricing memory upgrades for another friend's PC, which only had 72-pin SIMM sockets. It could accept either FPM or EDO SIMMs. I wanted to add 32 MB of RAM to her system, but the best price I could find on brand-name 16 MB SIMMs was $49 apiece. Crucial Technology was selling 32 MB DIMMs for about $59 at the time. It was just barely economical to go ahead and buy the SIMMs, but had she wanted to add more than 32 MB of memory, it would have made sense to replace her system with a motherboard that could accommodate the newer, more inexpensive memory.

With the exception of the Pentium II 366, Pentium II and Pentium III systems faster than 350 MHz can only use PC100 SDRAM—at least, if they use an Intel chipset—while Celerons and Pentium IIs 333 MHz and slower use PC66 SDRAM. PC100 SDRAM works in systems that use the PC66 variety; they just can't take advantage of the extra speed. Many current AMD K6- and Cyrix-based systems have jumpers to select between PC66 and PC100 memory. You'll get better performance from PC100, but if you find PC66 memory on sale or happen to already have a decent quantity of it on hand, it works. The performance difference between the two is less than 10 percent, a difference you can easily overcome by adding more memory.

You shouldn't try to future-proof your computer with your memory choices, because it's so difficult to do. Companies are fighting right now over what the next memory standard will be: will it be PC133 SDRAM, or will it be the slightly faster but more expensive Rambus? Intel is backing Rambus, but the majority of other industry players are lining up behind PC133 SDRAM. Most experts believe PC133 has more short-term momentum, but Rambus has the long-term momentum. Rambus may win eventually. Then again, something even faster and less expensive could come around.

For now, you're best off buying an adequate amount of PC100 or PC133 memory. There isn't much price premium on PC133 (between $5 and $20 per module), which makes it a better long-term investment. For now, there's no point in waiting for Rambus.

Speeding Up Your Memory: L2 Cache

Although RAM is far faster than a hard disk, modern RAM is still so slow as to handicap your CPU. Today's PC100 SDRAM has enough power to keep a 33 MHz 486 from having to wait on it, but our requirements have moved far beyond the abilities of that CPU. CPU speeds are just advancing too quickly for new memory technologies to keep up.

This phenomenon has always been present in PCs. The trick is to put some very high-speed memory between the CPU and the system's main RAM. This is known as cache. Cache is capable of running at speeds much closer to the rate a CPU wants to be fed, and because of the structure of programs, CPUs tend to linger for fairly long periods of time in the same area of memory before moving on. So beginning with 386-based computers, manufacturers started putting small amounts of cache on the motherboard.

Cache is referred to as Level 1, 2, or 3, depending on how far removed it is from the CPU core. Level 1 (L1) cache resides very close to the CPU core; the biggest reason why the 486 was faster than the 386 was its addition of 8K of L1 cache. Modern CPUs have much larger L1 caches; the Pentium II and Pentium III have 32K L1 caches, while some AMD and Cyrix CPUs have 64K L1 caches and some CPU manufacturers have been throwing around the idea of using a 128K L1 cache. In years past, L2 cache resided on the motherboard, but starting with the Pentium Pro, Intel started putting L2 cache in the CPU itself. AMD followed suit with its K6-III and Athlon CPUs.

L3 cache is relatively rare in PCs; AMD experimented with L3 cache with its K6-III CPU, but there is little indication that future CPUs from AMD, Intel, or any other manufacturer will incorporate this trick anytime soon.

The presence of L2 cache significantly speeds up the system—a system with L2 cache can easily outperform an otherwise identical system without cache by 20–30%. Intel caused a major brouhaha in 1998 when it released its much-maligned 266 MHz Celeron processor. Intel had moved the L2 cache onto the processor itself with the Pentium Pro and Pentium II processors, but the L2 cache was by far the most expensive aspect of those processors. So Intel created the low-cost Celeron by eliminating the costly L2 cache. People quickly figured out that a 233 MHz Pentium with L2 cache—any amount of L2 cache—significantly outperformed the 266 MHz Celeron, even though the Celeron contained numerous internal enhancements and had a higher clock rate.

Many Pentium motherboards—especially those in consumer-level systems—didn't have L2 cache present on them from the factory. Adding some L2 cache to the system will significantly improve the performance of these systems, but unfortunately, L2 cache can be difficult to come by.

Intel has made the L2 cache equation a bit more confusing, since the Pentium Pro, Pentium II, and Celeron processors have L2 cache as part of the CPU, rather than part of the motherboard. This improves performance but makes L2 cache impossible to upgrade without replacing the CPU.

The amount of L2 cache isn't a huge factor in performance. The speed jump from no cache to 128K of L2 cache is significant; the jump from 128K of L2 cache to 256K is smaller; the jump from 256K to 512K is smaller still, and the jump from 512K to 1 MB is still smaller. Intel illustrated this with the Celeron and the Pentium II. The Celeron has 128K of L2 cache that runs at the full speed of the processor. Pentium IIs have a larger 512K cache that runs at half the processor speed. For typical home and small-business uses, when running at comparable speeds, the smaller and faster Celeron cache gives equivalent or better performance.

If your system has L2 cache, increasing its size isn't a very cost-effective upgrade, especially under Windows 9x. However, if your board lacks L2 cache, adding it—or replacing the motherboard with one that does have cache—will give you a significant improvement.

Hard Drive Size and Speed

Hard drives are second behind memory in importance when it comes to system speed. High-speed CPUs spend a great deal of idle time waiting on hard drives to deliver data to them. Hard drive speeds have made tremendous strides in the past two years; even the slowest hard drives of today are a tremendous improvement over the drives that shipped in 486s from the factory. If your system has 32 MB of memory or more and still feels sluggish, before you plunk down $200 for an overpriced CPU upgrade, pick up an inexpensive hard drive. Prices keep dropping, but as of this writing, a 4.3 GB hard drive costs less than $90, while 12 GB hard drives sell for $140 or less. Mainstream hard drives should be at or below $10 per GB by the time you read this.

To determine whether your hard drive is a good candidate for upgrading, open your system and take a look at the drive. The top label will probably contain a date of manufacture. If it doesn't, take a look at the bottom of the drive. On the chips on the drive's printed circuit board, you should be able to find some silk-screened numbers. Look for some four-digit numbers that start with the number 9 (if the drive was manufactured in the twenty-first century, the numbers will start with 0). Many chips are labeled with a date of manufacture in the form YYWW, where the last two digits make up a week of the year. So most successful candidates will start with a 9, and the last two digits will be no larger than 52. If you find two or more chips on the drive with numbers that indicate they were made within a few weeks of one another, you can get a decent idea when the drive itself was manufactured. If the drive was manufactured before 1996, one of today's drives will be a tremendous upgrade. If it was manufactured before 1998, a modern drive will give your system a smaller, but still noticeable, boost.

Many pre-1997 systems, however, cannot identify a drive larger than 4.3 GB, and a large percentage of pre-1995 systems cannot identify a drive larger than 528 MB.

You can get around this limitation with software, which is usually included with the drive if purchased at retail. This software will reduce the amount of conventional memory you have available by a small amount, however, and it puts an extra layer between you and the system if you ever have to attempt data recovery on it.

To take full advantage of fast, modern drives with an older motherboard, you need a controller card that contains its own BIOS. Promise Technology (*www. promise.com*) is a good source of inexpensive controllers; similar cards are often available in retail superstores as well.

Be aware, however, that these controllers will not fit in most 486s because they're PCI cards, and if the card costs more than $50, it's coming dangerously close to the cost of a replacement motherboard. If you have a Pentium system and can salvage your CPU and memory, you're better off buying a new motherboard than one of these cards. Good Socket 7 motherboards start at about $65 and will give you the benefits of a modern disk controller, plus, in all likelihood, a bigger cache, a newer, faster chipset, an AGP slot, and other systemwide benefits.

What to Look for in a Hard Drive

It's very easy to get caught up in hard drive specs, trying to buy the drive that looks best on paper, and end up making the wrong purchase. Mark Twain didn't have hard drives in mind when he uttered his famous words, "There are lies, damned lies, and statistics." I suspect if he were alive today and aware of the situation in modern hard drives, he'd say something much more harsh.

In reality, there are a number of factors that go into making a hard drive fast, and many of them aren't printed on the box. It's easy to fall into the trap of buying a 7200 rpm drive because it sounds fast, but the best 5400 rpm drives outperform many 7200 rpm drives. It's easy to look at two identically sized drives, one with a 10 ms seek time and one with a 9 ms seek time, buy the second because it sounds better—it's 10% lower, after all, and lower seek times are theoretically better—and end up buying the slower drive.

PC manufacturers and magazines sometimes fall for the hype. In its March 20, 1999 issue, *PC Magazine* reviewed an AMD K6-III-based PC manufactured by Cybermax. *PC Magazine* found that after replacing the factory-installed 5400 rpm drive with a 7200 rpm drive, performance actually went down. Yet the 7200 rpm drive scored higher on certain benchmarks than the 5400 rpm drive. "AMD is flummoxed by this paradox, as we still are," *PC Magazine* stated.

This wasn't an anomaly with AMD processors. What *PC Magazine* discovered is what the hardware web sites had been reporting for a couple of years: some benchmarks do a better job of simulating real-world situations than others, and some hard drive specifications matter more than others. Rotation speed isn't everything. I was a little bit disappointed that AMD didn't pick up on this, seeing as AMD and Cyrix have made careers of producing CPUs that outperform Intel CPUs under some circumstances; but in all fairness, AMD is in the business of making chips, not analyzing hard drives. A 5400 rpm hard drive can outperform a 7200 rpm hard drive for the same reasons that an AMD K5 CPU running at 117 MHz blew past an Intel Pentium CPU running at 120 MHz and gave the 133 MHz Pentiums a run for the money. The K5 was more efficient, so it could make more use of its lower number of clock cycles. Sometimes less is more.

It's difficult to predict the speed of a hard drive, because so many factors go into it. There's the rotation speed of the drive, of course, plus seek time. Most people know to look for those. There's also the size of the drive's buffer—an on-drive disk cache—which of course makes a difference. If RAM is much faster than the hard drive, putting some RAM on the hard drive to cache it will speed the drive up. The density of the platters also makes a difference. When data is packed more densely onto the platters, the drive head doesn't have to move as far to get the data. But platter density is never printed on the box.

Some drive manufacturers boast of their drives being able to deliver throughput of 33 MB or even 66 MB per second. This is a truly worthless statistic—only the drive's onboard cache is able to deliver that kind of throughput. This is the speed of the drive's bus, not the drive itself, and the only time you're going to get those kinds of speeds is if you read the drive's cache over and over. The best sustained transfer rate in real-world tests that any drive can manage as of this writing is about 20 MB per second. That's an impressive figure, but far short of the advertised 33 MB/sec limit, and just a fraction of the 66 MB/sec limit. Besides, every modern hard drive has one of these two limits, whether the manufacturer boasts of it or not.

The drive's firmware can also make a difference. Some disk manufacturers are very adept at making drives that perform exceptionally well under Windows NT, but under Windows 9x, their performance is middling. The reverse is also true.

When it comes to gaming and other home use, the drive's interface—IDE versus SCSI—makes very little difference. SCSI has a theoretical advantage in that SCSI drives, when hit with a barrage of requests, can reorder them and execute them in the order that makes the most sense, whereas IDE drives simply perform each request in the order received. Under Unix-based systems that have good preemptive multitasking, this can yield a significant performance increase. Windows 9x multitasking isn't as sophisticated as Unix multitasking, however, so the difference won't be tremendous. The difference may be noticeable, but when a SCSI drive costs $100–$200 more than an equivalent-sized IDE drive and also requires an expensive drive controller, it's just not worth doubling or tripling the cost of the disk subsystem in order to improve system performance by 15%. You'd be better off buying a second IDE drive and splitting up your files between them—operating system on one, applications on the other, as described in Chapter 3, *Disk Optimization.*

The only way to know the true capabilities of a drive, unfortunately, is to use it, or at the very least, to simulate use with benchmarks. I never buy or recommend a hard drive without first going to The Storage Review (*www.storagereview.com*), an online repository of drive reviews and benchmarks. They've reviewed virtually every drive manufactured since late 1997, and have an online database that allows you to compare speeds between various drives. You can even compare IDE drives to SCSI drives, so you can fantasize about 10,000 rpm SCSI drives with 4.9 ms seek times, then find out that a drive that costs 20% as much will give you 80% of the performance. The Storage Review benchmarks will give you far more useful information than the specifications on the manufacturer's web site or on the drive's packaging. You still can't be absolutely certain that you're buying the perfect drive, since no benchmark can accurately simulate the mixture of programs on your system and how you use them, but you can make a much more educated decision.

Video Cards

The speed of the video card is a crucial part of overall system speed. Think about it: virtually everything the user does requires some type of graphical feedback from the system. Think of the video card as the CPU's personal assistant. A good personal assistant knows his or her job, and does what is asked when it's asked, quickly and without asking questions. The best video cards do just that. The CPU tells them to draw a line, and they do it. The CPU tells them to move the mouse cursor to some position on the screen, and they do it.

A bad video card is worse than a bad personal assistant, because a bad video card never learns. The CPU decides a line needs to be drawn between two points. The video card doesn't know how to do that on its own, so the CPU tells the video card to plot this point, and every other point along the line, until the entire line is drawn. While this is going on, the CPU can't get to the other pressing duties that are piling up, because the CPU is too busy doing the video card's job.

Before buying any video card, check out the manufacturer. Never, ever buy a video card without knowing who made it. I especially like David A. Karp's advice in his book *Windows 98 Annoyances* (O'Reilly & Associates). He says to look at the manufacturer's web site to see if the manufacturer still offers drivers and technical support for old video cards. The logic is that a manufacturer who's still willing to support a video card sold in 1994 is more likely to support a video card sold today in five years. That makes sense. You should also look to see if the manufacturer offers Windows 3.1 and/or OS/2 drivers for at least some of their video cards. This, too, is an indication of a company's commitment to supporting its products. If the company cares (or once cared) about the few hundred thousand OS/2 users left out there, it will definitely care about the few hundred million Windows 9x users like you out there.

There are a number of factors that indicate a video card's speed, but not all the factors matter all the time. This can make shopping for a video card confusing.

Video Memory

Here's the skinny on video memory: if one of your primary interests is games, get as much video memory as you can afford. In addition to the image on your screen, today's 3D accelerators store textures in video memory, because it's much faster to access the textures from video memory than from system memory. Some cards even store the textures in memory twice (a technique known as parallel texture mapping), which improves performance even further but makes the amount of memory on the card even more deceptive. Cards will use additional memory for double- or triple-buffering (displaying one image while drawing the next one in the sequence). Because of all these factors, that closeout 16 MB video card is probably no bargain.

If all you're interested in is basic productivity—word processing, email, and web browsing—video memory has little or no effect on speed, and the most significant advantage of having more video memory is higher-resolution displays with more colors. Generally speaking, the same wisdom holds for strategy games. A puny-sounding 4 MB video card has enough memory to drive a 19-inch monitor at 1280×1024 resolution in 24-bit color. If you want 1600×1200 resolution with 32-bit color, you'll need an 8 MB video card and a 19- or 21-inch monitor so you don't go blind. Since most of us still have 15- and 17-inch monitors in the home, huge amounts of video memory are overkill.

The Video Bus

The first thing to look at with video cards is their bus. The old ISA bus runs at 8 MHz, and you don't want to be running something as critical as your video card at 8 MHz if you can help it. The VESA local bus, introduced with the 486, improves the situation. It ran at speeds of up to 40 MHz. If you have a 486 and it has VESA slots, you want your video card to be in one of those slots. PCI wasn't really a technical improvement over VESA, but PCI cards tend to be faster than VESA cards, if only because at some point manufacturers quit putting their latest and greatest video chipsets on VESA cards and exclusively made PCI cards. PCI generally runs at 33 MHz or half the processor's bus speed, whichever is slower. (The newer revisions of PCI allow speeds of 66 MHz, but both the card and the motherboard have to support it.)

Modern video cards use a new bus called AGP. AGP is an extension of PCI but runs at much higher speeds (originally 66 MHz; AGP 2X runs at 133 MHz and AGP 4X runs at 266 MHz). AGP also has the ability to borrow memory from the main system when the onboard memory fills up. This is faster than handing off rendering duties to the CPU, but it's still faster to put an adequate amount of memory on the card.

AGP provides a number of benefits over PCI—notably, high-color displays run faster under AGP than they did under PCI. AGP is also faster than PCI for the same reason that PCI eventually became faster than VESA. Few manufacturers are still producing PCI video cards in quantity, and those who are generally aren't putting their newest and fastest chips on them. However, unless your system happens to have an empty AGP slot, upgrading from PCI to AGP will require a motherboard replacement.

Video Chipsets

The video chipset is the chip (or set of chips) that actually does the job of rendering the display on your screen. Not all chipsets are created equal. Some of the more common chipset manufacturers are 3Dfx, nVidia, ATI, Matrox, S3, SiS, Cirrus Logic, Trident, and Tseng. The chipsets from the various manufacturers do basically the same thing, but they vary more widely in capability than CPUs do, and they evolve every bit as quickly.

You're likely to see video cards advertised as 64-bit or 128-bit cards. This doesn't mean those cards do 128-bit color depths—that's overkill, seeing as the human eye can't perceive the 16.8 million colors a 24-bit display can render. This measurement refers to the width of the bus between the video memory and the chipset. Generally speaking, the wider the bus, the faster the card.

A good video chipset is a key component in system speed. One of my first PCs was a 40 MHz 386DX. When the time came to upgrade it, I went out and paid an obscene price for a Pentium motherboard and a 75 MHz CPU. I couldn't afford to do much more than upgrade those two components, but the price of the motherboard and CPU was less than one-third the cost of a new system, so it made sense to do it. I put the hard drive from the 386 in my 66 MHz 486, and put the 486's hard drive in the 386-turned-Pentium. The video in the 486 was integrated, so I had to either use the 386's old Paradise SVGA video card or buy a new one. I opted to make due with the old Paradise card, since the least expensive video card worth having (in my mind) cost about $300 at the time and I really didn't have the $300 to spend.

The resulting system loaded and executed programs far more quickly than anything I was used to, but the video was pathetic. I could set my two systems up side by side and watch the Pentium blow past the 486, but once I had my word processor loaded, the 486 was much more fluid. I was pretty sure the problem was the video card, but it didn't cost me anything to put all of the 486's memory in the Pentium to see if that made a difference, so I did it. It didn't help. So I called around and found a 32-bit Trident-based video card for $119. It wasn't what I wanted—I had my eye on a blindingly fast 64-bit video card with an S3 chipset—but I could afford it. It was a mediocre card in all the benchmarks I ran on it, but it blew away that ancient Paradise card, it was at least comparable to the 486's video, and it was capable of displaying more colors.

The Trident turned out to be a smart move. Two years later I bought a 64-bit S3-based card with 3D acceleration for $89—it was far superior in every way to the card I'd lusted after, and in 1997 it was a mid-range card. I really wanted a 128-bit card, but I figured I probably didn't need it, seeing as the inexpensive Trident card had served my needs for two years, this 64-bit card cost less than I'd paid for the Trident, and the card I really wanted cost about $300.

In October 1998, I built the system I'm writing this book on. It has an STB Velocity 128 card in it, based on the nVidia Riva 128 chipset. It, too, is far better than the $300 card I wanted in mid-1997, and I paid $79 for it. It's been a while since I've seen the Velocity 128 advertised, but I recently saw a Diamond Viper 330, which uses the same chipset, for $50. It's an awful lot of video card for the money.

Any advice I give on the best value-for-money chipset out there will be obsolete by the time you read this, but the general principle should be pretty clear. If your video performance seems a bit sluggish, replace the card, but don't go spending $300 on the most impressive-sounding card. This year's $100 card is better than last year's $300 card, and next year's $100 card will be better than this year's $300 card. Anything in the $75–$125 price range will be better than what you have now, so you're better off buying a mid-range card and replacing it in a year if you feel the need.

This principle doesn't work so well at the low end. Most of the $29 cards available today are slightly better than that old Trident video card I bought a few years back, but those cards were available a year ago and the price hasn't changed much. Don't buy a really low-end card unless you're really on a tight budget and are building a minimalist system. You'll probably have to move up to the $50 mark or so to avoid stagnant year-old inventory, and you'll be much happier if you do.

Other Factors

On high-end video cards, two other factors can come into play. Sometimes two cards that use the same chipset may use memory of different speeds. The card with the faster memory will give better performance.

The card's cooling system can also affect performance. High-end video chipsets tend to run very hot and require cooling systems just like the system's CPU. If a manufacturer can't devise an adequate cooling system, it might have to compensate by clocking the video card at a lower speed. This, of course, affects performance greatly. There are software utilities for overclocking certain types and brands of video cards, but generally a manufacturer had a good reason for clocking the card at a given speed, so I don't recommend prolonged use of these utilities.

3D Add-On Cards

With the current generation of video chipsets, the era of the 3D add-on card, which worked in conjunction with a regular video card and took over some 3D functions, appears to be over. Today's 3D accelerated cards pack more power than the 3D add-on cards of 1998, add regular 2D graphics for use in standard productivity applications, and sell for right around what a typical mid-range video card sold for in 1998.

For information on the state of the art in 3D acceleration, your best bet is to check one of the hardware-oriented web sites. The standard by which the others are judged is the venerable Tom's Hardware Guide (*www.tomshardware.com*). AnandTech (*www.anandtech.com*) and Ars Technica (*www.ars-technica.com*) are good secondary sources of information; they're not as well known as Tom's Hardware but tend to update more frequently. For recommendations on how to make specific games run well on your system (you're interested in more than Quake, aren't you?), check out Blue's News (*www.bluesnews.com*), or if you're into simulation and strategy games, CombatSim (*www.combatsim.com*). These technologies seem to change every other week, and there looks to be more competition in this field by the time you read this than there is currently. You can expect to pay $150–$175 for a good 3D-accelerated card as of this writing. Good gaming cards typically cost a bit more than cards intended for productivity work.

Sound Cards

People generally don't give much thought to the effect their sound card has on performance, because for years, the best advice on sound cards was to buy a Creative Labs Sound Blaster, period. You didn't worry about speed; you worried about compatibility.

Those days are largely over. DOS games no longer comprise the majority of titles we play, and Windows device drivers have conquered the compatibility problem. Overcoming that barrier allows us to talk about overhead and efficiency. These days, an ISA-based Sound Blaster or clone doesn't do the CPU any favors. If you're playing games and have an ISA sound card, your CPU is spending an awful lot of time pumping bits down a bus that's poking along at 8 MHz. The manufacturers of some PCI sound cards have claimed an ISA Sound Blaster can take up to 20% of your CPU time. That's more than the difference you get by stepping up another grade in CPU speed.

These days, PCI sound cards are cheap. The best cards cost between $50 and $100, but serviceable cards can be had for $35. Try to look for a card that provides DirectSound acceleration in hardware, especially if you're into gaming. The more work your system peripherals can do, the more time the CPU can spend doing other things.

Inexpensive PCI sound cards frequently load wavetable sets into system RAM, so they'll chew up more system memory than your old ISA-based Sound Blaster clone. ISA wavetable cards usually had SIMM slots for holding the wavetable sets. This made the cards more expensive, and since the cards sometimes used proprietary SIMMs, the memory for them was expensive too. All other things being equal, I like the idea of paying $35 for a card that uses system memory better than paying $99 for a card that has its own memory. I can spend the other $65 on an extra 32 MB of RAM. The sound card will use 8 MB of that memory at most; the other 24 MB goes to the system, increasing overall performance.

The big concern with PCI sound cards that people sometimes miss is the number of voices the sound card produces. This deals with the number of simultaneous sounds the card can play at once. Many cards that advertise 64-voice sound are actually only producing 32 voices in hardware. The other 32 voices come from mixing multiple sounds in software. That job falls to the CPU.

If you want the fastest possible system, be sure to get a card that produces its voices in hardware rather than with a combination hardware/software approach, and provides hardware DirectSound and DirectSound3D acceleration.

Modems

Most people don't give a thought to this, but certain modems can drain your CPU power. Windows-only modems, sometimes called Winmodems, rely on your CPU for most of their operation. This usually makes the modem slower than a hardware modem would be, and it drains some of your CPU power while you're online.

Unfortunately, Winmodems can be deceptive. They're attractive—the price is right, and frequently they're PCI, so they can be sold under the allure of having an all-PCI system. Modems have no need for PCI's extra bandwidth, however. So, if you plan to upgrade your modem, insist on a modem capable of working from straight DOS or Linux. I know you'll probably never use the modem from DOS, and you may have no interest in Linux either. But it's the only way to ensure your modem is in fact a hardware modem and not a Winmodem.

Never buy a modem you can't return without hassle. If the salesperson says it will run in DOS, don't believe it. Take it home and try it yourself. The most foolproof way to test whether a program can run in DOS is to download a DOS terminal program. Walter Cox's small, free terminal program called Wterm, though a relic from 1990, is more than up to the task. It's available at *www.access2k1.net/users/farquhar/wterm110.zip.* The download is only about 180K, so it will be fairly quick even on an old 14.4 modem. I will walk you through the process of testing with Wterm; if you already have another DOS-based terminal program, the procedure will be similar. Go ahead and unzip Wterm, then restart in DOS mode. It's important to run Wterm in DOS mode, not just in a DOS box within Windows.

Go ahead and launch *wterm.exe.* Wterm will look by default for a modem on COM1. Hitting Alt-S will take you to Wterm's configuration screen, where you can change the COM port where Wterm looks for a modem. DOS doesn't always put the modem on the same COM port as Windows does, so if you put your modem on COM1 and Wterm doesn't see it, don't panic yet. Go ahead and switch COM ports with the Alt-S-P-Esc key sequence.

Now to test the modem, we need to send it a command. Type ATZ and hit Enter. If the modem responds with OK, the modem works from DOS. If you want to be really sure, hit AT D and hit Enter. The modem should pick up the phone. Hit Enter again to hang up.

If you're not seeing any of the text as you type, chances are either the modem isn't DOS-compatible or you have the wrong port. Go ahead and type the whole command and hit Enter before you give up. If it doesn't work the second time, try again. Repeat the Alt-S-P-Esc sequence for COM1, COM2, COM3, and COM4.

Not getting a response from your modem in Wterm is a pretty good indication that the modem isn't DOS-compatible and therefore is relying on the CPU-based Windows driver to do most of the dirty work. It's not absolutely foolproof—a plug-and-play internal modem on an old non-plug-and-play system can fail to show up in DOS—but you can rest assured that if Wterm can see your modem, your modem thinks for itself and doesn't tax the CPU any more than necessary.

Once you've made your conclusion with Wterm, exit. Alt-X will take you back to the DOS prompt. Or if you want to get back to Windows fast, hit Ctrl-Alt-Del.

If you want to be really safe, buy an external modem. They're more expensive and they require a separate $9 cable to connect to the computer, but they're more reliable, virtually guaranteed to be hardware modems, and when something goes wrong, you can reset the modem just by cycling the power. That's something you can't do with an internal modem.

The thought of using some extra CPU cycles to make a device like a modem less expensive has a certain appeal, especially to cost-conscious computer manufacturers facing thin margins. Don't be seduced. Modem chipset manufacturer Lucent Technology's web site states that a 56K Winmodem can use up to 50 MHz of your CPU's valuable clock cycles. In effect, if you put a Winmodem in your brand-spanking-new 650 MHz PC, you've just turned it into a 600 MHz PC. The price difference between a regular modem and a Winmodem is $20–$50. The price difference between speed grades of CPUs varies, but it can be several hundred dollars if you're living on the cutting edge. It's usually just not worth it.

Remember, no matter what CPU you own today, within a year, it won't have any CPU cycles you're willing to spare. Get a modem that does its own work, so the CPU can concentrate on its work.

Printers

If the use of the CPU to power a modem wasn't enough, a number of printer manufacturers are making printers that rely on the host computer's CPU and memory. This is an old practice—pioneered by cost-conscious Atari in the mid-1980s with its Atari ST laser printer—but is pointless today. Printers are cheap, so there's no point in sacrificing your CPU power to save a couple of bucks. Pay the extra $10 or $20 for a printer that does its own work.

The way to avoid CPU-hogging Windows-only printers is the same as for modems: Insist on a printer that works from DOS or Linux. Testing a printer's DOS compatibility is very easy, and if the printer is connected to a computer in the store, you can do it right there. Restart the computer in DOS mode, then type the following series of lines from the command prompt:

```
COPY CON: C:\TEST.TXT
THIS IS A TEST PAGE FROM DOS.
Control-Z+Enter
COPY C:\TEST.TXT LPT1:
DEL C:\TEST.TXT
```

As long as the printer isn't a PostScript printer—and no inexpensive printer is—this is a quick, foolproof test of a printer's DOS compatibility.

The PCI Bus

Moving as many peripherals off the ISA bus and onto the PCI bus is an attractive idea. After all, CPUs get faster and faster, but the ISA bus keeps chugging along at 7 or 8 MHz. It's interesting that 33 MHz is one-quarter the speed of the current state-of-the-art CPU bus speed of 133 MHz. In the early 1990s when high-speed buses became common, ISA was running at one-quarter the bus speed of the fastest x86 CPU of the time—8 MHz versus 33 MHz.

Although PCI is starting to show signs of inadequacy, it's still a tremendous improvement over ISA, and the more peripherals you have on the PCI bus, the less time your CPU will spend waiting on it.

One trend among the do-it-yourself crowd today is to build PCI-only systems, on the thinking that eliminating the ISA bus will improve performance. How much difference this can make is uncertain.

The thing to remember is that ISA permeates the system. The keyboard port, the PS/2 mouse port, the serial ports, and the parallel port all operate on the ISA bus, as do most floppy controllers. To get a true all-PCI system, it's necessary to get a USB keyboard, mouse, printer and modem along with an IDE LS-120 drive. This makes such a setup impractical under Windows 95, all versions of which have spotty USB support at best.

Having these last few peripherals on the ISA bus is no big deal, however. The keyboard and mouse, of course, require very little bandwidth since they are user-driven. For these, 8 MHz is severe overkill. Modems, printers, and floppy drives aren't a big deal either.

These days, the only speed-critical peripherals commonly available on the ISA bus are sound cards and network cards. Buying PCI versions of these cards makes good sense. Going to the expense of buying a USB keyboard, mouse, and modem just to get your remaining peripherals off a bus you can't disable anyway seems unnecessary.

Straight Talk on CPU Upgrades

I mention CPUs late in the chapter because CPU power really is much less important than Intel would have you think. As inexpensive PCs started to become popular in late 1997, Cyrix executives were widely quoted as saying, "Megahertz doesn't matter." To a large degree, they were right, as illustrated by the systems reviews that appear every month in computer magazines. You'll frequently see reviews of systems that underperform, and the magazine might say that a 450 MHz system, "Performs like the average 400 MHz system." It's often more economical to surround a weak CPU with a strong supporting cast to get a fast system. Whenever I build a system, I literally pick out the case, memory, hard drive(s), video card, motherboard, and other components I want, then I buy a CPU with whatever money I have left over in the budget.

Straight CPU upgrades, with few exceptions, are rarely economical. Take, for instance, the 133 MHz upgrades that many companies offer for 486s at a cost of around $99. These CPUs can take your 33 MHz 486 and catapult it to approximately the same level of CPU power as a 75 MHz Pentium. That's a pretty big jump. But these upgrades sometimes don't work—I've had cases, usually in name-brand systems, where these upgrade CPUs refused to perform any better than a 66 MHz 486, no matter what I did. I also had one case where I plugged one of these CPU upgrades into a 486 but had pin 1 misaligned. Pentiums have a key pin so you can't plug them in the wrong way, but 486s lacked this feature. I blew the voltage regulator on the motherboard, rendering the entire system useless.

In all fairness, when these CPU upgrades do work, they provide a very noticeable boost, especially when upgrading a 33 MHz system. If you consider one of these upgrades, you definitely want to check your motherboard for jumpers to select CPU speed. Many 25 MHz and 50 MHz systems also contained a jumper for a 33 MHz clock. With the former clock rates, your CPU upgrade will only run at 100 MHz. With the latter, the upgrade runs at a full 133 MHz. A few 486s even contained a jumper for a 40 MHz clock. The chip in these upgrades is rated for 133 MHz, but it is well-known for being able to run at 160 MHz. If you have a 40 MHz clock, you can overclock this CPU to 160 MHz and give 90 MHz and 100 MHz Pentiums a run for their money.

You can get 486 upgrades for 386 systems, but they're generally not worth the hassle. These chips frequently had small onboard caches, or they had a 24-bit data bus, which limited them to 16 MB of RAM. If you have an old 386 and someone gives you a CPU upgrade for it, it might be fun for experimentation, but prepare to be disappointed and be aware that the chances are pretty good that it will be a waste of time.

Pentium upgrades tend to be very difficult. Unless they are based on Intel CPUs, they usually require a BIOS upgrade, which adds considerable risk factor—not to mention expense. The poor-performing IDT WinChip CPU became popular in CPU upgrades because it uses the same voltage levels as the non-MMX Pentium and most BIOSs mistake it for an older non-MMX Pentium or for an AMD K5. WinChips are also nice because they recognize the old 1.5x multiplier that 75, 90, and 100 MHz Pentiums used and clock themselves at 4X—so a WinChip-200 is a drop-in replacement for a Pentium 75 and a WinChip-240 is a drop-in replacement for a Pentium 90.

The problem with WinChips is they provide adequate integer performance but terrible floating-point performance. This feature makes them excellent for word processing applications and other productivity software, but a liability for 3D games.

The dirty little secret in CPU upgrade circles is the WinChip's price. When you buy one of these upgrades, you essentially pay $100 or more for a CPU, a fan, and tech support. A high-quality PC Power and Cooling CPU fan sells for less than $20. If you can find a clone shop that has one, a 240 MHz WinChip sells for about $35. So if you're willing to live with just the technical support from the store—who, admittedly, would much rather sell you an entire system—and you're looking for a way to get some extra life out of an aging Pentium-based system, pick up a WinChip if you can find one. Pocket the $40 you save, or put it towards some memory.

There are companies that have started to sell CPU upgrades on plug-in PCI cards. These upgrades usually contain an AMD or Intel CPU on a card with the supporting circuitry; they're almost a replacement motherboard that just uses the old mother-board's slots. Unfortunately, they're very pricey: $499. The only time these would even begin to make sense would be in very high quality business-class systems that are still under warranty. With Micron selling new Celeron-based PCs at $799, and Compaq selling Celeron-based business PCs for slightly more, it would make more sense to buy a low-end PC to replace the upgrade candidate. The upgrade candidate could sell for a couple hundred bucks, making up most of the price difference between the upgrade and a new PC—and the new PC would be covered by a brand-new warranty.

How to Tell if You Need a CPU Upgrade

The easiest way to figure out if you need a CPU upgrade is to load a word processor. Microsoft Word 97 is especially good for this testing because of its high demands systemwide, but Corel WordPerfect or Lotus Word Pro will do as well. Load a document about two pages long. If you don't have a document that length, load a shorter one, then copy and paste the entire document into itself until you generate a document of sufficient length. Now, scroll up and down the document. If the scrolling is fast and smooth, you probably don't need a CPU upgrade. I find that when I run this simple test with Word 97, a 75 MHz Pentium is about as slow as I'm willing to tolerate for producing a document of any significant length, and a 100 MHz Pentium isn't much of an improvement.

When typing, your computer may have difficulty keeping up with you—the words may lag behind your typing speed. This might be because your word processor is checking your spelling and/or your grammar while you type. If you want to rely on this feature, get a faster CPU. If the delay is only occasional—the computer keeps up most of the time, but occasionally falls behind—pay attention to what the computer is doing while you type. If you see the disk activity light or hear the hard disk trundling, the problem isn't your CPU. You need a faster hard drive. If your disk activity light is constantly going as you type, you probably have less than 32 MB of RAM. Upgrade your memory. In the case of either of these two latter scenarios, a CPU upgrade isn't going to solve the major problem.

Games: A Different Story

It's easier to tell when you need a hardware upgrade to run your favorite game. The game just feels sluggish. But while the diagnosis is easy, hardware upgrades to get games running faster and more smoothly present a unique challenge. Building a good gaming system is very different from building a good productivity system—a decent amount of memory, a fast hard disk, and a mid-range CPU is all it takes to improve a word processing program, for instance. But a serious Quake player will be seriously disappointed.

Strategy games are easier to speed up inexpensively. Most modern strategy games have a pretty 3D face up front, but the bulk of their calculations are behind the scenes and are usually integer operations. Any modern CPU can plow through AI algorithms without much trouble. You can put a 200 MHz WinChip and 32 MB of RAM into an aging Pentium 75 and play Alpha Centauri or Railroad Tycoon II pretty happily.

If you're into Quake II, however, you're not likely to be satisfied with any CPU upgrade on the market. An old Pentium CPU is a deficiency in 3D games—it can't crank out enough clock cycles to feed the other peripherals—yet its most important component, the floating-point unit, is far superior to the floating-point unit in any upgrade chip. If you can find a CPU upgrade based on an AMD K6-2 or an AMD K6-III that will work with your system, it will improve your gaming experience—especially if your game supports the AMD 3DNow! extensions. The WinChip-based upgrades just aren't very good for 3D gaming. Parts of the game will run faster with a WinChip, but the 3D rendering will suffer. Usenet is littered with messages from gamers cursing IDT WinChips.

If you're looking to make your games run faster, you need a better CPU. This means an AMD K6-III, an AMD Athlon/K7, an Intel Celeron, an Intel Pentium II, or an Intel Pentium III. Chances are you have a Socket 7 motherboard, so only a K6-III would plug into your motherboard. But the K6-III doesn't work in all Socket 7 motherboards, due to its low voltage and its BIOS requirements.

So, chances are you have to get a new motherboard. Your new motherboard may or may not take your old memory—it depends on the age of your system. Either way, you want 64 MB of memory, and more if you can afford it.

The last thing you want to do is pair up that great new CPU and motherboard with that year-old video card. Video cards improve in speed and come down in price even more quickly than CPUs do, so this year's entry-level card is probably better than last year's screamer.

So, now you've bought a motherboard, a CPU, some memory, and a video card. If your sound card, modem, hard drive, and CD-ROM drive are adequate, you can recycle those from your old system. But you've come very close to replacing everything in your system. If you're heavily into games, I think you're better off not trying to upgrade your computer. Put the optimization tricks you learn in this book to work, then buy a new computer and network it to your old one. If you're using the system you have now, it'll be good enough for multiplayer games. Have a friend over and fight over who gets to use the new computer, or switch off and fight over who gets to use the new computer first.

Overclocking

It's impossible to bring up the subject of hardware in the late 1990s without the controversial topic of overclocking (running the processor at more than its rated clock speed) coming up. Overclocking is touted as the ultimate in free upgrades, and dozens upon dozens of web sites talk about how to do it. Motherboard manufacturers boast of manufacturing boards more overclockable than their competition. The hysteria has even spread from the Web into print media. I saw a magazine cover on the newsstand recently that shouted, "Add 150 MHz of pure speed without spending a penny!" Soon after that, I saw an article in the *Boston Globe* under the headline, "Overclocking and Loving It." At one time, computer magazines wouldn't touch the topic; now it's even hit the mainstream press.

Overclocking stems from the way chips are produced. As of this writing, the fastest Pentium IIIs available are 650 MHz. Intel doesn't set out to manufacture a given number of 650 MHz Pentium IIIs. They make a batch of chips, look at the orders, and decide how many of the chips in a given batch will be 650s and how many will be 600s and now many will be 550s. Theoretically, once a product is mature, the difference between speed grades will be indistinguishable.

That's the argument for overclocking. The argument against overclocking is that the very fact it doesn't work all the time suggests that some 600s are failed 650s. The chip tested at 650, failed, and became a 600. Intel has done this in the past with earlier product lines—the 60 MHz Pentium came about because Intel couldn't get early versions of the chip to run reliably at 66 MHz. Similarly, the 75 MHz Pentium came about because Intel had difficulty producing Pentiums that ran reliably at 90 MHz.

For me, the biggest argument against overclocking is the issue of warranties. No manufacturer is going to honor a warranty if they know the system has been overclocked. Running the chip at higher speeds than its rated speed causes excess heat, which causes components to wear out more quickly. Overclockers frequently go to extreme measures to cut down on the heat, but sometimes the cures are worse than the disease. Taking your computer outside into the Ohio winter, opening the case, then pointing a box fan at it isn't exactly a good solution—especially when you consider that the hard drive and other components are designed to operate at room temperature.

Generally speaking, overclocking makes me leery. I don't have extremely strong feelings on the subject, but I know I'm not about to advocate you going and overclocking your CPU, because I can't make any guarantees that it will work and won't damage your system.

I admit I have overclocked in the past, and I am overclocking now. I have an elderly Pentium 75 overclocked to 90 MHz. I had another Pentium 75 that I overclocked as high as 120 MHz for a while. I stopped overclocking that system because its stability diminished over time. The overclocked Pentium 75 is not my primary computer, however. It's slightly overclocked, and I know if the CPU starts pouring out smoke one day, I can go buy a WinChip-200 for $30, drop it in, I'll still have a usable system, and I'm only out 30 bucks. And for as long as it works, I have 30 bucks I can use for something else. And, rest assured, though pieces of this book went through that computer during various stages of its existence, the bulk of the work took place on non-overclocked systems. The overclocked system isn't mission critical.

The most prudent advice on overclocking seems to be not to do it unless you're willing to lose your CPU investment. If you're going to replace your CPU every year anyway, why not buy the slow model for half price, clock it at the rate of the fast model, then replace it with something faster (and thus, more overclockable) at the end of a year? Likewise, if you have an older second computer that you'd like to get more oomph from, you might consider overclocking it, as long as it's not performing mission-critical operations.

But consider one last thing. Overclocking is often just a matter of changing jumpers—set your motherboard for the higher speed, power up, and go. But often it's not. In those cases, you play around with the voltage, feeding the chip more voltage to try to get a higher clock rate from it. Once you get into playing with voltages, overclocking becomes more of a black art. Running at higher voltages is absolutely, positively, 110% guaranteed to shorten the CPU's useful life. If you find yourself having to do this, I suggest backing off.

The overclocking party may come to an end soon. Both Intel and AMD know how to make CPUs operate only at a given frequency. Both companies are locking the multiplier on their CPUs, which severely limits the speed at which the processors run: to overclock a Celeron, you have to run it at a higher bus frequency. The Celeron 300 used a 66 MHz bus, so to overclock it, you ran it on a 100 MHz bus, yielding a Celeron 450. If the chip wouldn't run reliably at 450 MHz and your motherboard didn't have any frequencies between the two, you were stuck at 300.

I wouldn't be surprised to see Intel implement a clock-locking scheme within the next year or two. AMD is a bit less likely to follow, given its close relationship with overclocking specialist Kryotech, but the minute AMD decides overclocking hurts their bottom line, look for them to do likewise.

Motherboards

If you find yourself needing to change generations of CPU, you need to buy a motherboard. Unless you're lucky, you can't just go buy any old motherboard and drop it right into your system and expect to be up and running immediately. You have to make sure your board is the same form factor (roughly the same size and

shape) as your old board, as well as making sure your board has enough slots—
and the right type of slots—to accommodate your peripherals. You also want to do
some quality control. Cheap motherboards kill system stability and compatibility.

A motherboard swap used to be a great way to turn your old PC into a new one.
Back when new PCs cost $2,000 and a new motherboard cost a fraction of that, it
was practical to go to the time and expense. Whether a motherboard swap is practical now depends on your expectations. If you're buying a new motherboard so
you can turn an old computer into a new one, chances are you're going to end up
replacing just about all of the components inside. You'll eventually be dissatisfied
with the video card, and with the hard drive, and with the memory, and with the
CPU. Pretty soon, you've replaced everything but the case and floppy drive. You
won't save any money in the long run. In fact, if you can afford to replace the
whole system, it will probably cost less. But it's much easier to spend $100 here
and there to replace components on an as-needed basis than it is to spend $1,000
on a whole new system.

There are people who say there is never any reason to swap out a motherboard in
1999, that it's just not cost-effective anymore. I don't believe that's true yet. If you
have a well-built system that happens to use industry-standard components (Dell,
Micron, and Gateway quickly come to mind), replacing the motherboard is probably worthwhile. Sure, you could buy a whole new eMachines PC for a little bit
more than you pay for the motherboard, but the upgraded Dell/Micron/Gateway
will give you better expandability. The verdict isn't in yet on the reliability of eMachines PCs, but Dell, Gateway, and Micron all have proven reliability, and as long
as you put a quality motherboard in your proven system, its reliability won't
degrade at all.

Form Factors

Motherboards in desktop systems almost always come in one of five form factors,
two of which are commonly available, making them good candidates for upgrading. The two common motherboard types are Baby AT and ATX, while the less
common types are Micro ATX, LPX, and NLX.

Baby AT

Baby AT motherboards are an old standard. Although the power supply specifications differ slightly and the number of expansion slots has increased from
five to eight, the 8.5"×10"–13" form factor is essentially the same as the one
used in the original IBM PC in 1981.

The AT motherboard, introduced by IBM in 1985, was larger—12" wide rather
than 8.5". As motherboard chipsets became more integrated, it became possible to squeeze the components that make up a PC back onto the smaller
board, which reduced costs. Baby AT motherboards used the same power

supply as regular AT motherboards, and the case standoffs were in the same position, so a Baby AT motherboard fits in a full-sized AT case. Baby AT motherboards were the most common and popular motherboards up until 1997 or so.

There are three characteristics that make a Baby AT motherboard instantly recognizable. First, the expansion slots are perpendicular to the motherboard. The only port connectors present on the board itself will be the keyboard port and, in rare circumstances, a PS/2 mouse port. The keyboard port is almost always the older, larger 5-pin DIN connector, rather than the smaller 6-pin DIN connector the same size and shape as a PS/2 mouse. You can usually recognize the Baby AT architecture without even opening the case—if the keyboard plugs into a large hole near the center of the case and the serial and parallel ports are mounted either on the case itself or on the backplates of expansion slots, you've got a Baby AT architecture.

Baby AT boards are becoming harder and harder to find because their power supplies don't directly supply the voltages modern CPUs need. Modern Baby AT boards need extra power regulation to make up for this, which increases costs and complicates the design, slightly increasing the possibility of failure down the road. The placement of the port connectors also makes them harder to work on—the ports are on the board, but the port connectors get mounted on the case and connect to the motherboard via ribbon cables. If you reverse the ribbon cable, the board port doesn't work. This increases the time required to build or upgrade a system, so Baby AT has fallen from favor among system manufacturers.

Due to the difficulty of fitting a Slot 1 connector, an AGP card, and at least two full-length PCI slots on a single Baby AT board, it is very difficult to find a Baby AT Pentium II motherboard.

If your system uses a Baby AT motherboard, you can inexpensively upgrade it, but chances are this will be the last upgrade you make without replacing your case. Whether the motherboard replacement is practical depends on how many other peripherals you have to replace.

ATX

ATX, introduced by Intel in 1995, is the most common form factor in use today. An ATX board measures 12"×8.5"–10"—essentially the same size and shape as a Baby AT board, only rotated 90 degrees. This shape is much more convenient for today's designs. Gamers frequently want an AGP slot and two full-length PCI slots so they can put a fast video card and two video accelerators in their systems, and it is much easier to design an ATX motherboard to these specifications than it is a Baby AT board.

ATX motherboards are much more convenient to upgrade and work on than Baby AT boards because all of the I/O ports are mounted to the board itself. Installing an ATX motherboard takes much less time than installing an equivalent Baby AT motherboard. It also has some other advantages such as better airflow.

You can tell an ATX motherboard by looking at the back of the system. ATX design specifications call for a maximum of seven slots, so if the case has eight slots, it's definitely not ATX. The real telltale sign is the knock-out for the computer's I/O ports. If the computer's serial, parallel, keyboard and mouse ports are all contained within the same $6'' \times 2''$ area, you have either an ATX or Micro ATX motherboard. If you have more than four expansion slots, it's ATX.

ATX systems are probably the easiest to upgrade and have the widest variety of upgrade options now and for the foreseeable future. It's hard to go wrong upgrading an ATX system. Since ATX was introduced in 1995, any system with this architecture will have serviceable components inside. If you're trading up to a Pentium II, you'll probably have to replace your memory and CPU along with the motherboard, but your hard drive and video card will be adequate for another year or two. If your ATX system is a Pentium, you can get a new Socket 7 motherboard and use your old CPU and still see a small performance boost, then eventually replace the CPU and memory with newer technology on an as-needed basis.

Micro ATX

Micro ATX is a low-cost derivative of ATX. Micro ATX boards have four expansion slots, which allows them to be considerably narrower than ATX boards. Micro ATX boards are also likely to have video circuitry integrated onto the motherboard. If your system looks like ATX but has only four expansion slots, it's Micro ATX.

Micro ATX is frequently used in low-cost systems. The popular eMachines line of consumer-oriented PCs use a Micro ATX architecture.

Micro ATX motherboards usually have very low-wattage power supplies, which severely limits their expansion capabilities. If you want a very basic PC, Micro ATX is fine. But if you want to record CDs or get into heavy gaming, you'll be better off with an ATX architecture system. The peripherals may fit into the case, but that doesn't mean the power supply can feed it all enough juice to keep it running reliably.

You can buy new Micro ATX motherboards, but you're probably better off getting an ATX motherboard and case if you need to upgrade a Micro ATX system. Micro ATX systems usually skimp on the power supply, running them at near capacity and shortening their lifespan.

LPX

LPX was invented by Western Digital—yes, the hard drive manufacturer—for use in space-saving systems. Western Digital has been out of the motherboard business for years, but the LPX standard remained common. The LPX architecture became especially popular in the early 1990s, and virtually every name-brand system sold in consumer electronics stores from 1992 to 1997 used this form factor.

LPX has a number of characteristics that distinguish it from Baby AT and ATX. The expansion cards sit on a riser card, and usually the expansion slots will sit parallel to the motherboard. The serial, parallel, video, mouse, and keyboard ports are integrated onto the motherboard and sit right next to each other in a straight line near the bottom of the case.

If you have an old LPX-based system, it is possible to buy an LPX motherboard. The cost is usually prohibitive, however. Expect to pay twice the price of a comparable Baby AT or ATX motherboard. If you want to upgrade an LPX system, your best bet is to buy a new AT or ATX case and a motherboard to match it.

NLX

NLX, also introduced by Intel in the mid-1990s, was designed to replace LPX. Modern systems in low-profile cases such as those sold in consumer electronics stores typically use NLX motherboards.

From the outside, NLX has the same set of characteristics as LPX. The major difference is that NLX moved the drive connectors from the motherboard itself to the riser card. It's impossible to know for certain whether a low-profile system is LPX or NLX without opening the case, though chances are if it's a Pentium II or Celeron, it's NLX, and if it's a 486, it's LPX.

Replacement NLX motherboards tend to be easier to find and less expensive than LPX boards. Thus, it's more practical to replace an NLX motherboard than an LPX motherboard, but of course, since NLX systems are newer, an NLX system is less likely to need a motherboard replacement.

Occasionally, you will find an odd motherboard—especially in a tower system—that doesn't match the description of any of these types. These boards may well be proprietary designs. In that case, you won't be replacing the board. Salvage what you can from the system and buy a new motherboard and case, or buy another computer and network it to your old one.

Motherboard Brands

Before you waltz into the nearest clone shop and buy any old motherboard they have in stock, you want to make sure you're getting a quality part. Unfortunately, not all motherboards are created equal.

You by all means want to know who makes any motherboard you buy. You want to be able to go to the motherboard manufacturer's web site to get any new device drivers and BIOS updates that might become available, and to download the motherboard manual if the manufacturer updates it. You also want to know your motherboard manufacturer because there are some manufacturers that consistently make high-quality boards and have been doing so for many years. I've had outstanding success with motherboards made by Abit, AOpen, Asus, EPoX, FIC, and Tyan. And, of course, Intel makes reliable and compatible motherboards, being the largest of the motherboard manufacturers, although the six other manufacturers I mentioned can frequently design a motherboard with the same specifications as Intel but get better performance.

Resist the temptation to buy a cheap motherboard. Right now, high-quality motherboards tend to start at around $80. Cheap boards can be had for $40–$60, but those cheap motherboards are no bargain. In some cases, these cheap boards are just obsolete leftovers made by a quality manufacturer. For example, I recently saw a mail-order vendor hawking ATX Socket 7 motherboards made by FIC for $40 a pop. These are good quality boards; the problem is, they're an 18-month-old design. That's an eternity in the computer field. Who wants 1997's top performer when 1999's worst performer is faster? Pay the few extra bucks to get a modern design.

In some cases, these cheap boards are made by disreputable manufacturers and have severe reliability and compatibility problems. Even when the boards do work reliably, they frequently don't perform as well as a good name-brand board.

Over the course of the past six years, I've built hundreds of systems, using a variety of motherboard manufacturers. I've only seen four defective motherboards in this time. Two were name brand boards; back in mid-1998 when AMD K6-2 boards were in short supply we'd bought a batch of 20 and a batch of 25 and one board from each batch turned out to be bad. The other two boards were cheap knock-offs. I aspired to build sub-$300 systems back in 1996 when it was still difficult to build a sub-$1,000 system, and these dirt-cheap boards made me think it would be possible. Then both of the cheap boards I ordered turned out to be defective—they worked, but they crashed the system any time I tried to access the floppy drive. I replaced the knock-offs with costlier FIC boards, and the systems worked fine.

The safest way to buy a motherboard is to hit one of the many hardware-oriented web sites, such as AnandTech (*www.anandtech.com*) or Tom's Hardware Guide (*www.tomshardware.com*) and read their motherboard reviews in search of a board that will do an adequate job for what you want. These sites really push the limits of a motherboard, so if a board gets a good review from them, it's going to hold up under normal use. If you can't find a review of the board, don't buy it. It could be just fine. But you always want to know what you're getting into.

The other way to buy is to find out the makes and models of boards available locally, then look for reviews of those boards, and if they turn out OK, buy.

I know some PC clone shops will not tell you the make and model of the motherboards they sell. The reasons for this policy vary, but you don't have to put up with it. If the shop won't tell you what they're trying to sell you, tell them you're going to a shop that will. Shops that don't give you full disclosure don't need your business, especially when there are many shops that will tell you exactly what they sell, and they're even willing to talk about when it's better to buy an Abit motherboard over an Asus model or vice versa.

Power Supplies

In a perfect world, power supplies would have absolutely nothing to do with system performance. Unfortunately, we live in a world where people naturally gravitate towards the best price, and all power supplies pretty much look alike. However, many cheap power supplies strain under the load a hard drive places on them during intensive disk access (and unfortunately, some games can work the hard drive pretty hard), and without adequate power, the drive can't read in an efficient manner.

Cheap power supplies hurt system performance. If you're building a PC, be sure to pay the extra bucks for a good quality power supply. There are a number of companies that manufacture and/or sell quality power supplies. The biggest name in power supplies is PC Power & Cooling (*www.pcpowercooling.com*), but other good sources of quality power supplies include Zippy USA (*www.zippyusa.com*), California PC Products (*www.calpc.com*), and Sparkle Power International (*www. spi.com.tw*).

The wattage you need varies. If you have a standard configuration with a single hard drive and CD-ROM drive, 235 watts is plenty. If you decide to add multiple hard drives and/or a CD recorder, consider upgrading to a 300-watt power supply.

CD-ROM and DVD Drives

People occasionally ask me when they'll need to buy a DVD-ROM drive and they're annoyed when I respond, "When you need one." Then they ask how they'll know when they need one, which is an easy question. Once there's a software title you absolutely have to have that's only available on DVD, get one. Until then, there's no reason to spend $100 to get something that's just going to act like a CD-ROM drive that costs half as much, unless you want to watch DVD movies on your computer's 17" monitor.

The lone exception to this rule is when buying a new system. Back when the price difference between CD and DVD was significant, it made sense to just get a

CD-ROM drive and wait. The price difference is now less than $50. If poking around inside a PC isn't your idea of fun, it might be worthwhile to make sure your next PC has a DVD-ROM drive.

And as for CD-ROM drives, I saw an entire shelf full of drives the last time I went to a computer superstore, and I still have no idea why. I saw 50x drives selling for upwards of $100, and I couldn't figure out why anyone would want to buy one. To see my logic, just think about the things you use a CD-ROM drive for:

Installing and loading software

A faster CD-ROM drive definitely makes software install more quickly. A 40x CD-ROM drive can copy 400 MB worth of data in well under 10 minutes. But the typical software package is about 100 MB. Whether that software package took 10 minutes to install or two will not have any effect on your overall computing experience.

Playing audio CDs

It always amuses me to watch people plug a set of headphones into a $2,000 computer and use it as they would a $40 CD player. I like the irony. This is probably the most common use of a CD-ROM drive, and an ancient 1X CD-ROM drive from 1990 will play audio CDs every bit as well as that ultra-over-priced 50X CD-ROM drive on the computer store shelf.

Playing games

Many games on CD-ROM contain some full-motion video and they play the video off the CD in order to conserve hard disk space, but they generally install their speed-intensive components on the system's hard drive. If the video clips are jerky, it probably means you need to adjust your CD-ROM drive's buffering. See Chapter 2, *First Steps*.

Extracting digital audio from audio CDs

There are several possible reasons for doing this. You might want an audio file in *.wav* form to use in a presentation, or you might want to convert the CD's contents to MP3 format.

Unless one of your primary interests is digital audio extraction, there is little need to replace a CD-ROM drive unless it breaks. You just won't see enough benefit from a high-speed CD-ROM drive to justify the expense. There's a joke that says CD-ROM stands for "Consumer Device—Rendered Obsolete in Months." If you want your CD-ROM drive to go faster, you're far better off spending that money on more memory and changing your CD-ROM drive buffering. This will probably bring your CD-ROM drive performance up to an acceptable level, plus it will improve overall system performance.

And sometimes a slower CD-ROM drive is preferable. Low-speed CD-ROM drives are much less sensitive to the amount of ink on the top side of a CD, less sensitive to thinner-than-normal CDs (IBM has been known to use these thinner CDs at times), and much less sensitive to scratches. I've seen store-bought CD-ROM titles fail on a 32X drive but work just fine on an older 12X drive. And on computers that lack busmastering controllers, a low-speed CD-ROM drive uses far less CPU time than a high-speed one. There's a myth going around that a fast CD-ROM drive won't run any faster than 12X on a 486. That's not true—CPU speed makes no difference in how quickly a CD-ROM drive's motor runs. But a high-speed CD-ROM drive certainly will bog your CPU's performance down much more than a 12X drive would. I prefer not to put anything faster than an 8X drive in a 486, because it strikes a good balance between drive speed and the amount of CPU time used.

Another little-known fact about CD-ROM drives is the way speed is measured. Most drives rated higher than 12X are actually spinning the disc at variable speeds—slower on the inside part of the disc, faster on the outside parts. A 32X drive is only spinning at 32X on the outermost part of the disc, which is usually empty. On the inner parts of the disc, that 32X drive is no faster than a 12X drive would be. In addition, these ratings assume a sustained read, whereas many CDs contain a large number of small files. Put simply, you'll very rarely get peak performance out of any drive.

A small number of companies market so-called TrueX drives, which employ multiple lasers to get higher speeds, rather than just spinning the disc faster. A 40X TrueX drive will give you true 40X performance, but chances are you don't need it. Most reviewers have found these drives don't give much better performance than variable-speed drives.

I also get questions about CD-ROM and DVD-ROM brands. Quality does vary slightly, just as quality varies among floppy drives, but the variance isn't enough to worry about. This advice might sound strange and superficial: get a drive that looks good. The cheaper, lower-quality drives are going to look cheap. A manufacturer who still takes the time to get the small stuff right—and in this day and age of hiding CD-ROM drives behind panels, appearance is small stuff—is more likely to get the big stuff right too.

The exception to the brand recommendation rule is digital audio extraction. The first and last name in digital audio extraction as of this writing is Plextor. Plextor's high-end SCSI CD-ROM drives can extract digital audio at a blistering 24X rate. If you want to be able to convert a full CD into files on your hard drive in less than five minutes, Plextor is the way to go. Plextor's drives carry a price premium—you'll very rarely find them for under $90, whereas a bargain-basement drive can sell for as little as $35—and they also require a separate SCSI controller, which will run another $30–$100 depending on its feature set, but if digital audio is important to you, it's worth the price.

External Removable-Media Drives

If you're wanting to use an external high-capacity drive like a Zip, Jaz, or CD-R drive, you should shy away from plugging it into your parallel port. The parallel port is too slow to do a good job with these drives, especially CD-R drives.

In the case of Zip drives, you can get either a USB or a SCSI version. Either will be much faster than a parallel-port drive. In the case of Jaz or CD-R, get a SCSI card. You'll get far too many buffer underruns with a parallel-port CD-R, which of course ruins the CD you're writing to. The Jaz is intended to be a high-performance drive, so give it the bus it was designed for.

Scanners

People don't normally think of a scanner as having an effect on PC performance, and it usually won't. The parallel port wasn't designed for scanners, however, so given the choice between a parallel or USB scanner, you're better off going with USB. USB will give you better performance and require less CPU intervention, allowing your background tasks to run better. A SCSI scanner is even better, but SCSI cards aren't standard equipment. If the scanner comes with a SCSI card, the price premium isn't too high, and you have an available expansion slot, go that route.

Monitors

A monitor has no impact on system speed, but it can dramatically increase your productivity. A big monitor running at a high resolution lets you really multitask. Considering most people still work at 800×600 resolution, a 21" display running at 1600×1200 would allow you to easily have four or even more tasks running side by side. Of course, these monitors still cost more than most of us are willing to spend, but I suggest getting a monitor of sufficient size to allow you to run at 1152×864 resolution comfortably. That's enough resolution to have a word processor and a web browser open side by side at somewhat comfortable widths for writing research papers, or to have a web browser and an email client open side-by-side for online correspondence.

Don't buy a cheap monitor, however. In 15 years of computer ownership (most of it very heavy use), I've had nine breakdowns. Five of those were monitors. The others were a printer, a floppy drive, a keyboard, and a PC/XT motherboard—comparatively very minor, seeing as a new monitor costs at least $150 today, whereas most of these components cost closer to $20. In my microcomputer support career, I've seen far more problems with monitors than with any other piece of hardware. I've always supported sites with about 500 clients, and I see monitors die at a rate of about one a month. About once a month, I usually see about one other hardware failure of some sort—usually a component with moving parts, like a keyboard, mouse, or CD-ROM drive.

The monitor is the worst place to skimp, for a couple of reasons. Computer components can be replaced with money, but no amount of money will make your eyes what they once were. And while it may seem foolish to spend $400 on a monitor you're going to use with a computer that costs as little as $399, remember that computers become obsolete far more quickly than monitors do and depreciate more quickly. When that $399 computer has a market value of zero, that monitor may still be worth half its purchase price. I still use an NEC Multisync II I bought in 1991. It's on its fourth system today. I know the 17" Iiyama monitor I'm currently using as my main monitor isn't top-of-the-line, but its picture is good, it's been reliable, and I bought it fully expecting to still be using it in five years. I bought it with a system that I expect will receive a complete overhaul within a year.

I wish someone would start publishing service and reliability ratings for monitors like the PC service and reliability ratings *PC Magazine* and *PC World* publish every year. Since I haven't seen such a thing, I can only make recommendations from my own experience. I've never had any problems with any of the NEC monitors I've owned or administered, including the very first one I bought used in 1991. It was manufactured in 1988 and I still use it several times a week. NEC monitors cost more than most other brands, and their picture quality, while always good, is never quite the best—but I've never seen another monitor with a similar history to my ancient NEC Multisync II that's in nearly as good shape as my monitor.

I've also had good luck with Viewsonic and Iiyama monitors, as have other people I know.

The mere presence of a three-year warranty isn't enough to guarantee a monitor's quality. If you buy a 19-inch monitor and it dies with six months to go on its warranty period, are you likely to go to the trouble of finding a box big enough to ship it, then lug around and pay one-way shipping for an 80-pound package? When I saw a 19-inch monitor for sale recently for $299, I was reluctant to pass on it. But seeing as every non-Viewsonic, NEC, or Iiyama monitor I've ever owned broke, I passed.

Input Devices

Input devices likewise have no impact on performance besides their impact on the user. If the computer is waiting on you, it's not being productive. So input devices do matter.

I grew up around Commodore and Amiga computers and I loved them, but it was definitely in spite of their keyboards. Those keyboards were terrible. The first keyboard I liked was a Wyse keyboard that came with an old 286 I bought and intended to turn into a quick-and-dirty refurbish project. I got it cheap, planning to add some value to it and turn around and sell it for enough profit to make it worth my while. I never did it, because its keyboard was so much better than anything else I owned. When I finally did part with that system, it was an even-up trade for a system with a Northgate keyboard. I liked that keyboard a lot, but Northgate keyboards are virtually impossible to find anymore. A couple of companies make close clones, but they charge upwards of $150 for them. I found I liked the old-fashioned IBM clackety keyboards just about as much (the ones with the gray IBM logo are better than the ones with the blue logo), and I can still find them in used computer stores for between $10 and $20. That's the same price I'd pay for a typical new no-name keyboard of today.

By now you probably think I'm a nut because I harbor strong feelings about something as trivial as a keyboard. That may be because I'm a writer and a systems analyst—my livelihood depends on my keyboards. The very fact that I can tell you the worst keyboard I ever used and the three that I liked best suggests tremendous variance. Be sure to try out some different keyboards before you buy something. Like-priced keyboards can vary widely in feel. Also check out the used computer stores. Manufacturers used to care a lot more about keyboards than they do now. I love IBM's old keyboards, but I hate their current keyboard line. If you get lucky and find a Northgate or Zeos keyboard, buy it without even looking at the price tag. You're in for a treat.

You're probably thinking I must have a strong opinion about mice too. You're right. I like the old-fashioned U-shaped three-button Logitech mice, which Logitech now markets as the Logitech Wingman Gaming Mouse. (Don't let the name fool you—it's great for everything else too.) Pointing devices are very personal. Don't settle for that $5 bar-o'-soap mouse that shipped with your system. Spend some time on the mouse aisle at the computer store, looking for something that feels pretty good, then if you find something good, get it. If you don't like it, take advantage of the store's return policy and get something you do like.

Input devices aren't just limited to mice, either. The people I've met who like trackballs, touch tablets, and touchpads are rabid about them. If I ever get back into graphics or publishing work, I'll probably want a touch tablet with a stylus. Find something that you like and can work with. You wouldn't buy a car whose seat, steering wheel, and mirrors only had one position, especially if that position were best suited for someone taller or shorter than you. Depending on your job, you may spend as much time in front of a computer as you do in a car. Make sure your computer is as comfortable as your car.

Buying New Systems

There are times that it makes sense to just chuck it all and buy a new system. If your PC is more than three or four years old and still usable for some tasks but making you wait on others, you may well be better off replacing it instead of trying to upgrade it. Don't bother trying to sell an old PC—no one wants to give you anything for your Pentium 90 when new 300 MHz systems sell for $399 or less. Either network it to your old PC so that more of your family members can get computer time when they want or need it, or pass it on to a relative.

Whether you're buying a consumer-oriented PC from a superstore or a clone from a small local dealer, it's hard to know exactly what's inside the case and how well it will perform. You may not get a straight answer from the salesperson either. If you can talk the salesperson into letting you run SiSoft Sandra (covered in detail in Chapter 5, *Utilities*), you can find out a lot about any PC. You can find out how the performance of two similar brand-name PCs compares, and in the case of a generic clone, you can find out who made the motherboard, video and sound subsystems, and other important information. You can also find out how many free ISA and PCI slots the PC has, how many free memory slots it has, and get SiSoft's professional opinion on the system. It's not like taking me PC shopping with you, but in some ways it's better.

Most clone shops will be more receptive to letting you run Sandra than most superstores. Before you cause a scene declaring that there won't be any commissions today on account of a purchase from you if you don't get a chance to run your benchmark, remember that nobody's getting rich by selling PCs at retail these days. The margins are razor-thin; most large stores stock PCs strictly because they know that people are much more likely to buy high-margin items like ink cartridges and software from the same store that sold them their PCs. If "Well, maybe [name of the store's archrival] will," doesn't suffice, then go to the competition, and if the direct competition isn't accommodating either, then try Joe's Clones.

If you're buying a PC via mail-order from a vendor like Dell, Gateway, or Micron, you don't have the option of running Sandra. The sales representative will be able to tell you who made most of the components going into the system and other critical specifications like the number of available expansion and memory slots, but you definitely won't know as much about any PC you buy mail-order as you would something you found locally and were able to run Sandra on before purchasing. On the plus side, if you ask for an ATX-architecture system from most direct vendors, you won't have any trouble getting one.

Scavenging

If you work for a company that has older systems, or if you're a longtime computer user with some old systems sitting in the garage or attic, or if you know of a used computer store nearby or online that has good deals on used hardware, and you want to do a little souping up of an old system without spending a lot of money, you can take the scavenger's approach to upgrading.

One scenario for scavenger-style upgrading immediately comes to mind. If you have an old 486 that uses 30-pin memory and you absolutely must get 32 MB of RAM into it, you should embark on a search for a 386 or 486 with 16 MB of RAM or more. Chances are, you won't pay much more than $100 for it if you can find one, and you'll have some extra parts to scavenge as well. If you can find two such systems, buy both, then pool their components with the components from your system. Take the 4 MB SIMMs, then find the best motherboard, CPU, video card, CD-ROM drive, and sound card from the lot. Then you can build another system based around these components and the two biggest hard drives, then if you're strapped for cash, use the leftover parts to build a second system and sell it to help finance the upgrade—the price difference between a really good 486 and a really bad one is about $25, and the difference narrows tremendously in the case of 386s. You'll still have plenty of leftover parts to add to your spare parts bin.

Obviously, if you want to take this approach, it helps to have some computer knowledge already. If you're comfortable disassembling and reassembling systems, this is a cheap way to do some upgrading. When you're bottom-fishing, an entire system frequently sells for just slightly more than one of the key components would fetch alone, so you can do some upgrading by buying a system similar to yours, swapping whatever components are better, then either try to resell the now-downgraded system, or find another use for it.

When scavenging, there are two things to remember. First of all, if you can find a good second hard drive to put in the system you're tying to upgrade, you want to do it. Two drives are far better than one.

The second and perhaps more important thing is to remember that not all components are created equal. They never were, and they never will be. Two motherboards that support exactly the same CPUs may differ in performance by as much as 10%. On older systems, that's more than the difference you get from stepping up to the next grade of CPU. The performance of video cards can vary widely as well. If you're messing around with 386s and 486s, your video cards are likely to be on the old ISA bus, so you definitely want to keep the fastest video card you find.

What Do I Do with This Old 486?

While 486-based computers are frequently maligned these days, they can still be useful. With some work, they can run Office 97 and other productivity software, and many older games were designed for 486s. An optimized 486 can actually feel faster than a Pentium if, like most Pentiums, the Pentium is bogged down with excess sounds, animated cursors, screen savers, and other novelties.

All of the tricks in this book applied to a 486 won't turn it into a Pentium III-based powerhouse. And while hardware upgrades are certainly possible, they aren't extremely practical. I can turn a 486 into a Pentium III by adding or replacing enough hardware, but the same can be said for the toaster in my kitchen. A 486 with the maximum amount of memory it can take—common limits are 32, 48, and 64 MB—and a new, fast 8.4 GB hard drive will run pretty well. But adding this stuff, unless you already have some of it laying around and it's already paid for, just isn't very practical. For $500, you can soup up a 486. Add 32 MB of RAM, add a 133 MHz CPU upgrade, add a fast new 8.4 GB hard drive, maybe upgrade to Windows 98, and buy PartitionMagic and Norton SystemWorks to optimize it. But the upgrade is hardly cost effective. As I write, a new 300 MHz eMachines PC with 32 MB of RAM and a 3.2 GB hard drive sells for $399. While it won't come with PartitionMagic and Norton SystemWorks, the tools that ship with Windows 98 are good enough that this new PC will outrun any 486, no matter how you optimize it.

If the 486 is still too slow even after optimizing it and adding salvaged hardware to it, there's still something you can try. Try dedicating the machine to a single task. If you're only interested in using that PC for web browsing and email, make Netscape Navigator 3.04 your default shell. If you're interested in using that PC for word processing, make your preferred word processor the default shell. This will in essence turn the 486 into a single-task kiosk, but you may be surprised how well a 486 can do a single task.

The process is easy. Install the most basic Windows 95 setup you need to get the job done. Configure it—adding Dial-up Networking if you're using it for web browsing—and streamline it. When I say basic, I mean minimalist. It's possible to run other programs, but not very easily. Now optimize it—partition the drives strategically, and use the other tricks described in this book.

Next, install the application you're going to want to use, then launch it and configure it. Microsoft Word 97 doesn't run well out of the box on a 486, but it will run fine if you do a little configuration. Select Tools → Options → Spelling and Grammar. Find the box labeled Check Spelling As You Type and deselect it. Find the box labeled Check Grammar As You Type and deselect it as well. You might also go to Tools → Options → View and check the box labeled Draft Font. This makes Word substitute the Windows system font for the TrueType fonts onscreen. The result won't be true WYSIWYG, but the speed will be much better and Print Preview will give you a good idea of what the finished product will look like.

If you're looking to turn a 486 into a web kiosk, it's best not to expect it to run a fourth-generation browser. Fifth-generation browsers are expected to be faster than their fourth-generation counterparts, but it's best to stick with Netscape 3 or Netscape 5, or better yet, Opera. Be sure to configure it to use the temporary partition for browser cache.

Once your application is installed and configured, you need to modify *system.ini.* Go to Start → Run → `sysedit` → SYSTEM.INI. About the eighth line down, you will find a line that reads SHELL=EXPLORER.EXE. Almost any application can serve as the shell; your best bet is to simply try it. You need to use the short filenames to specify it, however. For instance, to make Word my default shell, I use the following line:

```
SHELL=D:\PROGRA~1\MICROS~1\OFFICE\WINWORD.EXE
```

This assumes that Word is installed in *D:\Program Files\Microsoft Office\Office.*

To make Netscape Navigator my default shell, I use this line:

```
SHELL=D:\PROGRA~1\NETSCAPE\PROGRAM\NETSCAPE.EXE
```

You may occasionally need to run another program, such as when you need to defragment your drive. Hit Ctrl-Esc, and the Windows Task Manager will pop up. Go to File → Run Application, and type DEFRAG. You'll now be able to defragment your drives. You can run any other program you like this way as well, but the lack of a Start menu makes it a bit tedious. This trick assumes that the decreased overhead by not keeping a separate Windows shell in memory will make the system's speed more acceptable. You save at least 4 MB of RAM, you save some CPU cycles as well, and making the computer load some useful program automatically when it's turned on will make it easier for some people to use.

If you've put a scheduling program on the PC to automate tasks such as defragmenting the drive or scanning for viruses, add a line to *system.ini* to run it—putting it in the *Startup* folder won't work, since *Startup* is tied to Explorer. For example:

```
RUN=C:\PROGRA~1\PLUS!\SCHEDULE.EXE
```

This will allow the 486 to still do some self-maintenance.

This trick may allow you to pull a 486 off the scrap heap and make it useful again for another year or so. Or, it may allow you to give it to a friend or relative who isn't especially interested in computers for any purpose other than keeping in touch. If that's the case, a 486 will be useful to them until it breaks. If it's receiving fairly light use, that could be several years from now. Why spend a few hundred dollars on a new PC when your old 486 or a used 486 available for under $100 will do just fine for this job?

Appendix: Useful Web Resources

There are literally dozens, if not hundreds, of useful web sites that provide information and/or utilities to help you get more out of your Windows-based PC. These sites were all invaluable resources to me when I was writing this book.

Commercial Software Vendors

These companies produce commercial software products that are mentioned in this book:

Lineo (formerly Caldera Thin Systems) (http://www.lineo.com)
    Providers of DR-DOS

Mijenix (http://www.mijenix.com)
    Producers of the Fix-It 99 utilities suite

Network Associates' McAfee division (http://www.mcafee.com)
    Providers of Nuts & Bolts, UnInstaller, and McAfee Anti-Virus

Opera Software (http://www.operasoftware.com)
    Makers of an alternative small-footprint web browser

PowerQuest (http://www.powerquest.com)
    Makers of PartitionMagic and DriveImage

Symantec (http://www.symantec.com)
    Producers of Norton Utilities, Norton AntiVirus, and Norton CleanSweep

WinGate (http://www.wingate.com)
    A utility for sharing an Internet connection among multiple Windows 95/98 computers. An unnecessary tool with Windows 98SE, which includes a WinGate-like tool.

Free Utilities

These sites provide free utilities mentioned in this book. By "free," I mean you
don't have to pay for these tools. Some of these tools are free in the truest sense
of the word, meaning their source code is available under the GNU public license
or another open-source license. Most of the tools are simply available free of
charge, and some of them do have strings attached.

Disk/File/System Utilities

Acceleration Software (http://www.accelerationsw.com)
> Providers of the Windrenalin disk speedup tool

FIPS (http://www.igd.fhg.de/~aschaefe/fips)
> A free nondestructive disk partitioning tool

Info-ZIP (http://www.cdrom.com/pub/infozip)
> A free command-line Zip utility, which is invaluable for backing up your Windows directory

SiSoft Sandra (http://www.sisoftware.demon.co.uk/sandra)
> A utility that gives detailed information about a system's internals

Cleanup Utilities

EasyCleaner (http://www.saunalahti.fi/tonihele)
> A free, thorough registry cleaning tool

Freemem (http://www.meikel.com)
> A free memory-recovery tool

Kevin Solway's Clean System Directory
(http://www.ozemail.com.au/~kevsol/sware.html)
> A free utility to find unused DLL and OCX files in your system directory

RegClean (http://support.microsoft.com/support/downloads/DP3049.ASP)
> A Microsoft utility to remove unneeded entries from the registry.

Startup Manager (http://www.delphifreestuff.com/freeware/files/sm-setup.exe)
> A utility for controlling what your system loads at startup

Windows Shells

EVWM (http://www.evwm.com)
> A replacement shell for Windows 9x/NT

LiteStep (http://www.litestep.net)
> A replacement shell for Windows 9x/NT

Sun Microsystems (http://www.sun.com)
> Providers of the StartOffice office suite/desktop

DOS Utilities

Jörg Weske (http://www.tu-chemnitz.de/~jwes/win95boot.htm)
> Jörg Weske's tool to patch Windows 95B to allow dual-booting with DOS

Slowdown (http://oak.oakland.edu/pub/simtelnet/msdos/sysutl/slodn101.zip)
> A free utility to slow your system down for running old DOS programs

UMBPCI (http://www.uwe-sieber.de/umbpci_e.html)
> A free DOS memory manager

XMSDisk (http://www.opus.co.tt/dave/index.htm)
> A DOS-based RAM disk program

Internet Utilities

Black Castle Software (http://www.blackcastlesoft.com)
> Makers of NetLaunch, a utility to automatically load and close sets of utilities as you connect and disconnect from the Internet

EasyMTU (http://members.tripod.com/~EasyMTU)
> A free utility for optimizing your modem

FastNet99 (http://members.xoom.com/gcriaco)
> A tool by Giuseppe Criaco to speed up DNS lookups

iSpeed Manager (http://www.hms.com/ispeed.htm)
> A free utility for optimizing your modem

Junkbuster (http://www.junkbusters.com)
> Free ad-blocking software

A Junkbuster blockfile (http://www.home.unix-ag.org/sfx/junkbuster/blockfile)
> Required for general use of Junkbuster

NetSonic (http://www.web3000.com)
> A web preloading and caching utility

Proxomitron (http://members.tripod.com/Proxomitron)
> Free ad-blocking software with a nice GUI interface

Shareware Utilities

These sites provide links to shareware utilities mentioned in this book. Most of these utilities provide a free trial period during which you can evaluate their usefulness for your purposes, and after which you are expected either to pay for them or to discontinue using them.

BinaryWork CPU controller (http://binarywork.hypermart.net)
> A $37 shareware utility to set the priority of your Windows tasks to adjust performance

Bremze (http://ansis.folklora.lv/bremze)
> A $10 shareware program to slow your system down for old DOS programs, by Latvian programmer Ansis Ataols Berzins

CTS Serial Port utilities suite (http://www.troubleshooters.com/ttools.htm)
> Utilities suite that tells you what kind of UART your system's serial ports are using

Golden Bow (http://www.goldenbow.com)
> Providers of the popular Vopt defragmentation utility

Memturbo (http://www.memturbo.com)
> A $20 shareware memory recovery tool from Silicon Prairie Software

Mo'Slo (http://www.hpaa.com/moslo/moslotry.asp)
> A $15 shareware program by U.S. programmer David Perrell, to slow your system down for running old DOS programs

98lite (http://www.98lite.net)
> Utility to install Windows 98 with varying degrees of Internet Explorer integration

Virtusoft (http://www.virtusoft.com)
> Producers of the Windows-based VRAMDIR RAM disk program

Device Driver Archives

If you can't find the disk that contained the DOS or Windows device drivers for your CD-ROM drive, mouse, or sound card, you can download them from these sites:

http://www.drivershq.com
> CD-ROM, mouse, and sound card drivers

http://www.geocities.com/SiliconValley/4421/drivers.html
> CD-ROM drivers

http://www.windrivers.com
> CD-ROM, mouse, and sound card drivers

Hardware Vendors

Most hardware vendors maintain some kind of web presence. The following vendors are specifically mentioned in this book.

Disk Controllers

Promise Technology (http://www.promise.com)
Makers of high-speed PCI IDE controllers for upgrading older PCs to take advantage of larger, faster hard drives

Power Supplies

California PC Products (http://www.calpc.com)
Manufacturer of high-quality PC power supplies

PC Power & Cooling, Inc. (http://www.pcpowercooling.com)
Supplier of high-quality PC cases, power supplies, and cooling fans

SPI Power Co., Ltd. (http://www.spi.com.tw)
Manufacturer of high-quality PC power supplies)

Zippy Shin Jiuh Corp. (http://www.zippyusa.com)
Manufacturer of high-quality PC power supplies

Information Sites

These sites contain useful information on a variety of computing topics.

Windows 95

Computer Clinic (http://www.compuclinic.com/osr2faq)
Sean Erwin's comprehensive FAQ about Windows 95 OSR2

Hardware Reviews

AnandTech (http://www.anandtech.com)
A hardware site that features more frequent reviews than Tom's Hardware Guide; also very popular.

Ars Technica (http://www.ars-technica.com)
Yet another hardware-oriented web site that updates more frequently than Tom's Hardware Guide.

Sharky Extreme (http://www.sharkyextreme.com)
The archrival to Tom's Hardware Guide.

Storage Review (http://www.storagereview.com)
A hard-drive–oriented hardware site that compares and reviews virtually every new hard drive that comes on the market.

Tom's Hardware Guide (http://www.tomshardware.com)
>   An extremely popular web site run by Thomas Pabst, M.D., which has caused
>   a wave of hardware-oriented web sites to spring up since 1996. Not necessar-
>   ily the oldest, biggest, or most prolific of hardware sites, but it's the standard
>   by which all others are judged.

Information for Gamers

Blue's News (http://www.bluesnews.com)
>   A gaming-minded hardware/software review site

Combatsim.com (http://www.combatsim.com)
>   Another gaming site, concentrating on simulation and strategy games

Index

Symbols

@echo off command, 87

Numbers

100-Base-T standard, 176
10-Base-2 standard, 176
10-Base-T standard, 176
32-bit drivers, 17
3Com, 177
3D accelerators, 227
3D add-on cards, 230
486 computers, optimizing, 252–254
98lite, running, 195

A

Acceleration Software, 71
accelerators, 3D, 227
accessing
    BIOS setup program, 89
    files
        moved to front of FAT, 54
        tracking in Windows 95, 52
    network drives, 185
activating compressed RAM disks, 216
ActiveMovie, 191, 195
ActiveX Cleanup, 107, 172
Add New Hardware Wizard, running, 197
AddStor, 74
ads, blocking, 165–168

AGP video bus, 228
align.bat, 70
aligning software, 69–71
AMD K6-III-based computers, performance
    of, 224
AmigaOS, public screens, 127
AnandTech, 230, 244
animations, disabling, 27, 35–36
anti-virus software, 9, 55, 107
AntiVirus utility, 108
AppEvents subkey, 33
applications (see software)
archives
    device drivers, 258
    storing file in, 70
Ars Technica, 230
ATX motherboards, 220, 241
audio, 230
autoexec.bat
    boot menus, 81
    boot process, 78
    configuring to run DOS programs in
        DOS mode, 142
    enabling through boot menu, 144
    increasing speed of, 87
    renaming, 17
    settings for running DOS
        games, 151–155
autoplay, disabling, 23
AutoScan=n setting, 80

B

Baby AT motherboard, 240
backing up
    .bak, .dot, .old, and .txt files, 45
    data before running FIPS, 66
    files, automating, 46
    registry, 34, 105, 118
    Windows configurations, 201
    Windows directories, 9, 199
backward compatibility
    drivers, Windows 95 and 98, 198
    FAT32 to FAT16, 58
.bak files, 45
batch files, 88
Bay Networks, 177
benchmarks, 11, 226
Berzins, Ansis Ataols, 149
binary value, 37
BIOS
    controller cards with, 224
    setup program, accessing, 89
Blank Screen screen saver, 26
blocking ads, 165–168
Blue's News, 230
.bmp files as wallpaper, 25, 45
boot disks, creating, 189
boot drives, including FAT16 on, 62
boot menus
    DOS games, 153–155
    enabling, 144
BootDelay=n setting, 80
BootGUI=n setting, 81
booting
    dual
        Windows 95 and 98, 204
        Windows 9x and true DOS, 145–147
    from RAM disks, monitoring progress
        of, 212
    increasing speed of, 76–92
    pseudo-dual, 143–145
BootKeys=n setting, 81
bootlog.txt file, 83
BootMenuDefault=n setting, 82
BootMenuDelay=n setting, 82
BootMenu=n setting, 81
BootMulti=n setting, 82
BootSafe=n setting, 80
BootWarn=n setting, 82
BootWin=n setting, 82

Bremze utility, 149
Brooks, Shane, 195, 197
Browse Master, 185
browser caches
    deleting, 15, 57
    resizing, 69
browsers
    deleting, 57
    Internet Explorer
        deleting, 191, 197
        installing Windows 98 without, 195
    tuning, 172
    which to use, 171
buffer count, Windows 95 and 98, 148
bugs
    in Network Server setting, 20
    Windows 95 filesystem, repairing, 38
building home networks, 178–181
buses
    PCI, upgrading, 233
    video cards, 227
buying (see purchasing)

C

C drive, 59
cabinets, 190
cables, home networking, 176
CabPack, 191
CacheSize key, 36–38
caching
    browsers, 172
    buffer count, disks, 148
    tools, 168
Caldera, 146
California PC Products, 245
Caps Lock key, 200
cards
    controller, with BIOS, 224
    video, upgrading, 226–230
CAT5 (Category 5) cables, 176
CD-ROM drives
    brands of, 247
    caches
        recovering wasted memory, 38
        tuning, 22
    disabling autoplay, 23
    mapping drive letters for, 59
    tuning Windows 95/98 to, 36–38
    upgrading, 245–247

Central Point Software, 95
central processing unit (see CPU)
charityware, 165
Chernobyl virus, 108
chipsets, video, 228
.chk files, 14
Chuck Yeager's Air Combat, configuring to
    run in Windows, 150
Clean System Directory, 114, 117
CleanSweep, 9, 106
cleanup tools, 114
click here to begin animation, disabling, 36
Client for NetWare Networks, deleting, 178
cloaks, 124
cluster numbers, sorting directories by, 52
clusters
    FAT16 vs. FAT32, 57
    lost, 14
CMOS, presence of floppy drives in, 90
coaxial cables, 176
code, aligning, 69–71
coders (codecs), 24
COM port, finding location of modem
    on, 158
CombatSim, 230
Command directory, 214
command.com, 85
commands
    autoexec.bat, 87
    for scheduling disk scans, 55
    LOADER, 146
common section, 144
compatibility
    98lite, issues with, 196
    backward
        drivers, Windows 95 and 98, 198
        FAT32 to FAT16, 58
    Superfassst and other software, 73
    with Windows 98
        Speed Start and, 71
        Superfassst and, 71
        Win-G and, 205
compressing
    disks, 74
    RAM disks, 112, 215
computers, basic steps for
        optimizing, 13–40
Config subkey, 33
ConfigFileAllocSize entry, 39

config.sys
    adding umbpci.sys to, 148
    boot menus, 81
    boot process, 77
    configuring to run DOS programs in
        DOS mode, 141
    renaming, 17
    settings for running DOS
        games, 150–154
configuration data, moving to
        winboot.ini, 86
configuring
    config.sys to run DOS programs in DOS
        mode, 141
    DOS games to run in
        Windows, 150–155
    EVWM, 124
    LiteStep, 129–133
    networks, 201
    RAM disks, 213
    swap files, 101
    Word 97 to run on 486 computers, 253
connections
    Direct Cable, installing components
        for, 178
    Internet, controlling, 169–171
    modems, optimizing, 157–173
    parallel, speed of, 175
    phone, 160
    serial, speed of, 175
    tuning through software, 161–163
Control Panel subkey, 33
control panels, network, 185
controller cards with BIOS, 224
controllers, SCSI, 90
conventional memory, 136, 138
conventional-memory games, configuring
        to run in Windows, 150
Cookie Cleanup, 107
cookies, deleting, 14
cooling systems, video cards, 229
copying
    shortcuts, 112
    Win95 directory to hard drive, 188
Cox, Walter, 232
CP/M operating system, 146
CPU (central processing unit)
    boot process, 76
    purchasing, 4

CPU (central processing unit) (*continued*)
  upgrading, 234–239
  usage, effects of LiteStep upon, 128
CPU Controller, 110
CrashGuard, 97
Criaco, Guiseppe, 163
crossover cable, 176
Crucial Technology, 219
CTS Serial Port Utilities suite, 159
Custom directory, 213
Cybermax, 224

D

D drive, 59
data
  backing up before running FIPS, 66
  compressing on drives, 75
  configuration, moving to winboot.ini, 86
  isolating, 62
  organizing on drives, 44
data compression, RAM disks, 112
dates, sorting directories by, 52
dblbuff.sys, 77, 84
dblspace.bin, 83, 85
DblSpace=n setting, 83
decoders (codecs), 24
Defrag
  abuse of, 53
  fast loaders and, 71
  running after uninstalling and
    reinstalling programs, 56
  running before FIPS, 66
  scanning drives instead of running, 51
  vs. Speed Disk, 97
Defrag Plus, 51, 102
deleting
  ActiveMovie, 191
  browser caches, 15, 57
  .chk files, 14
  Client for NetWare Networks, 178
  cookies, 14
  Exchange, 190
  files, 14, 56–57, 61
  floppy drive from boot order, 90
  fonts, 16
  Hosts file, 164
  ICW Internet Connection Wizard, 191
  Internet Explorer, 191, 197

Mscreate.dir, 45
msdos.sys, 86
MSN, 190
online services, 191
surrogate drives, 212
Demos, Norton Utilities, 98
density, platters, 225
desktop icons, replacing with hotkeys, 25
desktop schemes, disabling, 26
DesktopManagement subkey, 33
desktops
  redirecting to RAM disks, 112
  virtual, 127
device drivers
  archives for, 258
  copying into Win95 directory, 188
  installing, 197
devices
  IDE, detecting, 90
  input, upgrading, 249
  Plug-and-Play, 77
Dial-Up Adapter, IPX/SPX protocol, 180
Dial-Up Networking, 169
digital audio, extracting from audio
    CDs, 246
Digital Research, 74, 146
DIMMs, 219
Direct Cable Connection, installing
    components for, 178
directories
  Command, 214
  Custom, 213
  Help, 213
  Inf, 213
  Media, 213
  optimizing, 42–50
  organizing data and software on, 44
  RAM disks, deleting to save space, 213
  sorting by cluster number vs. access
    date, 52
  Sysbackup, 213
  Win95, copying to hard drive, 188
  Windows
    backing up, 9
    renaming, 199
DirectX enhancements, 189
DisableLog=n setting, 83
disabling
  animations, 27, 35–36

Browse Master, 186
CD-ROM autoplay, 23
desktop schemes, 26
drive mapping, 183
Java, JavaScript, and Active X, 172
loading of graphics, 173
pause in menus, 35
POST memory test, 90
power management, 24, 98
screen savers, 98
sounds, 26
tooltips, Windows 98, 27
disaster recovery, speeding process of, 62
disk caches
    buffer count, Windows 95 and 98, 148
    optimizing, 20
    tuning hidden settings, 21
Disk Doctor, 55, 97
disk space, increasing, 14–17
Disk Tune, optimizing disks with, 104
disks
    boot, creating, 189
    boot process, 77
    freeing space, 14–17
    optimizing, 41–75
        compression, 74
        directories, 42–50
        FAT, 57–69
        fragmentation, 50–56
        results from, 73
        tools for, 69–73
        with Defrag Plus, 102
        with Disk Tune, 104
        with Speed Disk, 99
        working within physical limitations
            of, 56
    partitioning, 59–69
    RAM, 111–114, 155, 206–216
    saving space with networks, 184
    scheduling scans of, 55
    using tools to improve performance
        of, 93
    (see also drives)
DLLs (dynamic link libraries), moving with
    Clean System Directory, 114
DNS (Domain Name System) lookups,
    increasing speed of, 163
.doc files, 45
dock windows, 127

documentation, lost, 143
Domain Name System (DNS) lookups, 163
DOS, 88
    optimizing, 134–156
    partition types, 59
    support for multiple primary
        partitions, 65
    testing modems in, 231
DOS games
    configuring to run in Windows, 150–155
    running from RAM disks, 155
DOS Protected Mode Interface (DPMI)
    memory, 138
DoubleBuffer=n setting, 83
DoubleSpace utility, 74, 112
doubling RAM, tools for, 109
downloading modem drivers, 161
DPMI (DOS Protected Mode Interface)
    memory, 138
DPMI games, configuring to run in
    DOS, 152
DR-DOS utility, 74, 146
Drive Image, 10
drivers
    32-bit, 17
    archives for, 258
    copying into Win95 directory, 188
    dblbuff.sys, 84
    installing, 197
    lost, 143
    modem, downloading, 161
    network, setting up, 182
drives
    boot, including FAT16 on, 62
    CD-ROM
        caches, 22, 38
        disabling autoplay, 23
        mapping drive letters for, 59
        tuning Windows 95/98 to, 36–38
        upgrading, 245–247
    copying Win95 directory to, 188
    data compression, 75
    defragmenting, 16, 50–56, 254
    deleting from boot order, 90
    DVD, upgrading, 245–247
    external removable-media,
        upgrading, 248
    features to look for, 224–226
    formatting, 64, 67

drives (*continued*)
   mapping, 59
   network, 184
   organizing data and software on, 44
   partitioning, 7, 43
   scanning for viruses, 108
   sizes and speed, 223
   surrogate
      deleting, 212
      setting up, 208
   uncompressing, 75
   using tools to improve performance
      of, 93
   (see also disks)
DriveSpace utility, 75, 112
DrvSpace=n setting, 84
dual-booting
   Windows 95 and 98, 204
   Windows 9x and true DOS, 145–147
Duplicate File Finder, 107
duplicating (see copying)
DVD drives, 245–247
DWORD, 36
dynamic disk caching, 21
dynamic link libraries (DLLs), 114

E

E drive, 59
EasyCleaner, 115
EasyMTU, 162
echo off command, 87
EDO memory, 219
eMachines, 242
EMM386, 138
empty keys, adding to run WALIGN
      properly, 69
EMS (expanded memory specification), 139
EMS games, configuring to run in
      DOS, 151
entries
   limiting in root directories, 42–44
   MenuShowDelay, 36, 39
   MinAnimate, 35
Enum subkey, 34
erasing (see deleting)
errors
   correcting in registry, 100
   defragmenting drives with, 51
   scanning drives for, 50

Ethernet cables, 176
EVWM, 123–125
Exchange, deleting, 190
executable files, moving, 47–49
expanded memory (see EMS)
Explorer, replacing, 119
Explorer Shell Extensions, 98
explorer.exe, 78
extended memory specification (XMS), 137
extended partitions, 59, 68

F

fans, CPU, 235
fast loaders, 71–73
fast page mode memory (FPM), 219
FastNet99, 163
FAT (file access table), 57–69
   character limitations of filenames, 42
   directories as linked lists, 42, 58
   disk fragmentation and, 50
   formatting drives with, 64
   moving files to front of, 54
FCC ID, finding for modems, 161
FDISK
   creating partitions with, 67
   FIPS as replacement for, 65
   partitioning drives with, 63–65
Felten, Edward, 195
file access table (see FAT)
File and Printer Sharing for Microsoft
      Networks, 181, 185
File Compare, 98
filenames, character limitations of, 42
files
   access to, tracking in Windows 95, 52
   align.bat, 70
   as wallpaper, 45
   autoexec.bat
      boot menus, 81
      boot process, 78
      configuring to run DOS programs in
         DOS mode, 142
      enabling through boot menu, 144
      increasing speed of, 87
      renaming, 17
      settings for running DOS
         games, 151–155
   backing up, 45
   batch, 88

.bmp as wallpaper, 25, 45
boot process, 77
.cab, 190
.chk, 14
config.sys
  adding umbpci.sys to, 148
  boot menus, 81
  boot process, 77
  configuring to run DOS programs in
    DOS mode, 141
  renaming, 17
  settings for running DOS
    games, 150–154
deleting, 14, 56–57, 61
EMM386, 138
executable, moving, 47–49
Hosts, 163, 165
.ini, 77
msdos.sys, 77
  changing, 78
  checking after running
    WinCustomizer, 103
  increasing speed of, 86
  options, 79–86
sorting, 54, 94
swap
  configuring, 101
  on RAM disks, 210
  optimizing, 18
system configuration, backup copies
  of, 46
system.dat, 30
system.ini, 46, 253
temporary
  isolating, 62
  resizing, 69
umbpci.sys, adding to config.sys, 148
unalign.bat, 70
Welcome.exe, 214
filesswap, isolating, 62
filesystems
  reducing fragmentation, 39
  repairing Windows 95 bug in, 38
Find Fast, 18
finding, 28
FIPS (First Interactive non-destructive
    Partition Splitting program),
    partitioning drives with,
    65–67, 209

Fix-It 99, 9, 91, 94–97, 101–103
floppy drives
  data compression, 75
  deleting from boot order, 90
folders (see directories)
fonts, deleting, 16
form factors, motherboards, 240–243
formatting drives, 64, 67
FPM (fast page mode) memory, 219
fragmentation
  amount reported by Speed Disk, 99
  disks, 50–56
  RAM disks, 207
  reducing in filesystems, 39
free software, 171
free tools, 256
FreeBSD, 123
freeing disk space, 14–17
Freemem, 109
freeware, 109–118

G

gamers, web sites with information for, 260
games
  DOS
    configuring to run in
      Windows, 150–155
    running from RAM disks, 155
    slowing speed of, 148
  installing and uninstalling, 105
  multiplayer, IPX/SPX protocol, 180
  playing from CD-ROM drives, 246
  uninstalling unneeded, 15
  upgrading CPUs, 236
Gates, Bill, 58
gdi.exe, 78
Gecko browser, 172
GEM operating system, 146
GIF images as wallpaper, 25
Gillum, Eliot, 123
GNOME, 123
GNU GPL, 65
Good Socket 7 motherboards, 224
goto statements, 145
graphics, disabling loading of, 173

H

hangs, Setup, 200
hard drives
    boot process, 77
    copying Win95 directory to, 188
    defragmenting, 16, 50–56
    features to look for, 224–226
    partitions, dedicating to single tasks, 7
    sizes and speed, 223
hardware
    role of in performance, 1–12
    upgrading, 217–254
    vendors of, 258
    web sites with reviews of, 259
hardware subkey, 34
Hederer, Lars, 191
Helenius, Toni, 115
Helix Software, 71, 95
Help directory, 213
hexadecimal numbering system, 37
hidden disk cache settings, tuning, 21
high memory area (HMA), 137
High Mountain Software, 162
himem.sys, 77, 144
HKCC (HKEY_CURRENT_CONFIG), 31
HKCR (HKEY_CLASSES_ROOT), 30
HKCU (HKEY_CURRENT_USER), 31–32
HKDD (HKEY_DYN_DATA), 32
HKLM (HKEY_LOCAL_MACHINE), 31, 33
HKU (HKEY_USERS), 31
HMA (high memory area), 137
home networking, 174–187
Hosts file, 163, 165
HostWinBootDrv=path setting, 79
hotkeys
    LiteStep, 132
    replacing desktop icons with, 25
hubs, 177
Hurricane program, 71
Hussein, Saddam, 206

I

IBM, 240
IBM keyboards, 250
ICE program, 129
icons, desktop, 25
ICW Internet Connection Wizard,
        deleting, 191

IDE devices, detecting, 90
IDE drives, 225
"ideal" operating system, 4
IE-Remove script, 197
ifshelp.sys, 77
Iiyama monitor, 249
images, disabling loading of, 173
importing Start menu, 124
Indeo, 24
Inf directory, 213
Info-ZIP, backing up Windows
        configurations, 201
.ini files, 77
inner tracks, disks, 56
input devices, upgrading, 249
installing
    98lite, 195
    device drivers, 197
    EVWM, 124
    home networks, 178–181
    LiteStep, 129–133
    NICs, 178
    Norton Utilities, 97
    software
        from CD-ROM drives, 246
        running SFC before, 117
        to network drives, 184
    Superfassst 98, 72
    Windows 98, 192–204
    XMSDISK, 111
InstallLocationsMRU subkey, 33
InstallShield, 105
Integrator utility, 97
Intel, 177, 241
Internet
    optimizing connections by
            modems, 157–173
    resources for optimizing Windows-based
            computers, 255–260
Internet Explorer, 94, 172
    caches, 14
    deleting, 191, 197
    disk space allocation by, 57
    installing Windows 98 without, 195
Internet Junkbuster, 166, 170, 173
Internet Service Providers (ISPs), matching
        modems with, 158
io.sys, 77
IP addresses, 164

IPX/SPX (Internetwork Packet Exchange/Sequenced Packet Exchange) protocol, 180
ISA sound card, 177, 230
ISA video bus, 227
isolating
  data, 62
  Windows 95/98 and applications to separate partitions, 61
iSpeed, 162
ISPs (Internet Service Providers), matching modems with, 158

J

Java and JavaScript, disabling, 172
Jaz drives
  upgrading, 248
  using as surrogate drives, 209
Jeopardy!, 141
Jmodem, 162
Johnson, Bret, 149
JPEG images as wallpaper, 25

K

Karp, David A., 226
KDE, 123
keyboard layout subkey, 33
keyboards, upgrading, 249
Kingston, 177
krnd32.dll, 78

L

L2 caches, optimizing, 221
LANs (local area networks), setting up, 181–184
laptops, power management and, 24
laser disc players, 23
Launch Rocket, speeding application load times, 105
launching applications, increasing speed of, 101
libraries, Visual Basic, 164
limitations of Windows, working within, 5
limiting entries in root directories, 42–44
linked lists, FAT directories as, 42, 58
Linux, 123
  FIPS, 65
  proxy servers, 95
  speed of compared to Windows, 4

LiteStep, 126–133
LiveUpdate, 98
Livingston, Brian, 11
LOADER command, 146
loading
  graphics, disabling, 173
  software
    changes in speed of after installing Superfassst, 72
    from CD-ROM drives, 246
    increasing speed of, 105
LoadTop=n setting, 85
local area networks (LANs), setting up, 181–184
logical front, disks, 56
logical partitions, 59
Logitech Wingman Gaming Mouse, 250
Logo=n setting, 85
logons, networks, 78
lost clusters, 14
lost drivers and documentation, 143
LPX motherboards, 243
Lucent Technology, 232

M

macro viruses, 108
Magic Mover, 43, 68
mail-order vendors, buying computer systems from, 251
mapping
  computers and printers, 183
  drives, 59
master boot record (MBR), 77
Maximum Segment Size (MSS) setting, 161
Maximum Transmission Unit (MTU) setting, 161
MaxMTU, 173
MBR (master boot record), 77
McAfee Office Suite, 71
Media directory, 213
Media Player, 196
media, removable, 75
Melissa virus, 108
memory (see RAM)
MemTurbo, 109
menus
  boot
    DOS games, 153–155
    enabling, 144

menus (*continued*)
  disabling pause in, 35
  pop-up, improving in LiteStep, 131
  Start
    reimporting, 124
    support for, LiteStep, 127
MenuShowDelay entry, 36
Micro ATX motherboards, 242
Microsoft, 54, 74, 97, 137, 195
Microsoft Exchange, deleting, 190
Microsoft Network (MSN), deleting, 190
Microsoft Office, susceptibility to viruses
        with, 108
Mijenix, 95, 101
MinAnimate entry, 35
Mo'Slo utility, 149
modems
  external, 232
  finding manufacturers of, 161
  optimizing connections to
        Internet, 157–173
  speed of, 175
  upgrading, 231–233
modes
  DOS, 141
  protected, 137
  real, 137
monitors, upgrading, 248
motherboards, 189, 198
  brands of, 243–245
  replacing, 224
  upgrading, 220, 239–245
mouse, upgrading, 250
moving
  DLLs, Clean System Directory, 114
  executable files, 47–49
  files to front of FAT, 54
  ms.dos to winboot.ini, 86
  shell directories, 49
  Windows 95/98 and applications to
        separate partitions, 61
Mscreate.dir, deleting, 45
MS-DOS, 74
  compacting registry with, 91
  dual-booting with Windows 9, 147
msdos.sys, 77
  changing, 78
  checking after running
        WinCustomizer, 103

increasing speed of, 86
  options, 79–86
MSInfo, 195
MSN (Microsoft Network), deleting, 190
MSS (Maximum Segment Size) setting, 161
MTU (Maximum Transmission Unit)
        setting, 161
multibooting Windows 95 and 98, 204
multimedia, optimizing settings, 23
multiple primary partitions, DOS and
        Windows support for, 65

N

NEC Multisync II monitor, 249
NetBEUI (NetBIOS Enhanced User
        Interface) protocol, 180
NetLaunch, 170, 173
Netscape browsers, 172
Netscape cache, 15
NetSonic, 168, 172
NetSpeed, 173
NetWare environments, IPX/SPX
        protocol, 180
Network Associates, 71, 95, 106
Network control panel, opening, 185
network interface cards (see NICs)
Network Server setting, bug in, 20
Network subkey
  HKCU, 33
  HKLM, 34
Network=n setting, 85
networks
  at home, 174–187
  configuring, 201
  logons, 78
  naming, 181
NeXTStep, 126
NICs (network interface cards)
  in home networking kits, 177
  installing, 178
NLX motherboards, 243
NoIDE key, 17
Noorda, Ray, 146
Northgate keyboards, 250
Norton Ghost, 10
Norton Utilities, 9, 91, 94–101
  default and custom installations, 97
  fast loaders, 71
  file reordering, 54

NoStartBanner value, 36
Novell, 146
numbers, cluster, 52
Nuts & Bolts, 9, 52, 54, 91, 95–97, 103–105

O

OEM Service Release (OSR2), 191
Office Startup, 18
.old files, 45
online registration programs, 105
online services, deleting, 191
OpenStep, 126
Opera browser, 172
operating systems
    DOS, optimizing, 134–156
    "ideal", 4
    speed of, Linux vs. Windows, 4
    tools for optimizing, 93–118
Optimization Wizard, 98, 100
optimizing
    486 computers, 252–254
    caches, L2, 221
    computers, basic steps for, 13–40
    data and software on drives, 44
    disk caches, 20
    disks, 41–75
        compression, 74
        directories, 42–50
        FAT, 57–69
        fragmentation, 50–56
        results from, 73
        tools, 69–73
        with DefragPlus, 102
        with Disk Tune, 104
        with Speed Disk, 99
        working within physical limitations
            of, 56
    DOS, 134–156
    modem connections to
        Internet, 157–173
    multimedia settings, 23
    operating systems, tools for, 93–118
    ports, 158
    registry
        with Fix-It 99, 102
        with Nuts & Bolts, 104
        with Speed Disk, 100
    swap files, 18
    Windows, theory of, 1–12

Options section, settings, 80–86
organizing data and software on drives, 44
Orphan Finder, 107
OS rot
    RAM disks, 207
    Windows, 7
OS/2, 88
OSR2 (OEM Service Release), 191
outside tracks, disks, 56
overclocking, 230, 238–239

P

packets, sizes of, 162
parallel connections, speed of, 175
parameters
    /t, 156
    WinBootDir, 77
Partition-It, 60
PartitionMagic, 43, 60
    partitioning drives with, 67–69
    RAM disks and, 209
partitions/partitioning
    disks, 59–69
    drives, 7, 43
    Unix, 6
passwords, assigning to networks, 182
PATH statement, 88
Paths section, settings, 79
pause, disabling in menus, 35
PC DOS, dual-booting with Windows
        9, 147
PC Power & Cooling, 245
PC Tools, 95
PC100 SDRAM, 220
PCI buses, upgrading, 233
PCI cards, 177
PerfectPrint, 89
performance tuning
    AMD K6-III-based computers, 224
    computers, basic steps for, 13–40
    disaster recovery process, 62
    tools for, 93
    video cards, effects of cooling systems
        upon, 229
Perrell, David, 149
phone connections, 160
PKZIP/UNZIP utilities, moving, 47
platter density, 225

playing audio CDs and games from CD-ROM drives, 246
Plug-and-Play devices, 77
Plug-in Cleanup, 107
Plus! Pack, scheduling programs, 55
Populous II
    configuring to run in Windows, 151
    running from RAM disks, 156
pop-up menus, improving in LiteStep, 131
PortMaster, 159, 161
ports, optimizing, 158
POST (Power On Self Test), increasing speed of, 89–91
post-installation, Windows, 201
Power Clean, 106
power management
    disabling, 24, 98
    laptops, 24
Power On Self Test (POST), increasing speed of, 89–91
power supplies, upgrading, 245
PowerToys (Microsoft), 35
Prefetch key, 36–38
preloading tools, 168
primary partitions, 59
printers
    setting up, 182
    upgrading, 233
Program Manager, 120–123
programs (see software)
Promise Technology, 224
protected mode, 137
Protected Recycle Bin, 98
protocols
    IPX/SPX, 180
    NetBEUI, 180
    TCP/IP
        modem settings, 161
        using as network protocol, 179
proxy servers, 95, 166
pseudo-dual booting, 143–145
public screens, 127
purchasing
    CPUs, 4
    hardware, 218
    new computer systems, 250

Q

Quake II, 237
Quarterdeck, 137

Quick Clean, 106
QuickTime (Apple), 24

R

Railroad Tycoon, 149
RAM disks, 111–114, 155, 206–216
RAM (random access memory)
    effects upon computer speed, 3
    increasing, 38
    LiteStep, 128
    optimizing, DOS, 135–140
    POST memory tests, disabling, 90
    recovering, CD-ROM drives, 38
    requirements for upgrading hardware, 218–226
    StarOffice, 126
    tools for doubling, 109
    video cards, 227
    (see also virtual memory)
ramdrive.sys, 111
random access memory (see RAM)
real mode, 137
Receive Window (RWIN) setting, 162
recovery, speeding process of, 62
redirecting desktops to RAM disks, 112
Redneck Rampage, 140
    configuring to run in Windows, 152
Redundant DLL Finder, 107
RegClean utility, 91, 115
Regedit, 30–35
    NoIDE key, 17
registry, 30–35
    backing up, 34, 118
    binary value, 37
    CacheSize key, 36–38
    compacting, 91
    ConfigFileAllocSize entry, 39
    DWORD, 36
    empty keys, adding to run WALIGN properly, 69
    MenuShowDelay entry, 36
    MinAnimate entry, 35
    NoStartBanner value, 36
    optimizing
        with Fix-It 99, 102
        with Nuts & Bolts, 104
        with Speed Disk, 100
    Prefetch key, 36–38
    using tools to improve performance of, 94

Registry Cleaner, 103
Registry Defrag, 103
Registry Editor (Norton), 98
Registry Fixer, 102
Registry Repair Wizard, 104
Registry Sweep, 107
Registry Tune-Up Wizard, 104
Registry Wizard, 104
reinstalling Windows, 188–205
RemoteAccess subkey, 33
removable media, data compression, 75
removing (see deleting)
renaming
    files, autoexec.bat and config.sys, 17
    Windows directory, 199
reordering (see sorting)
repairing Windows 95 filesystem bug, 38
repartitioning (see partitioning)
replacement shells, Windows, 119–133
root directories, optimizing, 42–44
RWIN (Receive Window) setting, 162

S

saving
    disk space
        by deleting directories from RAM
            disks, 213
        with networks, 184
    files, fragmentation and, 61
    RAM disks, 113
scaling, FAT, 57
ScanDisk, 14, 50, 97
    abuse of, 53
    finding, 190
    running before FIPS, 65
scanners, upgrading, 248
scanning
    disks, scheduling, 55
    drives
        for errors, 50
        for viruses, 108
scavenger-style upgrading, 251
Schaefer, Arno, 65
schemes, desktop, 26
screen savers, 26, 98
screens, public, 127
scripts, IE-Remove, 197

SCSI controllers, 90
SCSI drives, 225
security, home networks, 182
Security subkey, 34
serial connections, speed of, 175
settings
    finding appropriate, ConfigFileAllocSize
        entry, 39
    hidden disk cache, tuning, 21
    modems, 161
    msdos.sys, 79–86
    multimedia, optimizing, 23
    Network Server, bug in, 20
    video cards, finding fastest for, 28
Setup, troubleshooting hangs, 200
setver.exe, 77
Seven Cities of Gold, configuring to run in
        Windows, 151
SFC (System File Checker), 116
shareware, 109–118, 257
shell directories, moving, 49
shells
    replacement, Windows, 119–133
    setting Word 97 as default,
        system.ini, 253
shortcuts, copying, 112
Sieber, Uwe, 139
Silicon Prairie Software, 109
SIMM trees, 219
Simpson, Robert, 170
SiSoft Sandra, 19, 251
sizes
    clusters, FAT16 vs. FAT32, 57
    disk caches, 21
    hard drives, 223
    packets, 162
sizing clusters, 69
Slowdown utility, 149
small drives, partitioning, 63
software
    aligning, 69–71
    anti-virus, 9, 55, 107
    benchmarking, 11, 226
    BIOS setup, accessing, 89
    compatibility with Superfassst, 73
    DOS
        running in DOS mode, 141
        speed of, 140
    free, 171

software (*continued*)
    installing
        from CD-ROM drives, 246
        running SFC before, 117
        to network drives, 184
    isolating to separate partition, 61
    launching, increasing speed of, 101
    loading
        changes in speed of after installing
            Superfassst, 72
        from CD-ROM drives, 246
        increasing speed of, 105
    moving, 47
    organizing on drives, 44
    requirements for networks, 178
    scheduling
        automating defragmentation of drives
            with, 55
        running on 486 computers, 254
    tuning connections through, 161–163
    uninstalling, 15, 56
        running SFC before, 117
        tools for, 105–107
    upgrading, 8
    vendors of, 255
    word processing, testing whether CPU
        upgrade is needed with, 236
    (see also tools)
Software subkey, 33
Solway, Kevin, 114
sorting
    directories by cluster number vs. access
        date, 52
    files, 54, 94
sound
    digital, extracting from audio CDs, 246
    disabling, 26
    upgrading cards, 230
Sound Blaster, 230
space, disks
    allocation of, Internet Explorer, 57
    freeing, 14–17
    saving
        by deleting directories from, 213
        with networks, 184
Space Wizard, 98
Sparkle Power International, 245
speed
    aligned vs. unaligned applications, 70
    boot process, increasing, 76–92

CD-ROM drives, 246
changes in loading applications after
        installing Superfassst, 72
computers, 3
disaster recovery, improving, 62
DNS lookups, increasing, 163
DOS games, slowing, 148
DOS programs, 140
FAT16 vs. FAT32, 57
hard drives, 223
L2 caches, improving, 221
modems, 157–173, 175
OS rot, effects upon, 7
parallel connections, 175
phone connections, 160
ports, optimizing, 158
RAM disks, 206
serial connections, 175
video buses, 227
video cards, finding fastest settings, 28
Speed Disk, 52, 97–100
    commands for scheduling disk scans, 56
    optimizing disks with, 99
Speed Start, 71, 73, 101
stability
    LiteStep, 129
    Superfassst with Windows 95, 73
    Windows, improving, 148
Stac, 74
Stacker utility, 74
StarOffice, 125
Start menu
    reimporting, 124
    support for, LiteStep, 127
Startup groups, cleaning, 17, 87–89
Startup Manager, 115
statements
    goto, 145
    PATH, 88
step.rc, 128
Storage Review, The, 226
storing files in archives, 70
Stowers, Brad, 115
subkeys
    HKCU, 32
    HKLM, 33
subtrees, registry, 30–34
Sun Microsystems, 125
Superfassst, 71

surrogate drives
  deleting, 212
  setting up, 208
swap files
  configuring, 101
  on RAM disks, 210
  optimizing, 18
Symantec, 95, 97, 106, 137
Sysbackup directory, 213
system configuration files
  backup copies of, 46
System Configuration Utility, 116
System Doctor, 97
System File Checker (SFC), 116
System subkey, 34
system.dat file, 30, 46, 77
system.ini file, 46, 253
SystemReg=n setting, 85
SystemWorks bundle, 108

T

/t parameter, 156
Tank Wars, 149
tasks, automating on 486 computers, 254
TCP/IP (Transmission Control
        Protocol/Internet Protocol)
  modem settings, 161
  using as network protocol, 179
telephone connections, 160
temporary files
  deleting, 14, 57
  fragmentation and, 61
  isolating, 62
  resizing, 69
temporary swap, isolating, 62
terminate-and-stay-resident module, 88
testing
  modems in DOS, 231
  whether CPU upgrade is needed, 236
  with POST, 89–91
textures in video memory, 227
Time to Live (TTL) setting, 162
.tmp files (see temporary files)
toggling loading of graphics, 173
Tolstoy, Leo, 4
Tom's Hardware Guide, 230, 244
toolbars, Wharf bar, 127, 131

tools
  bundled with Windows 98, 115–118
  caching, 168
  charityware,' 165
  cleanup, 114
  defragmentation, 51
  fast loaders, 71–73
  FDISK
    creating partitions with, 67
    FIPS as replacement for, 65
    partitioning drives with, 63–65
  FIPS, partitioning drives with, 65–67
  freeware, 109–118, 256
  improving performance with, 93
  Magic Mover, 43, 68
  Norton Utilities, 94–101
  optimizing disk performance, 69–73
  optimizing operating systems, 93–118
  PartitionMagic, 43, 60
    partitioning drives with, 67–69
    RAM disks and, 209
  PowerToys (Microsoft), 35
  preloading, 168
  RAM doubling, 109
  RegClean, 91
  shareware, 109–118, 257
  undelete, 54
  uninstalling software, 105–107
  UnZip and Zip, storing files in
        archives, 70
  WALIGN, aligning software, 69–71
  WinAlign, 69
  XMSDISK, 111–114
tooltips, Windows 98, 27
touch tablets, 250
touchpads, 250
trackballs, 250
tracking file access, Windows 95, 52
tracks, disks, 56
Transmission Control Protocol/Internet
        Protocol (see TCP/IP)
Trident video card, 229
Trojan Horse, 108
troubleshooting
  errors in registry, 100
  hung Setups, 200
true DOS, dual-booting Windows 9x
        with, 145–147

TrueX drives, 247
Trumpet Winsock, 161, 169
TSR (terminate-and-stay-resident
      module), 88
TTL (Time to Live) setting, 162
tuning
      browsers, 172
      CD-ROM caches, 22
      connections through software, 161–163
      hidden disk cache settings, 21
      Windows 95/98 to CD-ROM
            drives, 36–38
turning off (see disabling)
TweakUI, 102
.txt files, 45

U

UART (Universal Asynchronous Receiver-
      Transmitter, 159
Uberto, Frank, 111
Ultima VII, configuring to run in
      Windows, 152
UMBPCI memory manager, 139
umbpci.sys, adding to config.sys, 148
UMBs (upper memory blocks), 137
unalign.bat file, 70
unaligned applications, speed of, 70
UNC (Universal Naming Convention), 185
uncompressing drives, 75
undelete utilities, 54
undo disks, 51
uninstallation programs, 9
UninstallDir=path setting, 79
UnInstaller, 9, 106
uninstalling
      software, 56, 105–107
            running SFC before, 117
            unneeded, 15
            unneeded games, 15
uninterruptible power supply (see UPS)
Universal Asynchronous Receiver-
      Transmitter (UART), 159
Universal Naming Convention (UNC), 185
Unix, 6, 137
UnZip utility
      backing up Windows directories, 9
      moving, 47
      storing files in archives, 70

upgrading
      hardware, 217–254
      software, 8
      to Windows 98, 94
upper memory blocks (UMBs), 137
UPS (uninterruptible power supply), 20, 38
URLs (uniform resource locators)
      device driver archives, 258
      drivers and documentation, 143
      finding for favorite web sites, 164
      free tools, 256
      gamers' information, 260
      hardware reviews, 259
      hardware vendors, 258
user.dat file, 30, 46
user.exe, 78

V

VCACHE, 21
VCPI (Virtual Control Program Interface)
      memory, 138
VCRs, 23
vendors
      hardware, 258
      mail-order, buying computer systems
            from, 251
      software, 255
version numbers, finding in Windows
      95, 21
VESA local video bus, 227
VFAT
      disk fragmentation and, 50, 53
      long filenames and, 42
video cards
      fastest settings for, 28
      upgrading, 226–230
Viewsonic monitors, 249
Virtual Control Program Interface (VCPI)
      memory, 138
virtual desktops, 127
virtual memory
      fragmentation and, 61
      optimizing, 18
Virtual Software, 114
viruses, 107
Visual Basic libraries, 164
vmm32.vxd, 78
voices, number of produced by sound
      cards, 231

Vonk, Ron, 162
Voodoo, 150
Vopt, 51
VRAMDIR, 114

W

WALIGN, aligning software, 69–71
wallpaper, 25, 45
warranties
    monitors, 249
    overclocking and, 238
web browsers
    tuning, 172
    which to use, 171
web sites (see URLs)
Web3000, 168
Weber, Meikel, 109
Welcome.exe, 214
Western Digital, 243
Wharf bar, 127, 131
WIN32S directory, 47
WinAlign, 69
WinBootDir parameter, 77
WinBootDir=path setting, 80
winboot.ini file, 77, 86
WinChips, 235
win.com file, 78
WinCustomizer, 102
WinDir=path setting, 80
WinDoctor, 100
Windows, 21
    configuring DOS games to run
        in, 150–155
    improving stability of, 148
    optimizing, theory of, 1–12
    OS rot, 7
    Regedit, 30–35
    registry (see registry)
    reimporting Start menu, 124
    reinstalling, 188–205
    replacement shells, 119–133
    speed of compared to Linux, 4
    Start menu, support for, 127
    support for multiple primary
        partitions, 65
    working within limitations of, 5
Windows 95
    batch file support, 88
    buffer count, 148

bug in Network Server setting, 20
Computer Clinic web site, 259
disabling window animations, 35
drivers, compatibility with
        Windows 98, 198
dual-booting true DOS with, 145–147
dual-booting with Windows 98, 204
Hosts file, 164
isolating to separate partition, 61
Plus! Pack, scheduling programs, 55
ramdrive.sys, 111
reinstalling, 188–190
repairing filesystem bug in, 38
running from RAM disks, 207, 215
stability of Superfassst with, 73
tracking file access, 52
tuning to CD-ROM drives, 36–38
undelete utilities, 54
upgrading hardware, 217–254
WIN32S directory, 47
Windows 98
    aligning software, 69–71
    batch file support, 88
    buffer count, 148
    compatibility
        Speed Start and, 71
        Superfassst and, 71
    disabling animations, 27
    disabling tooltips, 27
    drivers, backward compatibility with
        Windows 95, 198
    dual-booting true DOS with, 145–147
    dual-booting with Windows 95, 204
    Hosts file, 164
    installing, 192–204
    isolating to separate partition, 61
    RAM disks and, 214–216
    ramdrive.sys, 111
    scheduling programs, 55
    speed of FAT32 drives with, 58
    tools bundled with, 115–118
    tuning to CD-ROM drives, 36–38
    undelete utilities, 54
    upgrading hardware, 217–254
    upgrading to, 94
    WIN32S directory, 47
Windows 98 Setup Wizard, 200
Windows 9x (see Windows 95/98)
Windows directory, optimizing, 45–50

windows, dock, 127
Windows NT, batch file support, 88
Windows Registry Checker, 118
Windrenalin, 71
Win-G, compatibility with
        Windows 98, 205
WinGate, 95, 187
win.ini file, 46
Winmodems, 231
WinVer=s setting, 86
WipeInfo, 98
wizards
    Add New Hardware, running, 197
    ICW Internet Connection, deleting, 191
    Optimization, 98, 100
    Registry, 104
    Registry Repair, 104
    Registry Tune-Up, 104
    Space, 98
    Windows 98 Setup, 200
Word 97, configuring to run on 486
        computers, 253
word processing programs, testing for CPU
        upgrade, 236
WordPerfect, files added to Startup
        group, 89
writing (see saving)
Wterm, 232

X

Xenix, 137
XFree86 X Window system, 123
XMS (extended memory specification), 137
XMS games, configuring to run in
        DOS, 151
XMSDISK, 111–114, 155

Y

Y-splitters, 161

Z

ZBR (Zoned Bit Recording), 56
Zeos keyboards, 250
Zip drives
    data compression, 75
    mapping drive letters for, 59
    upgrading, 248
    using as surrogate drives, 209
Zip utility
    backing up Windows directories, 9
    moving, 47
    storing files in archives, 70
Zippy USA, 245
Zmodem, 162
Zoned Bit Recording (see ZBR), 56

About the Author

David L. Farquhar graduated from the University of Missouri with a degree in journalism and has been working as a systems analyst ever since. He has also been a weekly computer columnist for the *Columbia Missourian* newspaper. When not working on or writing about computers, Dave is a diehard Kansas City Royals fan, sound technician, Bible study teacher, and fiction writer.

Colophon

Our look is the result of reader comments, our own experimentation, and feedback from distribution channels. Distinctive covers complement our distinctive approach to technical topics, breathing personality and life into potentially dry subjects.

The animal on the cover of *Optimizing Windows for Games, Graphics, and Multimedia* is a roadrunner (*Geococcyx californianus*). The roadrunner is a ground-dwelling type of cuckoo bird found in the southwestern United States, including California, Arizona, Nevada, Utah, and south into Mexico. It stands about two feet tall, and can be 20–24 inches long. The roadrunner is possibly most famous for its long legs that carry it quickly through the open, desert environment at speeds up to 15 miles an hour. Though it has wings, the roadrunner typically flies only when in danger. Other characteristics include a long tail and bill, a crest of feathers at the top of its head, and a striped or spotted pattern, typically of brown and white, on its back and tail.

Roadrunners nest in bushes, low trees, or cactus. The male bird sits on the 4–8 eggs during incubation, and roadrunners are considered to be excellent parents. Their diet consists of bird eggs, insects, lizards, snakes, and small rodents. Roadrunners have three calls, the most popular of which sounds much like a dove's cooing.

Madeleine Newell was the production editor and Nicole Arigo was the copyeditor for *Optimizing Windows for Games, Graphics, and Multimedia*. Clairemarie Fisher O'Leary provided quality control. Jeff Holcomb, Abby Myers, Anna Kim Snow, and Maeve O'Meara provided production assistance. Mike Sierra provided FrameMaker technical support. Cheryl Landes of Tabby Cat Communications wrote the index, and Brenda Miller edited the index.

Ellie Volkenhausen designed the cover of this book, using an illustration created by Lorrie LeJeune. The cover layout was produced by Kathleen Wilson with QuarkXPress 3.32 using the ITC Garamond font. Whenever possible, our books use RepKover™, a durable and flexible lay-flat binding. If the page count exceeds RepKover's limit, perfect binding is used.

The inside layout was designed by Alicia Cech based on a series design by Nancy Priest, and implemented in FrameMaker 5.5 by Mike Sierra. The text and heading fonts are ITC Garamond Light and Garamond Book. The illustrations that appear in the book were produced by Robert Romano and Rhon Porter using Macromedia FreeHand 8 and Adobe Photoshop 5. This colophon was written by Nicole Arigo.

How to stay in touch with O'Reilly

1. Visit Our Award-Winning Web Site

http://www.oreilly.com/

★ "Top 100 Sites on the Web" —*PC Magazine*
★ "Top 5% Web sites" —*Point Communications*
★ "3-Star site" —*The McKinley Group*

Our web site contains a library of comprehensive product information (including book excerpts and tables of contents), downloadable software, background articles, interviews with technology leaders, links to relevant sites, book cover art, and more. File us in your Bookmarks or Hotlist!

2. Join Our Email Mailing Lists

New Product Releases
To receive automatic email with brief descriptions of all new O'Reilly products as they are released, send email to:
listproc@online.oreilly.com
Put the following information in the first line of your message (*not* in the Subject field):
subscribe oreilly-news

O'Reilly Events
If you'd also like us to send information about trade show events, special promotions, and other O'Reilly events, send email to:
listproc@online.oreilly.com
Put the following information in the first line of your message (*not* in the Subject field):
subscribe oreilly-events

3. Get Examples from Our Books via FTP

There are two ways to access an archive of example files from our books:

Regular FTP
- ftp to:
  ftp.oreilly.com
  (login: anonymous
  password: your email address)
- Point your web browser to:
  ftp://ftp.oreilly.com/

FTPMAIL
- Send an email message to:
  ftpmail@online.oreilly.com
  (Write "help" in the message body)

4. Contact Us via Email

order@oreilly.com
To place a book or software order online. Good for North American and international customers.

subscriptions@oreilly.com
To place an order for any of our newsletters or periodicals.

books@oreilly.com
General questions about any of our books.

software@oreilly.com
For general questions and product information about our software. Check out O'Reilly Software Online at **http://software.oreilly.com/** for software and technical support information. Registered O'Reilly software users send your questions to: **website-support@oreilly.com**

cs@oreilly.com
For answers to problems regarding your order or our products.

booktech@oreilly.com
For book content technical questions or corrections.

proposals@oreilly.com
To submit new book or software proposals to our editors and product managers.

international@oreilly.com
For information about our international distributors or translation queries. For a list of our distributors outside of North America check out:
http://www.oreilly.com/www/order/country.html

O'Reilly & Associates, Inc.
101 Morris Street, Sebastopol, CA 95472 USA
TEL   707-829-0515 or 800-998-9938
        (6am to 5pm PST)
FAX   707-829-0104

International Distributors

UK, EUROPE, MIDDLE EAST AND AFRICA (EXCEPT FRANCE, GERMANY, AUSTRIA, SWITZERLAND, LUXEMBOURG, LIECHTENSTEIN, AND EASTERN EUROPE)

INQUIRIES
O'Reilly UK Limited
4 Castle Street
Farnham
Surrey, GU9 7HS
United Kingdom
Telephone: 44-1252-711776
Fax: 44-1252-734211
Email: josette@oreilly.com

ORDERS
Wiley Distribution Services Ltd.
1 Oldlands Way
Bognor Regis
West Sussex PO22 9SA
United Kingdom
Telephone: 44-1243-779777
Fax: 44-1243-820250
Email: cs-books@wiley.co.uk

FRANCE

ORDERS
GEODIF
61, Bd Saint-Germain
75240 Paris Cedex 05, France
Tel: 33-1-44-41-46-16 (French books)
Tel: 33-1-44-41-11-87 (English books)
Fax: 33-1-44-41-11-44
Email: distribution@eyrolles.com

INQUIRIES
Éditions O'Reilly
18 rue Séguier
75006 Paris, France
Tel: 33-1-40-51-52-30
Fax: 33-1-40-51-52-31
Email: france@editions-oreilly.fr

GERMANY, SWITZERLAND, AUSTRIA, EASTERN EUROPE, LUXEMBOURG, AND LIECHTENSTEIN

INQUIRIES & ORDERS
O'Reilly Verlag
Balthasarstr. 81
D-50670 Köln
Germany
Telephone: 49-221-973160-91
Fax: 49-221-973160-8
Email: anfragen@oreilly.de (inquiries)
Email: order@oreilly.de (orders)

CANADA (FRENCH LANGUAGE BOOKS)
Les Éditions Flammarion ltée
375, Avenue Laurier Ouest
Montréal (Québec) H2V 2K3
Tel: 00-1-514-277-8807
Fax: 00-1-514-278-2085
Email: info@flammarion.qc.ca

HONG KONG
City Discount Subscription Service, Ltd.
Unit D, 3rd Floor, Yan's Tower
27 Wong Chuk Hang Road
Aberdeen, Hong Kong
Tel: 852-2580-3539
Fax: 852-2580-6463
Email: citydis@ppn.com.hk

KOREA
Hanbit Media, Inc.
Sonyoung Bldg. 202
Yeksam-dong 736-36
Kangnam-ku
Seoul, Korea
Tel: 822-554-9610
Fax: 822-556-0363
Email: hant93@chollian.dacom.co.kr

PHILIPPINES
Mutual Books, Inc.
429-D Shaw Boulevard
Mandaluyong City, Metro
Manila, Philippines
Tel: 632-725-7538
Fax: 632-721-3056
Email: mbikikog@mnl.sequel.net

TAIWAN
O'Reilly Taiwan
No. 3, Lane 131
Hang-Chow South Road
Section 1, Taipei, Taiwan
Tel: 886-2-23968990
Fax: 886-2-23968916
Email: taiwan@oreilly.com

CHINA
O'Reilly Beijing
Room 2410
160, FuXingMenNeiDaJie
XiCheng District
Beijing, China PR 100031
Tel: 86-10-66412305
Fax: 86-10-86631007
Email: beijing@oreilly.com

INDIA
Computer Bookshop (India) Pvt. Ltd.
190 Dr. D.N. Road, Fort
Bombay 400 001 India
Tel: 91-22-207-0989
Fax: 91-22-262-3551
Email: cbsbom@giasbm01.vsnl.net.in

JAPAN
O'Reilly Japan, Inc.
Kiyoshige Building 2F
12-Bancho, Sanei-cho
Shinjuku-ku
Tokyo 160-0008 Japan
Tel: 81-3-3356-5227
Fax: 81-3-3356-5261
Email: japan@oreilly.com

ALL OTHER ASIAN COUNTRIES
O'Reilly & Associates, Inc.
101 Morris Street
Sebastopol, CA 95472 USA
Tel: 707-829-0515
Fax: 707-829-0104
Email: order@oreilly.com

AUSTRALIA
WoodsLane Pty., Ltd.
7/5 Vuko Place
Warriewood NSW 2102
Australia
Tel: 61-2-9970-5111
Fax: 61-2-9970-5002
Email: info@woodslane.com.au

NEW ZEALAND
Woodslane New Zealand, Ltd.
21 Cooks Street (P.O. Box 575)
Waganui, New Zealand
Tel: 64-6-347-6543
Fax: 64-6-345-4840
Email: info@woodslane.com.au

LATIN AMERICA
McGraw-Hill Interamericana
Editores, S.A. de C.V.
Cedro No. 512
Col. Atlampa
06450, Mexico, D.F.
Tel: 52-5-547-6777
Fax: 52-5-547-3336
Email: mcgraw-hill@infosel.net.mx

O'REILLY®